Leadership and Negotiation in the Middle East

LEADERSHIP
AND NEGOTIATION
IN THE
MIDDLE EAST

Edited by
Barbara Kellerman
and
Jeffrey Z. Rubin

Foreword by Seymour Feshbach

Published in cooperation with the
Society for the Psychological
Study of Social Issues

New York
Westport, Connecticut
London

Library of Congress Cataloging-in-Publication Data

Leadership and negotiation in the Middle East / edited by Barbara
    Kellerman and Jeffrey Z. Rubin.
        p.   cm.
    ''Published in cooperation with the Society for the Psychological
Study of Social Issues.''
    Bibliography: p.
    Includes index.
    ISBN 0–275–92489–0 (alk. paper)
        1. Lebanon—History—Israeli intervention, 1982–   2. Middle East—
Foreign relations.   3. Political leadership—Middle East.
4. Politicians—Middle East.   5. Political leadership—Case studies.
6. International relations—Case studies.   I. Kellerman, Barbara.
II. Rubin, Jeffrey Z.   III. Society for the Psychological Study of
Social Issues.
DS87.53.L43   1988
956.92′044—dc19   88–10337

Library of Congress Catalog Card Number: 88–10337
ISBN: 0–275–92489–0

First published in 1988

Praeger Publishers, One Madison Avenue, New York, NY   10010
A division of Greenwood Press, Inc.

Printed in the United States of America

The paper used in this book complies with the
Permanent Paper Standard issued by the National
Information Standards Organization (Z39.48–1984).

10 9 8 7 6 5 4 3 2 1

CONTENTS

FOREWORD

The Society for the Psychological Study of Social Issues (SPSSI) is comprised of social scientists who have an abiding interest in applying the insights and techniques of social science to the analysis, amelioration, and, where possible, resolution of contemporary social problems and issues. SPSSI functions as a bridge between the detachment of the academy and the immediacy of social, political, and economic problems that confront the larger community, whether local, national, or international. In a sense, through the research activities of its members, SPSSI is continually testing the utility and social relevance of behavioral science theory and methodology. At the same time, these applied research activities frequently entail contributions to basic social science theory and data.

The present volume, edited by Barbara Kellerman and Jeffrey Z. Rubin, is very much within the SPSSI tradition. It utilizes the insights of social science to help illuminate the failures and possibilities of leadership during a particular international crisis: the June 1982 Israeli invasion of Lebanon and the four month period that ensued before a multinational peace-keeping force was put in place. Although the volume addresses an important historical event and merits our attention on historical grounds alone, it is more than a historical contribution. It is a pioneering volume that examines the nature of that Middle East crisis and the possibilities for compromise, negotiation, and resolution through the personalities and perspectives of national leaders of governments or organizations whose interests were strongly affected by the crisis. In reading the chapters on the Lebanese leaders, on Israel's Menachem Begin, on the PLO's Yasser Arafat, on Syria's Hafez al-Assad, and other Middle Eastern leaders, and on the superpower leaders, Brezhnev and Reagan, we develop a deeper understanding of the issues entailed in that Middle East crisis and of the role of these eminent figures in the events of that period.

More importantly, in terms of the broader social science objectives of this volume, we are provided insight into the interplay among the personalities and perspectives of the leaders, the interests of the groups they represent, and the constraints and flexibilities entailed in the crisis situation. Avoidance or resolution of the crisis was not necessarily in the interests of all parties. However, there were numerous instances in which a leader could have taken an action that would have facilitated the reduction of the conflict but, because of misappraisal or because of personality attributes, failed to do so.

These analyses of lost opportunities and of those occasions on which leaders did act effectively to foster negotiation and reduce conflict have implications that extend beyond the understanding of that particular crisis period. As one of the editors notes in an excellent concluding chapter, many of these leaders still occupy leadership roles. In addition, the Middle East continues to be highly vulnerable to crisis situations. Indeed, several crises exist in the area as this is being written and, unfortunately, it is likely that related crises will arise when this volume is published. The insights that this volume has provided into the character and world view of these leaders, the constraints under which they operate, and the manner in which they respond to crisis can serve to enhance the negotiating effectiveness of intermediaries in future crisis situations in this area. Related insights also bear upon general principles of leadership, compromise, and negotiation in crisis situations. These insights and principles are elucidated and critically evaluated in the introductory and concluding chapters by the editors, and in two overview chapters, one by a political scientist and the other by a psychologist. These more integrative chapters, in conjunction with the individual leadership–historical chapters, result in a unique and valuable volume.

At another level, the thesis set forth by Kellerman and Rubin, and elaborated in various chapters, bears upon fundamental views of history and political change: whether historical change is the outcome of inexorable economic and social forces, and leaders essentially serve to expedite or delay the inevitable; or, whether leaders (and their followers) can make a qualitative difference in the flow of historical events through timely and thoughtful action. This volume makes a strong case for the latter proposition. Those of us in SPSSI like to think that applied research and social action make a difference in the real world. We are encouraged by Kellerman and Rubin's *Leadership and Negotiation in the Middle East*.

Seymour Feshbach
President, SPSSI

PREFACE

This book has its origins in a friendship that goes back more than ten years. At the time we were both at Tufts University, teaching an interdisciplinary course on decision making. As part of the course, we spent several sessions focusing on the key decisions during the 1962 Cuban Missile Crisis. Barbara, a political scientist, chose to analyze much of what happened during that period in terms of leaders and leadership. Jeff, a social psychologist, instead concentrated on the situational and strategic components. Our joint presentation of the decisions made during these critical 13 days invariably led to friendly arguments and exchanges, grounded particularly in the role of various turning points in history. Over the ensuing years we have continued to argue with each other, as only good friends and longstanding colleagues can do with so much pleasure. While several hundred miles now separate us, our enjoyment of a good intellectual debate lives on, as manifested most recently in the pages of this book.

Leadership and Negotiation in the Middle East is the result of an ongoing exchange on the relative importance of individuals and situations in the settlement of international conflict. Can national leaders make a difference in international conflict? Would having a set of leaders with the "right stuff," with sufficient motivation, ability, political sensibility, and so on be sufficient to alter the course of conflict management in international affairs? Or is more variance carried by the situation itself, the set of circumstances that make it possible both for leadership to emerge and for such leadership to make a difference? More specifically, the key question this volume addresses pertains to the role of leadership analysis in negotiation theory. Should biographical case studies—studies sensitive both to the national leader and the situation—become routine data for those who seek to manage international conflict?

While this book does not purport to provide simple, straightforward answers to these questions, it is certainly designed to sharpen and continue the debate. We have been most fortunate in being able to draw into this exchange the services of a distinguished group of political scientists and social psychologists. Stirred by their joint insight and reflection, it is our hope that this collection will make it easier to evaluate the role in international dispute settlement of both the national leader and, indeed, the negotiation process itself.

A number of friends and colleagues have made wise comments along the way, and we particularly acknowledge the helpful observations of Randa Slim and J. William Breslin. Linda Underwood and Jean Intoppa lent much needed secretarial assistance at various points; without them this project would have taken even longer to complete. Finally, we are grateful to the Society for the Psychological Study of Social Issues (SPSSI) for sponsoring this book.

For us, the editors, this collection represents not an end but another step in an ongoing, friendly exchange between us. Our friendship preceded this book, and has lived to survive it. The arguing continues, as does our pleasure in bringing this collection to you.

Leadership and Negotiation in the Middle East

1

INTRODUCTION

Barbara Kellerman

On the face of it, maintaining peace should be easy. Political leaders are supposed to protect the public interest, and the public interest demands nothing if not the elimination of the death and destruction caused by war between nations. In fact, it can be argued that the first and foremost responsibility of the national leader is to keep the peace.

What is never quite clear is why political leaders have generally failed to carry out this fundamental charge. If men, women, and children everywhere want to live free from harm, why is it so difficult to refrain from doing battle? Put another way, why has a yawning gap existed in human history between what people want and what their leaders have provided?

"Imagine," Andrew Bard Schmookler has written,

a group of tribes living within reach of one another. If all choose the way of peace, then all may live in peace. But what if all but one choose peace, and that one is ambitious for expansion and conquest? What happens to the others when confronted by an ambitious and potent neighbor?

There are only four possible outcomes for the threatened tribes: destruction, absorption (and transformation), withdrawal (exile), and imitation (in order to defend itself, it will have to become like its foe). This "parable of the tribes" teaches that "no one is free to choose peace, but anyone can impose upon all the necessity for power."[1] In other words, since one or another tribe can always be relied on to be both ambitious and strong, all the others are essentially compelled to prepare to defend themselves—or risk extinction.[2]

The individual responsible for maintaining this strong defense is the group leader. It is thus the national leader—who derives his* authority from holding

---

*The masculine pronoun is used because all the leaders discussed in this book are men.

the highest office in a legally sanctioned national government—who is formally charged with protecting his state from incursion by other states.

This identification of the national leader with the state for which he is responsible suggests that the leader's raison d'être derives almost entirely from the needs of his own people—not from those of humankind more generally. In fact, the stronger the leader's bond to his followers in particular, and the more urgent his need to see them (and himself) prevail, the less likely he is to consider the welfare of everyone else unless it happens to coincide with his own.

Thus the leader–follower tie can reasonably be said to lie at the root of all international conflict. Leaders are charged with defending their national states against destruction, absorption, withdrawal, and imitation, and followers are willing to die at the leader's command so that national security is achieved. (In fact, when people are no longer willing to die on orders of someone else, international warfare must inevitably cease.) What results, then, is a world politics fueled by passions that are parochial rather than ecumenical, and conducted by leaders who are so tied to the nationals of their own states that they are virtually devoid of concern for everyone else.

While national leaders might reasonably be considered the primary locus of action in the international environment, as objects of study by experts in international relations they have been largely neglected. While the media have always lavished attention on leaders as "stars," scholars have been much less interested in the role of the leader in world politics. To be sure, leaders have figured prominently when there was no mistaking their pivotal role. In particular, Robert C. Tucker drew our attention to the importance of the dictator in the foreign policy systems of totalitarian states:

> When we confront the theoretical model of the totalitarian polity with what we now know about the factual situation in Hitler's Germany and Stalin's Russia, it appears that the model was seriously deficient in its omission of the personal factor from the dynamics of totalitarianism, its obliviousness to the impact of the dictator's personality upon the political system and process.[3]

For the rest, however, academics have tended to underplay (or even ignore) the human element, or to refer to it in ways that obscure rather than clarify the national leader's particular significance. Very little work has been done on how leader–follower relationships shape leaders' perceptions and decisions on foreign policy issues, on how the personality of national leaders impinges on their performances in international settings, or on how national leaders view and relate to each other.

In fact, many experts in foreign policy and international relations ignore the role of the leader altogether. Instead, some prefer to concentrate on foreign policy "systems," while others focus on the messengers (for example, bureaucrats, diplomats, and mediators) rather than on the power-wielders and decision-makers directly. Similarly, scholars often become so wrapped up in tactics and strategies that they neglect the psychopolitical imperatives governing those who must perforce initiate and implement them.

In fact, even those experts who acknowledge the role of the powerful individual, more often than not fail to use the proper nomenclature. Rather than describing the key players as leaders—which is what they really are—actions are described as having been taken by "decision-makers," "actors," "statesmen," or, even less precisely, by "the U.S.," "the Germans," "the Soviets," and so on.

To be sure, there is a virtue to using vague language: Anyone and everyone who has any impact at all on the foreign policy process is thereby included in the discussion. Moreover, there are, of course, times when the key player is not the national leader but rather, to take but one example, his deputy, such as the secretary of state. Furthermore, there are occasions when the major player regarding a particular foreign policy is an aroused public (at least in democratic states). Still and all, I would argue that on those foreign policy issues that are salient, most of the time it is the national leader who has by far the greatest impact on what happens. It is to him that we must look in order to understand what is being perceived and why one course of action is finally chosen over all the others. I propose, in short, that instead of continuing to ignore the key players in world politics we should place them center stage—and start by referring to them as the national *leaders* they literally are.

One of the few scholars who has pointed to the importance of the individual in world politics is Herbert Kelman. In an article titled "The Role of the Individual in International Relations: Some Conceptual and Methodological Considerations," Kelman discussed a whole range of people who have an impact on foreign affairs.

While agreeing that the nation-state remains the basic unit of analysis in international relations, I would stress that individuals constitute the ultimate locus of action. Individual decision-makers act, set the limits and define the mood within which decision-makers can operate; and individual actors carry out the official and unofficial interactions of which international relations consist.[4]

Although Kelman does not make what I consider to be a crucial distinction between the role of "ordinary citizens" and national leaders, he does raise the fundamental methodological question: How should the study of the role of the individual in international relations proceed? With regard to the impact on foreign policy of those whom he terms "individual decision-makers" (read national leaders), Kelman proposes what might be termed a basic social–psychological approach: Take account of both psychological processes and situational constraints.

This approach is in keeping with that taken by most contemporary leadership theorists, who argue that to understand the leadership process, at least three variables must be considered: the leader, the followers, and the situation at hand.

On the basis of these variables I have developed five propositions that suggest conditions under which the leader's role in international relations is likely to be pivotal.[5]

1. The leader's impact on foreign policy will vary according to the scope of his power, authority, and influence within his own nation state. The more power, authority, and influence he has, the greater his impact on foreign policy, and the greater his impact on foreign policy, the more his effect on world politics.
2. The leader's impact on world politics will vary according to the nature of his political role. The more his role demands an orientation to foreign policy, the greater his impact on world politics.
3. The leader's impact on world politics will vary according to the personal strengths, weaknesses, and inclinations of the individual actor. The stronger and more capable he is, and the more interested in foreign affairs, the greater his impact on world politics.
4. The leader's impact on world politics will vary according to the importance of foreign politics in general, or of a particular foreign policy issue, to the domestic politics of his nation state. The more important foreign politics is to domestic politics, the greater his impact on world politics.
5. The leader's impact on world politics will vary according to the size, power, and strategic importance of his nation state. The more powerful and important his nation state, the greater his impact is likely to be on world politics.[6]

The ultimate purpose of this volume is to make practical use of the proposition that the national leader is the primary focus of action in international politics. More specifically, the book is based on the following hypothesis:

Opportunity for the containment, management, and reduction of international conflict through negotiation will be significantly enhanced by the availability of information on the role, history, style, beliefs, policies, and situations that characterize or confront each pertinent national leader.

Analysis of negotiation obstacles and opportunities in the international system has generally been guided by the assumption that context—cultural, political, and economic—reigns supreme. Conflict resolution, this position argues, can proceed only as vigorously as contextual conditions will tolerate. In contrast, this book proceeds from the assumption that by highlighting the distinguishing and common features of the national leaders who occupy central roles in international conflict, it may be possible to discover new opportunities for dispute settlement.

The evolving relationship between Ronald Reagan and Mikhail Gorbachev provides strong evidence that the individual who is in power can make a big difference in how nations relate. For most of President Reagan's first term in the White House, he clung to what was for him the familiar image of the Soviet Union as an "evil empire." As to the Soviets, they had no one in residence long enough to provide the U.S. president with a proper foil. Leonid Brezhnev had died in 1982; his successor, Yuri Andropov, passed away a mere 14 months later, and Konstantin Chernenko, who replaced Andropov, himself died after only about a year in office. It was not until Reagan's second term in office that the situation stabilized. With Mikhail Gorbachev, the Soviet Union finally had a vigorous leader in place who, in accordance with the normal Soviet pattern, was expected to be in power for years to come.

The relationship between the aging U.S. leader and his relatively young Soviet counterpart has by no means been an easy one; but of the fact that a relationship of sorts has evolved, there can be little doubt. As of this writing they have had three face-to-face meetings. On the first occasion, they became acquainted in what was generally felt to be a cordial fashion. On the second, they met on uncommonly short notice and, after a series of what can most kindly be described as misunderstandings, parted in anger. Finally, at the third meeting, they made what would have to be described as substantial progress. A major arms treaty was signed, and fruitful discussions were held in several other areas of bilateral concern.

The point in any case is this: Both leaders, for their own personal and political reasons, were interested in improving the Soviet–U.S. relationship, in reducing the risk of war, and in establishing a basis for continued accommodation. Once their paths intersected in this regard, they were able together to do no less than alter the temper and tide of world politics.

Anwar Sadat's 1977 overture to Israel provides another obvious and relatively recent example of how leadership behavior is able to alter the context within which nations negotiate in a single stroke.

To break the psychological barrier, Sadat chose to do the daring, the imaginative, the dramatic, the unprecedented, and indeed, the inspired. . . . In his visit to Jerusalem, Sadat captured the attention and the imagination of the world, fired Israel's public opinion, and challenged fundamental assumptions of Israel's leaders about their Arab neighbor. The president succeeded not only in shattering the old but, more importantly, in putting new rules in place: the conflict between Egypt and Israel was normalized and made negotiable. . . . By this single act, through the exercise of will, the president of Egypt changed the fate of many in the Middle East.[7]

To be sure, we concede the importance of both leader and group, key decision-makers and institutional context, and present circumstances and past history in the determination of intergroup conflict outcomes. Still, we are convinced of the intellectual and perhaps also the ultimately practical value of deliberately focusing on those who are empowered to make the critical decisions.

This approach would seem to be especially promising in an area such as the Middle East, which has a long and continuing history of regional conflict, and which is populated almost entirely by states whose national leaders completely dominate the foreign policy process. As Janice Gross Stein has observed, many of the states in the Middle East are "rich in cultural and historical tradition but neophyte in political institutions, institutions put in place by a generation of founding leaders."[8] In fact, Stein continues, even their successors tend to wield authority and influence far beyond that of their counterparts in older and better institutionalized political systems. It is precisely because the autonomy and authority of political leaders has been so impressive in this area of the world that it serves as a perfect laboratory for the study of how individual leaders shape the course of international politics. Another aspect of the book's rationale is thus that serious discussion of dispute settlement in the Middle East must take account of the role of the region's national leaders.

For our intellectual experiment to proceed as we intended, we required a particular instance or case of international crisis, a frozen section of history that invited joint analysis in terms of leadership and dispute settlement. The desiderata of such a case included: a relatively clear demarcation of the points of origin and termination of the conflict "event"; the presence of highly visible leaders about whom it was possible to develop background information and insight— in effect, leader "briefing books"; and the prospect that the conflict—of which the case in question is but one example or time slice—is enduring and therefore of continuing interest and importance.

Several instances of crisis in the Middle East satisfy one or more of the above criteria. However, we became convinced that none better satisfies the set than the crisis that was initiated by the June 6, 1982 Israeli invasion of Lebanon. Since the crisis was terminated for the moment by the events of late September 1982, when the Israeli army handed West Beirut over to the Lebanese army and 45,000 soliders from the United States, France, and Italy positioned themselves in Lebanon to serve as a multinational peace-keeping force, the focus of our investigation is limited to a period of just under four months.[9]

It appears that Israel initiated the invasion in order to achieve four aims: (1) to drive Arafat and the PLO (Palestine Liberation Organization) out of Lebanon, thereby freeing Galilee from terrorist incursion and weakening the Palestinians enough politically to give Israel a free hand in the West Bank and Gaza Strip; (2) to expel the Syrians from Lebanon and remove the surface to air (SAM) missiles with which Syria was threatening to restrict Israel's freedom of move- ment; (3) to change the balance of power between Christians and Muslims within Lebanon, probably in order to help set up a new Christian-dominated government there led by the clan of Bashir and Amin Gemayel and protected by the Phalange which had been trained by Israel; and finally, (4) to rattle the Palestinians in the occupied territories sufficiently to make them leave or acquiesce to permanent Israeli domination.

Of these four goals, only one succeeded (albeit the victory was Pyrrhic); two backfired; and one failed catastrophically.[10] In their highly respected account of the 1982 war, Ze'ev Schiff and Ehud Ya'ari conclude that Israel's major achieve- ment was (and remains) the destruction of the PLO's "state-within-a-state" in Lebanon. However, in place of the PLO there emerged on Israel's northern border a militant Shiite Muslim enemy that has recently proven to be more deadly than the PLO ever was. Furthermore, while the Syrian missiles were in fact removed, the price paid was the promotion of Syria "from a sullen police state on the margins of recent Middle Eastern history to an imperial power . . . , a virtual Soviet arsenal, and a player in regional politics to which both superpowers regularly suck up."[11]

The war against the Palestinians backfired as well. They have certainly not budged from the occupied territories, and it may be reasonably concluded that the lesson they learned was that it is really quite possible to compel Israeli troops to evacuate occupied territories by killing a sufficiently large number of them. If the Lebanese Shiites had not thrown hand grenades at Israeli soldiers, the Israelis would not have withdrawn, or at least would not have withdrawn so rapidly.

Finally, it was the Israeli's political goals in Lebanon that eluded them altogether. For nearly a decade now, Middle East leaders and the leaders of the superpowers have been unable to successfully negotiate a settlement, thus condemning Lebanon to bitter, recurring civil strife. In the process, Lebanon has virtually lost its national identity, an outcome that to all appearances was only hastened by an Israeli invasion that failed utterly in its attempt to decisively strengthen the Christian position.

Clear in any case is that the 1982 war in Lebanon was a "watershed in modern Middle Eastern history."[12]

For Israel, it was the culmination of a disastrous obsession by the Begin Government with the Palestinians and a desire to knock them out of the Middle East equation. For the P.L.O., it was the culmination of the malaise that had set in years before and had transformed a once radical, ascetic guerrilla force into a semiconventional army, with an overweight bureaucracy, artsy posters and a Wall Street portfolio. . . . For Lebanon, the war marked the last gasp of a Christian Maronite oligarchy trying . . . to hold on to the perquisites of power to which their numbers no longer entitled them . . . [and] for the Arab oil states, the summer of 1983 unmasked the decadence that had set in from a decade of oil wealth.[13]

It is this turning point, then, that provides us with a richly textured opportunity to explore the role of national leaders, to see whether the analysis of their behavior can make a difference to theorists and practitioners of conflict resolution in the Middle East.

We decided to initiate the joint analysis of leadership and dispute settlement by developing case studies of each of the national leaders who played a significant role during the 1982 Lebanon war. Thus, eight of the nine following chapters provide separate discussions of each of eight leading players; these contributed essays have been written by scholars sensitive to leadership issues. The leaders are: Menachem Begin (Israel), Yasser Arafat (PLO), Hafez al-Assad (Syria), Hosni Mubarak (Egypt), King Hussein (Jordan), King Fahd (Saudi Arabia),

Leonid Brezhnev (USSR), and Ronald Reagan (US). Tellingly, the chapter that immediately follows this one—addressing leadership in Lebanon—does not focus on a single individual. Instead, it is a discussion that clearly reveals how the lack of leadership in that country contributed to its decline and fall.

The contributors' case studies of different national leaders contain information that can be roughly grouped into four different categories: (1) the general situation, (2) the leader's persona, (3) leader–follower relations, and (4) leader–leader relations.

THE GENERAL SITUATION

This material sets the stage on which the national leader's performance takes place. Erik Erikson's biographical work first drew widespread attention to the importance of the interrelationship between psychology and history. In his books on Martin Luther and Mohandas Gandhi, Erikson argued that for authentic leadership to occur, there must be a fit between the leader and the situation, between the passions and capacities of the man and the needs of the people. Components of the situation facing the national leader in particular include national character, political culture, prevailing ideology, dominant institutions and practices, and the political mood of the moment. In the case of a study such as this one—which concerns relations between states—beliefs, perceptions, and decision-making procedures pertaining to foreign policy systems are especially relevant.[14]

THE LEADER'S PERSONA

The student of leadership must also consider the leader; that is, the person filling the leadership role. What has been the course of his life history? What is his *Weltanschauung?*[15] What is the pattern of his political behavior: for example, how does he collect information? Who does he listen to, and under what circumstances? What is the quantity and quality of his interpersonal activity? How great is his proclivity to risk? What is his rhetorical style, and how does he generally communicate with his follows? How are his decisions formulated and implemented? What are his goals? Finally, there is perhaps the most important question: What are the leader's salient traits and personal characteristics?

Note that trait theories used to dominate the study of leadership. It was assumed that all leaders were endowed with superior qualities that could be identified and that offered a sufficient explanation for why leadership occurs. Although we no longer automatically assume that leaders are inherently superior, and although attention is now directed as much to the situation as it is to the leaders themselves, most leadership theorists still monitor the way the leader's personal traits affect his political style and the content of his decisions. Moreover, there are certain traits that are apparently associated with leadership in virtually all situations. Social skills such as speech fluency, and such traits as initiative, energy, and task-relevant ability, are hypothesized to be present whenever leadership takes place.

LEADER–FOLLOWER RELATIONS[16]

The degree of latitude enjoyed by the national leader depends on the extent of his formal and informal sources of power, and on the nature of both the political culture and his most important constituencies or followers. Formal sources of power are legally derived from constitutional and institutional arrangements. What, for instance, is the formal numerical distribution of leadership roles in the society? What are the legal means by which individuals gain access to these roles? How broad is the scope of the leader's authority? How severe are the constitutional constraints on the leader's freedom to act, and by what legal means can the national leader be stripped of his power?[17]

Informal sources of power are located in the leader rather than in the system. They are tools or tactics he acan employ—such as exuding charm to exert interpersonal influence, or using oratory to sway large crowds—to his own political advantage. Informal sources of power thus matter to the extent that the leader has the will and skill to mobilize them on his own behalf, and to the extent that the system allows them to have an impact on political outcomes. The U.S. presidency provides a good example of an office that is conducive to the use of informal sources of power. Because the president is constitutionally (formally) prohibited from legislating, he will, if he is politically skilled, use a variety of political tactics drawing on a variety of informal sources of power to get others, especially members of Congress, to do what he wants them to do.[18]

An even more vivid example of the importance of informal sources of power is provided by charismatic leaders and leaders of broad sociopolitical movements. Because such leaders—for example, Martin Luther King, Jr.—typically do not hold political office of any kind, and therefore lack formal power, their support is derived entirely from their personal capacity to mobilize followers on behalf of the view they espouse. Indeed, the nature of this personal rather than institutional support—support for the man rather than the office—can be so strong that, once generated, leadership is made relatively easy. Conversely, the leader who holds political office but who has little or no personal support will find his leadership task very difficult unless he can employ pressure or even force.

This brings us to the gray area of political culture. It can be argued that there are situations in which the national leader's ability to do what he wants does not depend only on his formal and informal sources of power. In these cases, it is the nature of the leadership system that is important. Certain political cultures endow their national leaders with a wide latitude, a latitude that is neither formally granted nor particularly earned but that seems rather to grow out of tradition, out of what has been considered the national norm. States that have had a pattern of strong authority figures, both in and out of government, are especially conducive to national leaders who are granted considerable leeway by what seems to be almost a kind of divine right. The patterns of authority that have dominated the Middle East for centuries make the area especially hospitable to strong national leaders who derive at least some of their power from a past in which the leader was not easily challenged, either by competing individuals or by rival factions.

LEADER–LEADER RELATIONS

Relations between national leaders can often be described as relations between people from two different worlds. Joseph H. de Rivera addressed the problem as follows:

> The difficulties inherent in communicating between two different worlds are usually underestimated. Most persons assume that their world is reality; consequently, they believe that the other's position must be based on the same "reality." They believe they understand the other's position, when in fact they have a pseudo-understanding achieved by distorting the other's motives. This illusion of understanding is preserved by the lack of contact that usually exists between alien worlds and the lack of motivation . . . [to change] one's own world.[19]

In his book, *Perception and Misperception in International Politics,* Robert Jervis explored the ways in which "decision makers' " views of the world actually diverge from reality, and described what were in many cases the frightful consequences of such misperception.[20] Jervis expressed particular concern about decision-makers' tendency to overestimate the other side's hostility—a tendency that has been particularly pertinent to the situation in the Middle East.

This is to not argue, of course, that the region has not been characterized by genuine and very deeply rooted conflict. Rather, is it to suggest that on those few occasions when there have been windows of opportunity for negotiation, the process has usually come to a halt in large part because of the inability of the different parties to imagine a reduction in the level of hostility that has characterized the situation. Indeed, both the Jewish and Arab states in the Middle East apparently continue to have a particular need for enemies. The problem is that this preoccupation with the enemy overshadows everything else. As a consequence, the longer it persists, the more difficult it becomes to eliminate or even reduce.

We are interested, then, in how Middle East leaders, each from a different world, see and behave toward one another. Further questions concerning the nature of leader–leader relations include: What are the formal arrangements and informal understandings between them? What are the channels of communication, and how often are they utilized? What are the similarities and differences between the national leaders and how do they affect the relations between states? How can relations between and among national leaders or their representatives generally be characterized?

Not surprisingly, space constraints have made it impossible for the authors of the nine leadership chapters to respond to all of the questions in each of the four categories described above. A complete case study is the stuff of a book, not a single chapter. However, taken together, the nine chapters provide an extraordinarily rich body of data. Based on these data, three experts on negotiation were invited to identify missed opportunities for dispute settlement.

More specifically, the three negotiation analysts were asked two classes of questions. First, there were questions bearing on the specifics of the four-month period in 1982: How might the negotiations, or lack thereof, have been handled differently by one or more of the leaders involved? What opportunities did they miss at several critical points? How might the discussions and negotiations have gone differently based on the leadership profiles provided? Second, there were questions bearing on the present and the future in the Middle East: What opportunity for conflict resolution do you now see in the Middle East? Based on the nine analyses of the 1982 leaders, what are the implications for future negotiation rounds involving these leaders or their successors?

Even now, scarcely a day passes in which the Middle East does not make front-page news. Moreover, the cast of characters in this region of the world has remained unchanged over long periods of time. As of this writing, Begin is out and Yitzhak Shamir is in, but all the other leaders in the region—Arafat, Assad, Mubarak, Hussein, Fahd, and even Amin Gemayel of Lebanon—hold the same positions of power as they did in 1982. (In some cases they were in leadership roles long before that.) As for the superpowers, Reagan will have had two terms in which to put his stamp on the Middle East, and while Brezhnev died in 1982, the history of Soviet leadership suggests strongly that Mikhail Gorbachev will have many years in which to make his mark on world politics, just as Brezhnev did before him.

This study of leadership and negotiation in the Middle East should therefore be pertinent for a long time to come. In fact, the Palestinian rioting that began in late 1987 prompted another look at the situation in which the leadership issue was key. As Thomas Friedman of the *New York Times* put it, "Ever since the Palestinian-Jewish conflict began, there have been two basic models for understanding it." The first affirms that it is an irreconcilable conflict that can be managed but never solved. The second grows out of Sadat's dramatic visit to Jerusalem, and assumes that, with bold leadership, Arabs and Jews can rise above their history and politics to break the cycle of violence and build a new relationship.[21]

Of course, the real problem with the second model is that it presupposes that there will be leaders on both sides with the vision and cunning to conceive and implement a new dynamic. However, as Israeli political scientist Yaron Ezrahi argues, there do not now appear to be any leaders either in Israel or the Palestine Liberation Organization who are capable of diagnosing today's problems or taking the necessary risks to reshape public opinion in a way that might bring about a solution. Alternatively, as a senior U.S. official put it, "Peres, Arafat and King Hussein have one thing in common: They all want a peace process without any pain or any political risks to themselves.''[22]

What we can say with some certainty, in any case, is that the potential role of leaders in resolving international disputes is likely to be newly scrutinized. The particulars of the dispute will change, as will, of course, the cast of characters, but the opportunities that leadership analysis affords may well be constant. In our view, there can be little doubt that placing the national leader in the middle of the action accords with the political and psychological realities of how the world really works.

NOTES

1. Andrew Bard Schmookler, *The Parable of the Tribes: The Problem of Power in Social Evolution* (Berkeley, Calif.: University of California Press, 1984). The quotes are from pp. 21 and 22, which contain the kernel of Schmookler's elegant and elaborately developed argument.

2. A brief discussion of the evolutionary perspective can also be found in Graham T. Allison, Albert Carnesale, and Joseph S. Nye, Jr., eds., *Hawks, Doves, and Owls: An Agenda for Avoiding Nuclear War* (New York: Norton, 1985). They argue that the "tendency of individuals, groups, tribes, and nations to fight among themselves has functioned adaptively . . . to provide access to food, water, and shelter, and to resolve disputes among groups" (p. 8). At the same time, they believe that the situation has now changed radically. Today we are in an environment in which "the species might destroy itself and the ecosystem" (p. 8).

3. Robert C. Tucker, "The Dictator and Totalitarianism," *World Politics* 17, no. 4, (July 1965): 555–83.

4. In the *Journal of International Affairs* 24, no. 1 (1970): 3.

5. A nod here to Fred Greenstein, who years ago formulated several similarly structured propositions on the links between personality and politics. See his *Personality and Politics* (Chicago: Markam, 1969), pp. 42 ff.

6. It should be noted that a powerful personality with a zealous passion for shaping world affairs can overwhelm objective factors such as the size of the state.

7. Janice Gross Stein, "Leadership in Peacemaking: Fate, Will and Fortune in the Middle East," *International Journal* 37, no. 4 (Autumn 1982); pp. 538, 539.

8. Ibid., p. 519.

9. Thomas Friedman, "Inside the Palestinian Bunker," *The New York Times Book Review,* December 15, 1985, p. 3. Friedman noted that a reasonably complete discussion of the 1982 war in Lebanon can be drawn from Ze'ev Schiff and Ehud Ya'ari, *Israel's Lebanon War* (New York: Simon and Schuster, 1984), and Rashid Khalidi, *Under Siege: P.L.O. Decision Making During the 1982 War* (New York: Columbia University Press, 1985).

10. See Leon Wieseltier's review of Schiff and Ya'ari, *Israel's Lebanon War,* in *The New Republic,* December 10, 1984, p. 85.

11. Ibid., p. 87.

12. The phrase is Khalidi's, in Khalidi, *Under Siege,* p. 1.

13. Friedman, "Inside the Palestinian Bunker," p. 3.

14. For more on what constitutes a foreign policy system, see Ofira Seliktar, "Iden-

tifying Belief Systems,'' in *Handbook of Political Psychology,* volume 2, ed. Margaret Hermann (San Francisco: Jossey-Bass, 1986), pp. 320–54.

15. For a discussion of general beliefs as they pertain specifically to political action, see Alexander L. George, ''The 'Operational Code': A Neglected Approach to the Study of Political Leaders and Decision-Making,'' *International Studies Quarterly* 13, no. 2 (June 1969); 190–222.

16. The word ''follower'' is used rather broadly here. That is, we assume that the political elite as well as the masses must follow the leader—or at least may not actively resist him—if he is to successfully initiate change.

17. For a description of what David Rosen has called the ''leadership system,'' see his chapter ''Leadership in World Cultures'' in *Leadership: Multidisciplinary Perspectives,* ed. Barbara Kellerman (Englewood Cliffs, N.J.: Prentice-Hall, 1984), pp. 39–62.

18. For an elaboration of this argument, see Barbara Kellerman, *The Political Presidency: Practice of Leadership* (New York: Oxford University Press, 1984).

19. Joseph H. de Rivera, *The Psychological Dimension of Foreign Policy* (Columbus: Charles E. Merrill Co., 1968), p. 279.

20. Princeton: Princeton University Press, 1976.

21. Thomas Friedman, *New York Times,* December 31, 1987, p. 6.

22. Both Ezrahi and the U.S. official were quoted in ibid.

2

LEBANON'S ELIAS SARKIS, BASHIR GEMAYAL, AND AMIN GEMAYAL

David M. Rosen

The Lebanese Constitution establishes the Lebanese presidency as one of the most powerful political positions in the country. Under the constitution, the president, who must be a Maronite Christian, is elected for a single term of six years. In theory, the president controls the principal centers of state power including the Lebanese army and the state bureaucracy. Despite these constitutionally derived powers, the Lebanese presidency is perpetually embroiled in a crisis of legitimacy that undermines its ability to serve as an integrating or stabilizing political factor in Lebanese society. This chapter is less a detailed historical study than an attempt to provide a model for analyzing the Lebanese presidency as a national force. I argue that Lebanese society is characterized by a dual leadership system whose internal contradictions prevent the successful emergence of viable national leadership. This leadership system has contributed to the recent history of political anarchy in Lebanon, and has helped create the conditions leading to the Israeli invasion of Lebanon in 1982.

THE LEBANESE LEADERSHIP SYSTEM

Presidential leadership in Lebanon, like leadership elsewhere in the world, must first be understood in terms of the social and cultural contexts within which it is embedded. The presidential role involves a set of rights and obligations, some embedded in law and others given by custom, which are tied to the leadership role. Lebanese presidential leadership, and the specific institutional supports and constraints within which it functions, constitute what can be termed the Lebanese leadership system.[1]

Analysis of the Lebanese presidency as part of a wider leadership system requires investigation of three broad areas: 1) the relation between presidential leadership and other principal leadership roles in Lebanese society; 2) the manner in which presidential leadership is attained and realized; and 3) the ways Lebanese presidents carry out their roles. It is useful to view Lebanese society as having a dual leadership system: a state-level leadership system on the one hand, and an ethnic or communal leadership system on the other. Although these two systems are in some respects highly integrated, their continued separate existences and contradictory demands give Lebanon its special political structure and determine the character of the presidency. To be a successful president in Lebanon, an individual must be a leader within both the national leadership system and the ethnic-communal leadership system. However, the conflicting demands and value orientations of these different systems continually undermine the legitimacy of presidential power and make it impossible to fill both roles properly.

THE NATIONAL LEADERSHIP SYSTEM

The formal national leadership system in Lebanon is embedded in a parliamentary form of government; the parliamentary body is known as the Chamber of Deputies. The current constitution of the country was put into place in 1926, during the period of the French mandate over Lebanon. Although the constitution has been modified in several respects, its provisions regarding the formal allocation of governmental leadership roles in society remain intact. The national leadership system, sometimes termed the confessional system, distributes political power along ethnic communal and religious lines. Traditionally, the primary power groups in this system have been Maronite Christians and their junior partners the Sunni Moslems. Other religious communal groups, most notably Shiite Moslems and Druze, have an important but subordinate role.

Under the original Lebanese Constitution, parliamentary seats were "equitably" distributed along ethnic communal lines. Immediately prior to independence in 1943, the Maronite leader and future President Bishara Khoury and the Sunni leader Riyad Solh created the so-called National Pact—an unwritten agreement with national and international dimensions. Within the framework of the pact, Christians and Moslems agreed to maintain the independence of Lebanon by renouncing Arab union and French protection.[2] Nationally, the constitutional provision for the equitable distribution of parliamentary seats was interpreted so as to provaide a 6-to-5 ratio in favor of the Christians. The same ratio was applied to positions within the executive branch of the government as well.

Within each of the broad religious groupings, there was an additional subdivision of seats along other communal and ethnic lines, so that Maronite Christians, Greek Orthodox, Sunni and Shiite Moslems, and Druze are all represented in varying ratios. As a result of this parliamentary structure, the principal leadership roles were allocated among the most powerful ethnic groups. Thus, the president was to be a Maronite Christian, the prime minister (appointed by the president) a Sunni Moslem, and the speaker of the chamber a Shiite Moslem. Under the National Pact the president was elected by a two-thirds majority of the Chamber of Deputies for a six-year term. However, while every candidate for the presidency had to be a Maronite Christian, it was impossible for any candidate to receive a two-thirds majority vote without finding some support among non-Christians.

Some of the provisions of the National Pact were amended in 1976 under the constitutional document of President Suleiman Frangieh. Specifically, seats in the Parliament were redistributed on an equal basis between Christians and Moslems—the president elected by a 55 percent majority after the first ballot, and the prime minister elected by a 51 percent majority vote. The distribution of the three principal posts of president, prime minister, and speaker remained the same under the Constitutional Document, which was merely regarded as an amendment to the National Pact.[3] Thus, the National Pact, in its amended form, remains the foundation upon which Lebanese national politics are constructed.

Historically, then, the national political system allowed religion and ethnicity to define the field of eligible presidential candidates, but also to block candidates who could not achieve some following among other non-Christian ethnic and communal groups. Typically, this following was achieved through the distribution of political and material rewards to non-Christian supporters. In addition, Christian power was required to stress, at least in the ideological and symbolic arena, its association with the Arab world, and to do so despite the strong tendencies of the Christian community to associate with Europe and the West. In the National Pact, for example, Lebanon was declared to be a country with an "Arab face," a term that stressed its association but not its union or total identification with the Arab world.[4] By and large, the national system tended to favor compromise candidates: people whose perspectives and policies were minimally acceptable to other ethnic and communal groups. However, this system essentially operated within a constitutionally and politically enshrined, asymmetrical set of power relationships in which Christian power dominated and few forces were sufficiently powerful to launch an effective challenge to Christian hegemony. In this sense, the Christian commitment to the Lebanese state was primarily constructed out of its dominant role in the state.

The National Pact was a crucial element in cementing the relationship between Lebanon and its more powerful northern neighbor, Syria. Syria, having long regarded Lebanon as part of "Greater Syria," has wielded its power and influence through the traditional Lebanese leadership system. As a result, it has usually regarded attacks on this system as a challenge to its regional domination. While Syria has often forcibly agitated for reform within Lebanese politics, it has also stood clear of commitment to radical social and political changes that might undermine its control.

The recent political history of Lebanon, most prominently the Civil War of 1975 and 1976, involved a sustained assault on the National Pact. In the early 1970s, Shiite Muslims, first under the leadership of Imam Sadr and later under the leadership of Nabbih Berri, began to launch an attack on the National Pact. More recently they joined a broad coalition composed of the Druze National

Front as well as Sunni leaders intended to openly challenge the Christian hegemony. The Sunni position in this coalition was an ambivalent one; they clearly
benefited from the National Pact, and primarily sought reforms that would expand
their power within the traditional system (for example, the elimination of Christian control over the presidency). They did not identify with the more radical
demands of their Shiite and Druze allies. As Itamar Rabinovich has pointed out,
the Civil War was carried out between two broad coalitions, neither of which
can be totally described on a religious or communal basis; rather, the largely
Christian camp attempted to maintain the status quo, while the largely Moslem
camp attempted its overthrow.[5] In the end, the growing power of the Shiites and
their allies has led to some reform of the National Pact. It has not, however,
lessened the resolve of the major conservative actors—Christians, Sunnis and
Syrians—to maintain the traditional system of plural confessional politics in
some form.

In a fundamental way, the assault on the National Pact has modified the
political relationship between the different ethnic-communal groups and the Lebanese state. Under the National Pact it was the Christian community that was
most profoundly committed to the Lebanese state. Now, however, with the vision
of the end of the pact in mind, it is the Moslems who are most committed to a
Lebanese state. The Christians, for their part, have increasingly come to see a
political future in separation and partition. Although partition is unlikely to come
about, Christian hegemony as it was known before the Lebanese Civil War and
the Israeli invasion can no longer be realized.

THE ETHNIC/COMMUNAL LEADERSHIP SYSTEM

The ethnic-communal leadership system can be understood by examining the
relationship between the various ethnic-communal groups and the Lebanese state.
Recently, Elie Kedourie has suggested that the European concept of political
organization breaks down in the Middle East, where the concept of the nation
as a natural entity has not taken root.[6] In Kedourie's view, the authority to rule
in traditional Middle Eastern societies does not derive from the electoral process;
rather, it derives from a combination of conquest and perogatives linked with
traditional status positions in Middle Eastern society. Thus, voting and electoral
processes per se have little, if anything, to do with the concept of leadership
legitimacy.

At the same time, the heterogeneous character of Middle Eastern societies
prompted the evolution of the so-called "millet system," by which minority
groups with no real claim to national leadership exercised internal control over
their communal affairs. Put simply, recognized customary subordinate status
carried with it rights and special claims upon the governing community. The
emergence of the modern state however has, in Kedourie's terms, transformed
the traditional minority into a national minority. The important difference between a traditional and a national minority is that the latter, having lost the basis

for communal autonomy and self-government, has become a body of pseudo-citizens who are citizens only in the barest legal terms. Because state citizenship provides few, if any, rights within the state political system, groups engage in ethnic mobilization in order to gain access to the benefits of the national society. In Kedourie's terms, state citizenship is meaningless, since it provides minority groups with little or no access to the principal political, social, and economic resources.[7]

Kedourie's model is provocative. It is not clear, however, even in a society as conflict-laden as Lebanon, that the absence of meaningful state citizenship renders the state political system meaningless, or that communal groups have lost control over their internal affairs. If state citizenship is not the dominant mode by which groups and individuals are linked to the larger society, issues surrounding the control of the state, its resources, and its governmental apparatus, still dominate Lebanese politics. Regardless of whether ethnic mobilization is the main political strategy, ethnic groups deal with one another within the framework of an existing state system. Even where the state exists only marginally, as a common communal political system governed by widely accepted norms, it exists, in a contradictory manner, as both a highly valued material and institutional resource, and as a potential threat to the political integrity and communal autonomy of the various subgroups of Lebanese society. In this sense, ethnic mobilization serves to advance the interest of particular ethnic groups within the state system, while protecting the interests of these groups against the power of the state.

In all these respects, then, state citizenship is an important category in Lebanese political life. Ethnic and political groups, not having the benefit of citizenship, cannot legitimately compete for state-controlled resources even where ethnic mobility is a viable option. A good example is the Palestinians in Lebanon who, having been denied Lebanese citizenship, created a semisovereign ministate. However, their de facto presence never afforded them legitimacy within the Lebanese state political system.

LEADERSHIP IN THE ETHNIC/COMMUNAL SYSTEM

The leadership that develops within a system of ethnic mobilization is totally dedicated to advancing the interests of that particular ethnic group. In Lebanon, local-level leadership is constructed around patron-client relationships, in which a patron (*za'im*) exercises power over varying sizes of groups of followers. The manner in which leaders actually come to power varies both within and between groups. Some patrons draw their strength from a long history of feudal control over agriculture, while others gain power within the more capitalized sectors of the Lebanese economy. Normally, the legitimacy of such leadership depends almost entirely upon the ability of a leader to gain and distribute economic and political rewards to the community of followers. However, such leadership can be partially transformed through participation in a national system that itself creates norms and values transcending the interests of particular groups.

For most communal leaders, the Lebanese state forms a political arena where communal groups, legitimized through state citizenship, compete with one another for power and resources. The benefits of participation in this system are balanced against the dangers that a powerful state system poses for communal autonomy. A powerful state leadership could potentially supplant and overrun the leaders of the independent communal groups. In theory this can occur where forces and leaders committed to the more universalist concept of the state replace the more particularistic forces and leadership of communal groups, but it can also occur where particular communal groups and leaders gain control of state structures and resources, and utilize the power of the state to enforce their own interests. Throughout the history of modern Lebanon, the main fear of the different Moslem communal groups and leaders has been that increasing state power and leadership would transform the state into a special instrument of the Christian community. Ironically, following the increasing gains made by the Moslem community in the years after the 1975–1976 Civil War, it has primarily been the Christians who, for similar reasons, had feared the growth of the Lebanese state. However, it is not only fear of control by an alien community that underlies the attempts of some ethnic and communal group leaders to keep the state at a distance. Any state system would ultimately subordinate communal interests to state interests.

The Lebanese state and its system of leadership must be regarded as a major resource toward which ethnic mobilization is directed. Involvement in the state implies both benefits and risks. Historically, communal groups and their leaders have sought to maximize benefits from the state system while minimizing the costs of participation. As a result, the relationship between ethnic groups and the Lebanese state is strikingly fluid: the communal perception of risks and benefits afforded by participation in the state system continually serves to alter the relationship between the communal groups and the state leadership system.

TYPES OF PRESIDENTIAL LEADERSHIP

In recent years, the history of the Lebanese state has been characterized by a struggle between leaders whose vision has involved a more universalist concept of the state, and those whose vision is primarily governed by strong communal interests. The ability of these two kinds of leaders to gain control of the state system has varied according to circumstances. Generally speaking, Lebanese politics has favored presidential candidates whose leadership has been secured through the ethnic-communal system. Normally, a period of peace makes it possible for this kind of presidential leader to emerge. In contrast, periods of war and conflict tend to generate leaders more clearly associated with political reform. When the Christian community has felt relatively secure in its hold over the country, a more particularistic leadership has emerged, but when significantly challenged, the same community has tended to promote reform candidates with a more universal and nationally oriented perspective. Because the bulk of the Christian community has primarily been concerned with preserving its prerogatives within the framework of the National Pact, it has never permitted reformist presidents to carry out substantive changes in the political structure.

Regardless of the type of leadership involved, the Lebanese presidency has been an extraordinarily weak institution—so weak, in fact, that it has a long history of appealing to outside sources of power. These have included the United States, France, Syria, and Israel, all of whom, at one time or another, have come to the military aid of a presidency and country in crisis.

This pattern reveals the contradictions inherent in the Lebanese leadership system: The most powerful leaders tend to achieve their leadership roles through the ethnic-communal system, and their primary identification and loyalties remain embedded in that system. With respect to the Lebanese presidency, these have been Maronite Christians who have obtained a strong following even in the context of a sharply divided and conflict-laden Maronite community. To be sure, the acceptability of such presidents to non-Christians has depended upon their ability to articulate a vision of the Lebanese state which, at least on the ideological and symbolic level, promotes the interests of all ethnic groups. At the same time, and in keeping with their constituencies, these presidents tend to maintain the status quo and the dominance of Christian power and authority. In contrast reform candidates, who have a more universal approach to Lebanese society, have remained weak and have lacked any real following.

Within these limits, the Christian community seems to have generated three types of presidential leaders. I term these the "broker," the "reformer," and the "militarist." Brokers have initially achieved positions of strength within the ethnic communal system but, in attempting to attain the presidency, have necessarily shifted their position from being strongly communal to being broadly nationalist. These relatively strong leaders have considerable support within the ethnic-communal system; their main problem is extending their legitimacy and authority into the state political arena. Typically they have done so through a classic combination of brokerage politics, and ideological and symbolic identification with the Arab community. This identification, however, falls short of any modification of the leadership system. I include Camille Chamoun, Suleiman Frangieh, and Amin Gemayal in this category.

The second, or reformist, type of presidential leadership, has emerged when the Christian community has been under assault. These are reform candidates who, as apolitical technocrats or bureaucrats, are firmly committed to the concept of an ethnically plural Lebanese state. Such leaders are generally more committed to national reform and to remedying the imbalance between the Christian and non–Christian communities through constitutional means. However, these kinds of leaders have lacked real legitimacy in the Christian communal sector, and have served primarily in a stop-gap capacity as arbitrators when the Christian community has been under attack. The position of such leadership has usually been a desire to create a strong Lebanese state with accommodation to all sides. However, such leaders have had little to build with, and their main sources of support have often come more from the international community than from Lebanon itself. I include Bishara Khoury, Fuad Chehab, Charles Helou, and Elias Sarkis in this category.

The third type of presidential leader—the militarist—emerged with the election of Bashir Gemayal. This type of presidential leader has great legitimacy within the ethnic-communal system but virtually none in the national system. Bashir Gemayal's primary goal was to promote directly and militarily the interest and power of the Christian community at the expense of the other communal groups. Bashir Gemayal's election, however, was an anomalous event brought about only because of Israeli intervention in Lebanon in 1982. His unacceptability within the framework of the national leadership system was made crystal clear by his assassination, prior to taking office, on September 14, 1982, by a member of the Syrian National party. In his place, Amin Gemayal, his brother and a classic broker, emerged as president of Lebanon.

In this chapter, I discuss neither the role of the Sunni prime minister nor the relationship between the president and prime minister, even though a discussion of both would be an important component in a total analysis of the Lebanese leadership system. Briefly, the presidency and the prime ministership are largely competitive and parallel leadership roles, although the president monopolizes a larger share of national power. Most of the weaknesses of the presidency, however, can also be found in the office of the prime minister. In contrast, a major cultural strength of the latter office is that the prime minister is a Moslem in an Arab country. To be sure, a major Sunni goal is to overturn that portion of the National Pact that provides the Maronites with a monopoly over the presidency. Whether a Moslem president would be stronger than a Christian one remains open to speculation

This next section discusses the three types of presidential leadership in detail. The focus is primarily on the last three presidents: Elias Sarkis (1976–1982), a reformist; Bashir Gemayal (1982) a militarist; and Amin Gemayal (1982–present), a broker. These three presidential leaders illustrate the nature and scope of Lebanese presidential power, as well as the circumstances affecting the ability of a president to lead the larger society. The careers of these men are illustrative of the crisis of legitimacy that has undermined the ability of the Lebanese presidency to act as an agent on behalf of the Lebanese state.

Equally important, however, the focus upon these three presidents is crucial for understanding the context in which the Israeli invasion of Lebanon took place. It is the weaknesses of the Lebanese presidency and the Lebanese state that combined to create the social and political environment in which the Palestinian refugee presence in South Lebanon evolved into a ministate whose growing autonomy and power invited the Israeli invasion. This phenomenon could only have taken place in a political environment in which the president lacked the ability to mobilize state power toward given ends.

ELIAS SARKIS: 1976–1982

Elias Sarkis was a compromise candidate who emerged during the Lebanese Civil War on the heels of the presidency of Suleiman Frangieh. Sarkis had been a candidate for the Lebanese presidency in 1970, when he ran against Frangieh. Sarkis was governor of the Central Bank and an advocate of political reform in Lebanon. Although both were Maronite Christians, Sarkis was perceived to be more sympathetic to Arab nationalism than was Frangieh. Sarkis lost this election, but he obtained the majority of the Moslem votes in the Chamber of Deputies. Frangieh had strong ties to Syria but was firmly committed to Christian control of Lebanon; he was also largely indifferent to the need to accommodate the growing power and dissatisfaction of Lebanese Moslems. Although he attempted some constitutional reforms at the end of his presidency, they were too little and too late; Lebanon was already embroiled in the 1975–76 Civil War, and the Christian community was in danger of a serious, if not fatal, military setback. It was precisely the immanent danger to the traditional Lebanese political system that invited Syrian intervention into Lebanon during the Civil War in 1976.[8]

There were many reasons why Syria was willing to rescue the Christian community in this conflict. First, Syria regarded Lebanon as part of "Greater Syria," and feared that a leftist Moslem takeover might undermine Syrian influence in Lebanon. Second, Syria also feared that a leftist takeover of the Lebanese state might lead to the partitioning of Lebanon into Christian and Moslem enclaves. This would have had a profound ideological impact on the entire Arab world since, in Syria's view, it would lend support to Israel's claim of the profound animosity in the Arab world toward non-Moslems. Third, a Moslem victory would make possible the strengthening of the PLO ministate in South Lebanon, an event Syria viewed as dangerous to Syrian interests.

It should be pointed out here that Syrian attitudes toward growing Moslem power, and especially the growth of PLO power in South Lebanon, were complex. Although Syria was supportive of the Palestinians, this was true to the extent that Palestinians could be mobilized in support of the Syrian struggle against Israel. Conversely, Syria was implacably hostile to the growth of any Palestinian power that was not subordinated to Syrian directives. Equally important, the Lebanese Civil War brought a new phase of Palestinian activity in Lebanon, namely direct military support of the Moslem Left in Lebanon. As a result, Syria was willing to intervene in Lebanon in order to both maintain the system of traditional politics and subdue the Palestinian presence in Lebanese politics.

The price to be paid by the Christian community for Syrian support was the election of a president who would accommodate Syrian involvement and institute sufficient political reforms to stave off the leftist attack. The person chosen for this job was Elias Sarkis.[9] The reforms he was to institute included equal Christian and Moslem representation in Parliament, the election of the prime minister by

Parliament, and equal representation of Christians and Moslems in top civil service and army appointments.

Sarkis was elected in May of 1976. In addition to his commitment to reform, Sarkis may also have been an attractive candidate to Syria precisely because, as he did not come out of the communal leadership system, he lacked both a mass base and military backing, and was therefore heavily dependent on Syria for support.[10] He was supported by the major Christian leadership as well as conservative Moslems, but he was not supported by more radical Arab factions. On May 8, 1976, Sarkis was elected president by a total of 66 votes on the second ballot in the Lebanese Chamber of Deputies. Twenty-nine deputies were absent. He was escorted to and from his election by the Syrian-controlled faction of Palestinians, *el-Sa'iqa*, who at the same time was engaged in a full-scale attack on the leftist-Palestinian alliance.[11] In June of 1976, a month after Sarkis's election, Syria intervened in Lebanon in hope of removing the Palestinians and leftists from Mount Lebanon and the coast prior to Sarkis's actual inauguration on September 23.[12]

With Syria providing the support for the presidency, the crucial goal for the Sarkis regime was national reconciliation. To achieve this, Sarkis appointed a non-political technocratic government to begin rebuilding the Lebanese infrastructure. The second goal of the Sarkis government was to reassert the power of the Lebanese state. However, the reassertion of state power required the achievement of a consensus among the very powers that found state power to be detrimental to their most vital interests: the communal leaders. Thus Sarkis's energies were spent trying to mediate among enemies.

For example, crucial to the achievement of national stability was the rebuilding of the Lebanese army. The rebuilding of the army was completely opposed by the National Front on the grounds that movement toward national stability might involve power sharing as envisioned by Shiite and Druze leaders. Syrian intervention left the Maronites militarily if not politically strong, and in no mood to effect the constitutional reforms involved in power sharing. Thus, although Sarkis attempted to assert the power of the Lebanese state and to create a centralized system of military and political power, the Sarkis period is best described as a political cease-fire in which the ethnic and communal factions of an increasingly divided Lebanon bolstered their military and political strength. Sarkis himself spent much of his presidency in a futile effort to curb the growing trends of militarism and radicalism in the various ethnic communities.

A principal preoccupation of the Sarkis regime was the growing power of the Palestinians. The growth of Palestinian military power not only invited possible Israeli intervention in Lebanon, but it also created an alliance between Israel and the Christian community. The Christians, who regarded the Palestinian presence in Lebanon as illegal, saw growing Palestinian power and the Palestinian-Lebanese-Left alliance as a direct threat to their control. Thus, in the months preceding Sarkis's election, the Christian community was engaged in two important actions: first, the Christian Phalange was making contacts with

Israel for military support; and second, it was developing the economic infra-structure of airports, roads, and communications to make partition from the rest of Lebanon feasible. However, Sarkis's and the Christians' attitudes toward the Palestinians were incompatible. The Christian community wanted the Palestinians out of Lebanon. Sarkis's mandate from Syria, however, was to control and stabilize the Palestinian presence under Syrian domination.

Because of the desperate military and political situation and the buildup of Christian, Palestinian, Druze, and Shiite forces, Sarkis found it impossible to halt the spiral of confrontation. In September of 1976, Sarkis reached an initial compromise in a meeting arranged between the most powerful of the Palestinian factions, al-Fatah, and the Christians, but the compromise was unacceptable to several "rejectionist" Palestinian factions. As a result, Syria launched a punitive attack on the Palestinians, delaying any possibility of compromise.[13]

However, Syria's main goal was to control, and not merely to punish the Palestinians. Sarkis was finally installed as president on September 23, 1976. One month later, Syria, along with other Arab nations and the Palestinians, signed the Riyadh Accord imposing strict regulations on the Palestinians. Enforcement responsibilities were assigned to the Arab peace-keeping forces, which were composed mainly of Syrians, and theoretically subordinated to Sarkis.[14] In addition, Syria began to rebuild the Lebanese army (not to be confused with the Christian Lebanese forces) with a nucleus composed of a pro-Syrian force named the "Vanguards of Lebanon's Arab Army."[15]

Sarkis's main approach to stabilizing the conflict was to place the Lebanese army, a symbol of state control, between the contending parties. Sarkis also hoped to employ the Arab League to maintain a truce between Lebanese Christians and Moslems. Syria, however, demanded that the Phalangists renounce their ties to Israel as a precondition for further efforts by the Arab League to find a peaceful solution. Sarkis was clearly unable to achieve this, and had to content himself with a patently false statement from Bashir Gemayal, then the leader of the Christian military forces, declaring that the Phalange Party had no relationship with Israel.

Sarkis did in fact have some success in the north of Lebanon. In January of 1977, he established the Board of Reconstruction and Development, paving the way for limited economic recovery. It was clear, however, that full recovery depended on political reconciliation.[16] Thus, in April of 1977, Sarkis ordered 4,000 Palestinian refugees out of a former Christian town in order to allow for Christian resettlement. In addition, the Sarkis government banned the entry into Lebanon of all Palestinians holding foreign passports so as to reduce by attrition the total number of Palestinians in Lebanon.[17] In July 1977, Sarkis reached an agreement with Yasir Arafat, who agreed to abide by the accords regulating Palestinian activities in Lebanon.

Sarkis's success in South Lebanon was much more limited. His goal was to use the Lebanese army or the United Nations forces to replace Palestinian forces, to provide a military buffer between Palestinians and Israelis, and to put an end to the possibility of Israeli intervention. However, Israel trusted neither the ability nor will of the Lebanese army or the United Nations to maintain peace on the border. Instead, Israel began to provide the autonomous self-defense capacity for Christians in South Lebanon, which paralleled its growing relationship with the Christian community in the north. This policy, while clearly linked to Israel's security needs in the south, served to effectively weaken the authority of the Sarkis government.[18] Moreover, the growth of the overall Christian-Israeli alliance prompted the Christians to threaten withdrawal of all support for Sarkis unless restraints on the Palestinians were enforced.

The years 1977 and 1978 involved a major transformation of Sarkis's relationship with Syria. It involved his increasing recognition that Syria was acting as a foreign occupier in Lebanon. As a result, his position began to shift closer to that of the Christian community.[19] In addition, Sarkis was concerned that the growing rapprochement between Israel and Egypt following President Sadat's visit to Jerusalem would result in a Middle East solution leaving the Palestinians in Lebanon. On January 6, 1978, Sarkis declared that Lebanon would not accept any kind of settlement permitting the Palestinians to remain in Lebanon.

However, Sarkis was unable to control Palestinian power in the south. Palestinian military activity against Israel led to the Israeli Litani Operation in March of 1978, in which Israel intervened in South Lebanon. One result of the Israeli intervention was the formal creation of the Army of South Lebanon, a Christian militia under the command of Major Sa'ad Hadad. In April 1977, Sarkis met with both Arafat and U.N. Secretary Kurt Waldheim; Arafat agreed to cooperate with the U.N. forces to secure Israeli withdrawal. However, Israel was now firmly committed to maintaining a separate Christian force in South Lebanon as a means of securing its northern border. Moreover, Palestinian military activity in the south continued to grow, which dictated that curbing the Palestinians would become the major preoccupation of the Sarkis regime.

In January 1981, in a speech to Islamic leaders attending a conference in Taif, Saudi Arabia, Sarkis pleaded that the growing Palestinian activity in South Lebanon was in violation of the PLO's commitment. In November 1981, Sarkis sought a moratorium on Palestinian guerrilla activity in South Lebanon, and a simultaneous takeover of the area by U.N. forces. At this point, Sarkis was quite aware that failure to control the Palestinians would lead to an Israeli invasion. In November of 1981, the leader of the Christian forces, Bashir Gemayal, had already declared his candidacy for the presidency in anticipation of the expiration of Sarkis's term of office in September 1982, Bashir Gemayal knew that he stood no chance of being elected without direct Israeli intervention.[20]

In April of 1982, Sarkis met with both U.S. and Soviet envoys to ask for their intervention to stave off the expected Israeli invasion. However, failure to control the Palestinians led to the strengthening of the Israeli-Christian alliance. As a result, Sarkis could neither prevent the Lebanese Christian–Moslem confrontation nor the Israeli attack on the Palestinians. Recruited as a compromise candidate, he lacked legitimacy at the ethnic-communal level; he could serve only as an arbitrator, unable to impose a solution on groups who saw their best interests served by military combat. The Sarkis presidency came to an end with the Israeli invasion of Lebanon and the emergence of Bashir Gemayal as president of Lebanon. Indeed, it may well be that the time of the invasion itself was meant to coincide with the expiration of Sarkis's term as president.

THE EMERGENCE OF BASHIR GEMAYAL

It was during the Sarkis presidency that Bashir Gemayal rose to prominence in the Christian community. Bashir Gemayal's goal was to bring the various Christian groups under the military and political authority of the Phalange party, which had been founded by his father Pierre Gemayal. First, Bashir Gemayal wanted to gain greater control of the territory under the rule of the Frangieh family, Sarkis's predecessor and the most important ally of Syria within the Christian community. On June 13, 1978, about a month after Suleiman Frangieh walked out of a meeting over this very problem, Phalangist forces surrounded the home of Tony Frangieh (Suleiman's son and leader of the militia); the Phalangists murdered Tony Frangieh, his wife, daughter, bodyguards, and do-mestic staff.[21] Two years later, on July 7, 1980, Phalange military units destroyed the military forces of former president Camille Chamoun and announced their intention to unify all the separate Christian militia into a single military force. Many of the Chamoun forces joined the Phalange, as did the forces of two smallera militia groups: the Organization and the Guardians of the Cedar.[22]

Although military contacts between Israel and the Christians began in 1975, they intensified in the period between 1978 and 1982. It has been estimated that some 250 Christian and 1,000 non-Christian officers were trained by the Israeli Defense Force in special training camps in the Negev. By June of 1982, at the time of the Israeli invasion of Lebanon, Bashir Gemayal had consolidated the separate Christian militias into the Lebanese forces—a military force of between 8,000 and 10,000 regular troops.[23]

To understand the Phalange party's election of Bashir Gemayal, it is important to note the historic political flexibility in its ongoing relationship with Moslem Arab interests. Unlike some other factions in the Christian community, the Phalange was often a willing participant in the numerous compromise solutions that characterized the pattern of Lebanese political life. Pierre Gemayal himself supported many of the reforms of reformist President Fuad Chehab and served in the government of Prime Minister Rashid Karami. The Phalange party believed that continued Christian hegemony depended on an amended National Pact which would preserve traditional alliances with conservative Moslem forces.

Two major forces within the Phalange movement sought to advance Christian interests and control in Lebanon: the Phalange party itself and the Lebanese forces. Although the Lebanese forces were dominated by the Phalange party, the forces were a far more militant strain within the Maronite community. In contrast to the party's overall political strategy of brokerage politics, the military saw a more expanded role for the Christian community through a military alliance with Israel. The Lebanese forces had been developed under the stewardship of Bashir Gemayal; it was he who converted the militia into a well-trained, disciplined fighting force. Bashir Gemayal wanted to move both the party and the militia outside the sphere of Syrian influence, and to enter into a tacit alliance with Israel. Moreover, he entertained a much more powerful role, based on military force, for the Maronite Christians.

From this perspective, Bashir Gemayal found an important ally in Ariel Sharon, the Israeli minister of defense in the Begin government, who had already developed a design to invade Lebanon and bring it within the sphere of Israeli influence. Sharon's view of the Lebanese problem was not limited to Israel's security concerns. Instead, he anticipated a new political order in Lebanon in which Israel and its Christian allies would both eliminate the PLO and sharply reduce Syrian and Moslem influence in Lebanon.[24] Thus Sharon began to plan the first offensive war in Israel's history.

Even under the dominance of Bashir Gemayal, the Phalange party was careful about its relationship with Israel. After the Israeli invasion, Sharon expected to receive clear political and military support from the Phalangists, especially in eliminating the PLO from Beirut. However, the Phalangists refused for two basic reasons: first, their knowledge that Israel would have to take on the PLO irrespective of Phalangist support, and second, the fact that public demonstration of an Israeli-Christian alliance would immediately undermine the ability of a Christian-controlled regime to govern post-invasion Lebanon. Even if Bashir Gemayal was ultimately willing to try governing Lebanon by force, he was, at the beginning at least, not prepared to do away with the appearance of commitment to the old style of rule.[25]

The Israeli invasion of Lebanon was the catalyst for bringing about Bashir Gemayal's brief dominance. Under the influence of Israel, Bashir was elected president—a clear victory for the pro-Israeli elements in the party and the Lebanese forces. It appears that some Israeli experts counseled against supporting Bashir Gemayal directly; they proposed supporting either a compromise candidate or a constitutional amendment extending Sarkis's presidency for another two or three years.[26] These experts may well have feared that his election would lack any real legitimacy in the Lebanese system. Moreover, there were several practical obstacles to Bashir Gemayal's election, especially the threat of a Moslem boycott of the election. However, Bashir Gemayal's campaign manager assured the Israelis that even if his candidate lost the election, the Christian forces would force Sarkis to appoint him prime minister, giving him presidential powers without the title.[27] Sarkis, never known for his leadership abilities, appeared to passively await the end of his regime.

In the end, Israel decided to fully support the election of Bashir Gemayal, which occurred on August 23, 1982. On September 14, a week before his scheduled inauguration, he was assassinated in an explosion set by a member of the Syrian National party; this was a small radical party which had split from the Phalange and supported both Syria and the PLO.[28] As a result, the Phalange party returned to the balancing strategies which served it well under the leadership of Pierre Gemayal. In this sense, the election of Amin Gemayal (Bashir's brother), following the assassination of Bashir Gemayal, was an attempt to return to the classic broker strategy of the Lebanese presidency, namely ruling Lebanon through an uneasy alliance with the Islamic Arab world.

CONCLUSION

This chapter has outlined types of presidential leadership in Lebanon in order to evaluate the president's ability to act as a national leader. As we have seen, the history of the Lebanese presidency casts doubt on the ability of Christian presidential leadership to serve effectively in a national capacity. The political energy required of the Lebanese presidency is drained by a struggle over its own legitimacy. Even if the current presidential system survives, it is unlikely that it will ever be able to extend its power and authority much beyond the sphere of the Christian enclave. Indeed, any future presidency will continue to be squeezed between the contradictory requirements of legitimacy at the state and communal levels. Given this inherent weakness in the presidential system, real leadership in Lebanon will continue to lie outside the formal structures of government for years to come.

NOTES

1. David M. Rosen, "Leadership Systems in World Cultures," in *Leadership: Multidisciplinary Perspectives,* ed. Barbara Kellerman (Englewood Cliffs: Prentice Hall, 1984), pp. 39–62.

2. Walid Khalidi, *Conflict and Violence in Lebanon: Confrontation in the Middle East* (Cambridge, Mass.: Harvard Center for International Affairs, 1979), p. 36.

3. Ibid., pp. 53–54.

4. Ibid., p. 36.

5. Itamar Rabinovich, *The War for Lebanon, 1970–83* (Ithaca: Cornell University Press, 1984), pp. 60–88.

6. Elie Kedourie, "Minorities and Majorities in the Middle East," *European Journal of Sociology* 25 (1984): 278.

7. Ibid., passim.

8. Khalidi, *Conflict and Violence in Lebanon,* p. 56.

9. Adeed Dawisha, "The Motives of Syria's Involvement in Lebanon," *The Middle East Journal* 38 (1984): 228–36.

10. B. J. Odeh, *Lebanon: Dynamics of Conflict* (London: Zed Books, 1985), p. 168.

11. John K. Cooley, "The Palestinians," in *Lebanon in Crisis,* ed. P. Edward Haley and Lewis W. Snider (Syracuse: Syracuse University Press, 1979), p. 41.

12. Rabinovich, *The War for Lebanon,* p. 55.

13. Cooley, "The Palestinians," p. 46; Lawrence W. Whetten, "The Military Dimension," in *Lebanon in Crisis,* ed. P. Edward Haley and Lewis W. Snider (Syracuse: Syracuse University Press, 1979), p. 81.

14. Whetten, "The Military Dimension," p. 82.

15. Itamar Rabinovich, "The Limits of Military Power: Syria's Role," in *Lebanon in Crisis,* ed. P. Edward Haley and Lewis W. Snider (Syracuse: Syracuse University Press, 1979), p. 66.

16. David Gilmour, *Lebanon: The Fractured Country* (New York: St. Martin's Press, 1984), p. 144.

17. Whetten, "The Military Dimension," p. 84.

18. Lewis W. Snider, "Inter-Arab Relations," in *Lebanon in Crisis,* ed. P. Edward Haley and Lewis W. Snider (Syracuse: Syracuse University Press, 1979), p. 97; Rabinovich, *The War for Lebanon,* p. 89.

19. Rabinovich, *The War for Lebanon,* pp. 110–11.

20. Ze'ev Schiff and Ehud Ya'ari, *Israel's Lebanon War* (New York: Simon and Schuster, 1984), pp. 45–46.

21. Ibid., p. 25.

22. Ibid., pp. 28–29.

23. Richard A. Gabriel, *Operation Peace for Gallilee: The Israel-PLO War in Lebanon* (New York: Hill and Wang, 1984), pp. 129–30.

24. Schiff and Ya'ari, *Israel's Lebanon War,* pp. 199–201.

25. Ibid., p. 233.

26. Ibid., p. 231.

27. Ibid., p. 232.

28. Ibid., p. 47.

3

ISRAEL'S MENACHEM BEGIN

Ofira Seliktar

INTRODUCTION: THE TRANSITION FROM SOCIALIST ZIONISM TO NEW ZIONISM

The foreign policy of Israel has been shaped by the continuing Middle Eastern conflict. Dating from the arrival of the first waves of Jewish immigration to Palestine at the end of the nineteenth century, this struggle has dominated the Israeli polity since the establishment of the Jewish state in 1948. Throughout most of this period, the actual conduct of foreign policy was dictated by the Socialist Zionist belief system. However, the 1977 victory of Menachem Begin's Likud party ushered in New Zionism as the dominant belief system of the society. New Zionism is a loose amalgam of Revisionism, neo-Revisionism and National-Religious Zionism, as well as broad historiophilosophical strands derived from the reevaluation of anti-Semitism and the Holocaust in contemporary Israeli thinking.[1]

New Zionism and Socialist Zionism offer sharply divergent visions of Israeli's foreign policy. The two major differences pertain to the modes of conducting foreign policy and the definition of Zionism. Foreign relations theorists argue that most nations adapt to the limitations imposed on them by the international system. *Realpolitik* is the term often used to describe the art of striking the delicate balance between the external exigencies and internal needs of a nation.[2] The modus operandi of the Socialist Zionist heirs of Theodor Herzl, founder of Modern Zionism, has always been plagued by tension between those who cautioned against policies that would exceed the limited means of the Jewish community and those who advocated a more audacious stand. Although Ben-Gurion was associated with the stand of "courage," we may accept Shlomo Avineri's

I thank Mary Arnett, the Research Coordinator at the Biodatabase Project of MERI, for her assistance.

argument that on the whole the foreign policy conduct of the Socialist Zionists was pragmatic, that is, based on the perception that there are limits to what Israel could implement and achieve.[3]

On the other hand, New Zionism and its chief ideologue, Begin, adopted an idealistic approach to foreign policy thinking. In terms of decision making, this modus operandi is based on two elements: high risk taking, and the calculation of probabilities of success based on standard means as well as such "intangibles" as motivation, destiny, or even the help of God. This mode also affects the balance between the initiative and reactive elements in the international behavior of an actor. While small actors are normally more reactive, this idealistic posture has led Israel under Likud to adopt a more initiating stand in foreign affairs.[4]

The second major difference between the two belief systems pertains to the definition of the concept of Zionism. Zionism is more complex than many other ideologies of national independence. It evolved outside a territorial base, and aimed to mobilize a Jewish Diaspora that was geographically dispersed and divided culturally, religiously, linguistically, ideologically, and socially. These conditions shaped the fundamental level of the Zionist belief system, emphasizing the coequality of its temporal and spatial dimensions. The temporal concept involved the perception of the state of Israel as the legitimate embodiment of the ancient Jewish state. The spatial concept focused on the unity of the Jewish people across geographical boundaries. In operational terms, Zionism advocated *hitnahlut* (settlement), which was designed to secure the territorial base for the state, and *aliyah* (immigration), which underscored the concept of "ingathering of the exiles."

The foundation of the state and the subsequent influx of immigrants shifted the focus from the temporal to the spatial dimensions of ingathering of exiles. The historical continuity between the ancient Jewish state and Israel was relegated to the area of collective symbols. *Eretz Israel* (the Land of Israel) was perceived as an important georeligious concept which legitimized the state of Israel but did not coincide with its international borders. The 1967 war reactivated the temporal concept of Zionism. The occupation of some 26,000 square miles of territory, especially the West Bank, reopened the preindependence debate on the desirable boundaries of the Jewish state.

The outpouring of religious feelings brought about by the renewed contacts with East Jerusalem, Judea, and Samaria, accelerated the spread of the normative view. This view emphasized the moral and religious significance of the West Bank. Developed by the rational religious leaders, Rabbis Abraham and Zvi Kook, and propagated by the *Merkaz Herav* Yeshiva, the spiritual center of the Gush Emunim leaders, this approach stated that settling the territories is a religious imperative that supersedes any strategic considerations. Begin, though strongly supportive of the strategic value of the territories, has incorporated this religious-normative vision. Indeed, the dominant long-term goal of Likud's foreign policy has been to turn the state of Israel into the Land of Israel.

The fundamental tenets of New Zionist ideology dictated the operational goals of the Likud government in the 1977–1984 period. We shall examine the hallmark of this policy, the war in Lebanon, through the psychological prism of Menachem Begin.

BEGIN AS A PERSON: THE EMERGENCE OF A HISTORICAL LEADER

From Brest-Litovsk to Jerusalem

Menachem Begin was born on August 16, 1913, the third and youngest child of Ze'ev Dov and Hassia Begin, in Brest-Litovsk. Ze'ev Begin was a highly active Zionist, whose circle of acquaintances included such early Zionist pioneers as Mordechai Sheinerman, the grandfather of Ariel Sharon, and Sheinerman's wife, who delivered Menachem. In his capacity as the secretary of the Jewish community, Ze'ev Begin often clashed with local authorities, thus providing a strong role model for the young Begin.

The historical border town of Brest-Litovsk was the focus of rivalry between Russia, Germany, and Poland. The Jews of Brest, in addition to suffering from the war were also suspected of divided loyalties and regularly expelled by the conquering powers. For instance, during World War I, Ze'ev Begin was exiled by the Russians for his alleged German sympathies. In 1919, the family returned to Brest, which was occupied by the Russians. When the Poles took over the city, they started a series of pogroms in which Begin's father was nearly killed.

The Begin home was religious with strong national overtones; national religious holidays, which were optional among Orthodox Jews, were celebrated. Young Begin started his education in the traditional religious school, the *Heder*, but after one year was transferred to the *Tachkemoni*, a more secular Jewish school. In 1925, Begin joined the socialist *Hashomer Hatzair* youth movement, but the older Begin objected to the downgrading of the national Jewish aspirations of the Socialist Zionists and terminated his son's membership. In 1928 or 1929, Begin switched to Betar, the youth organization of the Revisionist movement, which was established in 1923. At that time, he was a student in a Polish gymnasium (university-preparatory secondary school), where encounters with anti-Semitism deepened his national resolve.

In 1931, Begin left Brest-Litovsk to enroll at the law school at Warsaw University. His admission reflects an impressive high-school record, in view of the fact that Polish universities had a policy of quotas whereby only a limited number of Jews were accepted. During his studies, he worked as a coordinator for the Betar movement. By 1935, when the Revisionists left the World Zionist Organization and established the New Zionist Organization, Begin graduated and became a full-time organizer. In 1937, he was appointed the deputy commissioner of Betar for Poland, and in March 1939 he became the commissioner of Betar in Poland.

The beginning of World War II on September 1, 1939, presented the Betar leadership with a painful dilemma. While some wanted to stay on in occupied Poland, Uri Zvi Greenberg, the great Revisionist poet, urged Begin to leave. On September 5, 1939, Begin and his wife Aliza fled Warsaw, followed by most of Betar's officials. The Betar leadership settled in Vilna, which was taken over by the Russians as the capital of Free Lithuania. Although Begin was engaged in organizing escape routes for Betar members, leaving Poland exposed him to the criticism that he had abandoned the rank and file.

It is not entirely clear whether the Betar Commissioner was prepared to return to Warsaw once it became apparent that the war would be a protracted conflict.[5] In any case, in 1940 Begin was arrested by the People's Commissariat for International Affairs (NKVD, the predecessor to the KGB, active 1935–1942). After some months of interrogation in the Lukishki prison, he was sentenced in March 1941 to eight years in the Siberian labor camp of Pechora.

Following the Russian agreement with the Polish government in exile to create a Polish army under the command of General Anders, Begin, like many other Polish prisoners, was released from the camp at the end of 1941. He enlisted in the Anders army and in May 1942 was posted in Jerusalem to work as a clerk.

Begin's arrival in Palestine coincided with a major upheaval in the *Irgun Zvai Leumi* (Military National Organization, known as Irgun) which in 1941 lost its highly effective commander, David Raziel. After a period of collective leadership, Begin, the Betar leader, was asked to fill his place and officially assumed command on January 26, 1944. Amid growing evidence that European Jewry had been exterminated, and in the light of the British refusal to allow refugees into Palestine, Begin decided in January 1944 to start a revolt against the mandatory power. The Irgun engaged in numerous attacks against the British, including the bombing of the Mandate administration headquarters in the King David Hotel.

The dominant Socialist Zionist underground, the *Hagana,* viewed these activities as jeopardizing its control over the *Yishuv* (Jewish community in Palestine) and as detrimental to Jewish-British relations; the Hagana response was to declare the *Seison* (the hunting season). Between November 1944 and June 1945, the Hagana either detained or turned over to the British members of the Irgun. In spite of the subsequent reconciliation between the Hagana and the Irgun, and their cooperation during the War of Independence of 1948, the Seison created extremely bitter feelings between Begin and David Ben-Gurion.

These tensions were enhanced by the Altalena incident. On May 14, 1948, Israel declared independence, and Ben-Gurion became the head of the Provisional government. Begin accepted the Provisional government post on behalf of the Irgun, and on June 1, 1948, he negotiated an agreement to join the Israel Defense Forces (IDF). The ship Altalena, carrying weapons bought by Irgun supporters in France, arrived in Israel on June 15, 1948, and Begin informed Ben-Gurion about the cargo. Following a failure to negotiate terms for unloading the arms, on June 22, 1948, Ben-Gurion's cabinet ordered the IDF to sink the ship.

The Altalena incident prompted Begin to disband the Irgun and establish the

Herut party. Although the Herut party had an average of 11.8 percent of Knesset (Israeli Parliament) seats in the 1948–61 period, it was not legitimized among a majority of Israelis. Begin's call for active dissent against accepting the German reparations, which generated public violence during the Knesset debate in 1952, was highly damaging to Herut's image. The party gained respectability when it joined the General Zionists in 1965 to form the parliamentary bloc *Gahal*. Herut became fully legitimized when Gahal joined the National Unity government on the eve of the 1967 war. Although Begin decided to leave the cabinet in 1970 over disagreement with the Rogers Plan, his performance as a minister without portfolio, in addition to his well-known skills as a master oppositionist, established his credibility for constructive cooperation.

The 1973 Yom Kippur war accelerated the long-term erosion of the dominant Labor movement. Demographic changes—especially the emergence of the Oriental Jews, whom Begin cultivated since the early days of the state—finally led to the victory of *Likud* (formerly Gahal) in 1977. Although Begin, who suffered a major heart attack in March 1977, could not actively participate in the campaign, Likud was thoroughly identified with his name.

The Likud leader showed considerable adroitness in negotiating the first right-wing religious coalition in Israel's history. To preserve the continuity of policy making. Begin minimized personnel changes and invited Moshe Dayan to serve as his foreign minister. Like his Labor predecessors, the prime minister continued his informal contacts with Arab leaders in the search for a peace formula. The breakthrough occurred when President Sadat made the unprecedented decision to come to Jerusalem on November 19, 1977. In the ensuing negotiations, Begin's hard-line approach was tempered by Moshe Dayan and Minister of Defense Ezer Weizman. The Camp David accord reached on September 17, 1978, provided the framework for the peace treaty between Israel and Egypt, which was signed by Begin and Anwar Sadat in Washington in 1979. Both heads of state received the 1978 Nobel Prize for Peace. The prize provided a symbolic vindication of Begin and the Revisionist movement in Israel.

Throughout this period, Begin suffered repeated health problems. On July 20, 1979, he was hospitalized with a small blood clot in one of the arteries in his brain. The cardiac and encephalographic examinations proved negative, and the prime minister was discharged on August 3, 1979, with only a slight visual impairment. On November 26, 1981, Begin suffered a fractured thigh, and was hospitalized until December 14, 1981. In spite of his physical disabilities, Begin was fully involved in the government decision-making process. He instigated the annexation of the Golan Heights in December 1981, and was instrumental in planning the Peace for Galilee operation. However, the failure of the war in Lebanon undermined Begin's performance. The mounting Israeli death toll, the Sabra and Shatila massacre of September 1982, and the death of Begin's wife Aliza on November 12, 1982, are all credited with contributing to the prime minister's ill health and depression. Begin resigned at the August 28, 1983, cabinet meeting, and tendered his formal resignation to the president of Israel, Yitzak Navon, on September 15, 1983, after six years and three months in office.

Begin as a Political Actor: A Psychological Profile

The psychological profile of a political leader includes four facets: Weltanschauung, personality characteristics, intellectual level, and modes of political behavior. The extremely complex Weltanschauung or political belief system of Menachem Begin can best be analyzed by using a modified version of the operational code technique developed by Alexander L. George. Broadly categorized, the political belief system of an individual consists of philosophical issues, views of the contemporary world, and instrumental beliefs.[6] To overcome the methodological problems of autobiographical data such as Begin's *The Revolt* and *White Nights,* which are consciously designed for a wide audience, [7] I have relied on a variety of sources; this includes the four volumes of his clandestine writing, *In The Underground,* as well as later work and speeches which can be used to monitor changes in Begin's belief system.

The most important philosophical issue is the actor's perception of the fundamental nature of the political universe. There is no doubt that in Begin's vision, this universe is one of unremitting conflict. Begin derived this vision from what he described as "the rules of history," in which conflict leads to national sovereignty and international recognition. The many examples of his rule, "we fight ergo we exist," include the war of independence of the United States, the national revolutions in Europe, and finally Israel's independence.[8] Moreover, Begin openly questioned the philosophy of nonviolent resistance. Writing after the death of Gandhi, Begin acknowledges the greatness of the Indian leader, but pointed out that this philosophy was undermined even before Gandhi was assassinated.[9] The same perception was evident in Begin's address to the United Nations General Assembly in 1982. He defined pacifism as a "beautiful idea" which is "the greatest provocation inviting attacks, subjugation and destruction" in the world of "aggressive totalitarianism."[10] In other words, the Israeli leader viewed conflict as having a zero-sum game property in international relations, one that is necessary for historical progress.

The sources of this image apparently derive from Begin's dominant prism of Jewish identity. Whether consciously or not, Begin was the first Israeli prime minister to act as the representative of all Jews. He fully acknowledged the pious Talmudic tradition whch started after the destruction of the Temple and kept Judaism alive for two thousand years.[11] Nevertheless, he was acutely aware of the shortcomings of a pacifist stand which subjected Jews to continuous persecution. Expressing a widely held view in Israel, Begin regarded the Holocaust as both a culmination of Christian hostility and a reflection of the Jewish collectivity's lack of power to defend itself. In an analysis of the Warsaw Ghetto uprising, which he described as a "fight to die in dignity," Begin concludes that Jews historically allowed themselves to be herded into ghettos, neglected to learn the martial arts, and preferred "dreams over reality."[12]

The history of persecution and especially the Holocaust were a source of continuous anguish and bitterness in Begin's thought. As early as 1943, he issued warnings that millions had died, and in his June 1945 proclamation, the figure of six million deaths appeared.[13] Begin has consistently held the British, who refused entry into Palestine to Jewish refugees, responsible for the genocide along with the Germans.[14] Begin's discussion of the book by Arthur D. Morse, *Why Six Million Died,* implies that he also accused the free world of indifference and duplicity in the tragedy.[15]

Begin's image of the contemporary world derives from his conflict-oriented philosophical views. In this philosophy, the international system is almost exclusively based on power relations; countries that lack decisive power cannot influence the system and often are unable to survive.[16] However, Begin's instrumental view shows more flexibility. His attitude toward Communism and the Soviet Union is the most notable case in point. Contrary to the popular perception that the "Gulag left Begin with an enduring hate of Communism,"[17] his earlier writings indicate a certain sympathy for the Communist experiment in tackling the issue of distributive justice. Although Begin did not view Communism as a success, he fully acknowledged that the issue of social inequality should be solved.[18]

When the Soviet Union decided to support the 1947 UN partition proposal, and was among the first to recognize the state of Israel, Begin advocated close cooperation with Moscow. He felt that an actor cannot afford a rigid stand toward other international actors; the attitude should be based on the interests of the state.[19] As the Likud leader, Begin's growing anti-Soviet attitudes were apparently a reflection of his perception of the Soviet role in fomenting the Arab-Israeli conflict, as well as its mistreatment of Russian Jews.

Compared to their belief systems, the characteristics and traits of political leaders are more difficult to analyze because of methodological problems and lack of empirical data. Like many political leaders, Begin has normally avoided disclosure about his physical condition. The various biographies and the autobiographical accounts indicate that in spite of a rather frail physique, the young Begin had a high level of physical endurance. This trait was especially manifest during his imprisonment in the Lukishki prison and the sub-Arctic Pechora camp.

Like Gandhi and other independence leaders, Begin derived his physical endurance from a set of mental traits. In order to overcome the effects of sleep deprivation and the sense of isolation that normally lead people to break down and confess, he played "intellectual chess" with his NKVD interrogators in Lukishki. Begin's commitment to an overarching goal and his absence of doubts about the "ultimate justice" of his goals also helped him survive the harsh conditions in the underground. Begin's major vulnerability as a leader can be gleaned from his reaction to the loss of human life, especially Jewish casualties, caused by his policies. He withdrew from active politics after the bombing of the King David Hotel, and broke down during a public broadcast after the Altalena incident.[20] Similarly, the mounting the casualties of the war in Lebanon apparently contributed to Begin's depression and resignation.

A major problem in assessing Begin's personality is the recurrent allegation that he has suffered a variety of character pathologies, such as manic depression, or paranoia. David Guttman, a clinical psychologist who surveyed these various arguments, has found that the terms have been applied in a nonrigorous manner by the media, political foes, and even some biographers. In the absence of clinical data, the assumption of manic depression or paranoia cannot be validated.[21]

An equally plausible alternative is that Begin's alleged ''manic depressive'' state is a bimodal behavioral trait whereby a person can alternate between a passive accommodative stance and an eruptive assaultive stance. There is a dialectical relationship between the two stances that can both feed on and utilize political expedience. Unlike other Israeli prime ministers, Begin is characterized by fitful decision making. Following the 1977 election, he embarked energetically upon the annexation of the West Bank, and pursued the peace process with Egypt. After the signing of the Camp David agreement, he gradually lapsed into a passive stance, reaching a low point in 1979. However, with international attention focused on the invasion of Afghanistan, Begin began again to pursue an active policy that culminated in the annexation of the Golan Heights in 1981 and the decision to bomb the nuclear facility in Iraq. Again, another period of inactivity followed and ended with the decision to invade Lebanon.

There is more positive evidence to indicate that, while in office, Begin suffered several bouts of depression, which might have been related to his physical illness. According to an investigative report in *Haaretz,* Begin deteriorated after the death of his wife, which coincided with the problems in Lebanon. Between February and his resignation in September 1983, the prime minister had curtailed most of his activities, even canceling a trip to the United States.[22] Current evidence seems to suggest a lingering depression. The Israeli press recently disclosed that after a discussion with Begin's friends and former aides, the chairman of the Maccabean Games decided against inviting the former prime minister to open the ceremonies.[23]

A useful approach in assessing the intellectual level of a leader is conceptual complexity theory. Regardless of context and substantive area, there are stable personality traits that manifest themselves at the level of complexity of information processing and articulation.[24] Even without formal content analysis, Begin's writings indicate an impressively high level of cognitive complexity. They reveal a subtle understanding of the interaction between psychological and organizational features of political systems: For instance, in a comparison between Lenin and Stalin, he concluded that the excesses of Stalinism were personal in origin rather than systemic, and predicted that they would disappear after the dictator's death. Begin's analysis of the psychology of interrogation of the NKVD, which normally resulted in ''quiet disposal'' of high-ranking political figures to avoid creation of political martyrs, in another example of cognitive complexity.[25]

Begin's discussion of the psychology of occupation, terrorism, and resistance is perhaps the best sample of these cognitive skills at work. The then-Irgun leader appreciated the fact that terrorist activities have a powerful impact on public opinion at home and abroad.[26] The Irgun's "glass house" strategy was designed to hurt highly symbolic British mandatory targets, as in the bombing of the King David Hotel headquarters to humiliate the British empire. The whipping of British officers and the hanging of the sergeants was designed to stop equivalent acts against Irgun members. These tactics were instrumental in the British move to grant captured Irgun members a semi-POW (prisoner of war) status, and were apparently considered in Britian's decision to give up the mandate.

In spite of his high cognitive complexity, Begin often simplified and exaggerated his arguments. For instance, he compared the British House of Lords to the Nazi Reichstag and accused the British of using Nazi techniques against captured Irgun members.[27] In later years, he routinely compared the PLO to the Nazis, and used the Holocaust analogy to describe a variety of events such as the plight of the Maronites in Lebanon.

Begin's oratorial style of delivery can explain part of this cognitive pattern.[28] Another explanation is derived from analogous thinking; like other leaders, Begin has used historical analogies to explain current events. The dominance of the Holocaust experience in Begin's life apparently exacerbated this tendency, especially as the PLO or its affiliates have often reiterated their determination to "liquidate the Zionist entity, politically, economically, militarily, culturally and ideologically."[29] Whether the PLO really intended to carry out its threat or had the capacity to do so was a moot point for Begin who, like many Israelis, believed that in view of Hitler's *Mein Kampf*, any threat of genocide should be taken seriously.[30]

Yet another explanation is based on the existence of different modes of logical thinking. Begin's rationality seems to derive from formal logic. It operates internally within a self-consistent system, which at times is divorced from commonly held perceptions or empirical reality. This logic, combined with Begin's legal training, leads to a certain rigidity in conceptual constructs that cannot be corrected by dissonant realities. For example, Begin maintained that during the Yishuv period, the Jews were a de jure majority in Palestine since they were a de facto minority because of the restrictive British immigration policies.[31]

Begin's patterns of political behavior have varied according to specific activities and time periods. He is extremely effective at information gathering. In addition to his mastery of several languages, he has a wide knowledge of Western history and current events. He has been reported to read the Hebrew press and several foreign-language newspapers and journals daily. Begin's preparation for foreign visits was scrupulous. Before his first trip to Washington as prime minister, he studied the Brookings Report on the Middle East on the assumption that President Carter would use it.[32] At the same time, it is known that Begin took little interest in domestic affairs; he often came unprepared for cabinet meetings and left the decision making up to the relevant ministers.

Begin is well known for his propensity for risk taking. Decisions in the Irgun, such as the King David Hotel bombing and the hanging of the British sergeants, were both risky and highly controversial. The same pattern is evident in Begin the prime minister. In accordance with the New Zionist idealistic-initiative mode of foreign policy conduct, Begin bombed the nuclear facility in Iraq, annexed the Golan Heights, and decided on the war in Lebanon. These and other decisions carried a high risk of internal failure, as well as the potential for widespread international condemnation. On the other hand, Begin has been noted for some drastic changes of policy when faced with public pressure. For instance, he reversed his position on the German reparations issue, and was forced to establish a commission of inquiry into the Beirut massacre in spite of his initial claim of a "blood libel."

Begin as a Leader: A Master Politician

In performing the role of prime minister, Menachem Begin was constrained by the coalition system. The normally oversized coalitions have generated a smaller decision-making body or inner circle in the cabinet, known as the "kitchen cabinet." During Begin's tenure, two such groups emerged. The more formalized group consisted of Begin's deputy prime ministers, such as David Levy (Likud-Herut), Simcha Erlich (Likud-Liberals), and Yigael Yadin (Democratic Movement of Change); the foreign minister Moshe Dayan (Independent); the defense ministers Ezer Weizman and Ariel Sharon, and the finance ministers. The less formalized group included members of the "fighting family"; that is, Begin's associates from the Irgun underground, such as Transportation Minister Haim Landau, Security Adviser Amichai Faglin, and Yehiel Kadishai, the life-long friend and personal secretary of the prime minister. Observers are divided over the comparative influence of these two bodies on Begin's decision making. In the absence of conclusive evidence, it is only possible to note that at certain decisional junctures, such as Camp David, the more formalized body had an upper hand; in other situations, Begin relied on the informal circle.

There is a related difficulty in estimating the degree to which Begin sought or was bound by the advice of his aides. According to the testimony of the Irgun elite, the decision making was collegial and friendly. As the leader of Herut and as a prime minister, Begin was known to arrive at a crucial decision in an independent manner. Dayan's account of Camp David indicates that Begin was adverse to suggestions from other members of the Israeli delegation. However, after the accord was reached, Begin was highly skillful in deflecting any criticism during the cabinet debate.[33]

Begin's key role in the leadership of the Likud stemmed from his mastery of the recruitment and competition process in the movement. From its inception, Herut sought to diversify Labor's pattern of recruiting from the founding fathers' Ashkenazi elite and senior military circles. Likud's leaders derive from four sources: the predominantly Ashkenazi Revisionist and Betar movement, including the Irgun and Lehi undergrounds and known as the "fighting family" (Yitzhak Shamir and Yaacov Meridor); technocrats mostly associated with the Liberals (Yitzhak Mudai, Gideon Pat, Moshe Arens, and Yuuval Neeman); the military (Ezer Weizman and Ariel Sharon); and Oriental Jews who have risen through local politics (David Levy, Moshe Katzav and Meir Shitrit).

Competition in the Likud is intense and manifold. One reason for this is the rift between Herut and the Liberals. Another stems from the rivalry among different Herut factions. Some of the factions, such as the 'fighting family," which constitutes about 25 percent of the 950-member Central Committee of the Herut, are historical; others form around personalities, such as the Sharon group, the Arens group, and the Levy group.

Although often disruptive of the Likud coalition, the competition has never affected Begin, who was unanimously accepted as the leader of the movement. The sources of Begin's authority were both historical and personal. He was the heir of Ze'ev Jabotinsky, the founder of the Revisionist movement, and the leader of Irgun and Herut. Begin had a charismatic personality and was regarded as the major asset of his party. He bolstered his power through organizational means, including the exercise of complete authority over top Herut appointments.

Above all, Begin's authority derived from his relations with the masses. The most common styles in political mobilization are the elitist and the pluralistic. The former, evolved under the Socialist Zionists, tended to downgrade political cleavages and emphasized a broadly defined national consensus. The structure of popular commitment was focused on the dominant *Mapai* party and its charismatic leader, David Ben-Gurion. Pluralistic mobilization can either be constitutional or populist. The former, prevalent in Western democracies, is based on an orderly interplay between institutions, groups, and individuals. The latter is a mixture of patterns ranging from a referendum type of democracy to politicians' populism, that is, emphasis on a social division that the cohesive leader can overcome.[34] Israel's slow transformation from Ben Gurion's elitism into a pluralistic constitutional mobilization system was interrupted by Likud's victory. Begin's populist style of mobilization was particularly effective with the Oriental Jews, who constitute some 60 percent of the Jewish population in Israel.

Such mass popularity gave Begin a high degree of political maneuverability, and a corresponding degree of freedom to act. This political freedom, comparable to the stature enjoyed by Ben-Gurion, enabled Begin to negotiate the peace treaty with Egypt. Conversely, both Ben-Gurion and Begin were able to commit Israel to war—the Sinai in 1956 and Lebanon in 1982—with little constraint from the Israeli body politic.

Begin as a Regional Actor: Perceptions and Misperceptions of the Middle East Conflict

From its inception, the Revisionist ideology, as articulated in Vladimir Jabotinsky's *Iron Wall* articles, involved a zero-sum game perception of the Arab-Israeli conflict. Begin was deeply committed to the land of Israel and did not accept the Socialist Zionist policy of territorial compromise. In a 1948 speech, Begin declared that the homeland, that is, the land of Israel, is indivisible; failure to recognize Jewish rights to the entire territory is equivalent to the lack of recognition of any of the territories. In Begin's view, the artificial line between a "nation's state and a people's country" disappeared in 1967.[35] Like his mentor, Begin also believed that regardless of the size of the territory, the Arabs would not accept a Jewish state in their midst.

This cognition was fed by Begin's negative affective reaction to the Arabs. Unlike Ben-Gurion, Golda Meir and other early Socialist Zionist leaders, whose hostility was tinged by liberal ideology and fundamental feelings of guilt, Begin's mistrust of the Arabs was based on his experiences at the hands of the Gentiles. In spite of his erudition, there is no evidence that Begin made any effort to acquire a working knowledge of Arab culture. Unlike Jabotinsky, who understood the depth of Arab national feelings, Begin's preindependence writings reflect the common Socialist Zionist misperception of the Yishuv period. For instance, he viewed the Arab resistance as instigated by either the British or the Arab elite.

Begin showed little sensitivity to Arab suffering and blamed the Deir Yassin massacre by the Irgun on the local Arab command, which failed to evacuate the population.[36] Subsequent threats by various Arab actors against the Jewish state hardened Begin's hostility. Begin was often criticized for dehumanizing the enemy while showing extreme concern for Jewish suffering. The Beirut massacre apparently corrected some of this attitudinal imbalance. It is interesting that after this event Begin stopped equating the PLO with Nazis, and decreased the rate of Holocaust invocations.[37]

Throughout his career in the political opposition, Begin exhibited a relatively undifferentiated perception of the regional actors, whom he often labeled as "treacherous," "cunning," or "murderous." The PLO was the most frequent target of such descriptions. Begin was also highly derogatory in discussing the Syrian president Hafez al-Assad, the Libyan leader Mu'ammar Khaddafi, and the Saudi Arabian royal family, whom he described as corrupt. While some of these projections were related to oppositionist rhetoric, they undoubtedly reflected deep-seated beliefs.

Upon coming into power, Begin was able to overcome his lack of differentiation and mistrust to fashion a more creative foreign policy. While pursuing traditional informal communication with Arab leaders like King Hussein, either directly or through third-party intermediaries, Begin decided to break with the routine of Israeli intelligence. When the Israeli services unearthed a Libyan plot to assassinate President Sadat, he ordered them to bypass the CIA (Central Intelligence Agency) intermediary and deliver the communication through King Hassan.[38] This action might have been instrumental in Sadat's thinking about peace. When the Sadat initiative became known, Begin overruled a September 1977 report of the intelligence service concluding that the Egyptian polity was not ready to accept the Jewish state.[39]

Begin's intuitive grasp of the "historical forking" provided by the Egyptian overture was apparently enhanced by the psychological similarities between the two leaders. In their early careers, they were both overshadowed by political figures of great stature—Ben Gurion and Nasser. Although neither Begin nor Sadat projected a Churchillian or de Gaullian mastery of history, both had a sense of destiny born out of deeply held religious convictions. Because Jimmy Carter shared many of the same psychological traits, he was an ideal intermediary in the peace process.[40]

The peace negotiation with Egypt lends itself to theorizing about leaders as agents of foreign policy change. The criterion of internal validity (did Begin act as a catalyst for foreign policy change?) is confirmed by the event. The question of external validity; that is, to what extent the occurrence is generalizable to future events, is not confirmed. The probability of obtaining the psychological configuration of Begin, Sadat, and Carter is quite low, as opposed to more common situations where political actors either clash or are incompatible in vision or stature.

BEGIN AND THE WAR IN LEBANON, JUNE 1982– SEPTEMBER 1982: A CASE OF FAILED LEADERSHIP

The decision to invade Lebanon has fundamental roots in New Zionist ideology. The collective "cognitive map" deviated from the traditional Socialist Zionist policy of seeking peace with the Muslim political center in the region. Instead, various New Zionist ideologists advocated an alliance with the periphery, that is, Shiites and non-Muslim minorities. The ensuing operational tenet called for a strong Maronite government in Lebanon which would increase the probability of securing a peace treaty between the two countries.

The second consideration stemmed from long-standing strategic thinking in the IDF (Israeli Defense Forces), which sought to deny a territorial base to Palestinian resistance. The PLO established a "ministate" in southern Lebanon, and combined its own strategy of raids across the border with the tactical shelling introduced by the Syrians prior to the 1967 war. As a result it used Lebanese territory as a base to raid and shell the settlements of northern and western Galilee. Equally important, the Lebanese infrastructure helped establish the credibility of the organization in the occupied territories. Drawing on this widespread popular support, the PLO was widely perceived by the international system as a legitimate representative of the Palestinian people and a major actor in the

Middle East. Israel's effort to dislodge the PLO in the 1978 Litani operation failed, and the subsequent prestige of the organization hampered the Likud policy of de facto West Bank annexation. There was an apparent perception by the Israeli civilian and military elite that the organization should be eradicated in order to curtail its power in the West Bank and the international arena.

These underlying objectives had an important influence on the decision to invade Lebanon, yet foreign policy decisions are not automatic translations of the "cognitive image" of a belief system. Selection of any particular option depends on a number of factors, among which the perceptions and the interpersonal relations of the foreign policy elite are most crucial.

The four most important actors involved in the decision to launch Operation Peace for Galilee were Prime Minister Begin, Defense Minister Sharon, Chief of Staff Rafael Eitan, and Foreign Minister Shamir. The head of the Mossad, Yitzhak Hophi, and the chief of Military Intelligence, Yehoshua Saqui, played important secondary roles, while the cabinet was relegated to a relatively minor position. Begin, Sharon, Eitan, and Shamir were all committed to the New Zionist initiating-idealistic foreign policy, and the ensuing optional use of military power. The exact stand of the cabinet is difficult to determine, but it would seem that no major objections were raised against this modus operandi.[41]

A number of political and strategic developments in Lebanon prompted Begin to execute the long-evolving Lebanese policy. In the spring of 1981, the Syrians tried to implement their Program of National Reconciliation, which would have undermined the Maronites allied with Israel. To prevent this design, Bashir Gemayal provoked the Syrians into a major action at Mount Senin, overlooking the strategic town of Zahle in the Bekaa Valley. Following the April 28 Israeli attack on Syrian helicopters deployed against Maronites on Mount Senin, President Assad installed SAM–6 missiles in the Bekaa Valley. On May 11, Begin disclosed that atmospheric conditions had forced the Air Force to cancel a raid on the missiles. It is not clear whether the Israeli government tried to negotiate over the missile crisis before the military mission was planned. However, subsequent U.S. negotiations failed to resolve the problem, reinforcing Begin's resolve to use military power.

In a parallel move under guidance from Chief of Staff Eitan, Begin authorized the IDF to launch a campaign against the PLO, which had emerged as an important actor in the Program of National Reconciliation. Eitan intimated that the massive bombing of PLO strongholds in May was also planned to increase the costs to the organization of its action.[42] After the second round of air raids in July, the PLO retaliated with an artillery barrage in northern and western Galilee. Although Israel accepted a U.S.-mediated agreement with the PLO, the July shelling convinced Begin and his top advisers that the Palestinian organization should be eradicated.

The plan for the invasion of Lebanon, code-named Big Pine, was developed by the IDF over a period of time and presented to the cabinet by Begin on December 20, 1981. Reconstruction of the debate indicates that the cabinet focused on the "minimal version" of Big Pine; that is, a 40-kilometer incursion against the PLO. The two remaining contingencies—a medium-range invasion against the PLO and Syrians up to Beirut, and the maximalist "grand design," which envisaged a massive drive into Lebanon to create a pro-Israeli Maronite government—were touched on but not resolved. In fact, the "grand design" contingency, supported by Sharon and Eitan, came under subsequent criticism from several quarters. Three months before the war, the General Staff conducted a simulation of the expanded version of Big Pine. In March, a graduating course of brigade commanders carried out exercises to test its operational premises. The conclusion was that the war would result in some 200 casualties and would not solve the Shiite demographics.[43] These arguments were reiterated by Saqui, who opposed the "grand design," and may have changed the attitude of Mossad Chief Hophi, who initially backed a comprehensive incursion.

To bolster the chances for cabinet approval of the operation, Sharon bypassed Begin and Shamir and met in December with U.S. envoy Philip Habib and the chargé d'affaires in Israel, William Brown. The meeting was designed to convey to Washington Israel's determination to carry out a decisive action against the PLO. Intelligence chief Saqui reiterated this message to the U.S. Secretary of State, Alexander Haig, in February 1982. After Sharon met Haig in May, he conveyed to Begin a sense of U.S. collusion with the plan. Subsequent developments proved that Haig's attitude was not representative of the foreign policy system. However, his official, mildly worded letter to the Israeli government convinced Begin that the U.S. would not oppose a military solution in Lebanon.

The assassination attempt against the Israeli ambassador in London on June 3, 1982, was treated by the cabinet as a causus belli, and as a result the invasion was ordered. However, there are conflicting reports about the intended scope of the action. According to Ze'ev Schiff, the military correspondent for *Haaretz,* the cabinet decided on a 40-kilometer incursion, but this decision was not transmitted to the IDF.[44] Begin confirmed to the Knesset's Foreign Relations Committee that the IDF was not ordered to stop at 40 kilometers.[45] On the other hand, Eitan claimed that at a night meeting following the June 6 crossing of the border, the cabinet approved an IDF linkup with the Christians and the occupation of the Beirut-Damascus highway.[46] Given the inconclusive nature of the evidence, it is only possible to speculate that Begin, along with most of the cabinet, approved a 40-kilometer incursion but at the same time either neglected to consider or condoned the broader implications of the operation.

The cabinet deliberations reflect some of the legal problems in war-time Israeli decision making. Existing laws do not clearly define the relationship between the IDF and the cabinet. Formally, the armed forces are subordinate to the government through the minister of defense. He serves as commander in chief, although his office does not expressly carry this title. The minister of defense need not consult the cabinet or obtain Knesset endorsement before making major decisions, including mobilization of reserve forces.

Communication between the prime minister, the cabinet, the minister of defense, and the chief of staff is not well defined and is mostly informal. This dates back to the days when Ben-Gurion was both prime minister and defense minister. As a result, the question as to who should decide about the start of a war and its subsequent scope is fraught with ambiguity. For instance, Ben-Gurion started the Sinai Campaign in spite of the objections of leftist Mapai party ministers. During the Six-Day War, the cabinet, including Defense Minister Dayan, decided to stop the IDF short of the Suez Canal, but Chief of Staff Yitzhak Rabin ordered the IDF to reach the bank. Conversely, Dayan bypassed Rabin when he directed the commanding officer of the Northern Command to take the Golan Heights. The Agranat Committee, investigating the Yom Kippur War, recommended a reform of the consultation process, but experts rejected the idea of a legal device such as the American War Powers Act of 1974.[47]

Given this background, the cognitive dynamics involved in cabinet decision making illuminate some of Begin's leadership deficiencies. First, Begin was known to rely heavily on the military expertise of Sharon and Eitan. Saqui and Communications Minister Mordechei Tzipori—the only other minister with a military background—were in a subordinate relationship to Sharon; their opposition did not carry enough weight to sway the cabinet into making a mandatory decision in favor of the "minimal incursion" plan. Second, Begin did not act to counter Sharon's style of managing and interpreting information. Third, as Irving L. Janis and others have noted in group situations or "group-think," there may be a shift toward a risky solution.[48] In the absence of a strong opposition to the Sharon-Eitan team, and because Begin and the cabinet were conditioned by a collective belief system, a "risky shift" occurred by default. In other words, the cabinet did not take the necessary legal steps to safeguard against a maximal design.

The dynamics of the war further eroded Begin's leadership. His casual remarks about the "fresh mountain air" at Beaufort Castle, where a number of Israeli soldiers had been killed, showed his lack of understanding about the conduct of the war. Most crucial, Begin was not notified in advance and did not approve the IDF's entrance into Beirut on June 13. It was Habib, who met Begin on the same date, who informed the surprised prime minister of the IDF presence in Beirut.

The issue of dealing with the Beirut-based PLO unit imposed an additional burden on the decision-making process. On June 12, the first of a series of Israeli-PLO cease-fires began, with the IDF effectively laying siege to Beirut. On June 17, the U.S. envoy started the negotiation process that led Israel to accept the evacuation plan "in principle" on August 10. While Begin and the cabinet were committed to a negotiated withdrawal, there was disagreement over the amount of military power to be used in order to force the PLO's hand. Sharon's use of massive firepower, and the policy of cutting off supplies to West Beirut, apparently caught Begin by surprise once again.

Accounts of the June 25 cabinet meeting, in which the treatment of the PLO and the role of the Phalangists in a clean-up operation were discussed, reveal disagreements. Deputy Prime Ministers Simcha Erlich and Mordechai Tzipori claimed that the cabinet did not agree on entering Beirut or on empowering the Phalangists to participate in a clean-up operation.[49] However, a few days later, Shamir declared that the PLO should be uprooted rather than allowed to leave Beirut.[50] At the beginning of August, six ministers—David Levy, Yoram Aridor, Zevulun Hammer, Yosef Burg, Mordechai Ben-Porat, and Aharon Uzan—joined the original critics, Tzipori and Minister of Energy Yitzhak Berman, in expressing misgivings about the conduct of the war and Begin's failure to exercise control. However, the August 21–31 evacuation of the PLO and the Syrians from Beirut was perceived as a vindication of Sharon's ''iron fist policy.''

Begin's faltering became even more evident during the decision-making process that culminated in the Sabra and Shatila massacre. In testimony to the Kahn Commission of Inquiry, Begin acknowledged that he authorized Sharon to move the IDF into key positions in West Beirut in order to prevent bloodshed in the wake of Bashir Gemayal's assassination on September 14. Begin was apparently notified that Sharon authorized the entrance of the Phalangists into the camps at 8:30 P.M. the same day, but showed no interest in the event. However, the prime minister was not informed about the trouble in the camps; he finally learned about the massacre from a BBC broadcast on September 16. The Kahn Commission noted Begin's flawed performance but stopped short of commenting on its reasons.

Analysis of the decision making during the war in Lebanon demonstrates that Begin lost effective control of events in the opening week of the operation. There is no doubt that Sharon's maneuvering and the military dynamics circumvented the orderly process of government. However, Allan Shapiro, a legal expert who reviewed the Kahn Commission's finding and other accounts, claims that some of the disorder stemmed from efforts to spare Begin from dealing with troublesome problems.[51] Like some European democracies, Israel does not have legal provision for monitoring a malfunctioning head of state.

CONCLUSION

A psychological profile of Menachem Begin provides a number of insights into the opportunities for negotiation during his leadership. In opposition, Begin often expressed hard-line and uncompromising positions which were undoubtedly permeated by his zero-sum perception of international relations. As prime minister, Begin was able to negotiate the historical treaty with Egypt through a rare combination of political opportunities and psychological compatabilities with Sadat and Carter.

Neither of these conditions was present in the Lebanon case. Begin's image of Lebanon was shaped by traditional Revisionist beliefs about the alternative route of Israel's integration into the Middle East, as well as a personal commitment to uphold the Maronite government. The prime minister's negative attitude toward the Syrian and PLO actors was reinforced by the failure to negotiate a withdrawal of the SAM–6 missiles and by the PLO's strategic shelling. Whether a strong U.S. stand for a negotiated solution would have changed the course of events cannot be determined. In the absence of such a stand, however, Begin led Israel into the most costly war in the country's history.

NOTES

1. For a survey of New Zionism, see Ofira Seliktar, *New Zionism and the Foreign Policy System of Israel* (London and Sidney: Croom Helm, 1986).

2. James E. Dougerty and Robert L. Pfalzgraff, *Contending Theories of International Relations* (New York: Harper & Row Publishers, 1981), pp. 84–86.

3. Shlomo Avineri, *Essays on Zionism and Politics* (Tel-Aviv: Sifrei Mabat, 1977), p. 86.

4. Yuval Neeman, "National Goals," in *On the Difficulty of Being an Israeli*, ed. Alouf Hareven (Jerusalem: The Van Leer Foundation, 1983), pp. 257–74.

5. Eric Silver, *Begin: The Haunted Prophet* (New York: Random House, 1984), p. 23.

6. Alexander L. George, "The Operational Code: A Neglected Approach to the Study of Political Leaders and Decision-Making," *International Studies Quarterly* 13 (June 1969): 199–222.

7. For a methodological discussion, see William McKinley Runyan, *Life Histories and Psychobiography* (New York and Oxford: Oxford University Press, 1984), pp. 21–37.

8. Menachem Begin, *Be Machteret* (In the Underground: Writings and Documents) (Tel Aviv: Hadar Publishers, 1978), vol. 1, pp. 91, 150, 260; vol. 4, p. 327; Menachem Begin, *Hamered* (The Revolt) (Tel-Aviv: Achiasaf Publishing House, 1986), p. 36.

9. Begin, *Underground*, vol. 4, p. 328.

10. Quoted in *The New York Times*, June 19, 1982.

11. Begin, *Underground*, vol. 2, p. 108.

12. Ibid., vol. 4, p. 323.

13. Ibid., vol. 1, p. 233.

14. Begin, *Hamered*, p. 67.

15. Silver, *Begin*, p. 33.

16. Begin, *Be Machteret*, vol. 1, p. 31.

17. Silver, *Begin*, p. 33.

18. Begin, *Hamered*, p. 22; Menachem Begin, *Leilot Levanim* (The White Nights) (Tel-Aviv: Karni Publishers, 1953, reprinted 1978), p. 226.

19. Begin, *Be Machteret*, vol. 1, pp. 245–46.

20. Uri Milstein, *DeDam Vaesh Yehuda* (By Blood and Fire, Judea) (Tel-Aviv: Levin-Epstein Publishers, 1973); Uri Brenner, *Altalena Mehkar Politi Vetzvai* (Altalena, A Political and Military Study) (Tel Aviv: Hekibutz Hameuchad: 1978).

21. David Guttman, "The Aging Leader and His Boys," paper presented at the annual meeting of the International Society of Political Psychology, Washington, D.C., June 1985.

22. Orit Shohat, "Kesher Hashtika" (The Covenant of Silence), *Haaretz*, November 2, 1984.

23. *Haaretz*, July 10, 1985.

24. Peter Suedfeld, Philip E. Tetlock, and Carmenza Ramirez, "War, Peace and Integrative Complexity," *Journal of Conflict Resolution* 21 (September 1977): 427–43.

25. Begin, *Leilot Levanim*, pp. 64ff., 242, 246.

26. For instance, see Eli Tavin and Yona Alexander, eds. *Psychological Warfare and Propaganda: Irgun Documentation* (Wilmington, Del.: Scholarly Resources, Inc., 1982).

27. Begin, *Be Machteret*, vol. 1, p. 204, vol. 2, p. 48.

28. Michael Brecher, "Images, Process and Feedback in Foreign Policy: Israel's Decisions on German Reparations," *American Political Science Review* 67 (March 1973): 73–102.

29. Quoted in the *Manchester Guardian*, July 20, 1980.

30. *New York Times,* May 1, 1980.

31. Begin, *Hamered*, p. 371.

32. Aviezer Golan and Shlomo Nakdimon, *Begin* (Jerusalem: Edanim Publishers, 1978), p. 235.

33. Moshe Dayan, *Halanetzah Tohal Herev?* (Shall the Sword Devour Forever?) (Jerusalem: Edanim Publishers, 1981), pp. 132, 160.

34. J. P. Nettle, *Political Mobilization* (London: Faber and Faber, 1967), pp. 87–88; Margaret Canover, *Populism* (New York and London: Harcourt Brace Jovanovich, 1981), p. 137.

35. Quoted in *The New York Times,* July 17, 1977.

36. Begin, *Hamered*, p. v.

37. *New York Times,* September 16, 1983.

38. Sidney Zion and Uri Dan, "The Untold Story," *New York Times*, 21 January 1979.

39. Ezer Weizman, *The Battle for Peace* (New York: Bantam Books, 1981), p. 19.

40. Melvin A. Friedlander, *Sadat and Begin: The Domestic Politics of Peacemaking* (Boulder, Colo.: Westview Press, 1983), pp. 203–31.

41. Ze'ev Schiff and Ehud Ya'ari, *Israel Lebanon War* (New York: Simon and Schuster, 1984), pp. 97–131; Richard A. Gabriel, *Operation Peace for Galilee: The Israel-PLO War in Lebanon* (New York: Hill and Wang, 1984), pp. 60–74.

42. An interview in *Yediot Aharanot,* 14 May 1981.

43. *Haaretz,* May 30, 1985.

44. Ibid., January 21, 1983.

45. Ibid., January 25, 1983.

46. An interview in *Maariv,* 7 September 1983.

47. Amos Ben Vered, "Who Decides About Wars," *Haaretz,* 9 February, 1983.

48. Irving L. Janis, *Victims of Groupthink: A Psychological Analysis of Conflict, Choice and Commitment* (New York: The Free Press, 1972), pp. 12, 44, 75, 118; Amiran Vinokur, "Cognitive and Affective Processes Influencing Risk Taking in Group and Expected Utility Approach," *Journal of Personality and Social Psychology* 2 (1971): 472–86.

49. *Haaretz,* November 11, 1982.

50. *New York Times,* June 23, 1982.

51. *Jerusalem Post,* January 1, 1984.

4

THE PLO'S YASSER ARAFAT

Rashid Khalidi

THE GENERAL SITUATION

The Israeli invasion of Lebanon, which began on June 6, 1982, marked the severest test ever faced by the PLO and its leaders. The factions composing the PLO had started in the mid–1960s as tiny, underground groups opposed as bitterly by the Arab states and the USSR as by Israel and the United States. The intervening years saw defeats, such as that at the hands of the Jordanian army in 1970–71; indecisive conflicts like the 18-month Lebanese war of 1975–76; and diplomatic victories, notably the 1974 recognition of the PLO as sole legitimate representative of the Palestinian people by the Arab League and the U.N. General Assembly.

Difficult as the earlier phases of the PLO's existence had been, the four months of invasion, siege, negotiations, evacuation, and massacre from June to September 1982 were unique in terms of the uninterrupted pressure brought to bear on the Palestinians and the men who led them.[1]

Israel was a regional military giant which had several times defeated a combination of Arab armies. It fielded an air force of unmatched range and expertise, and a battle-hardened army with enormous mobility and striking power. Much of this force (8 of a potential 16 to 18 divisions) was pitted against the PLO.[2] Although debate continues as to the extent of U.S. foreknowledge and approval of Israel's plans, there can be no doubt that the Reagan administration approved of the general Israeli goal of eliminating the PLO as a factor in the region, and sought to make the invasion serve some other ends as well.

Against these two formidable opponents was ranged the PLO, which with its Lebanese allies fielded a few thousand irregular combatants and militiamen, some of them boys. In terms of numbers, organization, logistics, and armament, they were grossly inferior to the Israeli forces, which in addition enjoyed unchallenged control of the air and sea.

The PLO and its Lebanese allies were virtually alone in the field. Although Syria had large forces in Lebanon, its leaders apparently fell victim to Israeli deception at the war's outset, as Israel repeatedly affirmed that its invasion was directed solely against the PLO.[3] When Syrian forces were attacked on June 9, they suffered a rapid defeat, particularly the air force and antiaircraft defenses. Syria accepted a cease-fire on June 11, although Israel failed to respect it. Syrian forces were in action for only a few more days in the latter part of June, after which a definitive cease-fire between Syria and Israel went into effect for the rest of the war. Thus, with the exception of about two weeks when Syrian forces were engaged, the PLO, supported only by some Lebanese groups and Syrian army units besieged with it in Beirut, fought alone for most of the 70 days of combat, from June 4 until August 12, 1982.

Diplomatically, the PLO was equally alone. Facing earlier Israeli assaults, as in March 1978, it had benefited from Arab pressure on the U.S. to restrain Israel. No such pressure was forthcoming in 1982. In past crises, the balance of forces within the Arab system had worked in its favor, as genuine popular sympathy for the Palestinians combined with outbidding and mutual suspicion among the regimes led the Arab states to unify behind the PLO. As the Arab system that was consolidated in the early 1970s unravelled following Anwar Sadat's visit to Jerusalem, Iraq's distracting war with Iran, and the decline in Saudi power and consequent increase in that of Syria, this balance evaporated. With it disappeared any hope of a unified Arab stand of support for the PLO.

The Soviet Union, which formerly had been willing to confront the United States on behalf of Arab clients under attack by Israel, was unwilling to intervene in support of the PLO in Lebanon. This position had been conveyed explicitly to the Palestinians during the six years of PLO-Israeli clashes in Lebanon preceding the 1982 war, and was clearly understood by the core PLO leadership.[4] To make matters worse, the dying Leonid Brezhnev was in his last months as leader of the USSR, and the already slow and cautious Soviet policy-making process regarding the Middle East was further impaired.

Something perhaps more serious than all these external problems faced the PLO as it met the biggest challenge in its history. Most of the Lebanese among whom it existed, and on whose goodwill it ultimately depended for its freedom of action, had reached the end of their tolerance for the Palestinian military presence in their country. This Lebanese attitude was born of both subjective and objective factors. The former included PLO insensitivity to the sentiments of their Lebanese hosts, and indisciplined acts by armed Palestinians, such as taking protection money, conducting gun battles in urban streets, and establishing checkpoints on heavily travelled routes. The objective factors involved the post–1973 paradox of Lebanon, Israel's weakest neighbor, being forced to bear the entire weight of the Palestinian-Israeli conflict virtually alone, as Jordan, Egypt, and Syria successively pacified their frontiers with the Jewish state. If this was the dilemma facing the Palestinians after the war began, how did they see their situation on its eve, what aims did they hope to achieve, and what strategy were they following?

The objectives of Palestinian nationalism had come a long way since the founding of the PLO in 1964.[5] Its goal then had been the same as that espoused by the Palestinians since the establishment of a Jewish state in Palestine appeared possible. It could be summed up in two words: Arab Palestine. However, while in the context of the Mandate, this had meant no more than self-determination for the two-thirds Arab majority in its own homeland, and did not necessarily contradict the terms of the Balfour Declaration and the Mandate (which had called only for a Jewish "national home" in Palestine), after 1948 the same words meant a radical revision of the existing situation.

The Palestinian National Covenant was drawn up in 1964, when the PLO was founded by Palestinian politicians chosen by Egypt with the aim of heading off the growth of independent Palestinian nationalism. It embodied this traditional aim, with all the implications current in 1964: a reversion to the status quo ante 1948, with the concomitant "dismantling" of the Israeli state apparatus. This remained the formal objective of the PLO even after it was taken over in 1968–69 by the same independent nationalist factions, headed by Fateh (an acronym for the Palestinian National Liberation Movement), which Egypt's President Gamal 'Abd al-Nasser had sought to foil in 1964.

Soon afterwards a change emerged: the idea of a "secular democratic state" in Palestine was adopted in 1969 as an objective, first by Fateh and then by the PLO. This signified not a reversion to the situation of 1948 or 1917, but rather an entirely new idea whereby Jews and Arabs would have equal rights in a binational state, neither exclusively Israeli nor Palestinian in nature. A further and even more radical change came in 1973–74, as the PLO shifted to acceptance of a bistate solution, implying coexistence of a Palestinian Arab state in a part of Palestine, alongside Israel. This became official PLO policy in the resolutions of the 12th session of the Palestine National Congress (PNC) in 1974, and was further defined in those of the 13th, 14th, and 15th PNCs, from 1977 to 1981.

In his general assembly address of November 1974, Arafat had spoken of carrying an olive branch in one hand and a freedom fighter's gun in the other.[6] This metaphor aptly describes the PLO's approach in the years that followed. Whereas the National Covenant of 1964 (as amended in 1968) spoke of "armed struggle" as the sole means of regaining Palestine, Arafat's 1974 speech signified a dual approach, with the Palestinians continuing to resist occupation and carry out attacks against Israel from without, but at the same time seeking a negotiated solution.

In time, however, circumstances combined to tilt the balance in favor of the olive branch. On the one hand, in the years after the 1973 war, PLO leaders were convinced that the Arab-Israeli balance of forces as well as the international situation favored a peaceful settlement resulting in a Palestinian state. This hope lasted until it was shattered by Sadat's separate peace of 1977–79, which weakened PLO bargaining power and limited the Palestinians to no more than the "autonomy" which Menachem Begin and the United States were willing to allow them.

On the other hand, the pressure of Israeli retaliation combined with Lebanese dissatisfaction at the PLO presence and severe inter-Lebanese tensions to provoke the 1975–76 phase of the Lebanese war. This saw the PLO drawn into full-scale fighting with the Maronite militias and later with Syria, and forced the withdrawal of most PLO military forces from South Lebanon. The result of all this was a curtailment of PLO attacks on Israel.

By the time of the 1982 war, the Palestinian political elite, whether under occupation, in Lebanon, or in other parts of the diaspora, could be said to have reached a broad consensus about how to proceed. Evidence could be found in resolutions passed by large majorities of the PNC from the 12th session in 1974 to the 15th in 1981, and in the unanimity within the movement over the PLO's formal acceptance of the 1977 U.S.-Soviet joint communiqué calling for an international conference on the Middle East, and of similar Soviet peace plans in the years that followed. This consensus involved acceptance of a diplomatic solution to the conflict, ideally one brokered by both superpowers, which would end in the creation of a West Bank-Gaza Strip state alongside Israel. In official PLO terminology, this was described as the "provisional program," but given the time and effort that would have been necessary to achieve it and the lack of consensus on a realistic means to achieve any goal beyond it, the "program" can be described as the PLO's long-term goal. Its short-term goal was survival. The old (1968–69) aim of a secular, democratic state was still adhered to, but was seen less and less as a serious objective and more as a dream for the future.

It is important to note that the real pre–1982 configuration of political forces within the PLO, and the broader Palestinian nationalist movement that it represented, was quite different from that appearing on an organizational chart. Indeed, many of the groups listed on such a chart had no existence in terms of popular support. Aside from small factions that were essentially creations of the intelligence services of Arab regimes, there were four groups with a mass base. This meant that they had sufficient popular support to win votes in an election, whether within Palestinian popular unions, West Bank unions, or student political groups at universities in Beirut or the West Bank. The four groups were Fateh, the Popular Front for the Liberation of Palestine (PFLP), the Democratic Front for the Liberation of Palestine (DFLP), and the Palestine Communist Party (in both its West Bank-Gaza Strip incarnation, and via the separate Rakah party in Israel). These groups shared a commitment to the principles, described above, with various shadings and nuances. The PFLP was least committed to them, and Fateh the most. The relative weight of Fateh (which regularly got large majorities in every election or poll), and its appeal to the broadest spectrum of Palestinians, made its views decisive.   Fateh's strength lay in its wide geographic distribution, its extensive support among every sector and occupational group and every socioeconomic level of Palestinians, and a vague ideology that made it highly attractive to those moved primarily by Palestinian nationalist sentiment. These characteristics and Fateh's generally loose organizational framework were a source of weakness in certain circumstances, notably after the PLO's departure from Beirut. However, in the pre–1982 situation, they worked in Fateh's favor. Combined with the cohesiveness of the Fateh leadership and the preeminence enjoyed by its leader, Yasser Arafat, they made its position unassailable within the Palestinian polity.

YASSER ARAFAT, HIS FOLLOWERS, AND OTHER LEADERS

Arafat the Person

Yasser Arafat's life is far from an open book. The two existing biographies (both in English) agree on little. One is essentially a piece of character assassination, while the other was "written in co-operation with Yasser Arafat."[7] From these and other sources, a picture emerges of a man with more than one persona: the private one known to associates and close coworkers; the political one displayed in public to his followers; and the incarnation of evil popularized in the United States and Israel by his enemies.

The facts of Arafat's life are in many cases not fully established, but what is known can be summarized briefly. He was born in Cairo in 1929 to a merchant of the Qudwa family, which was distantly related to the prominent Husseinis of Jerusalem. After a youth spent partly in Jerusalem and partly in Cairo, during which, like many schoolchildren of his generation, he became deeply involved in politics, Arafat went to Palestine at the age of 19 to enlist in the fight for his country.

His experiences during the 1948 war were bitter. They included military defeat at the hands of the nascent Jewish state, and what his entire generation perceived to be treachery by Arab regimes claiming to be acting on behalf of the Palestinians, notably those of Jordan under King Abdullah and Egypt under King Farouq. The former was seen as having connived with Israel to suffocate independent Palestinian nationalism, and the latter as having failed to support its own army at the front in Palestine. These two aspects of the Palestinian dilemma, the hostility of Israel and of the Arab regimes, were to preoccupy Arafat and his colleagues throughout their political careers.

After the 1948 war, Arafat brought together in Cairo the core of what was to become Fateh. Many of them first met at Fuad I University, where Arafat was studying engineering and was also deeply involved in politics, winning election as president of the Union of Palestinian Students in 1952. Fateh was secretly founded in Kuwait in the mid–1950s after the activities in Cairo and Gaza of Arafat and some of his close colleagues, including Khalil al-Wazir (Abu Jihad) and Salah Khalaf (Abu Iyyad) had made them unwelcome to the Egyptian authorities. They had developed contacts with a number of the main forces in

Egyptian politics of the period, including the secret Free Officers group which eventually overthrew the monarchy in 1952; the Muslim Brothers; and the Egyptian Socialist party.

Under Arafat's leadership, Fateh grew during the years that followed into an underground nationalist movement with branches in several Arab countries where Palestinians were located. After a brief period working as an engineer in Kuwait while continuing his political activities, Arafat devoted all his time to the latter. He lived a dangerous clandestine existence during the 1950s and 1960s, often running afoul of the authorities in different Arab states, and spending brief periods of time in the prisons of Egypt, Lebanon, and Syria. Fateh set the pace of Palestinian nationalist politics during these years, but Arafat himself remained largely unknown outside Palestinian nationalist circles. He emerged from this relative obscurity to take over the chairmanship of the PLO Executive Committee in 1969, the year after the commando groups led by Fateh won control over the organization, wresting it away from the discredited former leadership.

From this point on, Arafat's fortunes and those of the PLO were intertwined, whether during its Jordanian period ending in 1970–71, or the following 11 years in Lebanon. In Jordan, he and his colleagues in Fateh resisted the pressure of the PFLP and other radical factions to openly oppose Egypt's military-diplomatic strategy and to confront the Hashemite regime. However, the outcome of the conflict in Jordan was ultimately determined by the confrontational tactics of the PFLP and the determination of the Jordanian regime and its U.S. backers to end the duality of power in Jordan, rather than Arafat's more conciliatory approach.

In Lebanon, fierce attacks on the Palestinian refugee camps in the Beirut area by the Phalangists and other Maronite right-wing parties made inevitable another confrontation, again one which Arafat tried to avoid. Its result was also negative for the PLO, if less so than that of the Jordanian civil war. Refusing to break his links with Syria, which had forcefully confronted the PLO, and at the same time refusing to abandon his Lebanese allies, as was demanded by Damascus, Arafat trod a thin line. The PLO survived, but at a fearful cost, and with many basic assumptions and elements of strategy in tatters.

Arafat had already begun to move away from his view that armed struggle in the context of resistance to occupation was the sole means for the liberation of Palestine. This had been part of a vision rooted in the realities of the 1950s and 1960s, whereby the Palestinians, by their daring actions, would involve the unwilling Arab states in a confrontation with Israel. In the wake of the October 1973 war, Arafat and others argued that another approach was possible and that, indeed, events made one inevitable. This approach consisted of an independent PLO position based in Lebanon, a diplomatic strategy in coordination with the Arab states, and ultimately a negotiated settlement of the Palestinian-Israeli conflict leading to the establishment of a Palestinian state in the West Bank and Gaza Strip.

In pursuit of this strategy, the PLO engaged in a diplomatic offensive in the years before 1982, which resulted in international recognition but did not seem to advance the Palestinians as far as their goals of self-determination and return to their homeland were concerned. Nevertheless, Arafat grew in stature among his own people, in the eyes of Arab public opinion and much of the rest of the world, even as his image in the United States barely improved. With his pragmatism and ability to make the best of a bad situation, he apparently matched a new mood among Palestinians, who felt that self-determination in a part of their homeland was preferable to a continuation of the existing situation.

Arafat himself had changed as well, from an activist, radical youth, to a combatant in Palestine, to a clandestine underground organizer, to a guerrilla leader, and finally to an Arab statesman treated on a par with kings and presidents. While his outlook was transformed in some ways, in other ways it remained the same.

In keeping with his upbringing in Egypt, Arafat saw the Palestinians' dilemma as in large measure a problem with the Arab regimes, just as it was a problem with the Israelis. This remained a constant in his world view. Another constant was his suspicion of political parties—an outgrowth of his Egyptian experiences during a period when political parties were generally discredited. Yet a third constant was his lack of illusions regarding the practical significance of Arab nationalism and Islamic and international solidarity. In this he differed from less pragmatic Palestinian leaders such as George Habash and Nayef Hawatmeh, both of whom were later to lead major factions of the PLO. This attitude was in keeping with Arafat's intensely practical rather than theoretical nature, his preference for mathematics and finances rather than liberal arts, and his professional training as an engineer in Egypt, which he had otherwise had scant opportunity to utilize.

Other tendencies, developed during the early years of student politics, lingered on. Among them was Arafat's affinity for back-room wheeling and dealing, although he could play the demagogue and the public leader with equal skill. Another enduring trait was his appreciation of loyalty above many other virtues in his associates. This explains the dedicated core of colleagues, associates, assistants, guards, and retainers who have remained with the Palestinian leader for so many years, as well as his tolerance of faults in some of those around him. Partly as a result of this, he is the object of intense loyalty on the part of those who work with him, even when they are critical of him or his failings.

Arafat is short, balding, nervous, and meticulous in his personal appearance (in spite of his apparently unshaven face, which is in fact due to his sparse beard). He is very active physically, rarely at rest, and often agitated in his mannerisms. He sleeps little, works best at night, and reads extensively, primarily in Arabic but also in English. He has maintained a grueling pace, averaging an 18-hour workday seven days a week without break, respite, or vacation for most of his adult life.

It could be argued that in addition to the considerable force of his personality, Yasser Arafat has maintained his primacy in Fateh and the Palestinian movement due to the fact that he works far harder than anyone else in the leadership, or indeed at any level of the movement. However, his personality alone is enough to explain much of his success. He is a hard man to say no to, and has been known to impose his will on colleagues, and even on opponents, by a mixture of charm, guile, and sheer willpower.

A target for assassination from many directions for many years, Arafat has a highly developed sense of danger, and directs some aspects of his personal security arrangements himself. The strain of constant peril and the frenetic pattern of his life have taken their toll. Arafat is graying, his face is lined, and he has lost the paunch which he formerly had. Prone to irritability, he has become more so in recent years. At the same time, he has come to prefer being surrounded by those who will impose on him the minimum possible strain, and preferably will not disagree with him. This has naturally had an effect on the quality of information and advice to which he has access, for although he has numerous formal and informal advisers, those nearest to him tend to have his ear much of the time, regardless of their ability or qualifications to tender advice.

In the five years before the 1982 war, Arafat revamped his office, installing two highly educated and dedicated professionals to direct the flow of information, paperwork, and people. This had the effect of routinizing, and in the long run simplifying, much of his work. It also made it possible for more people to have access to him, since his headquarters, although decentralized physically, now had a clear structure. These innovations did not make the system more bureaucratic or Arafat himself more inaccessible. He could still be seen by virtually anyone with a valid request, so long as he or she had the patience to wait for him to return from meetings, lightning-fast field trips, or consultations with his colleagues, which generally meant waiting until late at night.

Arafat himself keeps voluminous notes, tape records meetings (with the knowledge of those present), and has a highly organized personal and official filing system. As a result, he is rarely at a loss for a record or document. Some of the records of the Office of the Chairman were computerized in the years before the 1982 war. In spite of this apparently highly efficient system, blockages exist in the flow of information and advice. Associates are sometimes reluctant to relay to Arafat advice that they know will be painful or critical. Although he does not like to be contradicted, a characteristic shared with many other leaders who have held their positions for many years, it can be and has been done. On balance, Arafat probably receives more dissenting opinion and tolerates more criticism from subordinates, colleagues, and opponents than most other Arab or Third World leaders.

Arafat and His Followers

The most important aspect of Yasser Arafat's leadership style has always been his relationship with the close colleagues who founded Fateh together with him, and who dominate its 10-man Central Committee.[8] Arafat and these men—

notably those from the Cairo and Gaza days like Abu Iyyad and Abu Jihad, and others such as Farouq al-Qaddoumi (Abu Lutf) and Khaled al-Hassan (Abu Sa'id)—have worked together for well over three decades. This may make them the longest lasting core leadership group in the Arab world, and has a number of advantages and disadvantages.

On the one hand, the knowledge, tolerance, respect, and understanding that members of this group have for one another make it possible for them to differ vigorously without fear of a serious split. On the other hand, it also means that key decisions tend to be a result of consensus emerging at this level, to the exclusion of other members of the Fateh and PLO leaderships and lower levels of the movement.

It has also meant that when this core group is divided or undecided, Palestinian politics suffer from a drift whose real source is not always apparent. Since the beginning, Arafat has been primus inter pares, with a changing balance of power and influence between him and other leaders. On many issues, he has been able to count on Abu Jihad, probably the closest to him personally of the group, and at other times on Abu Iyyad and Abu Lutf, who tend to be allied with one another. Polarities within the entire Central Committee and in Fateh and the PLO as a whole have coalesced around relationships between these key individuals. In the last analysis, they have been the only ones able to restrain Arafat's freedom of action, whether by themselves or in coalition with others; indeed, on occasion, they utilized the democratic procedure of the Central Committee to reverse a decision of his or oblige him to take a certain stand.

Beyond the core Central Committee group, there exist other foci of decision making, power, and influence, but as a rule they are of much less importance; for the period before 1982, Arafat and the central Fateh leadership group were undoubtedly preeminent in Palestinian politics. These other foci include the leaders of the other PLO groups, notably the PFLP and DFLP; the military high command of the growing regular PLO military forces in Lebanon; senior leaders of several of the Palestinian popular unions; intellectuals, academics, writers and journalists, and other opinion makers; the mayors, notables, and popular leaders of the occupied territories; and many of the wealthy businessmen in the Palestinian diaspora.

All these groups and sectors of Palestinian society, effectively a cross section of its elite, are represented in the 400-plus member PNC. However, the infrequency of its meetings and its largely formal nature have rendered it primarily a ceremonial forum on all but exceptional occasions, or where the decisions to be taken have been of a strategic nature. Other formal structures of PLO decision making, whether the Central Council, which is smaller and meets more frequently, or the PLO Executive Committee, nominally the PLO "cabinet," share more in the substance than in the reality of power. Although Fateh's other internal structures are less important than its Central Committee, they are more active than the analogous PLO bodies, and one of them, the Fateh Revolutionary Council (with several dozen members), often plays a key decision-making role.

Although this reality is masked from outside observers, it is well known to Palestinians. The formal PLO organs of power have been undermined by the need to respect the touchy political balance between different Palestinian factions, some small and others basically fronts for Arab regimes, notably those of Syria, Iraq, and Libya. Because of these imperatives imposed on the PLO by the reality of its delicate position in inter-Arab politics, most serious political activity takes place within the four main groups, especially Fateh, or among members of the other important sectors represented in the PNC such as the unions, intellectuals, and businessmen. Most everyday issues are raised within such contexts rather than within formal PLO bodies, and the unions in particular often serve as forums for dissenting, radical, or minority views, as well as popular sentiment.

As a result, popular interaction with Arafat takes place either in meetings with individual petitioners or small groups, or in large public encounters and mass meetings. Until 1982, this meant that those living nearby or able to come and go with ease—Palestinians in Lebanon or where travel to Beirut was easy—had much more access than those who did not. The most disadvantaged were those under occupation and in Jordan, who had little opportunity for direct contact with Arafat and the PLO.

In spite of this, Arafat would seem to have enjoyed extensive popularity among Palestinians both under occupation and in the diaspora on the eve of the 1982 war. It was possible to see evidence of this in Lebanon, Syria, and the Gulf when the Palestinian leader met with large groups of his people. He was greeted with enthusiasm by crowds whenever he spoke, and was invariably listened to with respect, even by his political opponents. In areas where Palestinian political expression was banned, the lack of immediacy of contact was made up for by Arafat's symbolic importance as the living embodiment of Palestinian nationalism.

Many others have easy access to Arafat. These include union leaders, prominent writers and journalists, and leading intellectuals and businessmen. It is an important part of his coalition building to be in constant touch with opinion makers and other political figures. Arafat makes a point not only of doing so, but of doing so publicly, often taking with him on visits such figures as the poet Mahmud Darwish (since 1987 a member of the PLO Executive Committee), or dropping in on seminars and conferences of the General Union of Palestinian Writers and Journalists and delivering an impromptu address.

With important Palestinian businessmen, who like businessmen everywhere generally eschew publicity, Arafat also maintains contact, albeit in a different way. Since his days as an engineer in Kuwait, he has known many leading contractors in the Gulf, who constitute the backbone of the Palestinian bourgeoisie. He and other Palestinian leaders frequently meet them in their homes or in the homes of mutual friends, and socialize with them and their families—with all the limitations imposed by the need for tight security, constant movement, and clandestine comings and goings. Such links were important in Beirut and Kuwait in particular, where many leading Palestinian businessmen were located, and where it was possible for the Palestinian leadership to operate with relative freedom. They have provided an important input into PLO decision making, and onc which has been much underrated.

Thus, before 1982 the most extensive contact between leaders and followers took place with the group which formed the core of the PLO's mass base, that is, the Palestinians in Lebanon. Virtually all of them had met or at least seen Arafat as he criss-crossed the country, visiting refugee camps, military bases, hospitals, and schools, and addressing small groups, meetings, and rallies. In spite of threats from all directions, in many ways the roughly 400,000 Palestinians in Lebanon had never experienced better treatment: they enjoyed a high degree of autonomy and access to their national leadership.[9]Arafat and his colleagues were given credit for this situation, just as they were held responsible when times became troubled. On the eve of the 1982 war, the links built up between leaders and followers were to be tested as never before.

Arafat and Other Leaders

A key relationship between leaders in the Middle East system over the past decade or so has been that between Yasser Arafat and President Hafez al-Assad of Syria.[10] It was of particular importance during the 1982 war, for Syria was the PLO's closest ally, the only power that could have helped it against Israel, and the country through which any other external help had to come.

PLO-Syrian relations had been poor in the past, but in the period immediately before the war they were especially strained. Assad held the PLO, and Arafat in particular, responsible for obstructing Syrian aims in Lebanon by supporting various factions opposed to Syria, and more seriously, for aiding the Syrian domestic opposition. These disagreements led to such a serious rift that before the war there had been several visits to Damascus by a Fateh Central Committee delegation to smooth over relations. Significantly, Assad and Arafat were barely on speaking terms, and did not communicate personally throughout the course of the 1982 war.

There was a fundamental antipathy between the two leaders for many reasons, only one of which was the marked difference in their personalities. Where Assad was consistent, discreet, and methodical, Arafat was flamboyant, impetuous, and changeable. Their political outlooks also differed. Assad was a head of state, one who had grown in importance in the regional system since he had taken over power. After the 1973 war, his regime had gained a new domestic and Arab legitimacy; the resulting confidence still marked Assad's actions in 1982. Syria, moreover, had newly strengthened its relations with Moscow, which had no other major regional clients and thus depended greatly on the Assad regime. After 1974, Syria also had good relations with the United States.

By way of contrast, Arafat and the PLO had no established place within the regional system. Their standing depended on their precarious base in Lebanon, and on the equally uneasy balance between Arab regimes, many of them more or less hostile to PLO aspirations. They were thus less satisfied with the status quo, and felt a greater urgency about the need to change it than did Syria.

Furthermore, Arafat desired the greatest possible independence within the Arab system, and Assad wished to dominate his closest neighbors in "Greater Syria": Lebanon, Jordan and the Palestinians. For Syria, such domination was a means of obtaining geo-strategic weight to make up for the loss of its Egyptian ally after the peace treaty with Israel. To make matters worse, both Arafat and Assad had felt betrayed by Sadat when he went ahead with a unilateral settlement with Israel brokered by the United States. Each suspected the other of intending to do the same, something that explains much of their behavior not only before and during the 1982, but after it as well.

PLO relations were little better with other key regional actors. In 1977, Anwar Sadat had announced to the Egyptian National Assembly in the presence of Yasser Arafat that he was going to Jerusalem. This personal humiliation (by all accounts Arafat had no idea of Sadat's intention) preceded a separate peace that all Palestinians and nearly all Arabs perceived to be a political betrayal. Sadat's death four years later opened the way for a change. Arafat and Mubarak had already exchanged secret emissaries, but a normalization of PLO-Egyptian relations had not yet taken place by the time the 1982 war broke out; nevertheless, the war in fact did hasten it.

Within the Saudi leadership too there had been changes. The death in 1975 of King Faisal, who had been personally deeply committed to the Palestine cause, had been a blow to the PLO. His successor, King Khalid, was to die during June 1982, leaving power in the hands of King Fahd, who as crown prince under Khalid had played a major role in directing policy. Fahd was more responsive to the United States than had been either of his predecessors. This was naturally a cause of distress to Arafat and the PLO, particularly since their diplomatic strategy depended in some measure on Riyadh's influence with Washington, rather than vice versa. The fact that the prestige and power of Saudi Arabia were constantly declining during this period meant that the PLO was in effect deprived of yet another weapon.

Jordan played only a minor role during the 1982 war, due to its distance from the battlefield and the history of poor relations between it and the PLO. This did not prevent King Hussein from allowing some units of the Badr forces of the Palestine Liberation Army (PLA), which are raised in and controlled by Jordan, to move to Lebanon to join the PLO's forces fighting there. Before the war, some PLO leaders had argued for a "Jordanian option," contending that the situation in Lebanon was heading for a dead end, and that closer ties with Jordan would make up for this and bring the PLO closer to its West Bank and Gaza Strip constituency. However, although there had been some slight improvement in PLO-Jordanian relations before 1982, it was insufficient to make Jordan a major factor during the war.

In all these cases, the personality of the leader concerned was of great importance. Arafat, Assad, Mubarak, Fahd, and Hussein were all responding to imperatives from within their respective domestic constituencies, but each put his own imprint on policy. There were regime-determined reasons for the problems between the PLO and Syria, but the Arafat-Assad relationship was vital. Similarly, the presence or absence of a figure like Sadat was of great importance in determining the course of Egyptian policy. The successors to King Faisal had as much potential power as their elder brother, but their weaker personalities and the changed balance between them in his absence made them much less effective than he had been. As for King Hussein, his longevity in power, in spite of the precariousness of his regime, was due in large measure to his ability to judge the extent to which he had to appease or confront Palestinian nationalism.

In the case of the last and most important regional actor, Israel, it has been forcefully argued by Ze'ev Schiff and Ehud Ya'ari that personalities, specifically those of Sharon and Begin, were major determinants in the course of events leading to the 1982 war.[11] While there is some truth to this, it must also be recognized that structural factors and elements of perception regarding the Arabs that have been common to all Israeli leaders since Moshe Sharrett's prime ministership were crucial in this regard.[12] Indeed, every Israeli government since 1967 had chosen to deal with the Palestinians through force alone. In this Begin and Sharon and their colleagues differed only in degree, and in their ruthless pursuit of a common Israeli aim: to put the Palestinians out of mind, through elimination of their representatives if no other method was available.

Thus, between Begin and Sharon on the one hand and Arafat and his colleagues on the other, there could be no relationship except one determined by the course of events on the battlefield. As the July 1981 cease-fire between Israel and the PLO demonstrated, other outcomes might have been possible and would have been welcomed by the PLO. Arafat and his colleagues were eager to take part in Middle East settlement negotiations, showing far more willingness to compromise than was evinced by the Begin government. Clearly, the leaders of Fateh had come a long way since they publicly launched their movement 17 years earlier, proclaiming armed struggle to be the only path to the liberation of all of Palestine. Their view of Israel had changed to the point that, while it was still their primary adversary, they could now contemplate the ideas of participating in negotiations with it and of a Palestinian state alongside the Jewish one.

However, Israeli leaders, possessed by a slightly more extreme version of the worldview held by most Israelis, could not see things this way: Given their perception of the Palestinians as ''drugged roaches in a bottle'' (to use Israeli Chief of Staff Rafael Eitan's words), and of Arafat as a new Hitler in his bunker (to use Begin's), war was inevitable.[13]

ARAFAT AND THE 1982 WAR

When Israel began its attack on Lebanon with a two-day air, land, and sea bombardment of Beirut and South Lebanon, which preceded the invasion of Sunday, June 6, Yasser Arafat was in Saudi Arabia. He made his first decision before his return, ordering PLO artillery and rocket batteries to respond to Israeli fire.[14] He made this tactical decision on the advice of the PLO chief of operations, Brigadier Sa'ad Sayel (Abu al-Walid), a former Jordanian Army officer trained in the United States, who had gained greatly in stature since assuming his post at the height of the 1975–76 war.

Arafat was soon faced with far more difficult decisions, most of them involving options that ranged from undesirable to unimaginable. The PLO very swiftly found its forces in South Lebanon cut off, surrounded, overrun, in retreat, or fighting for their lives. In some places, such as the refugee camps east of the coastal cities of Tyre and Sidon or the mountainous region in the southeast of the country, they were able to put up a desperate fight. Elsewhere, they were simply overwhelmed by an Israeli force of several divisions which enjoyed approximately a 10-to-1 superiority in manpower and perhaps 10 to 20 times that advantage in firepower and equipment, as well as total command of the air and sea.

Few PLO decisions were necessary during the first week of the war, while this hopelessly unequal battle was fought out in the south. The first issue that arose requiring a clear stand from Arafat and the PLO was that of a cease-fire, which was offered by Israel on 11 June (specifying, however, that the offer applied only to Syrian forces, not to "the terrorists"). By this point, Israeli forces had reached the outskirts of Beirut, were on the point of encircling the city, had dealt a devastating blow to Syria's air defenses and air force, and were still advancing northward against Syrian and PLO forces in several parts of Lebanon.

At question was whether to agree to a cease-fire, which Syria had already accepted with alacrity. In fact, the issue was a purely theoretical one, since the Israeli army at no point stopped its advance, continuing to move forward for nearly 72 hours even after both Syria and the PLO had agreed to cease fire. However, it provoked a brief but major rift within the PLO leadership.[15] Some, notably George Habash and Nayef Hawatmeh, supported by some Fateh leaders, argued that it was wrong in principle to accept a cease-fire, especially with an enemy which was determined to destroy them, which the PLO claimed to be eager to fight, and which had specified that the Palestinians were not covered by its provisions.

Arafat was more aware than many of his colleagues of the weak international position of the PLO, and he argued strongly in favor of a cease-fire. He stressed that militarily there was no way the massively outnumbered Palestinian, Lebanese, and Syrian forces could halt the Israelis; that Syria had in any case accepted the cease-fire (without consultation with the PLO); and that after initially moving to support U.N. action to halt Israel, the United States now seemed to be actively supporting the invasion. All these reasons weighed in favor of acceptance. So did what Arafat perceived as the need to continue working to achieve international legitimacy via U.N. treatment as a full party to the conflict, as had happened during the cease-fires of 1978, 1979, and 1981.

Arafat ultimately carried the day, but only after one of the most intense leadership disputes of the war. It was the last time that he was seriously challenged by his colleagues, or that they disagreed violently over a course of action. This was fortunate, for a far more momentous problem was about to arise: how to respond to the Israeli demand, backed by the United States and the government of Elias Sarkis, that the PLO leave Lebanon.

Before the question posed itself in these stark terms, the PLO fell victim to a concerted campaign of psychological warfare. This was apparently designed to sow panic in Palestinian ranks to the point that organized resistance and clear-headed decision making were impossible. Central to the campaign were rumors that the PLO had accepted Israel's terms and was on the point of laying down its arms and evacuating Beirut, and that Arafat and his colleagues were dead, injured, hiding in a friendly embassy, or had fled.

In the midst of intense deliberations as to how to respond to the demands made on the PLO, in a situation where none of its Lebanese, Arab, or international allies could or would extend support, Arafat had to stem this tide of rumors that threatened to undermine his followers' morale. He did so mainly via a series of lightning tours of the front lines and rear areas, appearing suddenly and collecting crowds of combatants, civilians, and journalists. While not downplaying the perils of the situation, Arafat would explain how the PLO proposed to confront problems and would underline the difficulties facing Israel, before disappearing with his entourage.[16]

The Israelis mounted concerted attacks then and afterwards on every known headquarters and residence of Arafat and the top PLO leadership. In light of this, Arafat's tours were an exceedingly risky undertaking, particularly given the impossibility of knowing in advance whether enemy agents would be present at a given location. Such visits were perceived to be so vital that from June 14 onward they were made constantly by Arafat, Brigadier Abu al-Walid, Abu Iyyad, and Abu Jihad, who also made certain that they received extensive press coverage. This seemed to help assuage the concerns of Palestinians, convincing them that rumors of panic among the PLO leadership were untrue.

From this point on, the shaky Palestinian and Lebanese home front began to stabilize, as the Israeli psychological offensive failed, as Israel was unable to make spectacular new advances, and as the possibility that the war was not already over began to emerge. Nevertheless, the problem of how to respond to Israel's demands remained.

Regarding this key question, there were two broad lines of argument within the PLO leadership.[17] One group, headed by Fateh Central Committee member Hani al-Hassan, younger brother of Khaled al-Hassan, argued that a PLO withdrawal from Beirut was inevitable, and that what remained was to obtain the best possible terms. Advocates of this view called for an attempt to extract some compensation in exchange for this inevitable concession, getting some sort of political "plus" in return for a military "minus."

The other group, identified with Abu Iyyad, argued that it was too early to accept defeat. While certain concessions and some flexibility were undoubtedly necessary, further PLO resistance would lead to a stalemate that might allow for better terms to emerge in the future than were possible at the time. At the very least, they argued, it was vital to "talk tough." This would keep up popular morale and possibly convince the enemy that the PLO was not on the point of giving in to its demands, while actively searching for a way out of the dilemma.

Arafat's role in all of this was crucial. He authorized the first contacts with France by Hani al-Hassan to determine whether it was possible to obtain a political quid pro quo in exchange for certain military concessions from the PLO.[18] At the same time, Arafat led the chorus of tough statements which in mid-June stemmed the tide of defeatism caused by Israeli and Phalangist propaganda and by exaggerated or distorted reports about the magnitude of PLO concessions being offered during contacts with French, Lebanese, and other intermediaries who were negotiating with Philip Habib and the Israelis.

In the end, Arafat chose the middle ground, hoping, along with the hardliners, for a break in the bleak outlook facing the PLO, and delaying as long as possible unequivocal and irrevocable concessions. At the same time, he was aware that in the end there might be no alternative to PLO acceptance of at least some of its enemies' demands, and thus he sought to explore the best possible terms if such a distasteful eventuality came about.

Remarkably, Arafat was able to reconcile the divergent views within his movement, and to sustain high morale in seemingly hopeless circumstances. He managed further to win the confidence or at least the tolerance of many Lebanese Muslim and leftist leaders who initially seemed willing to go along with the demand for the PLO's immediate and unconditional departure. Finally, he succeeded in obtaining French mediation, which sought to link a major political plus for the PLO—a place in efforts for a Middle East settlement based on UN Security Council Resolution 242 and the right of the Palestinians to national self-determination—to its withdrawal from Beirut. These terms were embodied in a Franco-Egyptian draft Security Council resolution, which was the focus of PLO and French efforts for over a month during the siege.[19]

These limited achievements had a price. First, prolonging the siege cost Beirut and its weary inhabitants many more weeks of bombardment and deprivation. Second, postponing a decision meant that some Palestinians would become dissatisfied sooner or later, as happened when a split in the PLO emerged in 1983. Third, imposing on the goodwill of Lebanese Muslim and leftist leaders required promising certain concessions, as Arafat was forced to do at the beginning of July via a secret written pledge to Premier Shafiq al-Wazzan that the PLO leadership would leave Beirut. Finally, fourth, dependence on French mediation carried with it the risk that France's powerful ally the United States would sooner or later succeed in imposing its will at the United Nations and blocking it the one of its choice. This, of course, is what happened in the

)f this became clear, the PLO managed to hang on for two months after the June 13 cease-fire, holding off Israeli assaults and enduring heavy bombardment and repeated unsuccessful attempts to kill Arafat and its other leaders. The military editor of the Israeli daily *Ha'aretz* has confirmed that during the siege, Israeli planes bombed every site in Beirut where Arafat and his colleagues could have been located.[20] For nearly six weeks of fighting under these conditions, Arafat and the PLO attempted to find an alternative to the Israeli-U.S. terms, as these were eventually narrowed down to what came to be called the Habib plan. Until the end of July, the French Security Council initiative was the main focus of their attention.

As the continuing siege brought the PLO sympathy in Europe, strong opposition to the war arose in certain diaspora Jewish circles as well as in Israel, notably in the Peace Now movement. This was seen by many Palestinians as an encouraging if tentative sign that some solution other than the complete liquidation of the PLO which was sought by Begin, Sharon, and their cohorts, might be possible. In pursuit of an opening in this direction, Arafat made a public appeal to former World Zionist Organization President Nahum Goldmann, former French Premier Pierre Mendes-France, and former World Jewish Congress President Philip Klutznik (who had all condemned Israel's invasion), to come to besieged Beirut. They responded positively, but as the means to implement this idea were being worked out, Goldman and Mendes-France both died, aborting what might have been an important initiative.[21]

Simultaneously, it became clear in mid-July that the United States was intent on stifling the Franco-Egyptian initiative. In response, Arafat and his colleagues authorized an effort to achieve a breakthrough with the United States by Khaled al-Hassan, who was a member of an Arab League delegation to Washington which included the Syrian and Saudi Foreign Ministers, 'Abd al-Halim Khaddam and Prince Sa'ud al-Faisal. Once there, al-Hassan was advised by intermediaries that a PLO concession in the form of acceptance of Security Council Resolution 242 was the basic prerequisite for any progress in negotiations with the United States. In his dispatches to Beirut, he proposed compliance.

This was a key decision, for at the time it appeared that this was the last chance for a break in the situation. The problem was not Resolution 242 per se: this had been specifically mentioned in the Franco-Egyptian draft resolution which the PLO had wholeheartedly approved. Resolution 242 was presented there in the context of a balanced and carefully crafted agreement whereby the PLO received a quid pro quo in return for its concessions. However, as Arafat pointed out in a telex to Washington, in the proposal that al-Hassan was asking the leadership in Beirut to approve, there was no quid pro quo; there was no guarantee and not even an assurance that there would be any response if the PLO made this concession. In Arafat's words, the required quid pro quo was "a fish in the water" that had yet to be landed.[22]

In the end, Arafat refused to accept the advice of Khaled al-Hassan, who had been supported by some Fateh colleagues in Beirut. Arafat was justified in his action soon afterwards. Khaled al-Hassan's interlocutors in Washington eventually informed him that there was no point in the PLO making concessions. The United States was not prepared to change its demand for unconditional evacuation of the PLO from Beirut, or its insistence on excluding the PLO from a Middle East settlement.

This soon became clear on the battlefield, as Israeli attacks intensifed in late July, and a hard choice became necessary for the Palestinians: to accept Habib's terms or hold out for something better in the absence of hope on the horizon. A few PLO leaders counseled a last desperate message to Moscow and Damascus to ask if they could offer any alternative to withdrawal on Habib's terms. Arafat stalked disgustedly out of the meeting at which this proposal was made, stating that the Soviet and Syrian responses were a foregone conclusion. His skepticism was borne out when the Soviets soon answered that they could do nothing, and that it would be best for the PLO to accept the Habib terms. The Syrians failed to respond for several weeks, finally letting it be known that no response would be forthcoming.[23]

In the interim, Arafat had authorized negotiations over the details of the Habib terms, which were accepted in principle at the end of July and in their final form a few days after the guns fell silent in mid-August. In spite of the obvious difficulty of their situation, the revelation that they would be leaving Beirut was a shock to PLO fighters and cadres alike, as well as to the civilian population that would be abandoned to an uncertain future. However, all recognized that there was no alternative, and that Arafat and his colleagues had held out as long as humanly possible in the absence of any hope.

Significantly, if there were no voices of relief at this hard decision, there were also none of dissent. There was only bitterness at the passivity of the Arab states in the face of the longest Arab-Israeli war.[24] Before he left Beirut, Arafat met with many of those who would be left behind, and with several Lebanese leaders. The outpouring of emotion which ensued was all the more intense because all concerned knew that the guarantees for protection of the Palestinian and Lebanese civilian populations who would be left defenseless by the PLO withdrawal were paper-thin. They depended entirely on the will of the United States to keep its word to restrain Israel and the Phalange from wreaking a terrible vengeance.

In any event, these guarantees proved insufficient, as Israel's occupation of Beirut in violation of the Habib accords, and the ensuing Sabra and Shatila massacres, amply demonstrated. By this time, Arafat and the combatants and cadres of the PLO were already in their new places of exile, scattered to eight Arab countries.

In the process of evacuation, Arafat made his last decision of the war. This was to avoid going to Syria, as an indirect means of showing Palestinian anger at the passive role played by Syria and the other Arab states. Instead he made Athens his first stop, to demonstrate that the Greeks had done more than all the Arabs for the Palestinians.[25] While widely approved among his followers, Arafat's decision was to have far-reaching consequences. In the wake of the war, the PLO was vulnerable and dispersed, no longer subject to the same central direction as in Lebanon. Syria took advantage of this situation, encouraging dissidents within Fateh to launch a rebellion. Such a clash was probably inevitable. Nevertheless, by slighting Syria, and by remaining away from his forces in Syria and in Lebanon, Arafat gave the Assad regime a golden opportunity to undermine his position and split the PLO.[26]

Of all the wartime decisions made by the Palestinian leader, tactically this was probably the least wise: Most of his other decisions were probably sounder. In a situation where all the options were bad, (which the PLO had partly brought on itself but largely inherited), Arafat had generally made the least bad choices. Even if the war's results were ones that no Palestinian could have wished for, they fell short of the aims of the PLO's enemies.

Arafat may have missed some opportunities to achieve a different outcome to the war, although in view of the determined resistance of both Israel and the United States, it is hard to see how this would have been possible. In a variety of ways, he had tried to bring about a negotiated settlement that would have led to a more constructive result than obtained after the 1982 war. In this Arafat was rebuffed by his adversaries.

At war's end, the PLO was beaten but had survived to face an uncertain future under the leadership of a master of survival. This achievement for Arafat's leadership had to be balanced against the grim fact that at the end, the Palestinian people were no nearer to realizing their goal of self-determination in their homeland.

NOTES

1. The actions of Arafat and the PLO leadership in 1982 are examined in detail in Rashid Khalidi, *Under Siege: P.L.O. Decisionmaking during the 1982 War* (New York: Columbia University Press, 1985), which is based on research in the PLO archives in Tunis and interviews with several PLO leaders, including two with Arafat, and on interviews with American and French diplomats involved in the negotiations.

2. Ibid., pp. 43, 58, 73. See also Chaim Herzog, *The Arab-Israeli Wars*, revised ed. (New York: Vintage, 1984), pp. 344–45, as well as *The Military Balance 1982–1983* (London: International Institute for Strategic Studies, 1983), for information about Israel's forces committed to the Lebanon campaign and its military capabilities.

3. Ze'ev Schiff and Ehud Ya'ari, *Israel's Lebanon War* (New York: Simon and Schuster, 1984), p. 117, describes the Syrian army as "still unsuspecting" on the first day of the war.

4. Khalidi, *Under Siege*, pp. 34–35.

5. For more on the early years of the PLO, see Helena Cobban, *The Palestinian Liberation Organization: People, Power and Politics* (Cambridge: Cambridge University Press, 1984); Aaron David Miller, *The P.L.O. and the Politics of Survival* (New York: Praeger, 1983); and William Quandt, Fuad Jabber, and Anne Mosely Lesch, *The Politics of Palestinian Nationalism* (Berkeley: University of California Press, 1973).

6. *International Documents on Palestine, 1974* (Beirut: Institute for Palestine Studies, 1976), p. 143.

7. These are Thomas Kiernan, *Arafat, the Man and the Myth* (New York: W. W.

Norton, 1976), which is full of incorrect information; and Alan Hart, *Arafat, Terrorist or Statesman?* (London: Sidgwick and Jackson, 1984), which, in spite of its flaws, has the merit of being based on extensive interviewing. Other sources on Arafat's life include Abu Iyyad with Eric Rouleau, *My Home, My Land: A Narrative of Palestinian Struggle* (New York: Times Books, 1981), and Cobban's book, *The Palestinian Liberation Organization,* cited above, also based on interviews with several PLO leaders. Much of this section is based on these sources, especially Hart and Cobban.

8. At Fateh's fourth General Conference in 1980, a 15-man Central Committee was elected, 5 members for the first time. Of the entire group, 3, Khalil al-Wazir, Majed Abu Sharar and Brig. Abu al-Walid have since been assassinated, and 2, Abu Saleh and Qadri, have split from the movement to head dissident factions in Damascus. Three of these 4 were among those newly elected in 1980.

9. The position of the Palestinians in Lebanon before the 1982 war is dealt with in Rashid Khalidi, "The Palestinians in Lebanon: The Social Repercussions of the Israeli Invasion," *Middle East Journal* 38, no. 2 (Spring 1984); 255–66, esp. pp. 255–58. The pre–1982 situation of the PLO in Lebanon is covered in chapter 1 of Khalidi, *Under Siege.*

10. Recent phases of the PLO-Syrian relationship are discussed in Rashid Khalidi, "The Asad Regime and the Palestinian Resistance," *Arab Studies Quarterly* 6, no. 4 (Fall 1984); 259–66.

11. This is a central thesis of Schiff and Ya'ari, *Israel's Lebanon War.*

12. The genesis of the Israeli state's hard-line approach to the Arabs is analyzed in Avi Shlaim's important article, "Conflicting Approaches to Israel's Relations with the Arabs: Ben Gurion and Sharrett, 1953–56," *Middle East Journal* 37, no. 2 (Spring 1983); 180–201. See also chapters 1 and 2 of Tom Segev, *1949: The First Israelis* (New York: The Free Press, 1985), which covers Israel's early relations with the Arab states using newly declassified Israeli documents, as well as Avi Shlaim, *Collusion across the Jordan: King Abdullah, the Zionist Movement and the Partition of Palestine* (New York: Columbia University Press, 1988).

13. Eytan was quoted by Davis Shipler in "Most West Bank Arabs Blame U.S. for Impasse," *The New York Times,* April 14, 1983, p. A3; and Begin by Schiff and Ya'ari in *Israel's Lebanon War,* p. 39.

14. Most of the material in Section III is drawn from *Under Siege,* which gives full references to published sources, the P.L.O. archives or interviews. For details on the course of the fighting see chs. 2 and 3; for P.L.O. decisionmaking, see chs. 4 and 5.

15. For sources on this episode see Khalidi, *Under Siege,* p. 201 n. 23.

16. A photograph of Arafat on a front-line morale-boosting tour appeared on page 1 of the *New York Times* on June 15, 1982.

17. For more details on these two tendencies within the PLO leadership, see Khalidi, *Under Siege,* pp. 110–13 and ff.

18. That this was the case was confirmed in interviews with both Arafat, in Tunis, March 9, 1984, and with Hani al-Hassan, in Tunis, August 31, 1984.

19. This important resolution, discussed in Khalidi, *Under Siege,* pp. 135–42 and p. 209 n. 10, and based in part on a PLO proposal adopted without dissent by the entire leadership in Beirut at the time, represents one of the most important indications to date of PLO readiness for a negotiated compromise settlement of the Arab-Israeli conflict.

20. Ze'ev Schiff, "Is it Necessary to Kill Arafat?" *Ha'aretz,* 11 October 1985, p. 1. Schiff calls this episode a "manhunt," and notes: "The siege of Beirut was openly used to try to kill Arafat and other Palestinian leaders."

21. Klutznik's own account of the episode can be found in Meir Merhav, Philip Klutznik, and Herman Eilts, *Facing the P.L.O. Question* (Washington, D.C.: Foundation for Middle East Peace, 1985), pp. 14–15.

22. Khalidi, *Under Siege,* p. 157. The entire episode can be followed on pp. 154–63.

23. Abu Iyyad interview, Tunis, March 14, 1984, cited in Khalidi, *Under Siege,* pp. 164–65, 212 n. 68.

24. Ibid., pp. 147–48. See also Selim Nassib with Caroline Tidall, *Beirut: Frontline Story* (London: Pluto Press, 1983), p. 126.

25. Ibid., pp. 132–35 reproduces Nassib's interview, originally published in the French newspaper *Libération,* conducted with Arafat aboard the Greek ship which was carrying him to Athens, in which he expresses harsh sentiments about the Arab regimes.

26. In an interview in Tunis, March 9, 1984, Arafat disagreed with this assessment, stressing the inevitability of the Fateh rebellion irrespective of what he might have done, due to the determined opposition of the Assad regime to his leadership.

5

SYRIA'S HAFEZ AL-ASSAD

Margaret G. Hermann

Hafez al-Assad, current president of Syria, is an enigma to Western scholars and policy-makers. There is debate over how much control he has over the Syrian government; that is, how accountable he is to others in the government and society. Moreover, some see Assad as the puppet-master in Lebanon, maneuvering the situation to meet his goals; other view him as caught in his own quagmire—Syria's Vietnam or Afghanistan. Some see Assad as capable of and interested in helping shape peace in the Arab-Israeli conflict; others see him as primarily disruptive to the peace process. Finally, some see Assad's Syria as merely a Soviet pawn, while others suspect Assad of using the Soviet Union. The question becomes: Just who is Hafez al-Assad? That is, which of these portraits best characterizes him? What kind of leadership does he exert over the Syrian government and people, and in the Middle East? In this chapter we examine these claims and counterclaims, and seek to make Assad less inscrutable.

THE LEADERSHIP CONTEXT

Assad gained control of the leadership of the Syrian government in a coup d'état in November 1970, bringing to a close two decades of coups and countercoups. Calling his takeover the "Corrective Movement" to the Baathist party revolution of 1963, Assad consolidated his power in early 1971, being named president in a public referendum. With Assad's assumption of power, the military wing of the regional (Syrian) Baath party asserted control over the civilian wing of the party. Assad moved from defense minister to head of state. Interested in making his party a mass mobilization party analogous to Nasser's party in Egypt,

The author wishes to thank Charles Snare for his help in locating the materials on Assad used in preparing this chapter. Support for writing this chapter was provided by the Mershon Center, Ohio State University.

Assad formed the Progressive National Front, comprised of the five socialist parties in Syria at the time: the Arab Socialist Renaissance (Baath) party, the Syrian Arab Socialist Union (Nasserite), the Socialist Union, the Arab Socialist party, and the Communist party of Syria. Assad's goal has been to draw "the whole population together by striving to transcend communal and party differences."[1]

Given that Syria is one of the most heterogeneous nations in the Middle East, this goal has not been easy to attain. Although the Sunni Moslems represent the largest group in the population, the following religious minorities are also found in the population: Alawites, Druzes, Ismailis, Christians, and Jews. Among the ethnic—non–Arab speaking—minorities in Syria are the Armenians, Circassians, Kurds, and Turcomans.[2] Moreover, there are nomadic Bedouins and a large Palestinian refugee population. Many of these religious and ethnic minorities are found in specific regions of Syria. These regions often have a city at their center and are divided from other regions by a geographical boundary such as a mountain range.

Loyalties develop to these communities or regions, not to the nation as a whole. As Michael Van Dusen has observed,

This fact has meant that political and ideological loyalties reflect the local political situation in a particular agro-city. As a result, national parties have had to adapt to Syrian localism, becoming decentralized and cell-oriented; as a result, too, national parties continue to project inter- and intra-regional interests.[3]

As an Alawite, Assad represents a minority group. Until the revolution of March 8, 1963, when the Baath Party assumed power in Syria, most of the Syrian political leadership had come from the majority population of Sunni Moslems. Since 1963, power has shifted to the religious minorities. With this shift began a concomitant "shift in political power from the big cities to the provinces. . . . The small town and rural population and those who have left to try their fortunes in the cities are the constituents" of the Baath party.[4]

The goal of the Baath party is a united Arab socialist society, its ideology emphasizes pan-Arabism and socialism, and its motto is "Unity, Freedom, and Socialism." The party feels there is only one possible Arab nation in the Arab world; the present nations represent illegitimate and artificial creations of the colonial powers and are merely regions of the larger Arab nation. To achieve this end, the Arab people find themselves in a "struggle against colonialism, Zionism, and provincial and separatist trends," and involved in a "revolution against domination and exploitation."[5] To the Baathists, inter-Arab relations thus become essentially "domestic rather than foreign matters."[6] Interference in the internal affairs of other Arab states is considered appropriate in order to further coordination among the various regions in the Arab nation: "No Arab region can improve its condition in isolation from the other regions."[7] Given the socialist orientation of the Baath party, this interference has often been directed toward those Arab countries with a more conservative philosophy.

One characteristic of the Baath party that has led to problems in Syria is its secular nature. There has been an attempt by the party to separate church and state. Unlike the constitutions of other Arab nations, the Syrian constitution "does not state that Islam is the State religion, but merely stipulates that Islamic jurisprudence shall be the main source of legislation."[8] This secularization of the state is opposed by the Sunni Moslem majority in Syria, and has led to some of Assad's most critical domestic political crises. To the Sunni majority Islam provides a social, cultural, political, and legal program for living—and is seen as the only acceptable code. As noted Islamic scholar Muhammed Hussein Fadlallah has observed, Islam provides no distinction between what is political and what is religious.[9] Islamic nationalism and Arab nationalism are viewed as synonymous. The most vocal proponents of this view, and thus the most dominant opponents of the Baath party rulers, have been the religious leaders and the Moslem Brotherhood. They believe that the Baath Party and Assad have used secularization to diminish the power and authority of Islam and religion.

ASSAD THE MAN

Hafez al-Assad was born the oldest son of an Alawite farming family in a small town in the Latakia district of Syria in 1928 or 1930 (sources differ as to the date).[10] The Latakia district is also known as the Alawite region of Syria, and is located near the Mediterranean Sea in northwestern Syria. The Alawite religious sect has been certified as part of the Shiite Moslem community. Assad (whose name means "protector of lions") received his primary and secondary education in schools in the Latakia district. While still in secondary school, he joined the Baath party and became a student activist. In 1952, he entered the Homs Military College, which is an air academy. He graduated as a pilot and lieutenant in 1955, his flying talent winning him the best aviator trophy upon graduation. Like other Syrian young men of that time who were both poor and from a religious minority, Assad perceived the military as a way to improve his lot economically and socially. Three years after graduating from the military college, Assad went to the Soviet Union for special night-combat training.

When Syria merged with Egypt in 1959, Assad was sent to Cairo to be a squadron leader in the air force of the United Arab Republic. In Cairo, his political interests were reawakened as he became a "leader of the clandestine group of Syrian officers known as the Military Committee, who were sympathetic to Baath principles."[11] The Military Committee played a key role in the coup of March 8, 1963, which brought the Baath party to power in Syria, at which time Assad became the commander of the Syrian air force. In the series of coups that followed the Baathist revolution of 1963, Assad became successively minister of defense and then leader of the "military wing" of the Baath party while still retaining his command of the air force. When in November 1970 Assad and the military wing of the party appeared to be losing politically to the civilian wing of the party, Assad "ordered the military to occupy the offices of the civilian party section as well as those of the Baathist dominated people's organizations, and furthermore to arrest prominent civilian party leaders."[12] Assad assumed control of the government.

Assad's beliefs grow out of his party background; his power and authority come from his military background. Thus, during tenure as head of state in Syria, Assad has worked to achieve the goals of the Baath party while keeping himself in power through his leadership of the Syrian military. The importance of the party to Assad is evident in his assertion that he joined the party before the military.[13] Dawisha notes that "ideologically and emotionally" Assad has "accorded considerable respect and prestige to the party."[14] Although willing to be pragmatic in the means he uses to achieve his ends, Assad espouses the Baath principles of Arab unity and socialism and, in turn, he believes Syria is locked in a zero-sum battle with the forces of imperialism, Zionism, and exploitation.

Embedded in Assad's view of Arab unity is the notion of a "Greater Syria." Before the colonial powers divided up this part of the Middle East after World War I,

the term "Syria" tended to denote loosely the territory now forming the contemporary states of Syria, Lebanon, Israel and Jordan. Indeed, [W. B] Fisher maintains that "to the Ottomans, as to the Romans, Syria stretched from the Euphrates to the Mediterranean, and from the Sinai to the hills of Southern Turkey, with Palestine as a smaller province of this wider unit."[15]

To many among the Syrian leadership, the states of Syria, Lebanon, Israel, and Jordan were artificially created by the colonial powers and do not have "historical roots in Arab history."[16]

Assad has become particularly interested in the notion of "Greater Syria" since Egypt's disengagement agreement with Israel. Assad's activities since 1975 have been directed toward the Palestinian cause as well as toward making Syria indispensable in Lebanon. He has cooperated with Jordan's Hussein when the king has maintained a confrontational posture against Israel, and has become belligerent toward Jordan when Hussein has shown any indication of entering into negotiations with Israel or settling the Palestinian question on his own terms. Daniel Dishon suggests that Assad wants to "produce a situation in which Damascus is the place to which both Jordan and Lebanon, as well as the PLO, have to turn in order to clear major decisions."[17]

In conjunction with Assad's pan-Arab philosophy and interest in a "Greater Syria" goes an intense hatred of Israel. Assad has a "devil-image" of Israel—an inherent bad-faith image of the enemy.[18] Israel can do nothing right; one must always be suspicious of the motives of its leadership. Any cooperative gestures are made in reaction to the situation and forced on the Israelis; they are certainly not intended. Israel's goal is further expansion into Arab territory. Assad quotes Moshe Dayan's speech to the soldiers on the Golan Heights in 1973 to illustrate Israel's expansionistic tendencies: "Our predecessors made the Israel of the 1948 frontiers, our generation that of the 1967 frontiers, now it's up to you to make Greater Israel."[19] For Assad, Syria and Israel have a basic conflict of interest—both want the same land and both believe that their countries have innate leadership rights over this territory.

Assad's political style has the following characteristics: behind-the-scenes maneuvering, broad consultation, control of information and attention to detail, use of incentives, pragmatism, and patience. Assad maintains control over policy making within the government by being the center of the network of information, and by consulting on important decisions with those likely to be affected by any policies or actions. As defense minister, Assad is reported to have said: "Nothing goes on in the army without my knowledge, right down to the promotion or transfer of a private."[20] One way that Assad garners such information is through discussions with those involved with the issue or problem under consideration.

Very rarely, indeed extremely rarely, would the President take an important decision without prior evaluation and consultations within the Government and sometimes from outside it, such as university professors. Consultations usually centre on important members of the Party and sometimes the Progressive National Front. If there is no time, he will certainly make a point of at least contacting by phone some members of the party leadership. He rarely makes an instinctive decision.[21]

Through such contact, Assad can assess the positions of the actors and the nature of the support for what he wants to do. The stream of foreign visitors to Damascus suggests that Assad follows much the same procedure in foreign as in domestic affairs. Through personal diplomacy, Assad can "size up his opponents," getting a sense of their positions and just how committed they are.

With up-to-date information and a sense of who is interested in what, Assad knows where to apply the carrot and where the stick. "To his mind, everything has a price, but it is up to him to fix it. He does not bother with limits and boundaries set by others."[22] Tactics and strategies become tied to the specific situation and problem, as do the positive or negative nature of the incentives used to try to get what he wants. This pragmatism has led to Assad's perceived unpredictability in foreign affairs.

The above characteristics all benefit from Assad's basic patience and sense of political timing. He "built his power stone by stone; he never rushes."[23] In effect, Assad makes a move, then stops to assess the effect and consider the new situation and players before making another move. "He can bide his time, while strengthening his advantages and letting his foes tie themselves up in knots, then pick his moment with precision."[24] Assad has used his patience and sense of timing to great effect in what U.S. policy-makers have called his "decibel politics": "They heighten tensions for a few days, then lower them."[25]

Again, such behavior allows him to test the waters and estimate how far he can go.

Assad's political style is associated with a "workaholic" nature. Called the "night flier" for his nocturnal work habits, he has been known to "summon aides to meetings at 2 and 3 A.M.." and to work 18-hour days.[26] These work habits took a toll on his health in November 1983, when Assad suffered an apparent heart attack and was absent from his office for ten weeks. During his absence, there was some maneuvering for his position among three vice presidents appointed at the time to help with the conduct of foreign affairs, the party, and the military.[27] Although Assad has apparently recovered from his illness, the fact that he is mortal has not been lost on those in a position to challenge his power.

Assad has been called "the Arabs' Bismarck"[28] and "a modern Saladin."[29] Like Bismarck, who unified the disparate groups in the German empire, Assad is interested in unifying an Arab people who seem prone to "disunity, strife, and even fratricidal conflict" and to achieving such unity with himself in a position of leadership.[30] Like Bismarck, Assad understands the political maneuvering and shrewdness that his goal demands. Like Saladin, the Moslem leader who defeated the Christian invaders and the Crusader Kingdom and ruled Greater Syria, Assad appears to believe that he has "the dual obligation to rid the region of all foreign presence while preserving Damascus as the only focal point for Arab unity today."[31] Assad keeps a picture of the Battle of Hittin (where Saladin delivered the final blow to the Crusaders) on his office wall—perhaps as a reminder both to him and his visitors of what he wants to do.[32]

LEADERSHIP STYLE IN DOMESTIC POLITICS

Assad has built his regime around three institutions: the Baath party, the military, and the governmental bureaucracy.[33] By heading all three institutions, Assad sits at the apex of power, and through a series of checks and balances, he has tried to ensure the loyalty and support of those working in each of these institutions. Devlin observes that integral to Assad's power and authority is a unitary patron-client structure, with him as the chief patron.[34]

One of Assad's goals on assuming power was to broaden the base of support for the Baath party. "The party must reflect the masses or perish" and, thus, must operate "within broad ideals simply stated and easily understood by the public."[35] Having found its initial support among the rural and small-town population who felt exploited by the big-city merchants who formed the political and social leadership of Syria in the 1940s and 1950s, the Baath party has further cultivated this clientele. During Assad's tenure in office, substantial resources have been directed toward improving the quality of life of those in the countryside. Moreover, by organizing the peasants, youth, and workers at the grassroots level, the Baath party has developed a means to socialize the young, to promote its policies, to mobilize demonstrations of support, and to keep abreast of what is happening in the various regions and among the various ethnic and religious minorities in Syria.[36]

Assad has also worked to gain the support of the landowners, businessmen and merchants—who are generally of the Sunni majority—by relaxing some of the socialist restrictions that were imposed on these groups during the earlier Baathist governments.

There could be no doubt that the perceived need to win the support of this group formed part of the motivation behind Assad's post–1973 efforts to liberalize the economy, his quest for better understanding in Syrian-American relations, his very cordial foreign policy towards the conservative Arab states, particularly Saudi Arabia, and his relaxation of foreign trade restrictions.[37]

Moreover, Assad has moved to protect his power base in the military by "upgrading the pay, benefits, and prestige of the officer corps."[38] Under Assad, the size of the armed forces has increased, as has its professionalization and the sophistication of the weapons at its command. Defense spending has also increased, representing nearly a fifth of the country's gross national product and "one-third of all central government expenditures."[39] In addition to these incentives, Assad has developed an effective intelligence network within the officer corps to alert him to discontent and possible trouble. He has used the reshuffling of commands and officers as a way of preventing individuals from gaining too large a power base, and as R. D. McLaurin, Don Peretz, and Lewis Snider have observed, Assad has kept the strike forces and many key combat units primarily manned by Alawites loyal to him and his presidency.

The command and control of the Syrian armed forces, particularly the army, are also directly Alawite oriented. Even where unit commanders are not Alawite, the senior Alawite within the unit is directly tied to the higher command structure and quite closely linked to the presidential palace. In effect, then, there is an Alawite command structure parallel to and more effective than the formal military command structure.[40]

In this way, Assad has tried to safeguard himself against a coup. Nevertheless, on issues concerned with the military budget and war and peace, the military— in particular the officer corps—become a significant force that Assad must take into account in making policy. These are areas that members of the military regard as their domains of influence.[41]

Assad has counted on a set of trusted advisers with party and military responsibilities to keep him attuned to his various constituencies, to consult with him in the decision-making process, to bear some of the accountability for decisions that are made, and to implement what is decided. His advisers are expected to demonstrate undivided loyalty to Assad personally and to his presidency. Two individuals who have served Assad in this capacity throughout his tenure in office are Defense Minister Mustapha Tlas and once foreign minister, now Vice President Abdel Halim Khaddam. Assured of loyalty in his closest associates, Assad can afford to solicit their opinions and weigh their views and information about various constituencies in reaching a decision.

Up to this point, this discussion has focused on the ways in which Assad works to establish legitimacy and to gain support for his regime. In understanding Assad's relations to his various constituencies, we also need to examine how he deals with opposition. Assad copes with opposition differently depending on whether it is located inside his regime or in groups in the society at large; his response also varies depending on whether opposition is focused on a specific policy issue or is aimed at ousting his regime. With his interest in building a workable consensus with the party and military leadership, Assad is more tolerant of differences of opinion on matters of policy than of challenges to his authority. He has behaved in a harsh and repressive manner toward those whose actions suggest an interest in changing the regime.

In an attempt to prevent those with leadership positions in the party or military from gaining a sufficient base of support to challenge his authority, Assad restricts the roles of these individuals to one of the institutions of power (party, governmental bureaucracy, or military) and shuffles his cabinet, commanders, and party personnel periodically.[42] If these techniques are not effective, Assad may resort to sending those opposing him into temporary or permanent exile, placing them under arrest or in house detention, or assassination. A case in point is Rifaat al-Assad, the president's brother, whom some consider to be Assad's likely successor. Rifaat has served as vice president and head of the Defense Brigades (or praetorian guard). During Assad's illness in late 1983, Rifaat showed signs of challenging his brother's position. Assad temporarily exiled his brother to Geneva and reorganized the Defense Brigades, reducing their role and special privileges.[43] In effect, Assad scaled back his brother's base of support and power.

Assad uses two techniques to deal with opposition in the society: deflection and repression. Israel, Iraq, the Moslem Brotherhood, and at times the United States are the scapegoats on which he deflects internal problems by claiming that they are the enemy and are responsible for Syria's troubles. Assad has also used the Syrian people's support for the Palestinian cause to rally their allegiance, thereby diverting attention away from problems. The fact that Syria remains under the state of emergency declared during the 1973 October War—and, therefore, under continuous martial law—reinforces Assad's call to pull together to fight the common enemy as well as his ability to arrest and detain those viewed as aiding the enemy. Fred H. Lawson makes the case that Syria's intervention in the Lebanese civil war in 1976 represents an attempt on Assad's part to deflect attention from the building unrest in north-central Syria.[44]

When Assad is unable to diffuse the opposition in the society, he has resorted to repressive tactics. At various times in the late 1970s and early 1980s, the Defense Brigades and Special Elite Forces have been used to put down outbursts against the Assad regime. Generally the targets of these special security forces have been members of the Moslem Brotherhood.[45] The uprisings have been crushed ruthlessly and often have been accompanied by severe and random brutality. Assad has moved quickly and decisively to "suppress dissident organizations by force."[46] There is a difference of opinion over the effect Assad's repressive tactics have had on support for his regime. Some argue that Assad's increased dependence on repressive measures in recent years has reduced overall support for his regime and increased sympathy for the dissidents as well as increased internal security problems; others argue that most "Syrian villagers and their relatives in the cities, whatever their sectarian affiliation, are not prepared to risk the material gains of the past 20 years" and, therefore, support has not been appreciably eroded by such practices.[47] Antigovernment outbursts appear correlated with a downturn in economic conditions and blatant sectarian actions on the part of the Assad government.

VIEWS AND RELATIONS IN THE REGION

Assad's views and relations with other countries in the Middle East are based on current developments in the Arab-Israeli conflict. His major foreign policy goals since coming to power have been recovery of the territory in the Golan Heights occupied by Israel in 1967, guarantee of the rights of the Palestinians, and a leadership role in the region. As Karim Pakradouni has observed, Assad has pursued these goals through a strategy of interchangeable alliances—he "takes care to hit the adversary without knocking him out and help the friend without really bailing him out, for the roles could be reversed one day."[48] Robert Neumann has alluded to this strategy as the "traditional Middle Eastern game of opposing and cooperating at the same time."[49] Assad has a reputation in the region for "intricate maneuvers combining daring action with a desire to take minimal risks."[50]

Since taking office in 1970, Assad has experienced several major changes in the region and in the nature of the Arab-Israeli conflict that have affected Syria's fortunes and policies. Among these are: the change from a bipolar to a multipolar system in the region, the ascendance of the role of the United States in the region, the adoption by the United States of the "one step at a time" approach to settling the Arab-Israeli conflict, the increasing ambivalence among Arab countries in the region over whether diplomacy or armed struggle is the best strategy in dealing with Israel, and the growing calls for an Islamic revolution. Within the constraints that his goals put on him and on Syria, Assad has endeavored to act pragmatically in dealing with these various changes. His reactions to these developments provide insights into Assad's views and relations in the region.

The Shift from a Bipolar to a Multipolar System

Before the 1973 October War, Israel and Egypt were the dominant military and diplomatic powers in the Middle East. Up to this point, "what mattered most in determining political outcomes in the Middle East were the predispositions and activities of the Egyptians and the Israelis. Other regional actors could on the whole be ignored or controlled by these two powers."[51] Since the October War, however, there has been a shift toward a more multipolar system. Lawson suggests four reasons for this shift.[52] First, other Arab countries were increasing their quantities of sophisticated arms at a faster rate than Egypt. Second, the Arab oil-producing states, buoyed by the success of their oil embargo and their growing economic strength, were becoming more influential in the region. Third, both the United States and the Soviet Union were directing more attention toward other actors in the region, and fourth, there was growing disagreement among the Arab nations about how to deal with Israel as Egypt went its own way in signing a peace agreement with that country.

In such a changing environment, "there is greater ambiguity about the relative distribution of capabilities among countries" and the chance for the nations whose influence is increasing to form a dominant coalition.[53] Furthermore, "less powerful countries whose relative position is improving—such as Syria during the mid–1970s—have both incentives and the capabilities to carry out assertive, if not aggressive, foreign policy initiatives."[54] There is an incentive to become part, if not leader, of the predominant coalition, and to gain control over conflict-laden situations that have long-term implications for future security—to take advantage of the opportunity for influence while it is available.

Lawson proposes that Syria's intervention in Lebanon in 1976 was just such an initative. It was an attempt to exploit the situation in such a way as to gain influence and the ability to give direction to any changes that were going to occur in Lebanon, as well as to increase its own security vis-à-vis Israel.[55] Assad's renewed interest in building a coalition among the "Greater Syrian" nations in the post–Sinai II period is also evidence of an attempt to take advantage of changes in the polarity of the region. As a leader of such an alliance of the Arab East, "Syria's interests could not be lightly disregarded."[56]

Ascendance of the United States in the Region

Dankwort Rustow has observed that a comparison of the Middle Eastern scene in the early 1970s and 1980s reveals a change in the role of the United States vis-à-vis the Soviet Union. Whereas in the early 1970s there was

hostility toward the United States and close relations with Moscow—with Egypt, Syria, and Iraq vying for leadership of this broad trend, . . . in 1984, by contrast, pro-Western forces were in the ascendant. Egypt, Jordan, and Saudi Arabia were engaged to varying degrees in military cooperation with the United States, and Washington had resumed full diplomatic relations with all Arab governments except Libya and South Yemen.[57]

Syria's relations with the superpowers, however, have shown the mirror image of the superpowers' general role in the area. Relations with the United States have worsened across the decade from their high during and just after Henry

Kissinger's shuttle diplomacy, while relations with the Soviet Union have grown closer. Most within the Syrian leadership remain wary of the United States for what is perceived to be its imperialistic ventures in the Middle East and its role in "establishing and sustaining Israel."[58]

Meanwhile, the Soviet Union is viewed as Syria's "international patron."[59] Although Assad's own pragmatism leads him to want to maintain an independent and nonaligned course in East-West relations, the practicalities of the situation have forced him closer to the Soviet Union.[60] "Assad recognizes that Syrian military forces depend on Soviet materiel and training, and that there is no near-term prospect of replacing that Soviet function."[61] Nonetheless, he has tried to maintain some independence from Moscow economically and diplomatically, realizing the dominant role that the United States plays in the region. Assad has worked to diversify the economic aid coming to his country from outside the Comecon countries and "has not been reluctant to displease the Soviets when it suits Syria's purpose."[62] Assad has been able to maintain this semblance of independence because Syria remains the Soviet Union's one major entrée into playing a role in any settlement of the Arab-Israeli conflict.

The "One Step at a Time" Strategy of the United States

Neumann observes that "there is a widespread impression in America that peace in the Middle East can be achieved 'one step at a time' or perhaps 'one peace at a time.' "[63] To the Arabs, this strategy is a disaster. It suggests to them "a nightmare image of increasingly impotent Arab states having to cut unfavorable deals with an overpowering Israel."[64]

Assad feels particularly threatened by this strategy since "under this scenario Syria would be the last and therefore the weakest to sign up."[65] Given Syria's poor relations with the United States, its ties to the Soviet Union, and the pan-Arab and nationalistic fervor of its people, Assad believes that this U.S. strategy places him in a no-win, highly isolated, and militarily vulnerable situation. Assad's perception is that peace with Israel can only come through

the strength of a united Arab front that includes: Egypt and Jordan, the two other Arab belligerents bordering on Israel; Saudi Arabia, as the financial backbone and the country with leverage on Israel's primary external supporter; and the Palestinians."[66]

For Assad, "the key factor likely to persuade Israel to negotiate withdrawal from the occupied territories" is this combined strategic threat.[67] Without such a strategic threat, Assad believes there is no chance of getting back the Golan Heights because it is so crucial to Israel's national security and demand for secure borders. Yet "Syrian sovereignty and the termination of Israeli control over the Heights are a sine qua non of any settlement" for the Syrians.[68] Assad's fallback position since the Camp David accords and Egypt's single-front settlement with Israel has been to try to spoil other bilateral peace initiatives with Israel and to concentrate on developing a united eastern front "with elements weaker than (and therefore dependent on) Syria"—a modern-day "Greater Syria."[69]

Increasing Arab Ambivalence over Armed Struggle Strategy

Across the decade of the 1970s, there was an increasing realization among the Arab countries that the "three nos" of the Khartoum Arab summit of 1967 were growing less viable as a strategy for dealing with Israel. "No peace with Israel, no negotiations with Israel, no recognition of Israel" was no longer a realistic rallying cry. With Egypt's withdrawal from the status of a confrontation state, with Israel's continued military superiority and backing by the United States, with the exile of the main bodies of the PLO from the area, and with the increasing numbers of Israeli settlers in the occupied territories, there has come a "greater willingness to recognize Israel and in some fashion to deal with it."[70] This mood is best reflected in the statement adopted at the Arab Summit in Fez in September 1982, which gave endorsement to the "drawing up by the Security Council of guarantees for peace for all the states of the region, including the independent Palestinian state."

In effect, Assad tacitly recognized Israel when he signed a disengagement treaty with Israel in May 1974. "Syria's disengagement committed it to the negotiation process."[71] The issue has become what is to be negotiated and who is to be involved. In each of the peace plans that have been proposed for ending the Arab-Israeli conflict, however, Assad has perceived that his interests were minimized. Egyptian, Jordanian, and Palestinian interests were the predominant focus. Given the preeminence the Arab world gives to the Palestinian problem in any discussions of a resolution to the Arab-Israeli conflict, one way to make sure that Syrian interests become part of the peace process is to control all or part of the PLO—the Arab League's designated representative of the Palestinians.[72]

Several factors make this strategy relevant and feasible for Assad. Given that "there is a sizable and influential Palestinian community in Syria, linked by a multitude of ties to Syrians," there has been continual popular support and pressure toward Syria's participation in securing rights for the Palestinians.[73] Moreover, since Syria

played an instrumental role in the formation of the Palestinian resistance movement and has been a major source of its military and political support, . . . Syria has seen itself—perhaps rightly—as the main champion of the Palestinians in the Arab world.[74]

Assad has used his control over al-Saiqi, the Syrian-based Palestinian group which "has emerged as the second most powerful group in the PLO," as a way of gaining and maintaining influence over PLO decisions.[75] The 1980s have seen both a cold and a hot war develop between Assad and the PLO, in particular

Arafat and Fateh, as Assad has moved to consolidate his control.[76] He is interested in eliminating the PLO as "an independent factor to be reckoned with in Lebanon. . . . If there is any negotiating to be done regarding Palestinian civilians, Palestinian military activity, or anything else pertaining to the Palestinians in Lebanon," Assad wants to do that bargaining.[77] In effect, Assad wants to gain control over all the PLO forces presently located on Israel's borders.

Growing Call for an Islamic Revolution

With the consolidation of the Khomeini Islamic revolution in Iran, a cry has gone up among Moslems throughout the Middle East for an Islamic revolution. "Toward the end of the 1970s, fundamentalist Islamic movements mushroomed throughout the area."[78] Those urging an Islamic revolution had the "conviction that Islamic beliefs, sentiments, and aspirations should be channeled into radical political action" and were generally Moslems caught in a changing world they did not understand, and in which they increasingly found themselves alienated and discriminated against.[79]

Assad began to feel the effects of the growing revolutionary fervor as the Moslem Brotherhood increased its attacks against his government in the late 1970s and 1980s. The increased attacks were accompanied by the growth of the Amal Shiite Movement in Lebanon during the civil war. As noted earlier, Assad took harsh repressive measures against the Moslem Brotherhood in Syria. His approach with the Amal movement has been somewhat different. Assad has done the same thing with the outside Islamic fundamentalist forces that he has done with the PLO—worked to gain control over what they can do in territory over which he exercises leadership. He has followed this strategy by allying himself with Iran. Emphasizing that as an Alawite he is a member of the Shiite sect and, thus, has a common religious heritage with the Iranians, Assad has worked to develop good relations with the mullahs in Iran. He understands the influence that the Iranian mullahs have over the Shiites in Lebanon, and knows that "a Lebanese Shia community actively opposed to Syrian interests could make Damascus's position in that country very difficult."[80]

Assad has also used his support of Iran as a way of harming Iraq. As Devlin observes, "any enemy of Iraq is a friend of Syria—most of the time."[81] Iraq would seem the best possible natural ally for Syria since it borders on that country, is militarily powerful, has oil, and is under the control of a wing of the Baath party. Instead, intense rivalry and mutual suspicion have usually characterized the relationship between Assad and Saddam Hussein, the Iraqi leader. "Leadership conflict, historical intraparty quarrels, and until recently, Iraqi rejection of a political settlement with Israel" have divided these two nations.[82] Tries at collaboration have ended in open hostility and in each country's leadership subverting the other.

Although Syria's support of Iran helps in dealing with the Shiite Islamic fundamentalists in Lebanon and thwarts Iraq, Assad runs the risk of alienating other parts of the Arab world whose help he needs through this behavior. In particular, the Gulf states, which have provided money to the Assad regime, fear Islamic revolts in their own countries should Iran succeed in its war with Iraq. Support from Saudi Arabia has become increasingly important to Assad in his desire to pursue both his military buildup and his economic development programs. Moreover, Saudi Arabia is important to Assad's united-front plan for dealing with Israel, since it "alone among the Arab states has real leverage over Washington."[83]

ASSAD AND THE ISRAELI INVASION OF LEBANON

Background

To understand Assad's leadership of Syria from its intervention in Lebanon in January 1976 to the present, one must understand the historical relationship between Syria and Lebanon, Assad's perceptions concerning the strategic importance of Lebanon for Syria, and Assad's need to control or influence those other entities in the Middle East that can affect what happens to Syria.

Assad has often observed that "the Syrians and Lebanese are one people, their past is one and the same, their history is one and their future is one and the same."[84] Like many Syrians, Assad believes that "Lebanon and Syria are integral parts of Greater Syria and that the divisions between the two countries were artificially created by the French to serve their own colonial interests."[85] In 1920, the French, under their mandate over Syria and Lebanon, took most of what is now northern, eastern, and southern Lebanon from Syria to create the present-day state of Lebanon. The territory added to Lebanon was predominantly Moslem, whereas the population in the "smaller Lebanon" was predominantly Christian (Maronite and Greek Catholic).[86] Syria has "never given up its implicit claim over Lebanon, or at least the parts added to it in September 1920."[87] As evidence of the close ties between the two countries, neither has an embassy in the other's capital, people travel freely from one country to the other, and both Syrians and Lebanese have sought safety and jobs in whichever country was more secure and prosperous at the moment.[88] Assad has indicated that "it is difficult to draw a line between Lebanon's security in its broadest sense and Syria's security."[89]

Indeed, a stable Lebanon is of strategic importance to Syria since in a weakened state it provides Israel with a way to outflank Syria's main defense line on the Golan Heights. After watching the Syrian forces go down to a humiliating defeat in the 1967 war with Israel, Assad has followed the strategy of engaging Israel only when Syria and any allies it may have are militarily close to parity with Israel; diplomatic maneuvering is the chosen strategy when Syria is militarily vulnerable. Assad wants to choose the time and place of any encounter with Israel so it will be his advantage. In Assad's view, "Egypt's decision to negotiate directly with Israel created a 'strategic gap,' that left Syria in a position of weakness vis-à-vis Israel."[90] Thus, the turmoil in Lebanon has posed a strategic problem for Assad. A military victory by the Palestinians or Lebanese leftist forces

would embitter the Maronites against the Arab world, drive them into the arms of Israel, and escalate partition, further balkanizing the Arab world. . . . The Syrians also feared a radical state in Lebanon sponsoring guerrilla warfare against Israel would only give the Israelis an excuse to evade pressures for a peace settlement, destroy the fedayeen presence in southern Lebanon, and realize their historical ambition to seize this area. Israeli intervention, whether in response to Maronite distress or against radical forces, would drag Syria into a war on terms favorable to Israel, in which the Israelis could threaten Syria's soft Western flank.[91]

For these reasons, Assad intervened militarily in Lebanon in 1976, preferring "a situation in which Syria could play the role of balancer between the two rival communities and hence exercise hegemony in Lebanon"[92]—in effect, "to prevent partition and a victory for one side, . . . to produce a solution which would preserve the main features of the pre-war Lebanese system,"[93] and hopefully to limit the chances of being drawn into a war with Israel not of his choosing.

The turmoil in Lebanon has also provided Assad with an opportunity. It has enabled him to extend his influence and "to draw Lebanon under Syria's political-strategic wing."[94] By playing an arbiter role in Lebanon, Assad has become a more important player in Arab politics. As Raymond Hinnebusch observed, by being in Lebanon, Assad has put Syria in a stronger position to resist rival Arab forces and to harness the PLO to Syrian objectives.[95] He has some ability to heat the Lebanese situation up or cool it down when things are not going well for Syria elsewhere in the Middle Eastern arena. In other words, he can use the Lebanese situation to flex his muscles and draw attention to his cause. Assad has positioned himself in Lebanon so he can have some leverage over what might otherwise have posed an intolerable strategic threat to Syria and over turmoil that might have spilled into Syria.

Setting the Stage

In gaining some perspective on Assad's reaction to the Israeli invasion of Lebanon in June 1982, a brief review of events from Syria's intervention in Lebanon in the winter of 1976 to the time of the invasion may prove instructive.

As the conflict in Lebanon between the Maronite Christians and the Moslem-Palestinian coalition built during the summer and fall of 1975, Assad became more and more involved as a mediator through his foreign minister, Abdel Halim Khaddam, and frequent visits of Lebanese leaders to Damascus. Although the Syrian attempts at mediation generally had some positive effect on the situation, the effect was usually short-lived. The Syrian position changed in January 1976 when the Maronites began what appeared to be a concerted effort to rid their enclaves of "foreigners and alien elements"—namely, to destroy the Palestinian camps and Moslem slums in the so-called "Christian Heartland."[96] Assad and his advisers became increasingly concerned that the Maronites would succeed in partitioning Lebanon. They perceived that if they did not act quickly, the time for action would be past. After wide consultation with party and military leaders, on January 19, 1976, Assad sent troops from the Yarmouk Brigade of the Palestine Liberation Army and al-Saiqi guerrillas into Lebanon to aid the Moslem-Palestinian coalition and as a warning to the Maronites to stop their movement toward partition. By sending in members of the Palestine Liberation Army (PLA) and not Syrian armed forces, Assad hoped to threaten the Maronites without generating Israeli retaliation. Along with the PLA troops, however, went the threat that Syrian Foreign Minister Khaddam voiced: "Any movement toward partition would mean our immediate intervention. . . . Lebanon was part of Syria before the French mandate. Syria will recover it the moment a serious partitioning attempt gets under way."[97]

Assad tied the entrance of Syrian PLA troops into Lebanon with a proposal of a set of reforms whose purpose was to ease the conflict and reestablish the status quo, that is, the balance between Maronites and Moslems in the government. The program of reforms called for representation in the parliament to be 50:50 Christian-Moslem as opposed to the 60:40 division that had previously been the rule. Moreover, it was proposed that the "Sunni prime minister would no longer be chosen by the Maronite president but would be elected by parliament; and civil service posts would be awarded on merit and not according to confession" (or religious preference).[98] The Moslems felt the proposals did not go far enough, and with the mutiny of Moslem officers from the Lebanese army they began to launch an offensive of their own against the Maronites. The Moslems under the leadership of Kamal Jumblatt began to talk about "a total and irreversible military campaign that would lead to full military victory and total revolution."[99]

Trying to defuse the situation, Assad found himself and the Syrian-supported guerrilla forces having to fight their former allies—the Moslem-Palestinian coalition. As noted earlier, Assad did not want a radical Moslem state in Lebanon anymore than a partitioned Lebanon. To maintain some influence over the deteriorating situation without sending in troops, Assad and his advisers decided to discontinue supplying arms to the Moslem-Palestinian coalition in Lebanon, and began a mobilization of Syrian troops on the Lebanese border.[100] "We are ready to move into Lebanon to stand against any aggressor, irrespective of his religious pretentions," threatened Assad.[101] Assad and his advisers became increasingly convinced that "military intervention was the only remaining option" to saving Lebanon.[102]

To ensure that Syria's actions would be understood if a military intervention became necessary, Assad undertook a "concerted diplomatic offensive to inform other states of Syria's intentions and goals in Lebanon, namely to save Lebanon and preserve its unity."[103] In addition to conferring with the leaders of other

Arab nations and Palestinian and Lebanese leaders, Assad also kept the U.S. ambassador informed of what was happening in order to convey through the United States to Israel that "any Syrian intervention was not aimed at Israel but was meant to save Lebanon."[104] Assad received tacit approval from the United States for its attempt at restoring order in Lebanon; he also learned through the United States of Prime Minister Yitzhak Rabin's statement that "Israel was in no hurry to intervene in Lebanon."[105] At that time, the Israeli leadership was preoccupied with the peace process with Egypt and wanted nothing to interfere with its culmination. However, the Israeli leadership did exact a quid pro quo from Assad through its U.S. intermediaries: Syria could intervene with no Israeli reaction as long as it "would not dispatch forces south of the Litani River, would not use its air force, and would not deploy ground-to-air missiles on Lebanon's territory."[106] A "red line" was drawn in Lebanon separating Syrian and Israeli interests.

On June 1, 1976, Syrian armed forces moved into Lebanon to counter the offensive of the Moslem-Palestinian coalition. Initially, the Syrian forces met with heavy resistance, but as the summer wore on they became more successful. However, the fact that Assad and his regime were, in effect, fighting their own Arab brothers and allying with the Maronite Christians raised a hue and cry throughout the Arab world, in the Soviet Union, and within the Syrian population. Saudi Arabia cut its aid to Syria, the Soviet Union reduced the arms coming to Syria, Iraq sent forces to the Syrian-Iraqi border, and the Sunni majority in Syria became aroused. To counter the criticism and try to deal head-on with the growing dissension in Syria, on July 20, 1976, Assad detailed the Syrian decision-making process regarding their policies in Lebanon in a dramatic speech to members of the newly elected Syrian provincial councils. [107] In the speech, he blamed events in Lebanon on an Israeli plot to partition that country: "Israel wishes the establishment of sectarian statelets in this area so that Israel can remain the stronger state."[108] In his speech, Assad also expressed concern about the Palestinians concentrating so hard on maintaining their position in Lebanon that they forgot their fight for Palestine—without continued world attention focused on the liberation of Palestine, Assad saw a reduction in his own ability to secure the Golan. He was worried about a repeat of the Black September revolt in Jordan, when the PLO tried to overthrow the Hussein government.

Periodically during the summer and fall of 1976, in order to reduce the casualties on both sides and not destroy the Moslem-Palestinian forces, Assad stopped the advance of the Syrian armed forces and sought a cease-fire—only to be rebuffed. Each rebuff was followed by a new offensive. By October 12, the Moslem-Palestinian coalition "was on the verge of total defeat."[109] At this point, under pressure from Saudi Arabia for an end to the fighting, Assad joined with leaders from Egypt, Kuwait, Lebanon, Saudi Arabia, and the PLO in a minisummit at Riyadh. Assad left the Riyadh meeting with both the "diplomatic and economic backing of the Arab world (with the notable exception of Iraq) for the Syrian role in Lebanon."[110] Among the decisions made at the Riyadh summit were an immediate cease-fire followed by a gradual normalization with 30,000 Arab troops—primarily Syrian—acting as a deterrent force to maintain peace and order. The Arab deterrent force would be supported by the oil-producing Arab states. In effect, the Syrian presence in Lebanon was legitimated by the Arab League. Assad and the Syrian government had been made "the final arbiters of power in Lebanon's domestic politics."[111]

The cease-fire and normalization did not last long. The Maronites perceived that "the Syrians were indeed determined to prevent first the partitioning of Lebanon and second the total defeat of one indigenous party at the hands of the other."[112] With the signing of the Camp David accords and Egypt's removal from the united front against Israel, and with the election of Menachem Begin as prime minister, Israel turned its attention to securing its border with Lebanon— a process that included an alliance with the more militant Maronite leaders and the building of an elaborate defense system along the Lebanese border. Furthermore, the PLO began exercising its authority over a region of territory in southern Lebanon extending from West Beirut to the Litani River, which became a virtual state within a state. Again they began border attacks on Israel, incurring retribution raids from Israeli forces. The assassination of Kamal Jumblatt, the dynamic leader of the Moslem-Palestinian coalition during the civil war, left a vacuum in the leadership of the Lebanese Moslem militias. Trying to distance himself from the embarrassment of Syria's alliance with the Maronites during the civil war, which fostered a domestic crisis in Syria, Assad improved his relations with the PLO and Moslem groups in Lebanon. To quell the domestic crisis, however, Assad was required to redeploy his troops in Lebanon, keeping some "troops in Beirut and along the Beirut-Damascus road, and concentrating the bulk of his forces in the Bekaa Valley"—the vulnerable flank that needed protection from a possible Israeli invasion into Syria.[113]

Thus, from October 1976 through May 1983, three forces were engaged in a battle to define the nature of Lebanon's political system—the Maronite-Israeli coalition, Assad and the Syrian forces, and the PLO under the leadership of Yasser Arafat. There were clashes between the Israelis and the PLO, including an Israeli incursion into southern Lebanon as far as the Litani River, a confrontation between Syria and the Maronite Phalange militia at Zahle in the Bekaa Valley on the highway to Beirut, and a cold war between Syria and Israel over Assad's emplacement of ground-to-air missiles in Lebanon, as well as several futile attempts by Assad and his representatives to help the Lebanese government establish a military foothold in southern Lebanon.

Operation "Peace for Galilee"

As the battle over Lebanon heated up, Assad gave signals to the Israelis that Syria did not want a war with Israel at this time. "It is no secret that Israel's military force is now larger than Syria's; therefore, the possibility of Syria's turning to a full-scale war at a time and place determined by Israel should be excluded.''[114] To forestall the Israelis being brought into the Maronite assault on Zahle and the Syrians' counterattack, Assad had emplacements dug—but not filled—for ground-to-air missiles in the Bekaa Valley south of the city. The missiles were only deployed after an Israeli air strike against Syrian helicopters. Moreover, in response to the Israeli annexation of the Golan Heights into Israel in December 1981, Assad worked diplomatically through the United Nations to condemn Israel's breaking of the disengagement treaty, but did not respond militarily to the challenge. Throughout the spring of 1982, Assad used various means of signalling warnings urging the Begin government that if it staged an operation, "it should at least limit its scope and enable Syria to minimize its own participation.''[115] Even after Israeli forces poured into Lebanon on June 6, 1982, Assad held back his Syrian troops, providing only limited support to the PLO in southern Lebanon. Assad received signs in return from Begin that "Israel would not attack Syria's forces unless attacked by them first.''[116]

Assad and his Syrian forces, therefore, were taken by surprise on June 7 when two Syrian radar stations in Lebanon were destroyed by the Israeli air force. Still not wanting to provoke an attack, the Syrian general staff did nothing toward reinforcing its troops in the Golan Heights or in the Bekaa Valley. The Israeli forces engaged Syrian troops on Tuesday, June 8, as the Israelis deployed troops in a pincer movement around the Syrian position in the Bekaa Valley in an attempt to reach the Beirut-Damascus road and cut the Syrians off from Beirut, as well as cut the troops in the Bekaa Valley off from their Damascus supply route and thus slow reinforcements. As the Syrians realized what was happening, the Syrian general staff began to reinforce its troops and to bring in more missiles and helicopter gunships. Wishing to appear as the attacked and not the attacker, the Syrians continued to fight holding actions trying to stop the Israeli advance now coming at them from two directions. On Wednesday, the Israeli air force was dispensed to destroy the missiles. The Syrian general staff sent up groups of interceptors in an attempt to stop the Israeli planes, but by nightfall, both the Syrian missiles and air force were rendered ineffective.

With the loss of his air defense system, Assad turned to Moscow for help, asking for a Soviet "air umbrella" with which to slow the Israeli advance. Although a Soviet direct intervention was not forthcoming, the Soviet leadership did begin stockpiling military equipment in the southern part of their country with the clear implication that it was to go to Syria, and began to exert pressure on the United States to engineer a cease-fire.

Philip Habib was dispatched by U.S. President Reagan to seek a way to end the invasion. Visiting Assad, he offered a cease-fire under the condition that the "Syrians see to the removal of the Palestinian forces huddling under their wing in the Bekaa Valley"—a condition that Begin wanted before a cease-fire could take place.[117] Assad accepted the offer of a cease-fire, hoping to save much of his position in the Bekaa Valley, but rejected Begin's condition, giving instead a countercondition that the Israeli forces be withdrawn forthwith. While the U.S.

leadership was prepared to accede to a condition like this, the Israeli cabinet only agreed to the cease-fire after attaching more conditions of their own in order to gain the time needed to get their troops to the Beirut-Damascus road. Fighting continued, with Syrian forces slowing the forward progress of the Israeli troops, and causing casualties to Israeli men and equipment as the Israeli forces pushed toward their objective.

A cease-fire was imposed on Israel by the United States with Assad's acquiescence by noon on Friday, June 11. As Ze'ev Schiff and Ehud Ya'ari observe,

The Syrian force in Lebanon took a thorough drubbing, but it was not utterly destroyed or even driven out of the country. . . . It had succeeded in holding up the Israeli advance in both the central and eastern sectors, and had prevented the Israeli forces from taking the main road all the way from Beirut to the Syrian border.[118]

These authors propose that Assad probably learned two lessons from the limited war with Israel: (1) if Syria can get an antidote to "Israel's superiority in the air, it can afford to be far more daring in tackling the Israelis on the ground," since (2) the "army met the test of holding the Israelis at bay when it counted most."[119] Disturbed by the ease with which the Israeli air force destroyed their ground-to-air missiles, the Soviets—at Assad's urging—have increased the sophistication of the air defense weapons at Syria's disposal and have provided Soviet technicians to man the equipment, a factor that may involve them more directly in Syria's military behavior in the Middle East in the future.

Although Syria's limited war with Israel had come to an end on June 11, Assad and the Syrian troops were engaged elsewhere during the ensuing three months as the battlefront changed to Beirut. The Syrian forces in and near Beirut "fought fiercely against the Israelis and made a considerable contribution to the creation of the stalemate in the area in mid-June."[120] It was a last-ditch effort with the PLO to stop an Israeli-Maronite victory in Beirut, and helped to mute the criticism Assad received for not helping the PLO when the Israelis first crossed the border into southern Lebanon.

Assad also became involved in shaping the plan for the withdrawal of the PLO from Beirut in mid-July. He first rejected a U.S. proposal to take a large contingent of Palestinian fighters—saying he would only host the PLO's senior leadership (and, as Arafat observed, get them under his control) since Syria could not sustain a large number of Palestinian fighters and their families. However, Assad's determination relaxed somewhat when Israeli troops began massing north of Beirut and he feared a possible attack on Syrian forces in the northern Bekaa Valley. Assad agreed to take "4,000 or so Palestinian fighters for whom no other refuge had been found," facilitating the formation of the U.S. plan for the evacuation of the PLO and defusing a possible attack on his troops.[121] Itamar Rabinovich suggests that Assad may also have viewed the situation as engendering a U.S. debt and as evidence of Syria's continued interest in helping the Palestinians (as well as gaining control over another group of PLO fighters).[122]

Although Assad's position in Lebanon seemed considerably weakened after the cease-fire in mid-June, by the end of 1982 he had gained back much of Syria's power and control over what happened in Lebanon. With the assassination of Bashir Gemayel, the Israeli-backed Maronite leader designate for Lebanon, and the Maronite massacre of Palestinians in the Sabra and Shatila camps under the eyes of Israeli soldiers, Israel lost its base of power and was forced by Israeli and world public opinion to withdraw from Beirut. In the meantime, Assad had begun to form an alliance with the Shiite and Druze Moslem militias, to work on securing the cooperation and submissiveness of Amin Gemayel's government, and to make the positions of the Israeli and U.S. forces untenable. Moreover, the Soviet Union had begun to replenish the Syrian arsenal. With the PLO losing its autonomous base in southern Lebanon and "the advantages offered by territorial concentration," Syria and Israel remained the two foreign forces contending for Lebanon at the close of 1982.[123] "Six years after drawing the original 'red lines,' Syria and Israel again confronted one another in Lebanon."[124]

CONCLUSION

Henry Kissinger is reported to have said about the Middle East that "no war is possible without Egypt, and no peace is possible without Syria."[125] Hafez al-Assad's leadership of Syria is directed toward ensuring that the latter half of this statement remains true. In his own words, "Syria is the core of the problem and the key to the Middle East solution."[126] He has attempted to position himself and his country so that Assad and Syria will not be left out of any negotiated settlement to the Arab-Israeli conflict, and has shown a willingness to play the role of leader or spoiler depending on whether Syria is being included or excluded from the peace process. Assad is patient, shrewd, and pragmatic, constantly monitoring what is happening and testing the waters for new ways of dealing with Syria's problems. He believes that the stakes are high—Syria's security and his own power are on the line. Furthermore, he is determined to stay the course. Assad has worked hard to provide Syrians with a period of stability, "a rising standard of living, an independent foreign policy, and a pride in being Syrian and Arab."[127] He clearly intends to continue his efforts to forge a leadership position for Syria in the Middle East.

NOTES

1. Anne Sinai and Allen Pollack, eds., *The Syrian Arab Republic: A Handbook* (New York: American Academic Association for Peace in the Middle East, 1976), p. 29.

2. All these groups are described in some detail in Nikolaos Van Dam, *The Struggle for Power in Syria* (London: Croom Helm, 1979); Sinai and Pollack, *Syrian Arab Republic*; and Richard F. Nyrop, eds., *Syria: A Country Study* (Washington, D.C.: Government Printing Office, 1979).

3. Michael H. Van Dusen, "Political Integration and Regionalism in Syria," *The Middle East Journal* 26 (1972): 127.

4. John F. Devlin, "The Political Structure in Syria," *Middle East Review* 17 (Fall 1984): 17.

5. A copy of the Constitution is found in Sinai and Pollack, *Syrian Arab Republic*, pp. 167–70.

6. Richard F. Nyrop, ed., *Area Handbook for Syria* (Washington, D.C.: Government Printing Office, 1971), p. 171.

7. Sinai and Pollack, *Syrian Arab Republic*, p. 47.

8. A. R. Kelidar, "Religion and State in Syria," in *The Syrian Arab Republic: A Handbook*, ed. Anne Sinai and Allen Pollack (New York: American Academic Association for Peace in the Middle East, 1976), p. 52.

9. Interview with Shiite religious leader Muhammed Hussein Fadlallah, in *Foreign Broadcast Information Service Middle East and Africa Report*, October 29, 1984, p. 52.

10. For descriptions of Assad's background see *Current Biography* (New York: H. W. Wilson, 1975), pp. 16–19; Majid Khadduri, *Arab Personalities in Politics* (Washington, D.C.: Middle East Institute, 1981); Stanley Reed, "Syria's Assad: His Power and His Plan," *New York Times Magazine*, February 19, 1984, pp. 42–43, 56–59.

11. *Current Biography*, 1975, p. 17.

12. Van Dam, *Struggle for Power*, p. 88.

13. Nyrop, *Area Handbook*, p. 160.

14. Adeed I. Dawisha, *Syria and the Lebanese Crisis* (London: Macmillan Press, 1980), p. 52.

15. Dawisha, *Syria and Lebanese Crisis*, p. 37; see also W. B. Fisher, "Syria: Physical and Social Geography," in *The Middle East and North Africa, 1976–1977*, 23d ed. (London: Europa Publications, 1976), p. 563.

16. Daniel Dishon, " 'Greater Syria': Reviving an Old Concept," in *The Syrian Arab Republic: A Handbook*, ed. Anne Sinai and Allen Pollack (New York: American Academic Association for Peace in the Middle East, 1976), p. 83.

17. Ibid., p. 85.

18. For a discussion of the inherent bad-faith image of the enemy in the context of the Middle East, see Daniel Heradstveit, *The Arab-Israeli Conflict: Psychological Obstacles to Peace* (Oslo: Universitetsforlaget, 1979).

19. Andre Fontaine, "An Interview with Syria's President Assad," *Manchester Guardian Weekly* 131 (August 12, 1984): 11.

20. Karim Pakradouni, "Hafez al-Assad—The Arabs' Bismarck," *Manchester Guardian Weekly* 129 (December 11, 1983): 14.

21. Dawisha, *Syria and Lebanese Crisis*, p. 179; this quotation is from an interview with Dr. Adib al-Dawoodi, Assad's adviser on foreign affairs. Dawisha notes that al-Dawoodi's comments were supported in interviews with Ahmad Iskander, the Syrian minister of information; Mohammed Khidr, director-general of the Department of Arab Affairs in the Ministry of Foreign Affairs; and Adnan Omran, Syrian ambassador to the United Kingdom.

22. Pakradouni, "Hafez al-Assad," p. 14.

23. Ibid.

24. Ibid.

25. James Kelly, "Bidding for a Bigger Role," *Time* 122 (December 19, 1983): 34.

26. Ibid., p. 26; Pakradouni, "Hafez al-Assad," p. 14; Reed, "Syria's Assad," p. 57.

27. See Devlin, "Political Structure," pp. 15–21; "War of Succession in Syria: A New Victory for Assad," *Manchester Guardian Weekly* 131 (August 26, 1984): 11, 13.

28. Pakradouni, "Hafez al-Assad," p. 14.

29. Jimmy Carter, *The Blood of Abraham* (Boston: Houghton Mifflin, 1985), p. 81.

30. Raphael Patai, *The Arab Mind*, rev. ed. (New York: Charles Scribner's Sons, 1983), p. 338.

31. Carter, *Blood of Abraham*, p. 81.

32. Saladin and Assad are similar in several ways—like Assad, Saladin did not come from a princely family or from the ruling class. Moreover, like Assad, Saladin eschewed material wealth but sought positions of power and leadership. Furthermore, Saladin is viewed as a hero in Syria like Assad wants to be. In some sense, Saladin may serve as a role model for Assad. See Geoffrey Hindley, *Saladin* (London: Constable, 1976).

33. See Devlin, "Political Structure," and Dawisha, *Syria and Lebanese Crisis*, Chapter 3.

34. Devlin, "Political Structure," p. 17.

35. From a public address by Assad on January 17, 1971, as reported in Nyrop, *Area Handbook*, p. 160.

36. See Devlin, "Political Structure."

37. Dawisha, *Syria and Lebanese Crisis*, p. 56; see also Fred H. Lawson, "Syria's Intervention in the Lebanese Civil War, 1976: A Domestic Conflict Explanation," *International Organization* 38 (Summer 1984): 451–80.

38. R. D. McLaurin, Don Peretz, and Lewis W. Snider, *Middle East Foreign Policy: Issues and Processes* (New York: Praeger, 1982), p. 255.

39. Nyrop, *Syria*, p. 220; see also Dawisha, *Syria and Lebanese Crisis*, p. 54.

40. McLaurin, Peretz, and Snider, *Middle East Foreign Policy*, p. 256.

41. Raymond A. Hinnebusch, "Revisionist Dreams, Realist Strategies: The Foreign Policy of Syria," in *The Foreign Policies of Arab States*, ed. Baghat Korany and Ali E. Hillal Dessouki (Boulder: Westview Press, 1984), p. 302; McLaurin, Peretz, and Snider, *Middle East Foreign Policy*, p. 254; Nyrop, *Syria*, Chapter 5.

42. McLaurin, Peretz, and Snider, *Middle East Foreign Policy*, p. 252.

43. "War of Succession," pp. 11, 13.

44. Lawson, "Syria's Intervention," pp. 459–80.

45. Devlin, in "Political Structure," p. 18, notes that the Moslem Brotherhood began subversive actions against Assad's regime in 1976, allied themselves with other militants as the Islamic Front in 1980, and joined with some secular groups in 1982 to become the National Alliance for the Liberation of Syria.

46. Lawson, "Syria's Intervention," p. 471.

47. Devlin, "Political Structure," p. 18. Contrast Itamar Rabinovich, "Full Circle—Syrian Politics in the 1970s," in *Middle East Perspectives: The Next Twenty Years*, ed. George S. Wise and Charles Issawi (Princeton: Darwin Press, 1981) and Lawson, "Syria's Intervention," with Devlin, "Political Structure" and Pakradouni, "Hafez al-Assad." For observations on both sides, see Eric Rouleau, "Behind the 'Socialist' Face of Assad's Syria," *Manchester Guardian Weekly* 129 (July 17, 1983): 12, and Eric Rouleau, "Syria—Clubbing Together to Beat the System," *Manchester Guardian Weekly* 129 (July 24, 1983): 12, 14.

48. Pakradouni, "Hafez al-Assad," p. 14.

49. Robert G. Neumann, "Assad and the Future of the Middle East," *Foreign Affairs* 62 (Winter 1983/1984): 256.

50. Ibid., p. 253.

51. Lawson, "Syria's Intervention," p. 453; see also Dankwort A. Rustow, "Re-alignments in the Middle East," *Foreign Affairs* 63 (Spring 1985): 581–601.

52. Lawson, "Syria's Intervention," pp. 453–55.

53. Ibid., p. 455.

54. Ibid.

55. Ibid., p. 456.

56. Hinnebusch, "Revisionist Dreams, Realist Strategies," p. 310; see also Assad's interview with Patrick Seale of March 6, 1977 in the *Observer*.

57. Rustow, "Realignments," pp. 599–600.

58. Hinnebusch, "Revisionist Dreams, Realist Strategies," p. 291.

59. Ibid., p. 293.

60. For an example of Assad's desire to follow a nonaligned strategy, see his speech to the Fourth Conference of the Heads of State of Non-Aligned Countries in Algiers, September 1973, available from the Syrian Arab News Agency, Damascus.

61. McLaurin, Peretz, and Snider, *Middle East Foreign Policy*, p. 282.

62. Charles Snare, "Adaptation and Application of Barber's Model: A Psychological Analysis of Kaddafi, Sadat, Hussein, and Assad," Master's Thesis, Ohio State University, 1985, p. 219; see also John F. Devlin, "Syrian Policy," in *The Middle East Since Camp David*, ed. Robert O. Freedman (Boulder: Westview Press, 1984), pp. 138–39; Neumann, "Assad and the Future," p. 243.

63. Neumann, "Assad and the Future," p. 240.

64. Ibid.

65. Ibid.

66. McLaurin, Peretz, and Snider, *Middle East Foreign Policy*, p. 275.

67. Ibid., p. 274.

68. Ibid., p. 272.

69. Ibid., p. 276.

70. Devlin, "Syrian Policy," p. 140.

71. Hinnebusch, "Revisionist Dreams, Realist Strategies," p. 309.

72. For a further exploration of this argument, see Aaron David Miller, "PLO," in *The Middle East Since Camp David*, ed. Robert O. Freedman (Boulder: Westview Press, 1984), pp. 193–229.

73. Hinnebusch, "Revisionist Dreams, Realist Strategies," p. 295.

74. Ibid.

75. Miller, "PLO," p. 197.

76. For a fuller discussion of this conflict, see Alain Gresh, *The PLO: The Struggle Within* (London: Zed Books, 1985); Rashid Khalidi, "The Asad Regime and the Palestinian Resistance," *Arab Studies Quarterly* 6 (Fall 1984): 259–66; Miller, "PLO."

77. Khalidi, "The Asad Regime," p. 264.

78. Shimon Shamir, "The Arab World Between Pragmatism and Radicalism," in *Middle East Perspectives: The Next Twenty Years*, ed. George S. Wise and Charles Issawi (Princeton: Darwin Press, 1981), p. 68.

79. Ibid., p. 69.

80. Devlin, "Syrian Policy," p. 128.

81. Ibid.

82. Hinnebusch, "Revisionist Dreams, Realist Strategies," p. 297.

83. Ibid., p. 299.

84. "An Interview with President Assad," *Time* 123 (April 2, 1984): 29.

85. Dawisha, *Syria and Lebanese Crisis*, p. 72.

86. Itamar Rabinovich, *The War for Lebanon, 1970–1983* (Ithaca: Cornell University Press, 1984), pp. 21–23; see particularly map on p. 23.

87. Ibid., p. 36.

88. David Gilmour, *Lebanon: The Fractured Country* (New York: St. Martin's Press, 1984), p. 130.

89. Interview with Assad as recorded in the British Broadcasting Corporation, *Summary of World Broadcasts*, June 28, 1975, ME/4941/A/7. Quoted in Dawisha, *Syria and Lebanese Crisis*, p. 89.

90. Rabinovich, *The War*, p. 111.

91. Hinnebusch, "Revisionist Dreams, Realist Strategies," p. 312.

92. Ibid.

93. Gilmour, *Lebanon*, p. 157.

94. Hinnebusch, "Revisionist Dreams, Realist Strategies," p. 311.

95. Ibid., p. 312.

96. Dawisha, *Syria and Lebanese Crisis*, p. 95. The discussion in the present chapter will follow Dawisha in referring to two opposing groups in Lebanon: the Moslem/Palestinian coalition and the Maronite Christians. Dawisha argues that these two distinctions, though not completely accurate, represent the designations that "were paramount in Syrian perceptions" (p. 12).

97. Interview with Abdel Halim Khaddam reported in the Kuwaiti paper, *al-Rai al-'Amm*, January 7, 1976, and reported in *Facts on File*, January 10, 1976, p. 1.

98. Gilmour, *Lebanon*, p. 131.

99. Ibid., p. 134.

100. Dawisha, *Syria and Lebanese Crisis*, pp. 128–29.

101. Ibid., p. 130.

102. Ibid., p. 134.

103. Ibid.

104. Ibid.

105. Ibid., p. 181.

106. Rabinovich, *The War*, p. 106; see also Reed, "Syria's Assad," p. 59.

107. This speech, as recorded by the Foreign Broadcast Information Service on July 20, 1976, is presented in an appendix in Rabinovich, *The War*, pp. 183–218.

108. Ibid., p. 189.

109. Ibid., p. 55.

110. Dawisha, *Syria and Lebanese Crisis*, p. 164.

111. Ibid., p. 186.

112. Ibid.

113. Rabinovich, *The War*, p. 113.

114. Ibid., p. 149. This quote is taken from the February 13, 1982 broadcast of Louis Fares, the correspondent from Radio Monte Carlo located in Damascus, who, in turn, indicated he was quoting a high-ranking diplomat in the Syrian government. Rabinovich notes that Fares has often been used by the Assad regime to unofficially convey its views (ibid., p. 148).

115. Ibid., p. 148; see also Ze'ev Schiff and Ehud Ya'ari, *Israel's Lebanon War* (New York: Simon and Schuster, 1984), p. 70.

116. Rabinovich, *The War*, p. 135; Schiff and Ya'ari, *Israel's Lebanon War*, p. 152.

117. Schiff and Ya'ari, *Israel's Lebanon War*, p. 189.

118. Ibid., pp. 189–90.

119. Ibid., p. 307.

120. Rabinovich, *The War*, p. 149.

121. Schiff and Ya'ari, *Israel's Lebanon War*, p. 224.

122. Rabinovich, *The War*, p. 150.

123. Ibid., p. 172.

124. Ibid., p. 173.

125. Kelly, "Bidding for Bigger Role," p. 34.

126. Pakradouni, "Hafez al-Assad," p. 14.

127. Milton Viorst, "Assad May Be Key To Mideast Peace," *Columbus Dispatch* (August 12, 1985), p. 7A; originally printed in the *Christian Science Monitor*.

6

EGYPT'S HOSNI MUBARAK

Kenneth Dana Greenwald

As Beirut was being bombed during Israel's Lebanon war, Shimon Shamir, director of the Israel Academic Center in Cairo, picked up his ringing phone. The caller was an Egyptian judge, a friend of many Israelis, whose liberal views stirred Islamic extremists to repeatedly threaten him with death. Now, referring to Israel's use of force in Lebanon, his voice was tear-choked: "You have sacrificed not only them but also us, your friends in Egypt; I won't be able to show my face to those who have disagreed with me and now are proven right."[1]

Those who had all along disagreed with the judge did indeed feel that their position had been confirmed by recent events. The conclusion reached by opposition journalist Muhammad Sid Ahmad was typical: "Israel's 'peace' with Egypt is authorization to commit the ugliest crimes and wreak havoc with impunity."[2]

As suggested by such statements of both a friend and a foe of Egypt's peace with Israel, a wide spectrum of Egyptians and other Arabs held Egypt's 1979 treaty with Israel partially responsible for Israel's invasion of Lebanon on June 6, 1982. The charge was not lost on Egyptian president Hosni Mubarak. As Herman Eilts, U.S. ambassador to Egypt from 1973 to 1979 and an intimate acquaintance of Mubarak, has remarked, the Israeli invasion presented the Egyptian president with "his most difficult hour."[3]

What were the Egyptian president's responses to the invasion, and why did he fashion them as he did? Mubarak was, of course, personally angered by the Israeli action and well aware of similar outrage among the Egyptian public. As a military man for almost half his life he had for many years dedicated himself to Egypt's long struggle against Israel. As president, he was under considerable political pressure—from both supporters and opponents—to respond vigorously to the Israeli action.

However, the fact was that since 1979 Egypt was bound by treaty to stay on the sidelines. Moreover, Mubarak could readily see the vital benefits that peace had brought. First, as a former combat pilot, the president knew first-hand the costs of the state of war with Israel; now innumerable casualties were being spared. Second, as head of state, he no doubt recognized, along with much of the Egyptian public, what the return of the Suez Canal and Sinai, the newly quiet border with Israel, and sudden U.S. magnanimity meant for an Egyptian economy that needed all the help it could get. Third, Mubarak no doubt felt honor-bound to his mentor and predecessor, Anwar Sadat, to uphold the peace that the former president had done so much to bring about. Fourth, the new president's ''Sadatist'' core following expected him to ensure the survival of at least Sadat's major policies, and finally, the treaty was popular with leaders in the military, the essential underpinning for any Egyptian regime. Thus, Mubarak's responses to Israel's Lebanon war had to strike a delicate balance: energetic and sharp enough to reflect his own sense of outrage as well as that of the Egyptian public, but also sufficiently restrained and tempered to maintain the peace.

This chapter will focus on Mubarak's attempt to walk that fine line. However, to more fully understand the leader in the context of the Lebanon crisis, we will begin with an overview of Mubarak's personal experiences and ties, political style, and policies, with reference to both his supporters and opponents.

"HE KEPT LOOKING AT THE SKY"

''I remember that he was . . . serious in his behavior, in class and at sports,'' a former schoolmate of Mubarak has recalled. ''He always observed long silences and was always thinking and constantly looking up. When we asked him why he kept looking at the sky, he said, 'Tomorrow you will learn why.' ''[4]

Muhammad Hosni Mubarak was born May 4, 1928, to a middle-class family, the third of five children, and enrolled in the Air College as soon as he could. After his graduation as a fighter pilot in March 1950, he was chosen to remain at the college as an instructor. Some time later he was selected assistant head of instructors at the War College. ''I remember his [combat] flying hours were much more numerous than other instructors,'' recalled one of Mubarak's colleagues.[5] In all, he flew close to 6,000 hours while in the air force,[6] a number of them as commander of the bomber force in the Yemen civil war (1962–67).[7] The result was that Mubarak came to be viewed by his superiors as ''an excellent officer from all standpoints,'' a young patriot who had demonstrated discipline, orderliness, industriousness, and integrity.[8]

His reputation would bring its own rewards. The highly touted officer became director of the Air College in 1967. Two years later, he was appointed chief of staff of the Egyptian air force.

"A YOUNG MAN WHOSE LIKES I WOULD LIKE TO SEE EVERYWHERE I GO"

Sadat had reportedly taken note of Mubarak as early as the 1950s when, as a cavalry officer, he noted that he had "met a flight officer Second Lieutenant Hosni Mubarak, an intelligent, active patriotic young man whose likes I would like to see everywhere I go."[9] By 1972, President Anwar Sadat was in a position to promote the air force chief of staff to commander. From that point on, in preparation for the 1973 war, meetings between the two men were frequent.[10]

Mubarak's formidable performance during that war was directly responsible for his ascent to the vice presidency in April 1975. Sadat stated that he chose him as vice president because he represented "the generation of October . . . the spirit, environment, and climate of October 6, the day our armed forces transcended every impossible obstacle and wall in the name of the people and the motherland."[11]

Sadat also declared repeatedly that he expected Mubarak to be his eventual successor.[12] Accordingly, during his years as vice president, Mubarak's political responsibilities were substantial. At home he oversaw the day-to-day affairs of the ruling National Democratic party. He was also active in foreign affairs, travelling to 40 countries in the course of 30 diplomatic trips during his vice presidency.[13] In addition, he was placed in charge of police and intelligence matters.[14] In short, by the time of Sadat's violent death, Mubarak had gained some relevant experience.

"IT SO HAPPENED THAT THIS IS MY FATE TODAY"

After Anwar Sadat was assassinated on October 6, 1981, the National Democratic party wasted no time nominating Hosni Mubarak to succeed him, and the People's Assembly followed suit almost immediately.[15] Mubarak himself then organized an early election. In the referendum held on October 13, Mubarak was the only candidate, and 98 percent of the eligible voters said "Aye."[16] "It has so happened that this is my fate today," remarked a tearful Mubarak at his inauguration, where he was introduced as the hero of the October War.[17]

Despite this quick and apparently smooth transition, there was a strong sense of uncertainty and instability in the immediate aftermath of the killing of Sadat. In the Nile city of Asyut, Moslem fundamentalists reacted to the news of Sadat's death by challenging the security forces in a three-day gun battle that left 54 troops and policemen dead. An armed revolt on this scale had not been witnessed in Egypt since the 1952 revolution.[18] In addition, there were rumors of new assassination plots;[19] Sadat's funeral was held in a secluded spot for security reasons;[20] and government officials warned against displays of mourning over Sadat's death, lest they provoke anti-Sadat and antigovernment riots.[21]

Hence, the new president's first task was to restore calm and confidence in the national government. Toward this end, he ordered the arrest of 700 Muslim militants considered by the government to be security risks, instructed army troops to man the streets of Cairo, and applied an iron fist to the uprising in Asyut.[22] Mubarak's experience as head of police and intelligence matters under Sadat no doubt stood him in particularly good stead during this tenuous initial period.

The public took note. One frequently heard joke had him in a movie house watching a newsreel when a scene of his inauguration appeared on the screen. Everyone applauded except the president, whose wife grew nervous, saying, "Hosni, applaud, or you'll get arrested."[23]

Such a reputation for selective use of force was politically desirable.[24] After several decades of strong central authority,[25] most Egyptians had grown comfortable with it and were made uneasy at the prospect of its decline.

Yet it still remained for Mubarak to more convincingly consolidate and legitimize his hold on power. That would entail more than the selective use of force. He would have to shape an agreeable political persona and he would, of course, have to formulate and implement satisfactory public policies.

"HE IS A PRESIDENT WHO SPEAKS OUR LANGUAGE"

Mubarak's public persona differs markedly from that which Sadat brought to the presidency. One of the first signs of this fresh political style came directly after the new president's inauguration, when he announced to the press that his wife would not be in the public eye as Jihan Sadat had been. This pointed announcement was probably intended to promptly convey Mubarak's conformity to traditional beliefs about the proper place and role of women, and also an image of no-nonsense presidential industriousness divorced from any desire for royal family privilege. In any case, this public relations message greatly enhanced the new president's domestic political position.[26] Similarly, the Egyptian people appreciated the words with which Mubarak addressed them: his fraternal "my brothers and sisters" contrasted sharply with Sadat's paternalistic "my sons and daughters."[27] The favorable comparison with Sadat was the implicit theme of an essay that appeared in the right-wing neo-liberal opposition paper *Al-Ahrar* during Mubarak's first year as president. The writer sought to convey the "common man's" perceptions of the differences in style between Mubarak and his immediate predecessor:

When it was decided that there would be no vacation homes and resorts in the area of the Pyramids in Giza, people saw with their own eyes that the president's house there was the first to be removed . . . and, for the first time, people saw that the peak of power was subject to what the rest of mankind was subject to . . . without lies or favoritism. . . . Hosni Mubarak was in practice a president who would not go before the people on television unless he really had something to say, and when he said it, chose the briefest words. . . . This president's mouth does not water whenever he sees a photographer's lens or a television camera. He is a president who does not fabricate things and does not react excitedly. He is a president who refuses to have his aides call out to him every minute. . . . He is a president whom we have not seen living in palaces, rushing after the friendship of millionaires, or hastening with his wife to meet Prince Charles. . . . He is a president of whose wife and children we have known nothing, because he wants to raise them the way any ordinary family in this country raises its children. He is a president who you tell from the clothes he wears is actually living off his salary. . . . He is a president who does not say 'I' but says 'we' . . . who does not tell people 'follow me' but tells them 'be with me.' He is a president who speaks our language and does not embezzle what is beyond our means for his benefit.[28]

Others related similar thoughts about Mubarak, though without necessarily implying a favorable comparison to Sadat. Former United States ambassador Eilts, for example, described Mubarak as an ''Inspector-General'' who preferred to attack problems head on, with as little circumlocution as possible.[29] Similarly, an adviser to the Egyptian president observed that ''he goes to the subject directly, like a machine gun.''[30] Indeed, Sadat himself was known to have chosen Mubarak as vice president partially because the air force commander had a reputation for avoiding the limelight.[31]

The new president's public persona, then, was generally viewed with favor. As a consequence, it helped to establish his political legitimacy and strengthen his grip on government.

"THE POLICY OF SADAT IS GOING ON . . . [BUT] I CAN'T STAND STILL"

Early in Mubarak's presidency, it became clear that although he listened carefully to the views of his closest advisers (especially to those of Osama al-Baz), final decisions were made by him alone.[32] As for the substance of those decisions, Mubarak explained that the ''policy of Sadat is still going on,'' but that he could not ''stand still.''[33] Accordingly, it was soon evident that Mubarak would try to strike a balance: he would largely continue Sadat's policies but at the same time set himself apart from his predecessor. The essentials of Sadat's legacy—the economic ''Open Door'' and the treaty with Israel—would proceed apace, but there were substantive departures from Sadat, most prominently in the new president's positions toward the domestic opposition, other Arab states, the United States, and corruption. This identification with the most basic of Sadat's policies, accompanied by notable departures from the former president, enabled Mubarak both to meet the expectations of his ''Sadatist'' core following and to earn credentials with the opposition.

Despite the economic woes that had persisted under Sadat—including a 30 to 40 percent inflation rate along with huge disparities in income distribution—Mubarak showed no signs of significantly altering his predecessor's ''Open Door'' economic program.[34] To the contrary, in his first speech marking the anniversary of the July 23 revolution, he stressed that ''the government is committed to encouraging the private sector . . . there will be no return to the fettered and closed policy.''[35] Accordingly, Egyptians as well as foreigners were still given free rein to engage in private enterprise and continued to receive government incentives such as tax exemptions and reduced or eliminated customs duties on imported capital equipment. As for the peace, Mubarak's position was summed up soon after he replaced Sadat, when he told an American reporter that he felt like displaying a large placard reading "No Change in Our Relations With Israel."[36]

To be sure, Mubarak's maintenance of his predecessor's two most prominent policies was to a considerable extent attributable to the loyalty the new president felt for Sadat and the influence Sadat had had on him. At his presidential inauguration, Mubarak called the former president his "teacher."[37] However, there was also a compelling political reason behind Mubarak's continuation of the two cornerstones of "Sadatism": his most important supporters wanted and expected to see the fundamentals of Sadat's legacy left intact. This Sadatist core constituency included many of the most influential and powerful members of Egyptian society: newspaper and magazine editors and columnists; heads of mass communications networks; business leaders; and high officials in education, government, and the military.[38]

As mentioned above, Mubarak did, however, diverge from Sadat in other areas of importance. The first sign that Mubarak would depart from Sadat's combativeness toward the political opposition[39] in favor of a conciliatory approach came during his inauguration speech: "I shall put my hand in yours, those of you who have supported me and those of you who have opposed me."[40] He would soon give credence to his announcement: approximately 50 percent of the roughly 1,600 political dissidents incarcerated in the months just before Sadat's assassination would be released during Mubarak's first half-year in office; nearly 100 of these would promptly be invited to the president's office to exchange views, and a number of them would continue to consult with him on a regular basis.[41] Sadat, by contrast, had been criticized for "listening to the Israelis while disregarding Egyptian politicians."[42]

In fact, Mubarak provided for more freedom of expression generally: large protests were permitted; virtually all of the 127 journalists and university professors who had been removed from their posts by Sadat were reinstated by January 1982; and by May 1982, four prominent opposition newspapers were allowed to publish again.[43] Mubarak, then, relied on imprisonment or suppression only when violence, treason, or their advocacy were suspected.[44]

Although it would be presumptuous and probably wrong to suggest that Mubarak's policy toward the opposition had nothing to do with personal inclination and everything to do with political expedience, there is no gainsaying that such a conciliatory approach to the opposition made political sense. It provided the president with a measure of goodwill, not enjoyed by his predecessor, that contributed to the stabilization of his hold on power. To be sure, the new president's fresh approach to the opposition did not lead to complete harmony. Voices of dissent were still heard, especially concerning the economy, relations with the United States, Egypt's regional policies, and remaining cracks in the democracy.[45] However, the atmosphere of conciliation did have the predictable effect of improving government-opposition relations. A Muslim Brotherhood leader released from prison declared that Mubarak had "initiated a promising era."[46] Labor Party Chairman Ibrahim Shukri, attacked by Sadat but given a private audience with the new president, spoke for a large part of the opposition when he favorably compared Mubarak to his predecessor and called him a "great hope for the Egyptian people."[47] Indeed, when opposition criticism did come, it consisted almost entirely of implicit advice or, at times, exhortation, in contrast to the vituperation frequently directed at Sadat.[48]

Again, Mubarak's policy toward other Arab states has been another point of departure from his predecessor. Sadat was inclined to ridicule leaders of Arab countries that broke with Egypt after the peace.[49] At one point, he even went so far as to proclaim that Egypt was "the only state in the area worthy of that name."[50] Mubarak, conversely, declared that he would not assail any Arab state or insult its leader.[51] The press, similarly, was ordered to refrain from such attacks, "even" against Libya.[52] In fact, Mubarak announced the withdrawal of some army units from the Libyan border, stating that he was not expecting a military confrontation with his Arab neighbor.[53] In addition, he declared Egypt's readiness to assist other Arab states in defense of the Gulf.[54]

Here, too, one should refrain from assuming that divergence from Sadat stemmed entirely from political expedience and had little to do with personal predisposition. After all, Arab fraternity is a value with a long tradition in Middle Eastern politics and culture, which we may assume that Mubarak shares. Even as vice president, he privately took issue with Sadat's verbal attacks against Saudi Arabia.[55] Yet again, the political benefit of the new president's divergence from his predecessor's Arab policy was irrefutable; the erosion of Egypt's inter-Arab position under Sadat had been notoriously unpopular. The new president's more fraternal attitude toward other Arab states, the arming of Iraq in its war with Iran, and his well-known refusal to either visit Jerusalem, yield on Taba, or sign an autonomy agreement unsatisfactory to the Palestinians, were all welcomed domestically, as they manifestly had the desired effect of improving Egypt's position in the Arab world. Enrollment of Arabs in Egyptian universities increased. In April 1982, Morocco and Jordan congratulated Egypt for regaining the Sinai.[56] That same month, Egypt was courteously received when it called for mutual Palestinian-Israeli recognition at a conference of non-aligned states in Baghdad.[57] In June, Mubarak was welcomed to Saudi Arabia to express his condolences upon the death of King Khaled, and was visited by Morocco's foreign minister, marking the first sojourn to Cairo by an official from an Arab country that had broken relations with Egypt.[58] Finally, in September of that same year, Egypt's influence may have been felt when the conferees at Fez accepted a modified form of the Fahd plan, implicitly recognizing Israel's right to exist.[59]

Sadat had also drawn widespread criticism for being too closely identified with the United States, and Mubarak's departure from him on this score made sound political sense as well. This divergence from his predecessor with respect to the United States was clearly implicit in his first July 23 anniversary speech, when he declared the following objectives: rejection of all forms of foreign domination; loyalty to the principles of non-alignment; and rejection of both foreign alliances and foreign bases on national soil.[60] Accordingly, while maintaining close ties with the United States, Mubarak agitated Washington by permitting roughly 60 Soviet experts to return to Egypt to finish work on projects they had started before being expelled by Sadat.[61] Again, there are no grounds to believe that Mubarak shifted from Sadat's policy solely to reap a political return, but if he was in fact more personally comfortable with a policy of greater distance from the United States, his personal predisposition clearly coincided with what was politically advisable.

Finally, Mubarak scored points with the Egyptian public by strongly emphasizing law and order, and by combatting corruption. He cautioned members of his family not to trade on the family name, and in his first address to the nation he stressed that there would be "no privileges for relatives or non-relatives."[62] He also warned his ministers against accepting gifts, and instructed the police to enforce even minor infractions of the law.[63] Such statements and policies were appreciated by the Egyptian public, especially since many Egyptians had perceived the Sadat government as corrupt. According to one Egyptian analyst, Mubarak's vigilance against favoritism and graft won him the "wide support of the masses."[64] Another observer reported that political figures as disparate as the Progressist Khaled Mohieddine, the Laborite Ibrahim Shukri, and the Nasserite Abdel Maguid Farid applauded not only Mubarak's Arab policy, but also his "probity."[65]

The result of Mubarak's successful search for a balance between aligning himself with Sadat and striking out on his own was the gradual affirmation both of governmental stability and his own political legitimacy. Both would stand in good stead during his "most difficult hour"—the Israeli invasion of Lebanon.

"HE HAD TO WALK A VERY FINE LINE"

Even before the Israeli invasion, there was widespread dissatisfaction and skepticism in Egypt concerning the peace with Israel. A survey taken before the Camp David agreement indicated that even among the political elite—Sadat's main base of support—there was considerable opposition to a peace that did not stipulate Israel's return of all occupied territories.[66] A survey of the same group conducted nine months after the peace agreement revealed that fully 36 percent of the respondents opposed the treaty.[67] Of course, those outside of Sadat's main constituency were even more critical of the terms to which he agreed in March 1979. As a *New York Times* correspondent observed, Sadat "had to struggle to realize the peace treaty, not only with other Arab countries but inside Egypt."[68]

When Mubarak succeeded Sadat, most Egyptians still harbored strong doubts about the terms of the peace—yet another sign that Israel's Lebanon initiative would strike a sensitive nerve. To be sure, most Egyptians had come to appreciate the accord with Israel because of its clear and important benefits: Egyptian soldiers were spared casualties; revenues flowed both from Sinai oil and the Egyptian-operated canal; and Egypt gained a magnanimous benefactor—the United States. Still, there was considerable discontent concerning other facets of the peace. For example, most Egyptians were socialized to regard their country as the central supporter of Palestinian demands. From this perspective the West Bank-Gaza accord was seen as a "sellout," especially as Israeli settlements on the West Bank multiplied and autonomy talks continued to languish.[69] There was displeasure as well with Egypt's ostracism from the Arab League, evidence of its compromised position in inter-Arab politics.[70] Even the status of the Sinai was not regarded as altogether satisfactory, as Egypt's forces there were to be limited and its air bases commercialized.[71] Such unfavorable sentiment toward the peace was not enhanced by Israeli Prime Minister Menachem Begin's widely-known tendency to indelicacy, nor by his directive to target the Iraqi nuclear reactor for sharpshooting just days after meeting with the Egyptian head of state.

Such doubts and frustrations concerning the peace were brought to the surface by the Israeli invasion of Lebanon, for many Egyptians, as noted above, saw their country's peace with Israel as partially—if indirectly—responsible for Israel's summer offensive. Indeed, none other than the Israeli Chief-of-Staff General Rafael Eitan had given credence to that view. In November 1981, he was quoted as having said that the treaty with Egypt and the security arrangements in the south "will enable the IDF [Israeli Defense Forces] . . . to free forces for the Eastern front."[72] A writer in a popular Egyptian magazine was, then, only agreeing with the Israeli chief of staff when he argued that Israel's invasion plans derived from its "confidence that Egypt will be loyal to the spirit of the peace treaty."[73] Similarly, in the Laborite opposition paper *Al-Sha'b*, former Egyptian foreign minister Ibrahim Kamel cited the invasion as evidence that Israel's objective at Camp David was to "neutralize Egypt and impose its hegemony on the region."[74]

Anger at the Israeli offensive was amply demonstrated. In addition to opposition press conferences that called for abrogation of the peace treaty and a campaign against the "Zionist-American" presence in Egypt, there was, for the first time, a public protest against Mubarak's Israel policy. Although Israel was the main target of this June 18 Cairo demonstration, Mubarak was to receive a distinct message. The *imam* giving the Friday prayer at *al-Azhar* mosque, where the protest commenced, regretted that "we have stood with our hands tied, refusing to raise a challenge while our Palestinian brothers, without supporters, have gone into exile. The Egypt of today is not the Egypt of yesterday. It is now a single bloc."[75] At the same demonstration, in a comment clearly directed at the government, the secretary general for the opposition Grouping party insisted that "there is no room for talk, just action."[76] Similarly, also at the protest, Labor Party Chairman Shukri appealed to Mubarak to take "a much tougher stance."[77] Finally, with placards reading "They Are Slaughtering Egypt in Lebanon" in hand, the demonstrators approached the Presidential Palace, where they had to be dispersed by riot police and karate experts dressed in civilian clothes.[78]

The challenge to public order presented by such protests was not lost on Mubarak nor on Egyptian officials, one of whom noted that there would have been more demonstrations if schools were not in summer recess.[79] It has been suggested, in fact, that Mubarak's refusal to give sanctuary to the Palestinian Liberation Organization (PLO) evacuees was largely determined by his concern that their presence in Egypt would spark further public protests against Egypt's regional policy.[80]

Nor was the opposition alone in feeling incensed and humiliated by the events in Lebanon. *Al-Ahram*, a daily paper that reflects prevailing views in the ruling party, called the Israeli invasion an act of "barbarism even more violent than that of which Nazism was accused."[81] U.S. diplomats said they had been informed by Egyptian contacts that Mubarak was under considerable pressure from his supporters to respond vigorously to Israel's "barbarism."[82] A 1983 public opinion poll of 500 Egyptians of various political, economic, and social groups reflected the broad cross section of Egyptians who attached great importance to the Israeli invasion and its aftermath.[83]

In part, this deep concern with the invasion among a wide spectrum of Egyptians was attributable to fear that Egypt would soon suffer the same fate as Lebanon. In advocating an active Egyptian response to Israel's Lebanon incursion, the Socialist Labor party's Kilmi Murad maintained that,

By defending Palestine and Lebanon we are defending Egypt and Egyptians. The day Israel achieves its goal in Lebanon and liquidates the Palestinian resistance, it will turn on us and try to humiliate us, and nobody will be able to confront it.[84]

According to one journalist, "The man in the street shared these fears." Reportedly representative of such common concern was the question of a 35-year-old farmer from a Nile Delta village: "What prevents Israel from retaking Sinai . . . when it sees that the Arabs have not raised one finger against it?"[85]

Furthermore, we can assume that the Israeli action in Lebanon weighed heavily on the president personally. After all, he had spent most of his adult life in the military, living daily with Egypt's unquestioned position in the vanguard of the struggle against the "Zionist enemy." Now, as president, the former air force officer was relegated to remaining at arm's length as Israeli Defense Minister Ariel Sharon persisted in his push north.

To be sure, Egypt, opposing Syria's presence in Lebanon and resenting its leadership of the "rejectionist" front, may have experienced some pleasure at witnessing Syrian President Hafez al-Assad's comeuppance at the hands of the Israelis. However, any such satisfaction was manifestly outweighed by Cairo's outrage at the fact that Israel had launched a prolonged offensive against Arabs across its border, thereby putting the Egyptian government in an extremely difficult political position.

Clearly, such strong reactions to the Israeli operation would have to be reflected in Mubarak's responses to the crisis. Abrogation of the peace was not, however, a viable option. First, it would put an end to the benefits that, as we have seen, earned the peace broad approval despite discontent over some of its components. U.S. aid, for example, would be curtailed or drastically reduced because Washington did not consider the invasion a violation of the Egyptian-Israeli treaty, which it viewed as essentially standing on its own.[86] Moreover, the amount of U.S. assistance since the Camp David accords had not been small. U.S. economic and military aid to Egypt came to $2 billion in 1981–82, and the Mubarak government was promised a 20 percent increase for 1983–84.[87] U.S. arms sales to Egypt amounted to $3 billion between 1979 and 1982.[88] To be sure, there would be some compensation in the form of renewed aid from Arab states. But the United States was far more reliably generous and could also deliver state-of-the-art defense equipment.

Furthermore, this decline in U.S. support would be accompanied by the threat of an Israeli campaign to retake the Sinai. Such a development would not only lead to renewed Egyptian casualties, it would also have severe consequences for the already struggling Egyptian economy. Revenues from Sinai oil and the Suez Canal would be in serious jeopardy. Moreover, there would be a significant increase in defense expenditures that would be particularly unwelcome. As it was, the Mubarak government was spending 50 percent of Egyptian gross national product on defense, and 75 percent on defense and food subsidies combined.[89] It is difficult to imagine Mubarak and his aides seriously contemplating a move that would revise these figures upward and simultaneously alienate the United States. Mubarak's prime minister, Dr. Fu'ad Muhyi al-Din, served notice on this point: "We are not ready to subscribe to a decision that would harm Egyptian interests. . . . We are not ready to sell Egypt's interests for the sake of any problem."[90]

Another reason why Mubarak could not have thought long about abandoning the Camp David accord was that his two most significant sources of domestic support—his Sadatist core following and the military—firmly backed the peace treaty and expected to see it continue along with the "Open Door" policy.

We have already seen that the president's Sadatist base of support included the most powerful and influential members of Egyptian society. As for the armed services, the president clearly understood that their backing was nothing less than a prerequisite to the stability of any regime. Even as vice president he had prepared for his tenure as head of state by appointing military commanders who would be beholden to him. The death of 13 of Sadat's generals in a helicopter crash gave Mubarak the opportunity to fill the vacancies with men who were his reliable supporters.[91] In any case, Sadat had generally left it to his vice president to appoint key personnel, enabling the future president to replace military commanders who were his potential competitors with officers securely behind him.[92] Defense Minister Abdel Halim Abu Ghazzala, for example, was an appointee of the vice president, and this is presumably one of the reasons why the popular military figure has been viewed as faithful to Mubarak.[93] Later, as president, Mubarak took particular care to ensure that the 24 men implicated in Sadat's death be treated as fairly as possible because many of the suspects were members of the army.[94] Yet perhaps the main reason Mubarak would come to enjoy the solid backing of the military was support for his policies at the highest levels of all the armed services—and the peace figured prominently here.[95] The treaty had led to more and better equipment from the United States,[96] and Mubarak's ability to procure such arms because of his assertiveness with the Pentagon was especially appreciated.[97]

Abrogation of the peace might, then, jeopardize what had come to be a firm underpinning of the regime—military support.

Finally, we should also recall that despite years on the front line against Israel, Mubarak had strong personal reasons for maintaining the peace. As a former combat veteran, he was especially aware that Camp David had spared potentially large numbers of Egyptian casualties. He also presumably felt a sense of loyalty to Sadat—the man whom he called his "teacher"—and to the accord Sadat had so laboriously crafted.[98]

Thus, the balance Mubarak had to strike in responding to the invasion was clear. Although some observers of Egyptian affairs have perhaps gone too far in assessing the Palestinian-Israeli conflict as a potential threat to Mubarak's hold on power,[99] the Egyptian president clearly was under political and personal pressure to address himself to the anger and humiliation aroused by Israel's war against Palestinians in Lebanon. At the same time, Mubarak had compelling political and personal reasons to preserve the peace. He therefore had to fashion responses to the Israeli operation that would reflect Egyptian (and his own) outrage without unduly alarming Israel and the United States. As put by Alfred (Roy) Atherton, U.S. ambassador to Egypt at the time, Mubarak "had to walk a very fine line."[100]

"NOTHING HE COULD DO BUT WHAT HE WAS DOING"

The fine line was walked. Mubarak's responses to the invasion established the balance that was called for—energetic and forceful, yet tempered and restrained. These responses all fell into one of four categories: specific overtures to end the war; emphasis on Arab solidarity; denunciation of Israel; and near freezing of relations with Israel.

During the first eight months of Mubarak's presidency, the civil war in Lebanon raged on but Egypt demonstrated little interest. Its "Lebanon policy," if indeed it had one, was hardly well-known.[101] In the wake of the invasion, however, Egyptian officials suddenly became very vocal on the subject of Lebanon, appealing throughout the summer for Lebanese unity, independence, and territorial integrity, and for the withdrawal of all foreign forces from the country. In midsummer 1982, for example, State Minister Butrus Ghali advocated a neutral

Lebanon that would not be a part of regional "storms" and international disputes; such neutral status, he maintained, would be in the interest of the Lebanese people.[102] Several weeks later, Foreign Minister Kamal Hassan Ali pronounced Egypt's hope that former Phalangist militia leader Bashir Gemayel could, as the newly elected president of Lebanon, bring unity to the war-torn country and rebuild it.[103] In mid-September, after expressing "great concern and regret" over the assassination of Gemayel, the Egyptian government released a statement emphasizing "again the utmost necessity of the withdrawal of all foreign forces from Lebanon for the sake of its unity, independence, and territorial integrity."[104] Several months later Ghali outlined how Egypt would help Lebanon achieve such objectives: it was prepared to assist with diplomatic efforts, working through the United Nations and with all interested states, and it was ready to contribute to the rebuilding of Beirut by offering technical expertise.[105]

Egypt's most prominent and specific diplomatic initiative with respect to the invasion itself consisted of a rather well-publicized proposal developed in the beginning of July 1982 in conjunction with France. This Franco-Egyptian proposal, issued after consultation with the PLO, called for a mutual Palestinian-Israeli withdrawal "with dignity," Palestinian self-determination, and the preservation of Lebanon's independence and territorial integrity.[106] With the aim, no doubt, of increasing support for this plan, the Mubarak government let it be known that it was working to establish a neutral zone in West Beirut to be manned by an international force of which Egypt would be a part.[107] Indeed, it appeared that both France and Egypt were quite intent on seeing their joint plan realized. It was submitted to the United Nations Security Council, and special attempts to gain backing for it were directed at the governments of England, Italy, and above all, the United States.[108] At the same time, the Mubarak government urged Palestinian and Lebanese leaders to keep the situation "contained" as Egypt worked to gain support for its proposal.[109] In this spirit, Mubarak himself warned Phalangist leader Bashir Gemayel not to join the Israelis in their fight against the Palestinians in Lebanon, lest the chances for Lebanese unity suffer another grave setback.[110]

Mubarak's emphasis on Arab solidarity also proved to be an important component of his overall response to the invasion. The Egyptian president repeatedly stressed that his country wished to be part of a unified stand against the Israeli operation, and in mid-July he called for a meeting to develop such a joint position.[111] Earlier, in fact immediately after Israel's initial June 6 offensive, Mubarak had sent messages to the heads of Oman, Morocco, and the Sudan appealing for a unified response to the invasion.[112] Another key component of this emphasis on Arab solidarity was the Mubarak government's newly vigorous support of Palestinian demands. According to State Minister Dr. Butrus Ghali, in the weeks following the invasion there was much official Egyptian contact not only with a number of Arab countries, but also with the PLO, which was invited to form a government-in-exile in Cairo.[113] On July 24, 1982, Egypt affirmed that the withdrawal of Palestinian forces from Lebanon should be linked to a comprehensive settlement of the Palestinian problem.[114] Also at the end of July, Mubarak let it be known that he had been writing President Ronald Reagan for two weeks, urging the United States to meet directly with the PLO and to explicitly support the Palestinian demand for self-determination.[115] In addition, the Egyptian president even made the gesture of calling on Israel to recognize the PLO.[116] Yet the most striking evidence that the Mubarak government had gone to unprecedented lengths in its support of the Palestinians were reports in the beginning of July that Ghali had gone so far as to appeal to Lebanese Phalangist leader Bashir Gemayel to fight alongside the PLO.[117]

Accompanying this support of the Palestinians were Mubarak's repeated denunciations of the Israeli invasion.[118] In a television address to the nation in July, Mubarak called the invasion a "violation of the very spirit of the peace."[119] In the aftermath of the Sabra and Shitila massacres, the president's words reflected his own outrage as well as that of the Egyptian public: he warned Israel that its "policies of murder . . . will have very bad results" and for the first time as President spoke of Israel as a potential threat to Egyptian security.[120]

Mubarak backed up such verbal condemnation with specific measures that amounted to halting the "normal" Egyptian-Israeli relations brought about by the peace. According to Foreign Minister Kamal Hassan Ali, relations were "99 percent frozen."[121] To wit, the Mubarak government cut off official discussions regarding Palestinian autonomy; refused to proceed in facilitating transport between the two countries; canceled visits of official student, labor, and technical delegations; and markedly decreased contacts with the Israeli ambassador in Cairo, who complained to no avail.[122]

Other steps may have been more strongly felt in Israel. For example, in 1981, Egypt imported $50 million of Israeli goods and the amount was expected to be even higher in 1982[123]—but in response to the invasion, the Mubarak government decided to halt such imports.[124] Furthermore, Egypt's withdrawal of its ambassador from Tel Aviv following Sabra and Shatila met with almost as much irritation in Jerusalem as agreement in Cairo.

Despite—or perhaps because of—these demonstrations of anger at Israel, Mubarak made a point of affirming that the treaty itself was not in jeopardy. Forty thousand barrels of oil continued to be sent to Israel throughout the summer, and the president refused to yield to pressure to withdraw his ambassador from Tel Aviv until Sabra and Shatila.[125] He maintained that "in a time of crisis we need an ambassador in Tel Aviv even more than in periods of calm."[126] Even after Shabra and Shatila, he reaffirmed his country's commitment to peace, and praised those Israelis "who had condemned the massacre that stand against all the basic ideals of Judaism."[127]

These responses apparently filled the order: the peace did not suffer a crisis of confidence in the most relevant countries abroad, Israel and the United States, nor did Mubarak's support decline at home. The three major dailies that support the governing National Democratic party—*Al-Ahram*, *Al-Akhbar*, *Al-Gomhouriyya*—all lauded the government's insistence on bringing the invasion to an end and its focus on the Palestinian question as the crux of the problem.[128] The ruling party formally praised the president's responses to the invasion.[129] As for those outside the government, an article in the neo-Liberal journal *Al-Ahrar* was also laudatory: the government was achieving "unequivocal and tangible successes in foreign policy."[130] Even when critical, opposition commentary was almost always advisory rather than pejorative in tone, a marked change from the Sadat period. Shukri, for example, called for a "tougher stance" against the Israeli action, but not before making clear that the opposition "appreciates Mubarak's condemnation of the invasion."[131] Similarly, a June 29, 1982 piece in *Al-Sha'b* expressed disappointment that Mubarak "does not decide anything," yet began by praising his statements condemning the Israeli invasion and concluded in a way that would have been particularly unimagineable one year earlier: "Rely on God, Mr. President, may he bless your steps, help you and keep you."[132]

It is worth mentioning here that Mubarak's domestic position could have only been helped by the fact that his responses to the invasion met with sharp Israeli denunciation and enthusiastic Arab and PLO approval. One sector of the Israeli press, for example, expressed concern that Egypt, the only Arab country at peace with the Jewish state, reacted as forcefully to "Operation Peace for Galilee" as any other Arab state.[133] By contrast, in early August the Jordanian government went on record affirming that Egypt's diplomatic initiatives deserved "Arab and international appreciation."[134] And in an interview that appeared in *Al-Ahram al-Iqtisadi* shortly after the Sabra and Shatila massacres, a PLO military commander stated that he wished to "relay to the Egyptian people all the feelings of friendship and appreciation. . . . Since the first moment of the invasion, President Mubarak took a responsible pan-Arab stance."[135] Even Yasser Arafat himself sent Mubarak a message welcoming Egypt's decision to recall its ambassador from Tel Aviv following Sabra and Shatila.[136] As one observer of Middle Eastern politics was led to conclude, Mubarak's responses to the invasion had "the effect of evidencing anew Egypt's credentials to its Arab brothers."[137]

Thus, Mubarak's responses to the invasion had found the requisite balance: multifaceted and vigorous without being alarming, they went some distance toward venting the president's own anger, satisfying the Egyptian public, and impressing Arab neighbors and the PLO—all without causing a U.S.-Israeli crisis of confidence in the peace. By this criterion, an Egyptian official's description of Mubarak in the wake of the invasion appears to be accurate: "There was nothing he could do but what he was doing."[138]

How much difference did it make, then, that Mubarak held Egypt's highest office at the time of the invasion?

From one perspective, next to none. We all know that despite Mubarak's condemnations, sanctions, and diplomatic initiatives, Israel's "Operation Peace for Galilee" raged through the summer and took fully three years to phase out. Certainly the Egyptian president's influence on events on the ground could not compare to that of the leaders of the parties directly involved—Begin, Sharon, or Arafat—nor even to that of President Ronald Reagan, with his singular leverage over Israel.

From another standpoint it made but little more difference who the Egyptian president was. Given both the manifest anger and humiliation aroused by the invasion *and* the overwhelming national interest in preserving the peace, it is difficult to imagine an Egyptian head of state failing to follow at least the general guidelines described above in responding to the invasion.

From a third vantage point, however, it mattered considerably who the Egyptian leader was. After all, one of the cornerstones of Egypt's foreign policy—its peace with Israel—was considered at least partially responsible for the Israeli operation. The hour, then, was a particularly sensitive one, and it was of no slight importance that Mubarak was a president who could approach the difficult period with political legitimacy; he had established an agreeable public persona, earned credentials with the opposition, reassured his core following, and solidified the support of the military. ''Mubarak's most difficult hour'' would have been more trying still for a president facing the stores of ill will that Sadat did, or for one with a shaky hold on power. For example, it is hard to imagine that Sadat would have received the Jordanian and PLO praise that helped Mubarak at home, even if his responses to the invasion proved similar to Mubarak's, and it is easy to imagine the former president feeling compelled to carry out massive arrests in the wake of the domestic unrest precipitated by the Israeli operation, thus making the situation more volatile. Mubarak, then, was not only able to define the balanced response to the invasion that was required; considerably more difficult, he was able to achieve it quite smoothly.

Ironically, what began as Mubarak's ''most difficult hour,'' primarily because of the uncomfortable light cast on Egypt's recently revolutionized regional posture, perhaps ended up drawing Egypt closer to the ''Arab-state system.''[139] Egypt's assertive diplomacy with both the United States and Israel was appreciated in other Arab countries, especially because it represented a comparatively notable contribution: as one analyst observed, ''No Arab state, including Syria, really put the Palestinian cause and that of Lebanon before its own.''[140] Indeed, many Arabs, including members of the PLO, gave Egypt credit for being one of the few Arab states that tried to help during the Lebanon war by using its singular link with both Israel and the United States to exert pressure for an end to the invasion that would encompass a solution to the Palestinian question.[141]

Mubarak's responses to the 1982 Lebanon war indicate that the Egyptian president is sensitive to Egyptian and greater Arab political sentiment while also aware of the benefits of Cairo's current relationship with the United States and Israel. There is also reason to assume not only that Mubarak sees the political wisdom of working within this balanced framework, but also that doing so accords with his personal predisposition. This point is important to bear in mind in gauging the current Egyptian president's probable responses to future crises and negotiations in the region.

Indeed, Egypt's improved position in the inter-Arab arena, combined with

Mubarak's evident ability to achieve a difficult balance and to maintain channels of communication with both the United States and Israel, suggest that there is potentially a significant leadership role for the current Egyptian president in such regional crises and negotiations. To be sure, the political legitimacy that Mubarak achieved in the months before Israel's Lebanon war also helped him during that particular regional crisis, and the 1986 police uprising has been cited by some as evidence that the Mubarak government has lost a serious measure of this domestic support. In particular, growing impatience has been reported among intellectuals and members of the military, focusing on the president's alleged lack of strong leadership in the face of grave, interrelated demographic and economic problems that are exacerbated by the oil glut and the decline in tourism from its peak of several years ago.[142]

Nevertheless, it would be premature to conclude that Mubarak has lost his political legitimacy at home, or that such a loss is inevitable. It is important to note that the police violence of early 1986 was condemned by the overwhelming majority of the Egyptian public and political opposition, and that the government had the confidence to allow full media coverage of the revolt without laying the blame on a conspiracy.[143] Mubarak has been given credit by Egyptians for this forthrightness and for the relative openness of Egyptian society and politics generally.[144] In addition, the Egyptian army's efficient quelling of the police riots indicates that the military was operating unhesitatingly in support of the regime, and Mubarak continues to enjoy the loyalty of the armed forces' premier figure, Defense Minister Ghazala.

As for Egypt's economic woes, it is true that the Mubarak government will have to address this central problem with a program that is forceful yet not disruptive of the delicate balance of subsidies that Egyptians depend on day to day. A failure to fulfill this order could present serious problems for the Mubarak government, even though Egypt's economic tribulations are seemingly insoluble in any case.

Mubarak may be expected to maintain his domestic political legitimacy, along with his avenues of access to both the United States and Israel. Moreover, the restoration of diplomatic ties between Cairo and several Middle Eastern capitals, in the context of substantial Egyptian support of Iraq in its war with Iran, bodes well for Mubarak's inter-Arab prospects. Even so, Mubarak's limited impact on events in the Lebanon war raises the question of whether, and under what circumstances, he will be able to draw on these assets to emerge as a *regional* leader.

NOTES

1. *Ha'aretz*, October 5, 1982.
2. *Al-Ahali*, August 25, 1982, as translated in *Joint Publication Research Service* (*JPRS*), #81790.
3. Hermann Eilts, interview with the author, November 8, 1984. However, Eilts

would probably adhere to the consensus view that the recent police uprising has since surpassed the Israeli invasion of Lebanon as Mubarak's "most difficult hour."

4. *Al-Musuwwar*, October 1981, as translated in *JPRS*, #79566.

5. Ibid.

6. Ibid.

7. P. J. Vatikiotes, "After Sadat," *Policy Review*, Winter 1982.

8. *Al-Musawwar*, October 1981, as translated in *JPRS* #79566.

9. Ibid. It is, of course, possible that this article contained some embellishment.

10. Ibid.

11. Ibid.

12. Ibid.

13. Ibid.

14. Stanley F. Reed, "Dateline Cairo: Shaken Pillar," *Foreign Policy* 45 (Winter, 1981–82); 183.

15. John G. Merriam, "Egypt under Mubarak," *Current History* 82 (1983); 27.

16. *The New York Times Magazine*, January 31, 1982.

17. Ibid.

18. Reed, "Dateline Cairo," p. 182.

19. *The New York Times* (*NYT*), October 16, 1981.

20. Ibid.

21. Ibid.

22. *The New York Times Magazine*, January 31, 1982, p. 34.

23. Ibid.

24. Eilts interview.

25. See Barry Rubin, "What Mubarak Inherits," *The New Republic*, (October 28, 1981): 20.

26. Eilts interview.

27. *Middle East Contemporary Survey* (*MECS*), 1981–82, p. 443.

28. *Al-Ahrar*, October 25, 1982, as translated in *JPRS* #82693. These comments had originally been printed in another publication several weeks earlier.

29. Eilts interview.

30. *The New York Times Magazine*, January 31, 1982, p. 48.

31. Mubarak did not let Sadat down on this score. Eilts, for example, remembers that Vice President Mubarak did not take his advice and issue a statement affirming that the peace under Israel would continue no matter who was president. Vice President Mubarak was concerned that such a statement might be misinterpreted by the president and make him suspicious (Eilts interview).

32. Ibid.

33. *The New York Times Magazine*, January 31, 1982, p. 26.

34. See Vatikiotes, "After Sadat," p. 43. The seemingly chronic economic disarray persisted, yet Mubarak did not suffer the virulent opposition attacks concerning the economy that had been Sadat's portion, in large part because the new president's general political style and forthrightness about economic travails contrasted favorably with his predecessor's public persona and wildly optimistic pronouncements concerning economic prospects. (See *MECS*, 1981–82, pp. 454–55, 458–59).

35. *The Middle East*, September 1982, p. 12.

36. *The New York Times Magazine*, January 31, 1982, p. 50.

37. *NYT*, October 15, 1981.

38. Saad-Eddin Ibrahim, "The Struggle for Mubarak's Soul," *Journal of Arab Affairs* 2, no. 2 (October 1982); 92.

39. The term "opposition" is used here to refer to the Mubarak government's political opponents, who belong to a variety of parties and organizations. Ibrahim (ibid.) includes among the regime's clear opponents "Nasserists" (those who remain committed to the Nasserist tenets of non-alignment, Arabism and socialism); the "Old Left" (composed of Marxists and non-Marxist Labor Party members who bitterly opposed Sadat); and "Muslim Militants" (avowedly committed to the overthrow of the regime, their activities are often illegal).

40. *NYT*, October 15, 1981.

41. *MECS*, 1981–82, p. 452, and *The Middle East*, October 1982, p. 11. In a related development, the minister of interior, a key figure in carrying out Sadat's arrests, was dismissed from office in what was probably nothing other than an additional step toward distancing the new regime from the previous one.

42. *MECS*, 1981–82, p. 452, and Merriam, "Egypt under Mubarak," p. 26.

43. Ibid.

44. The government also sought to nip in the bud potential practitioners of such illegal tactics: it embarked on a campaign to reorient "straying" youth. *Shayks* of *al-Azhar* were designated to speak at universities and schools about "true" versus radical Islam. A number of sports clubs, cultural centers, and public service projects were set up to "keep [young people] busy and contribute to their skills and experience." See *MECS*, 1981–82, p. 452.

45. Ibid., p. 454.

46. Ibid., p. 453.

47. Ibid.

48. Ibid.

49. *The New York Times Magazine*, January 31, 1982, p. 50.

50. *MECS*, 1980–81, p. 358. For a number of Sadat's similar comments about a variety of Arab states, see *MECS*, 1980–81, pp. 358–59.

51. See Vatikiotes, "After Sadat," p. 54.

52. *The New York Times Magazine*, January 31, 1982, p. 50.

53. See Vatikiotes, "After Sadat."

54. Louis Cantori, "Egyptian Policy," in *The Middle East Since Camp David*, ed. Robert O. Freedman (Boulder, Colo.: Westview Press, 1984).

55. Reed, "Dateline Cairo," p. 185.

56. Cantori, "Egyptian Policy," p. 186.

57. Ibid. and *The Middle East*, September 1982, p. 13.

58. Cantori, "Egyptian Policy," p. 186.

59. Ibid.

60. *The Middle East*, September 1982, p. 14.

61. Ibid.

62. *The New York Times Magazine*, January 31, 1982, p. 26, and Abd Elsattar Eltawila, "Egypt's Expectations of President Mubarak," *New Outlook*, March 1982.

63. *MECS*, 1981–82, p. 345.

64. Eltawila, "Egypt's Expectations."

65. Eric Roleau, "Mubarak's Cumbersome Heritage," *New Outlook*, April 1982, p. 22.

66. See Raymond A. Hinnebusch, "Children of the Elite: Political Attitudes of

Westernized Bourgeoisie in Contemporary Egypt," *Journal of Arab Affairs* 2, no. 1 (October 1982).

67. See Bahgat Korany, "The Cold Peace, the Sixth Arab-Israeli War, and Egypt's Public," *International Journal* 33, no. 4 (Autumn 1983); 661.

68. *NYT*, October 2, 1981.

69. Eilts interview.

70. Ibid.

71. Ibid.

72. *MECS*, 1981–82, p. 127.

73. Ibid.

74. Korany, "The Cold Peace," p. 667.

75. *Al-Ahali*, June 23, 1982, as translated in *JRPS*, #81381. The *imam* is referring to Egypt's alleged "Egypt first" outlook of recent years.

76. Ibid.

77. *MECS*, 1981–82, p. 345.

78. Ibid. and *Al-Ahali*, June 23, 1982, as translated in *JPRS*, #81381.

79. Dr. Abdalluh-Fouad Hafez, director of press and information in the Egyptian Embassy in Washington, interview with the author, December 19, 1984.

80. See Cantori, "Egyptian Policy."

81. *Middle East News Agency*, July 5, 1982, as translated in *JPRS*, #81289.

82. *NYT*, June 13, 1982.

83. Those polled also represented a broad geographic cross section.

84. *The Middle East* (September 1982); 13.

85. Ibid.

86. Eilts interview.

87. *MECS*, 1981–82, p. 466.

88. Jennifer Seymour Whitaker, "They Don't Miss Sadat," *Atlantic Monthly* 249, no. 1 (January 1982); 18.

89. John Kimche, "Mubarak: Sadat's Heir or Liquidator?" *Midstream* 28, no. 6 (June 1982); 5. Cutting food subsidies was not an option: Mubarak remembered the 1970s food riots well, if for no other reason than that his house burned down in one of them.

90. *Al-Ahram*, June 9, 1982, as translated in *JPRS*, #81104.

91. Reed, "Dateline Cairo," p. 184.

92. Ibid. and Eilts interview.

93. Reed, "Dateline Cairo," p. 183.

94. Merriam, "Egypt under Mubarak," p. 26.

95. *Middle East Focus*, November 1982, p. 10; also see *NYT*, October 16, 1981. Although there are a number of Nasserists and other opponents of the regime in the lower levels of the military, it is considered unlikely that a successful *coup d'état* could emerge from a complexly organized army of 450,000 unless touched off by generals. See *NYT*, October 16, 1981.

96. Eilts interview.

97. Ibid. Indeed, the new president was quite confidently aware that the military was solidly behind him. Shortly after becoming President, in the presence of Ambassador Eilts, he upbraided Defense Minister Abu Ghazala, a figure of great popularity and influence in the armed forces. As Eilts himself later noted, such berating of Egypt's top military figure in front of the U.S. ambassador was the mark of a president not even the least bit unsure of the armed services' support.

98. Mubarak has in fact continued to demonstrate loyalty to the peace agreement his predecessor initiated, and has worked toward widening it to encompass other parties in the region. We may assume that he will proceed along this path, at least in the absence of any unforeseen, major Israeli provocations.

99. See, for example, Cantori, "Egyptian Policy," and Hinnebusch, "Children of the Elite." Cantori, in a confusing concluding paragraph, strongly suggests that the durability of Mubarak's presidency may depend on the degree of energy and skill he demonstrates in working toward a solution of the Palestinian question. Hinnebusch is less dramatic, speculating that bourgeoise loyalty to Mubarak, essential to his ability to survive a political crisis, may be dependent on his willingness to strengthen Arab ties and increase coolness toward Israel (p. 560).

100. Alfred (Roy) Atherton, interview with the author, December 20, 1984.

101. Neither the *Foreign Broadcast Information Service* (FBIS), *JPRS*, nor *The New York Times* includes so much as a single Egyptian statement on Lebanon in the eight months preceding the invasion.

102. *Middle East News Agency*, July 30, 1982, as translated in *FBIS*, August, 2, 1982.

103. *NYT*, August 24, 1982.

104. *NYT*, September 16, 1982. This statement was similar to several issued by the Sadat government in May 1981. Sadat, however, was more direct and vituperative in denouncing Syria in particular, accusing it of "wreaking havoc" with its "oppressive aggression" (see *FBIS*, May 7, 1981). According to the Voice of Palestine radio broadcast in Lebanon, the Sadat government was providing arms to the Phalangists who, of course, also wanted Syria out of Lebanon (see *FBIS*, May 6, 1981).

105. *Cairo Domestic Service*, November 27, 1982, as translated in *JPRS*, #82442.

106. See *NYT*, July 11, 1982 and July 29, 1982.

107. NYT, July 29, 1982.

108. *Al-Akhbar*, June 29, 1982, as translated in *JPRS*, #81289; *NYT*, July 29, 1982.

109. *NYT*, July 27, 1982.

110. *Al-Musawwar*, July 22, 1982, as translated in *FBIS*, July 24, 1982.

111. *NYT*, July 27, 1982.

112. *Al-Ahram*, June 9, 1982, as translated in JPRS, #81104.

113. *Al-Musawwar*, July 2, 1982, as translated in *JPRS*, #81658, and *The Middle East* (September 1982): 13.

114. Korany, "The Cold Peace," p. 671.

115. *NYT*, July 27, 1982.

116. *NYT*, July 16, 1982.

117. *Middle East News Agency*, July 2, 1982, as translated in *JPRS*, #81289.

118. The national press also severely criticized the United States for its veto of the Franco-Egyptian proposal, accusing Washington of a lack of evenhandedness toward the major political issues of the region. See Korany, "The Cold Peace," p. 663.

119. *NYT*, July 26, 1982.

120. *MECS*, 1981–82, p. 84.

121. Merriam, "Egypt under Mubarak," p. 25.

122. *Al-Rayah*, July 7, 1982, as translated in *FBIS*, July 8, 1982.

123. *NYT*, July 20, 1982.

124. *Al-Rayah*, July 7, 1982, as translated in *FBIS*, July 8, 1982.

125. Anthony McDermott, "Empty Relationship," *Middle East International*, no. 187, November 12, 1982, p. 8.

126. *MECS*, pp. 81–82.

127. Merriam, "Egypt under Mubarak," p. 25.

128. Korany, "The Cold Peace," p. 663.

129. *Cairo Domestic Service*, August 15, 1982, as translated in *FBIS*, August 18, 1982.

130. *Al-Ahrar*, July 11, 1983, as translated in *JPRS*, #84248.

131. *MECS*, 1981–82, p. 456.

132. *Al-Sha'b*, June 29, 1982.

133. Korany, "The Cold Peace," p. 671.

134. *Al-Dustur*, August 4, 1982, as translated in *JPRS*, #81628.

135. Interview with Abu al-Zaim in *Al-Ahram Al-Iqtisadi*, October 25, 1982, as translated in JPRS, #82403.

136. *MECS*, 1981–82, p. 345.

137. Cantori, "Egyptian Policy," p. 189.

138. Hafez interview.

139. See Cantori, "Egyptian Policy," p. 189.

140. Ibid.

141. *The Middle East* (September 1982): 13.

142. *NYT*, March 9, 1986.

143. Tahseen Basheer, Egyptian ambassador to Canada, 1981–85, in lecture at Harvard University, April 3, 1986.

144. Ibid.

7

JORDAN'S KING HUSSEIN

Aaron S. Klieman

Jordan has always exhibited a distinct preference for a low profile in Middle Eastern affairs as the best assurance of state security and survival. This lesson is anchored in Jordan's basic geopolitical position as a small state prone to weakness and vulnerability, but it is also reflected and reinforced by historical experience: both that of the country as a whole and in the personal biography of His Majesty King Hussein.

While the Lebanese conflict produced no real winners, Jordan arguably qualifies among the very few indirect beneficiaries. Certainly the immediate postcrisis period 1983–85 found King Hussein better positioned in each of the four political relationships that vitally affect prospects for his Hashemite Kingdom: Israel, the Palestinian national movement, other Arab leaders, and the superpower of the United States.

At first, King Hussein and his advisers were caught largely unaware by both the scale and the intensity of the 1982 crisis. Once having recovered from the initial surprise, however, they proceeded to conduct an understated but effective brand of diplomacy. As a result, Jordan's leadership did more than merely weather yet another Middle East political storm, it actually managed to convert a potentially threatening situation into political gain, through a series of moves and responses on the regional chessboard. Furthermore, it did so without any major commitment, concession, or fundamental change in Jordanian bedrock policies.

THE GEOPOLITICAL SITUATION: A HISTORICAL OVERVIEW

The history of Jordan, covering 66 years, divides into three distinct periods, each differentiated by a watershed event involving a singular act of political boldness by a Jordanian leader. The periods are as follows:

- 1921–47: emergence of a Transjordanian entity;
- 1948–67: the expanded kingdom of Jordan, and
- 1968–present: the constricted state.

Of the three initiatives undertaken by Jordan's rulers (to be discussed here briefly), only the first two were crowned with success. Still, all three—the failures as much as the triumphs—continue to dominate the collective memory of the Hashemite state and to shape its political behavior.

Modern Jordan's origins lie in the unanticipated appearance on the east bank of the Jordan River in 1921 of Abdullah ibn Hussein, son of an Arabian prince and wartime ally of Great Britain. By his very entry and presence in what was then a geopolitical vacuum at the interstices of Anglo-French imperialism, Abdullah prompted nervous British strategists to accommodate him in their postwar plans for the Middle East.[1] From such modest beginnings, he succeeded in carving out a kingdom for himself and imposing a hereditary Hashemite monarchy on the indigenous Bedouin tribes. The evolutionary process of the state in the making saw Transjordan progress from a British-mandated eastern Palestinian province to an emirate and semisovereign desert kingdom before achieving full independence in 1946.

Abdullah was never content with this achievement, however, and remained alert to opportunities for enlarging his realm and widening his personal prestige. Such an occasion presented itself in 1948 due to Arab-Jewish intercommunal strife in western Palestine. If forcing Great Britain's hand in 1921 was the first bold act of Abdullah's career, the second came when the Hashemite monarch combined statecraft with force of arms to gain control over "west bank" areas designated for a Palestinian Arab state by the 1947 U.N. General Assembly partition resolution. In a unilateral act of defiance of international and Arab public opinion, Abdullah formally annexed these areas to what was then renamed the Hashemite Kingdom of Jordan.[2]

In effect, Israel and Jordan were left as copartitionists and successor states in former Palestine. Abdullah would pay with his life in July 1951 for this betrayal of the Palestinians and because he dared conduct secret negotiations with Israel. Despite his assassination, the territorial legacy bequeathed by Abdullah to his young successor, Hussein, would endure, at least for another 16 years.

In the second stage of Jordan's development, and following King Hussein's ascension to power in 1953, the Hashemites consolidated their gains on the West Bank and systematically sought to obliterate all remaining vestiges of a Palestinian national consciousness.[3] This era of an expansive kingdom straddling both sides of the Jordan also represents a period of acute stress, punctuated by domestic and external crises that brought the country to the brink of disintegration.[4] Hussein and the kingdom were able to preserve themselves against enemies from within and outside Jordan, only to then lose possession of the West Bank in 1967 through a miscalculation of profound dimensions.

This third and most calamitous independent decision in Jordan's history occurred when Hussein joined a military pact with Egypt and Syria against Israel on the eve of the Six-Day War. The Israeli counteroffensive pushed the Jordanians eastward back across the river to what in effect had been the original confines of Abdullah's realm. The 1967 fiasco opens the third phase of Jordan's political history, featuring a constricted kingdom forced to live with the price of error and defeat. However, once again one encounters a paradox in Jordan's general situation. Although reduced in physical size, Jordan in the years since 1968, but in particular after the 1970 suppression of a PLO challenge to Hashemite authority, has experienced a period of unprecedented diplomatic respectability and economic prosperity under King Hussein. So does it also enjoy a greater degree of social consensus and political stability, on the surface at least, then ever before.

It stands to reason, therefore, that these achievements could easily be jeopardized and possibly forfeited by either of three undesirable situations: first, a deterioration in Jordan's position arising from an alteration of the status quo in any one or more of the four key foreign-policy arenas mentioned at the outset; second, and alternatively, a break with the country's cautious approach in which a fourth bold initiative by the leaders of Jordan (such as rejoining a war coalition against Israel or unilaterally seeking a peace accord with Israel) would carry with it the risk of ending up as the second strategic miscalculation by Abdullah's successors; or third, the spectre of Hussein's own demise, posing a crisis of political succession for the kingdom.

KING HUSSEIN: THE LEADER AS A PERSON

The necessity for choice ultimately lies with King Hussein. So, too, he deserves the credit for much of Jordan's recent stability, although it was he who compounded the Jordanian predicament by his fatal decision in the 1967 crisis. This aside, however, for more than three decades the incumbent monarch has provided both a sense of direction and firm leadership, epitomizing Walter Bagehot's model of "the pilot of the storm." Furthermore, while the course of action or inaction followed by Jordan in 1982 may be explained in terms of geopolitical situation and historical experience, it is fully consistent with, and indeed mirrors, Hussein's own world view.

The 53-year-old monarch is the principal wielder of power in Jordan, the authoritative spokesman for his country and its ultimate foreign policy decision-maker. King Hussein of Jordan's special place in regional politics as much as in internal affairs is owed first to sheer durability. Not quite age 50 at the time of the 1982 crisis, he was in fact one of the world's elder statesmen in years of service, and few can recall a Jordan without him as head of state. Second, his place is attributable to the personal courage and the crisis leadership demonstrated by Hussein when at several critical junctures it appeared as though he alone stood between the combined weight of internal challenges and foreign intrigue and the destruction of Jordan. In maturing through experience, the young monarch advanced beyond mere bravery or luck, developing the administrative, negotiating, and leadership talents required of a national leader. Consistent with the demands of a political system built on personalized rule, the king has known how and when to wield his authority, and he assumes a close, active role in directing national affairs. He is assisted in this by other members of the royal family, the most prominent being his brother and heir apparent, Crown Prince Hassan, and his own son, Prince Abdullah.

Hussein is neither an innovator nor a risk-taker. His manner and style are those of a conservative who combines intuition with suppleness and an exceptional sense of timing. He has known when to alternate coercion with persuasion; when to advance, to retreat tactically or, even better, to move sideways (again with the notable exception of 1967) in order to avoid confrontation or hard choices. These qualities perhaps best explain the respect for Hussein abroad and his popularity at home, popularity described as "the almost mystical attachment of the Jordanian populace to its King."[5]

Life History

Because the bond between king and country is strengthened in the instance of Hussein and Jordan by overlapping national and personal histories, one cannot possibly comprehend Jordanian policies without understanding the king's own political orientation. This, in turn, derives from a number of formative experiences in both his private and public life.

A brief biographical sketch provides the following data:

* Hussein ibn Talal born November 14, 1935;
* educated in Amman and Cairo, then public school at Harrow, England;
* also attended the Royal Military Academy, Sandhurst (1952–53);
* succeeded to throne, August 11, 1952, following father's abdication; formally crowned, May 2, 1953;
* married four times: Dina (divorced), Muna (marriage dissolved), Alia (killed in helicopter crash, 1977), Nur;
* hobbies: aviation and swimming.

Missing from this profile are perhaps as many as six or seven turning points in his life: dramatic events in which Hussein was either a direct participant or close observer. Even now these events and influences must impress themselves on Hussein's political thinking and behavior, helping to account for his well-known caution.

The dominant figure in Hussein's life was King Abdullah, under whose shadow he was raised. Hussein himself admits that his grandfather above all men had "the most profound influence on my life."[6] It was Abdullah who ingrained

Hashemite aspirations and pride in the young, impressionable Hussein, who decided on his education, and who groomed him for kingship. The grandson stood at the old king's side when Abdullah was shot as they entered the Al Aqsa mosque in July 1951.[7] As Hussein wrote in a 1962 autobiography, "My life has been very lonely since that Friday morning, and I have often wondered what lay behind the thousands of bland smiles and fervent expressions of loyalty I have acknowledged since then."[8]

The early years following Hussein's ascension to the throne were exceptionally difficult and turbulent. In each of the years 1956, 1957, and 1958, the inexperienced and as yet uncertain monarch was tested by three consecutive crises. In 1956, under pressure from Arab nationalists, the king dared to dismiss General John Bagot Glubb as commander of the Arab Legion, precipitating a diplomatic crisis that threatened to isolate Jordan from its principal benefactor, Great Britain. Next, in 1957, he dramatically put down a threatened army mutiny. In this so-called Zarqa Affair he personally visited military encampments where he earned the loyalty of his troops; he has labored to preserve this loyalty ever since through many public appearances in military uniform, as well as visits to military sites and army maneuvers.[9] Then, in July 1958, Hussein was jolted by events in Baghdad. During a bloody military coup, the entire Iraqi royal family was murdered, including Hussein's young cousin, King Faisal, with whom he had had a close relationship. This left Hussein as the head of the sole surviving branch of the Hashemite dynasty.

A decade later, in June 1967, decisions by King Hussein cost him control over the West Bank. From his perspective, this represented far more than merely a question of territory. It was, first and foremost, a matter of personal honor: he had sullied Arab pride and, at the same time, had thrown away the greatest Hashemite legacy passed on to him by the grandfather he so revered and emulated.

The post–1967 dislocation led eventually to still another decisive moment in Hussein's reign. After having permitted the PLO (Palestine Liberation Organization) to increase its influence on the East Bank, to the point of constituting a virtual "state within a state," the king apparently was pressed into action by his generals. "Black September" 1970 and the months that followed saw Hussein not only face down a threatened Syrian invasion but regain full mastery over his kingdom and its majority Palestinian constituency. Hussein accomplished this through a violent show of armed force, thus making possible the extended domestic tranquility and improved diplomatic position that he has known since then.[10]

Perhaps it was Black September that emboldened Hussein in 1972 to set forth his scheme for restructuring future Hashemite-Palestinian relations (in the event of an Israeli withdrawal from the West Bank) along the lines of a federal union.[11] Jordan's fortunes reversed themselves in 1974, however, when Hussein was dealt a personal setback at the Rabat conference. The Arab summit unanimously voted to acknowledge the PLO, and not Jordan, as "sole, legitimate representative'' of the Palestinians. Particularly galling for Hussein personally in this political embarrassment and isolation was the reversal of position by Egypt's President Anwar Sadat, who earlier had seemed to endorse the Jordanian position. This reciprocal lack of personal esteem or confidence between the two leaders may partially explain Hussein's refusal in 1978–79 to support the peace initiative toward Israel taken by Sadat, or to join the Camp David negotiation.[12] The demise of the Egyptian leader and rival in 1981 might have been a source of gratification to Hussein were it not that the violent manner of Sadat's death stands as yet another reminder of the high risks inherent in Arab-Israeli peace making.

In retrospect, Hussein of Jordan has survived many challenges and setbacks. He has known personal danger, including at least 11 documented assassination attempts. He has experienced personal sadness and tragedy,[13] and in recent years he has had health problems in addition to periodic bouts of depression. All this has left the king acutely aware of his own mortality and the limits of time. Three goals remain unattained: (1) to guarantee a smooth succession; (2) to put Jordan's security and well-being on a sounder footing; and (3) to redeem himself—in Arab eyes, to the memory of Abdullah, and in his own esteem—by successfully regaining the West Bank.

A point of personal satisfaction for Hussein, and arguably his greatest triumph given so many constraints, is the mere fact that he has survived. As a result, when the 1982 Lebanese crisis erupted, it found the Hashemite monarch once more negotiating in Middle East politics from a position of strength. Thirty years of rule had transformed the once frivolous, ''plucky little king'' with a penchant for racing cars and air stunts into an experienced, senior Arab statesman and world figure. Adept at crisis leadership, Hussein was even able to recover from the 1974 Rabat setback. In adjusting to the new Middle East realities of the 1970s, he patiently steered a middle course consisting of a reopened dialogue with the PLO; a central, albeit indirect, role in the daily life of the West Bank that continued under Israeli military administration; open channels to the other Arab countries, particularly the wealthier, oil-producing nations such as Saudi Arabia, Iraq, and Kuwait; ingratiating himself with successive U.S. administrations; and, of course, overseeing domestic order and economic development.[14] King Hussein accomplished all of this while honoring the wish for Arab consensus, and without openly diverging from the pro-PLO Rabat resolutions.

Characteristics and Outlook

Hussein is frequently referred to as diminutive, yet he more than compensates for a lack in physical stature by a strong presence. Hussein conveys both warmth and a sense of dignity. That he comports himself like a true monarch may owe to the confidence that comes with experience, but it owes even more to upbringing. His erect military bearing, among other physical traits, may be seen as the product of the two cultures that influenced Hussein: the Bedouin culture, and the English officer training received in his youth. Similarly, the king's public presentations are phrased in the flowery oratory of classical Arabic, emphasizing such traditional themes as chivalry, bravery, sacrifice, and loyalty, although without much of the emotional delivery usually associated with Arab politics. This moderation favorably impresses those who meet Hussein, especially Westerners. Israelis, too, have emerged from secret encounters with Hussein having found him honorable, pragmatic, candid, and anything but extremist or irrational.

King Hussein is reported to be an intensely private man, relying on no one. Still, he has effectively employed close advisers in governing Jordan, signalling tactical shifts of internal or regional policy by changing prime ministers and cabinets at will. This sense of isolation and the inability to fully trust others can be traced to his childhood. Here is more of Hussein's own recollection of the traumatic scene of Abdullah's murder in 1951:

I saw from the corner of my eye . . . that most of my grandfather's so-called friends were fleeing in every direction. I can see them now, those men of dignity and high estate, doubled up, cloaked figures scattering like bent old terrified women.[15]

He ends this 1962 autobiographical account: "That picture, far more distinct than the face of the assassin, has remained with me ever since as a constant reminder of the frailty of political devotion."

Hussein's sense of isolation was probably reinforced by reports of intrigues against him in earlier years from within the royal court. The principal alleged conspirator in the 1957 aborted mutiny was Ali Abu Nuwar, previously a close confidant of the king. Again, Hussein felt betrayed by Nasser in 1967 and by Sadat both in 1974 and in 1977, when the Egyptian leader paid his surprise visit to Jerusalem. Loneliness is thus a powerful theme in the worldview of the king of Jordan.

Personal isolation, by extension, carries over to Jordan. Here, too, Hussein sees the Hashemite kingdom facing formidable threats and having to defend the just Arab cause by itself. To cite one illustration, in a 1984 *New York Times* interview, Hussein emphasized that "Jordan has always been on its own."[16] At the time he expressed criticism of U.S. policy in unusually sharp terms on the grounds that it, too, was abandoning Jordan; "I now realize," he declared, "that principles mean nothing to the United States."

Hussein's perception of the precariousness of his existence, and that of his monarchy, is reflected in his interesting and revealing choice of a title for his early memoirs: "Uneasy Lies the Head." That the opportunity now exists for a sequel to this book can only be a source of satisfaction for Hussein, and a surprise to him as well as to antagonists.

Since authoring his autobiographical book in 1962, Hussein's career has been extended by an additional quarter of a century, making it possible to map his operational code. Rather than attempt a comprehensive picture of the king's worldview or political relationships with Arab or world leaders, two or three of his more salient values have been singled out for mention.

The Jordanian monarch possesses a distinctive and strict personal code of honor. Perhaps the most powerful impression he conveys is the sense of duty. When responsibility was thrust upon him prematurely in 1952, he later candidly admitted, "I hated the idea." More than anything else, he wished to live a normal life. In his own words,

I wanted to finish my education and then get a job on my own merits. It did not matter what it was; I wanted to prove that I was capable of holding down an ordinary job, not to impress other people. . . . [To this he adds ruefully:] It was a dream I never realized.[17]

Hussein returns time and again in his 1962 autobiography to this theme of denial and responsibility imposed upon him and the consequent need to sacrifice himself and his personal wishes to this larger obligation of service. Once reconciled to the responsibilities of royalty, the king dutifully acknowledges: "On no occasion have I felt I was indispensable to Jordan. I am its servant, not its master."[18] He concludes his first volume of memoirs by praying for a long life "to work for the land we love so well, and to prove ourselves worthy descendants of the Hashemite dynasty."[19]

Arguably, one should be skeptical about accepting political leaders' professions of selflessness, sacrifice, and commitment, yet Hussein must be credited with a sense of dedication to country and to family that is as genuine as it is all-consuming. Having long since resigned himself to the challenges and risks of occupying the Hashemite throne, Hussein has worked hard at being king.

If duty stands at the center of King Hussein's Weltanschauung, then resignation—to the burdens, the deficiencies of Jordan and, above all, the force of circumstance—conceivably has led to a second influence on his personal and political belief system: namely, a sense of pessimism or stoicism that borders on fatalism. This belief system found expression, for example, in a recent observation by the king of his fervent desire to provide his people with "something I never had: confidence in the future."[20] Over the years, Hussein has developed a tendency to swing from moods of heightened expectation to depths of despair, sometimes with prolonged periods of withdrawal and depression in between.[21] Years of service have left Hussein more relaxed and mature, but also with a growing sense of mortality.

The result is an activist and highly visible monarch, yet one characterized by a basically negative outlook. Whenever rebuffed, as he was in 1974 at Rabat by his fellow Arab heads of state, Hussein has threatened to throw up his hands in resignation, absolving both himself and his country from responsibility for the Palestinian cause, and vowing to leave it to history to pass judgment.[22] Increasingly of late, Hussein has accompanied each step of Middle East diplomatic activity with gloomy pronouncements about this being the "last chance" or "the last opportunity" for peace.[23]

Hussein's commitment and fatalism, his feelings of isolation, and his personal and political desire to avoid censure, are so prominent as to have invited comment by others. Less appreciated, and only alluded to here, is one final noteworthy attribute: the similarity and the bonds between Hussein and Abdullah. His grandfather's memory still maintains a powerful hold over Hussein, always confronting him with the need to measure up to the high expectations and political legacy of his predecessor.

The king relates that only three days before the 1951 assassination, his grandfather took him aside and confided:

I hope you realize, my son, that one day you will have to assume responsibility. I look to you to do your very best to see that my work is not lost. I look to you to continue it in the service of our people.[24]

Hussein returned to this episode in a 1983 interview: "My grandfather always told me 'so much has gone before you, don't be the disappointing link.' "[25]

Few would disagree that Hussein has done his best to carry out Abdullah's wishes and political testament courageously as well as honorably. In the last analysis, however, he betrayed this legacy by his action in 1967. Hence his overwhelming dilemma: whether or not to seek atonement by regaining mastery over the lost territories. While success would redeem him, there is also the very real danger that instead of recouping the loss, his gamble could end in failure.

Conceivably, both a separate, fully independent Palestinian state or, alternatively, an East Bank-West Bank confederation (or federation) dominated by the Palestinians would run contrary to Abdullah's strategy for Hashemite hegemony; it could even spell the end of Hashemite control over the more restricted East Bank. Consequently, Hussein is torn between: (1) biding his time, like Abdullah, even though time is running out as he ages and as Israel widens its presence in the disputed territories; (2) lowering his sights and confessing the unattainability of his larger aspirations; or (3) risking everything in a last attempt at vindicating himself.

These, then, represent Hussein's three tiers of personal and state goals. His immediate priority must be to protect against a recurrence of the 1967 mistake. He allowed himself then to be pressed by others and by force of circumstance into a situation not of his own choosing; a repeat would bear the prospect of unintended consequences without the comfort of knowing the outcome in advance. Hussein's second goal probably involves a set of intermediate achievements to leave behind as his legacy: a smooth succession and power transition, and the secured existence of Jordan even in its truncated present form. Finally, there remains the ultimate objective: the reassertion of Jordan's right to, and authority over, the West Bank.

THREATS TO THE SOCIAL AND POLITICAL EQUILIBRIUM

Under Hussein's leadership, Jordan has known impressive domestic calm and economic growth since the traumatic period of readjustment in the years 1967–

71.[26] Hussein and his followers seem to have largely succeeded in repairing relations strained by the 1970–71 civil war and in achieving social integration. Such cohesion is all the more remarkable in light of two demographic facts: (1) Jordan's population has more than doubled in 20 years; and (2) this East Bank transformation derives from the influx in stages of West-Bank Palestinians, to the point that they now constitute 60 percent or more of the total population.[27]

Immediate Tasks

Having reached his present plateau by laboring to register social, diplomatic, and economic gains, Hussein has set the prevention of instability as his immediate goal in the 1980s, for while his policies have worked exceedingly well in recent years, beneath the surface calm certain unresolved issues and strains still exist both domestically and in foreign policy. Hussein is sensitive to the fragility of the recent equilibrium, and therefore maintains constant vigil against the spectre of a gradual or even sudden deterioration in the country's position.

Tensions accompanying the process of change at home are one definite source of concern for Hussein. First, there remains the problem of legitimacy in the Hashemite Kingdom, where the process of building state and nation is as yet incomplete and where Jordanian identity is still a fairly nebulous concept. There may be those, for instance, who deny the symbolic role of the royal house as the unifying agent; they view its members as alien and uninvited rulers who represent a small Hashemite minority or as reactionary agents. By exercising his royal prerogative, and by sticking to the centrist approach of accommodating both traditionalists and modernizers, Hussein, like the late shah of Iran, has unavoidably made enemies within his own realm.

Second, even though the traditionally loyal security forces built on a strong tribal base are acknowledged to provide the only ultimate insurance against overthrow of the monarchy, they too face several problems. Instances of barracks disloyalty are acknowledged to have taken place before. Insubordination has been discouraged, but at the price of concessions to the military by the king and his government.[28] As the army becomes less tribal and increasingly professional, resentment could grow in response to being used in domestic repression under the martial law apparatus. The potential for greater politicization of the armed forces is also reflected by the increasing numerical prominence within their ranks of Palestinian recruits. Such changes, when taken in the aggregate, make the army somewhat less reliable from the standpoint of the palace.

Third, the importance of tribal consciousness appears to be waning in the civilian sector as well. Replacing it are a variety of potentially explosive social conflicts under the heading of: rural–urban, north–south, royalist–leftist, and secular–religious.[29] Palestinian and other educated citizens, concentrated in and around the capital city of Amman, have had a genuine impact on the country's commercial and cultural life. Their support for Hussein, however, is not nearly as unconditional as that of the southern Bedouins. Loyalty is very much contingent upon King Hussein remaining at the helm, upon the continued protection of the monarchy, and upon material rewards. What might happen were any of these to be removed remains an open question.

Fourth, since for most Jordanians economic advantages and opportunity are a key in preserving internal stability, recent signs of an economic slowdown are also a matter of doubtless concern. The level of foreign remittances by Arab states and by Jordanian nationals employed in the Persian Gulf and elsewhere, began to decline by the time of the Lebanon crisis. Amman has become vulnerable to the recessionary effects of this substantial reduction in aid. No less worrisome is the possibility that many passport-carrying Jordanian citizens, finding themselves jobless and unwelcome in other Arab countries, have given thought to returning to the East Bank. Restless and more aware politically, this group could aggravate existing problems of unequal economic distribution and swell the numbers of unemployed, especially among the Palestinians.[30] Moreover, after the events of 1982, the PLO once again sought to replace Beirut with Amman as the operational center for its political and military activity. Increased Palestinian prominence in the life of Jordan can be expected to pose yet another potential source for destabilization of Jordan as well as of the border status quo with Israel, so long as the PLO leadership holds to an independent, militant course.

No issue has such potential for tearing apart the body politic reconstructed on the East Bank in the aftermath of the 1970 crisis as does the constant testing of Hussein's subjects in Amman and the adjacent refugee camps in terms of their true loyalty to the Hashemite crown and to the concept of a Jordanian entity. As tribalism continues to recede and is replaced by nationalism as the chief unifier, the ground is being laid for a clash between two competing and possibly antithetical nationalist allegiances: a Jordanian identity and a Palestinian one. To the extent that such a confrontation is forced out into the open, it could well threaten to expose Jordan as a divided society and a dual monarchy. So long as this issue remains dormant, East Bank Palestinians and their true political loyalties will remain the great enigma to the Hashemite Kingdom and the Jordanian political process.

Two auxiliary props which fall under the rubric of external affairs require ongoing attention and constant nurturing as well. One is Jordan's centrality in Arab world politics; the other is the international support it enjoys.[31] Appreciation for the political importance and strategic value of the country is in striking contrast to earlier periods of rejection, condemnation, or severe attack from different quarters, during which the kingdom was shaken by the crosscurrents of Arab and global politics.[32] This position has now reversed itself, as Jordan and its leaders have learned to ride the crest of Arab divisiveness and shifting alliances. Again, through a major diplomatic effort paralleling the one made on the domestic front, by the start of this decade Jordan came to be perceived by other Arab state actors as filling a multiple role.

Accordingly, King Hussein labored to preserve a special relationship with the

United States, and a positive image of the kingdom and himself in U.S. public opinion. Relations with Iraq and Saudi Arabia were also improved; and Amman showed a willingness to consider restoring ties with Egypt, opposition to the Camp David accords and the 1979 Israel-Egypt Treaty notwithstanding. Disconcerting to the Saudis, Iraqis, Egyptians, and Hashemites alike was the new threat by 1980 of Khomeinism, with its encouragement of revolution against conservative Sunni regimes in the Arab heartland. This shared concern, heightened by the Iran-Iraq war, gained further urgency with the intensification of the Lebanese conflict because of its potential for spreading instability and altering regional balances, particularly in relation to Syria, Israel, and the PLO.

These three political actors have always had special sensitivity for Hussein; even now, much of Jordanian diplomatic energy centers on preventing the ascendancy of any one of them. As we shall see, it is this threefold concern that informed immediate responses by Hussein to the crisis events that unfolded in late 1982. For the moment, however, it is worth keeping in mind that if Hussein's foreign policy is often compared to walking a tightrope, given the limits of his power and resources, the same analogy holds equally true for his domestic policies.[33] Internal–external linkages, in short, dictate a preoccupation with the most immediate, short-term, specific national tasks, yet this in no way precludes a clear conception of intermediate and even long-term objectives.

Strategic Goals

The king's advisers are agreed on at least three self-evident, permanent state interests. They fully realize that since the demise of the Arabian and Iraqi branches of the family, Jordan has no natural allies; it is the sole surviving representative of Hashemite dynastic ambitions and rulership. Hence, it is essential first, to ensure the physical survival and political sovereignty of Jordan as a state; second, to preserve its Hashemite character against those who argue that "Jordan is (or ought to be) Palestine"; and third, to accomplish both by eschewing boldness and avoiding extremes, thereby retaining for Jordan its present protected status, influence, and privileged position within regional alignments. This much is consensus.

Where differences appear is in how best to operationalize this strategy. In conceptual terms, Jordan's earlier history may have caught up with it. The 1921 initiative and period of the desert kingdom thrust Transjordan onto the center of the Middle East map and into a competitive Arab state system. The act of aggrandizement in 1948–49 implicated the Hashemites directly in a Palestinian problem that refuses to go away. Forfeiture of the West Bank in 1967 then set the stage for the present period, with its own challenges and imperatives.

How strongly, for example, ought Jordan to commit itself to the Palestinian quest for territorial liberation and political self-determination? Particularistic Hashemite goals, as confirmed throughout Jordan's history, do not exactly assign the highest priority to fulfilling (as opposed to espousing) the legitimate rights of the Palestinians. As a result, the Jordanian elite appears to be divided over the proper direction and means for the country to take in pursuing an overall strategy. Sets of contradictory poles are easily identifiable: for example, involvement versus disengagement on the Palestine question; seeking West Bank repossession or being content with East Bank consolidation; and perceiving Israel as a threat to the Arabs or a strategic ally of the kingdom. These remain the salient predicaments for Jordan as a state.

In sum, Jordanian policy expresses the interaction of a state, and its national interests and goals, with the general situation, be it one of crisis or non-crisis. However, if as the "individuals-as-actors" approach argues, individual leaders are a critical factor, this is particularly true of the Hashemite Kingdom. As mentioned at the outset, state and monarchy are so closely identified in Jordan that it is hard at times to distinguish between the institution and the person of the monarch.

This background may help to account for the pains that Hussein takes to keep open lines of communication with other Arab leaders (Mubarak of Egypt, Saudi Arabia's King Fahd, Iraqi strongman Saddam Hussein, and even Syria's President Hafez al-Assad) even as he keeps them at arm's length, always mindful of the element of distrust so prominent in recent Arab and Jordanian history.[34] It also explains why timidity is one of his more enduring characteristics.[35] Finally, it explains Hussein's noncommital policy in each of the four most recent military or diplomatic crises in the Middle East: the Yom Kippur war in 1973; the 1977 Sadat surprise dialogue with Israel; the 1982 Lebanese war; and the 1982 Reagan initiative.

FROM PERIPHERY TO CENTER STAGE

The crisis behavior of King Hussein and Jordan in 1982 was unexceptional in comparison with the equally marginal input of other leading Arab countries (like Egypt and Saudi Arabia) in easing the Lebanese tragedy or bringing the civil war to an end. Furthermore, the peripheral role played by Jordan in Lebanon was consistent with its performance in other Middle East crises, particularly over the last decade and a half.

Whether for reasons of necessity, expediency, or possibly both, Jordan and King Hussein sought to give the impression of real concern and direct involvement. The record, however, suggests otherwise. Policy toward Lebanon was esasentially defensive and declaratory, relying to a great extent on verbal or symbolic action. Jordan condemned military intervention and insisted on the prompt withdrawal from Lebanon of all armed forces, Syrian as well as Israeli, and even making this another precondition for any resumption of the Arab-Israeli peace process. Jordan also appealed for international aid to alleviate the human suffering, and participated in rounds of inter-Arab consultation aimed at a consensus on some form of mediation. Perhaps nothing better epitomizes the low degree of commitment by Jordan than Hussein's symbolic gesture of goodwill in August 1982, when he accepted 265 Palestinian fighters evacuated from Beirut instead of the 2,000 or more he had been asked to accept.[36]

Nevertheless, from the perspective of King Hussein and Jordan, the events of June through September 1982 posed a twofold threat. As guardians of the sensitive Middle East equilibrium which serves as the Hashemite Kingdom's best protection, they couldn't help but view with concern the deteriorating state of affairs in Lebanon. They were particularly nervous because the war reopened the question of the Palestinians' fate at a time when Jordanians continued to be uncertain themselves about the best course to follow on the issues of the West Bank and peace with Israel.

The significance of the Lebanese crisis for Jordan, and the leadership role shunned by Hussein, divides chronologically as well as politically into two distinct time frames: June 6 through August 31, 1982, and September 1 through April 10, 1983. The initial phase found Hussein in the position of a secondary or even tertiary actor, whereas in the weeks and months after September 1, he moved from the margins of the conflict in the Middle East to a place of centrality. While for some of the participants the crisis may have begun to abate by September, once the military moves shifted to a lower plateau and were superseded by diplomacy, the various pressures and risks conspired to produce for Hussein a more stressful situation. What brought about this dramatic transformation was the outline of a Middle East peace plan offered by the United States and President Reagan on September 1, which was premised on an unequivocal commitment by King Hussein.

June to September

In the first period of Israel's invasion, clash with the Syrians, and siege of Beirut, Hussein successfully pursued his preferred ''low-profile'' strategy, making any commitment contingent on a wider Arab consensus. Again, solely from the perspective of Jordan, there were several causes for concern.

First, Lebanon offered the disturbing precedent of ethnic strife leading to the subversion of a weaker Middle Eastern country by stronger neighbors, in clear violation of its sovereignty and borders. Second, the ineffectual Arab response reminded Jordan's ruler of how unrealistic it would be for him ever to premise the security of his country on Arab League protection. Third, Hussein was concerned that the Begin government might adopt an alleged ''Sharon plan'' by seeking to divert and redirect a PLO displaced from Lebanon toward the East Bank, with the ultimate aim of bringing about the ''Palestinization'' of Jordan. Finally, the king was leery of an imperialistic Syria. Were the Assad regime to consolidate its position by dominating Lebanon, the fear was that it might then feel emboldened to turn against Jordan with the dream of achieving a ''Greater Syria.''[37]

While genuine, these concerns were more in the nature of long-term contingencies, whereas the trend by late August in Lebanon was not without salutary, immediate gains for Jordanian policy. It could be argued that Israeli credibility, enhanced by what then seemed an effective demonstration of force, indirectly strengthened Jordan's security against Syrian military encroachment. Again, in terms of Syria and Jordan, Damascus was too deeply involved in Lebanon to concentrate on intimidating its neighbor to the south or diverting troops, thereby conceivably providing Hussein with a greater degree of diplomatic latitude.

The direct benefits were clear. The first was that Assad and the Syrian army had suffered a military setback inflicted by Israel in June. The second benefit followed from the first. The Kremlin was thrown on the defensive. Above all was the third benefit of a now demoralized PLO. More than anything else, the military action by Israel meant the loss of Lebanon as a territorial base of operations. Politically, Arafat and the Palestinians were dependent as never before on the goodwill and good offices of the Hashemites. To Hussein this also implied that were he able to play his few cards well, the prospect now existed for the first time since 1974 of revoking the PLO insistence on sole representation.

That this new opportunity and improved Jordanian political fortunes arose at all from the ruins of Beirut is noteworthy in itself. Even more impressive is that it was accomplished during July and August without King Hussein really having to do anything; it was all done by others and required no tangible commitment by Amman. If the Hashemites said little during the height of the crisis, they did even less. Jordan committed itself only to the bare minimum of what seemed necessary or expedient, such as condemnation of Israel, expressing regret at the bloodshed, and voicing solidarity with the plight of the Palestinians.[38] Even the admission into Jordan on August 22 of the 265 guerrilla fighters, instead of the 2,000 or more he had been asked to absorb, has to be regarded in this context as a token gesture by King Hussein.[39] The Reagan peace initiative changed all this, however, for it put Hussein in a compromising position in more than one sense.

Hussein's Diplomatic Crisis

By the end of August 1982, the general situation surrounding Lebanon seemed favorable for an initiative by Washington. The conflict offered definite signs of having entered into a postcrisis phase. The safe exit of the last PLO resistance fighters from Beirut had been successfully negotiated, and the stature of both the PLO and Arafat had been appreciably reduced. Leaders in Damascus and Moscow would be preoccupied for some time to come with damage assessment of their respective policies and joint relationship. Israeli security concerns on its northern border certainly seemed satisfied, and the Lebanese appeared to be on their way to effecting a national reconciliation under the strong leadership of Bashir Gemayel.

At that opportune moment, the Reagan administration sought to convert the Lebanese tragedy into a positive gain by inducing movement on the comprehensive Arab-Israel dispute. In taking the unprecedented step of volunteering a detailed plan of its own for resolving the conflict, the White House focused on the centrality of Jordan. The working premises at each stage of formulating the new policy emphasized: (1) the critical need to overcome Hussein's well-known reluctance to become directly involved; and (2) the excellent chance that with an explicit pledge of U.S. support, Hussein's consent for the proposals and firm commitment to be a direct, active participant would be forthcoming. Both considerations explain the clear reference in the Reagan plan to a pro-Jordan solution. Following the withdrawal by Israel from the territories negotiated with Jordan, the final disposition and status of the West Bank and Gaza would be resolved through their being governed in close association with the Hashemite Kingdom of Jordan.[40] Never before had Jordanian claims or dominance, in direct opposition to the idea of a separate Palestinian state, been stated so categorically.

On the surface, such U.S. assurances should have been most welcome in Amman. Indeed, in a sense they were viewed as both flattering and gratifying. Nevertheless, to King Hussein, such an open invitation to seize the opportunity for achieving the maximum goal of restoring Hashemite rule over the West Bank had the immediate effect of placing him squarely in the center spotlight. This sudden prominence represented something of a mixed blessing, forcing Jordan out of the shadows; or, as the *Wall Street Journal* phrased it at the time: the Palestinian defeat in Lebanon thrust Jordan "back into the hot seat of Middle East politics."[41]

Just as it would be inaccurate to describe Jordanian officials as ungrateful, so is it wrong to say that they were caught entirely by surprise. Since the element of surprise is generally regarded as one of the essential characteristics of international crises, it is important to note that King Hussein had ample reason and sufficient warning to anticipate a move by Washington. One of the first to grasp the potential for a wider diplomatic response to the Lebanese crisis was Henry Kissinger. As early as the tenth day of the fighting, the *Washington Post* published an article by the former secretary of state in which he urged the United States to lead with decisiveness and imagination. Specifically, he wrote of Jordan:

So far King Hussein has stood aside, conscious of his vulnerability, reluctant to bear the brunt of fighting the PLO and of resisting Syrian pressures, frankly dubious of America's understanding of the issues or its resolve to deal with them.

Following this sympathetic appraisal of Jordan's delicate position, Kissinger went on:

But he [Hussein] is much too wise to wish for a PLO state on the West Bank whose initial objective must be his overthrow. And he is much too shrewd not to recognize that the PLO defeat in Lebanon and the demonstration of the limits of Syrian willingness to run risks have given him a window of perhaps two years to take charge of his future.[42]

In addition, efforts by the Reagan administration to stiffen Hussein's resolve led U.S. officials to consult personally with the king during the late summer of

1982.[43] They emerged from these meetings with the distinct impression that Hussein was favorably inclined and would endorse the initiative shortly after its public announcement by the president of the United States.

Then, after a seemingly auspicious beginning, Hussein wavered as the full extent of his predicament became apparent. Even at the risk of inviting U.S. disappointment and impatience, his first sensitivity was to the strenuous opposition expected within Arab circles. The former could be countered by invoking U.S. understanding, and especially by citing the culpability of others: Israel, extremist Arabs, and Arafat. However, Arab critics could only be mollified by moving slowly, by carefully planning each and every tactical move, and by offering assurances that Jordan would continue to operate within the Arab fold.

Intimations of resistance were immediately forthcoming, each acting as a reminder of Hussein's—and Jordan's—vulnerability. Libya and Syria were outspoken in condemning the U.S. plan, and in labeling as traitors any Arab leader who would dare to defect from the Arab resistance front against Israel; this message was clearly received in Amman. Nor was the Israeli government prepared to make Hussein's task any easier by pledging territorial concessions in advance of peace negotiations; indeed, Premier Begin promptly and summarily dismissed the plan out of hand. Moreover, in December, Hussein headed a nine-member Arab delegation to Moscow; there he had to suffer the indignity of having Yuri Andropov denounce the Reagan proposals as "aimed at splitting the Arab countries in order to impose on them decisions beneficial only to Israel and the United States . . . and . . . to prevent the creation of an independent Palestinian state."[44] The Soviet leader was diplomatic enough not to mention the potential benefits for Jordan. Still, Soviet determination to oppose the peace initiative was conveyed to the king in no uncertain terms.

Besides, Hussein was preoccupied on a different front: bilateral Hashemite-PLO relations. To the extent that his earlier optimism owed to an assessment of Palestinian impotence in the wake of Beirut, and hence a softening of PLO intransigence, the king was proven wrong once more. After a series of deliberations in February 1983, both among the PLO constituent groupings and in bilateral conversations between Arafat and Hussein, the Palestine National Council rejected the Reagan plan on various grounds. Among these was the fact that it denied Palestinian statehood; also, as one senior PLO official explained, there was strong opposition to granting Jordan and the king a proxy to negotiate in their stead.[45] In a subsequent interview, Arafat himself stressed two points of major objection: first, "It is unacceptable to ask to delegate our authority of representing the Palestinian people to anybody else;" and second, "It is unacceptable to become a province of somebody else's government."[46] The inferences to Jordan here are unmistakable.

This multiplicity of negative factors or disincentives explain why King Hussein wavered. Upon circulation of the Reagan plan, one palace spokesman commented: "The president has put the Palestinian issue into a Jordanian context and given us a pivotal role. We like that, but it causes problems."[47] This overriding sentiment was even better described by the perceptive U.S.-Arab expert on the Middle East, Fouad Ajami: "From its inception in the 1920s the desert kingdom has had a difficult and tangled relationship with the Palestinian world to its west. It coveted that world and feared it."[48] Summarizing conversations with high officials in Amman in February 1983, Ajami reported, "men in Jordan must again worry and wonder, men in Jordan know that the passions of the Palestinian issue can kill." He found that "in Jordan men have to be persuaded that powers from afar and other Arabs and Palestinians asking them to take on the burden of Palestine are not inviting them to participate in their own ruin."

By this logic, any genuine search for Arab-Israeli peace inherently poses a deep crisis for Hussein and Jordan. In 1982, each voice of opposition to Jordanian emulation of Egypt reminded the king that neither he nor his country had ever been, or was soon likely to be, a free agent. However well intentioned and predisposed, the Reagan plan confronted the Hashemites with the limits of the possible, as the golden opportunity came to be nullified by countervailing political risks.

In the end, Hussein refused to be entangled. He also refused to be stampeded. Having diligently mended his political fences, the Jordanian leader was not yet prepared—nor could he afford—to climb down off the fence and join the United States and Israel in providing the Middle East peace-making process with renewed momentum.

That judgment having been made, the challenge for King Hussein lay in extricating Jordan from an awkward and stressful situation that was not of the country's own making. To do this, in March 1983 he adopted a mixed strategy: to make clear Jordan's ultimate commitment to peace, but also to remain ambiguous over precise procedural and substantive issues. As part of this strategy, the Jordanian government attached fresh preconditions before it could take the first but really critical step. Besides requiring total Israeli withdrawal, not only from southern Lebanon but also from the entire West Bank and Gaza under the principle of "peace for territory," Amman insisted on receiving from Washington detailed guarantees of an Israeli freeze on settlements.[49]

On top of this, King Hussein knowingly stipulated that Jordan would not move without first being given both inter-Arab and PLO endorsement, even though it was obvious as early as September 1982 that no such consensus existed or could be crafted. The idea, however, was quite simple: to absolve the Jordanians of all responsibility and guilt for the present failure. At the same time, the blame had to be assigned to other parties for refusing to give Hussein the all-important mandate. Finally, after showing good form in persisting with a Jordanian-PLO dialogue, the Jordanian cabinet, at a meeting presided over by His Majesty King Hussein himself, issued a long, carefully worded communiqué on April 10, 1983, explaining Jordan's refusal to endorse the U.S. initiative. The text of the document reviews efforts by Jordan on behalf of the Arab cause, and ends by asserting the intention of Jordan, in light of the no-war and no-peace situation, to take "all steps necessary to safeguard our national security in all its dimensions." Accordingly,

We leave it to the P.L.O. and to the Palestinian people to choose the ways and means for the salvation of themselves and their land, and for the realization of their declared aims in the manner they see fit.[50]

As of 1988, the Jordanian strategy executed by King Hussein during the Lebanese crisis has proved successful, but in a limited sense. It has not enabled repossession of the West Bank by Jordan. It has not dispensed with the ever-present Palestinian quandary. Nor has it resulted in a full peace with Israel. But then the very essence of Hussein's approach to Middle East politics has always been to avoid confrontation and especially crises, imposing as they do the necessity for clear, unambiguous choice. Quite possibly this is Jordan's larger contribution to the study of leadership. The true test of a crisis leader lies, from the very beginning, in preempting the crisis and in taking evasive action in order to be spared the costs of a showdown.

In the case of King Hussein, satisficing has prevailed over the logic of maximizing. Owing to this realism, translated into a subtle strategy of elegant evasiveness, Jordan, for the present, continues to enjoy internal stability, to retain a foothold in the Israeli-administered territories, and to be at the center of Middle East diplomacy. True, the credibility of Jordan and of King Hussein personally as the key to a U.S.-brokered peace breakthrough may not have emerged completely unscathed in the post-Lebanon period. What really matters, though, is that the Hashemite Kingdom of Jordan remains a viable actor. Given its vulnerabilities, this is no small feat.

NOTES

1. Jordan's origins are detailed in Aaron S. Klieman, *Foundations of British Policy in the Arab World* (Baltimore: The Johns Hopkins Press, 1970). Subsequent political development of the East Bank is dealt with by Uriel Dann, *Studies in the History of Transjordan, 1920–1949* (Boulder and London: Westview Press, 1984).

2. The only countries to recognize Abdullah's unilateral annexation of territories were Great Britain and Pakistan.

3. On Hashemite policies toward the Palestinians in the conquered West Bank, see Joel S. Migdal, ed. *Palestinian Society and Politics* (Princeton: Princeton University Press, 1980); Shaul Mishal, *West Bank/East Bank* (New Haven: Yale University Press, 1978); and Avi Plascov, *The Palestinian Refugees in Jordan, 1948–1957* (London: Frank Cass, 1981).

4. Hussein's earlier crises are recalled in Benjamin Shwadran, *Jordan: A State in Tension* (New York: Council for Middle East Affairs, 1959).

5. Paul A. Jureidini and Ronald D. McLaurin, "The Hashemite Kingdom of Jordan," in *Lebanon in Crisis*, ed. P. Edward Haley and Lewis W. Snider (Syracuse: Syracuse University Press, 1979), p. 150.

6. *Uneasy Lies the Head, The Autobiography of His Majesty King Hussein I* (New York: Random House, 1962), p. 13. He adds, "So too, had the manner of his death."

7. According to popular versions of the assassination, and by Hussein's own account, he was spared the same fate when a bullet aimed at him was deflected by a medal on his chest.

8. Hussein, *Uneasy Lies the Head*, p. 9.

9. The Zarqa episode is related in Richard F. Nyrop, ed., *Jordan: A Country Study* (Washington: Foreign Area Studies, The American University, 1980), p. 31.

10. Almost all the analysis of the 1970 crisis is from an American perspective. See William B. Quandt, *Decade of Decisions* (Berkeley: University of California Press, 1977), and Henry Kissinger, *White House Years* (Boston: Little, Brown and Company, 1979).

11. Hussein's 1972 federation scheme is reprinted in *The Arab-Israeli Conflict*, ed. John Norton Moore (Princeton: Princeton University Press, 1977), pp. 814–21.

12. Sadat's visceral distrust of Hussein is commented on by Henry Kissinger, *Years of Upheaval*, (London: Weidenfeld & Nicolson, 1982), p. 1140. Kissinger notes also the mutual personal distrust, p. 219, and is supported in this by Moshe Zak in his enlightening article, "A Survey of Israel's Contacts with Jordan," in *Israel in the Middle East*, ed. Itamar Rabinovich and Jehuda Reinharz (New York: Oxford University Press, 1984), pp. 337–41.

13. One of the worst tragedies was the death of his third wife, Alia, in a helicopter crash.

14. On Amman's foreign policy since Rabat, see Adam M. Garfinkle, "Negotiating By Proxy: Jordanian Foreign Policy and U.S. Options in the Middle East," *Orbis* 24, no. 4 (Winter 1981): 847–80.

15. Hussein, *Uneasy Lies the Head*, p. 110.

16. Judith Miller, "Excerpts from Interview with the King of Jordan," *The New York Times*, March 15, 1984.

17. Hussein, *Uneasy Lies the Head*, p. 36.

18. Ibid., p. 247.

19. Ibid., p. 306.

20. Judith Miller, "King Hussein's Delicate Balance," *The New York Times Magazine*, April 22, 1984, p. 24.

21. Hussein's family history reveals a pattern of mental disorders and depression going back to his great-grandfather the Sharif Hussein of Mecca, and including his own father, Talal, who was forced to abdicate because of schizophrenic behavior. See James Morris, *The Hashemite Kings* (New York: Pantheon Books, 1959).

22. This theme of the "last chance for peace" was underlined by King Hussein during his visit to Washington in May 1985, including remarks on the White House lawn following a meeting with President Reagan on May 29. Text courtesy of the Jordan Information Bureau.

23. He used this approach in capitulating to the 1974 Rabat summit conference resolution on P.L.O. representation.

24. Hussein, *Uneasy Lies the Head*, p. 6.

25. In an interview with Karen Elliott House, "Hussein's Decision: Fear for His Kingdom, Sense of History Drove Monarch to Seek Peace," *The Wall Street Journal*, April 15, 1983.

26. Three useful surveys of Jordanian contemporary society and politics are Peter Gubser, *Jordan: Crossroads of Middle Eastern Events* (London: Croom Helm, 1983),

Arthur R. Day, *East Bank/West Bank* (New York: Council on Foreign Relations, 1986), and Robert B. Satloff, *Troubles on the East Bank: Challenges to the Domestic Stability of Jordan* (New York: Praeger, 1986).

27. From 900,800 people in Jordan proper in 1961, by 1980 the figure rose to 2,223,000. See Ali S. Zoghal, "Social Change in Jordan," *Middle Eastern Studies* 20, no. 4 (October 1984); 53, citing U.N. and Jordanian sources.

28. On the Jordanian armed forces, see P. J. Vatikiotis, *Politics and the Military in Jordan* (London: Frank Cass & Co., 1967). A more recent profile of the army is in Nyrop, *Jordan*, in ch. 5, "National Security." The role of the tribes in the functioning of the monarchy and government as well as of the army and the society-at-large is the theme of a recent monograph by Paul A. Jureidini and R. D. McLaurin, *Jordan: The Impact of Social Change on the Role of the Tribes*, Washington Paper no. 108, (New York: Praeger Publishers, 1984).

29. These diversities are set forth in Nabeel A. Khoury, "Leadership in Crisis: A Comparative Study of Lebanon (1975–1979) and Jordan (1970–1971)," in *Leadership and Development in Arab Society*, ed. Fuad I. Khuri (Beirut: American University of Beirut, 1981), pp. 105–8.

30. Nasser H. Aruri and Samih Farsoun, "Palestinian Communities and Arab Host Countries," in *The Sociology of the Palestinians*, ed. Khalil Nakhleh and Elia Zureik (London: Croom Helm, 1980), p. 118.

31. The author has argued that tacit functional understandings with Israel are maintained by Jordan, such as the open bridges policy and policing of the borders. See Aaron S. Klieman, *Israel-Jordan-Palestine: The Search for a Durable Peace* (Berkeley: Sage Publications and the Georgetown University Center for Strategic and International Studies, 1981).

32. On the nature of Arab political dynamics at the interstate level, see Malcolm H. Kerr, *The Arab Cold War, 1958–1967*, 2d edition. (London: Oxford University Press, 1967); and Michael C. Hudson, *Arab Politics* (New Haven: Yale University Press, 1977). The effects on Jordan are surveyed in M. Graeme Bannerman, "The Hashemite Kingdom of Jordan," in *The Government and Politics of the Middle East and North Africa*, ed. David E. Long and Bernard Reich (Boulder: Westview Press, 1980).

33. In his autobiographical *Years of Upheaval*, Henry Kissinger likens Jordan to a "precarious balancing act" (p. 217).

34. One of the explanations given for refusals by Hussein to commit himself is the retaliatory actions expected of other Arab countries: the Saudis would cut off financial assistance—about $1 billion a year in direct and indirect aid; the moderate Arab regimes might isolate and boycott Amman; Palestinian terrorism inside the country would be incited from outside; and the militant Syrian regime might even stage an invasion.

35. This is described, for example, in "The Man Who Wouldn't Be King," *The New Republic*, November 29, 1982, p. 8.

36. Jordanian reactions to the war in Lebanon are described by Asher Susser in his essay, "Jordan," in *Middle East Contemporary Survey*, vol. 6, ed. Colin Legum, Haim Shaked, and Daniel Dishon (New York: Holmes & Meier, 1984), esp. pp. 680–81, 685.

37. In November-December 1980, the two countries were poised on the brink of war as Syria deployed an estimated three divisions on its border with Jordan. Details in Mark Heller, ed., *The Military Balance in the Middle East* (Tel-Aviv: Yediot Aharonot, 1983), pp. 28–31; Anthony H. Cordesman, *Jordanian Arms and the Middle East Balance* (Washington, D.C.: Middle East Institute, 1983), pp. 3, 39, 183.

38. Mordechai Gazit, "The Middle East Process," pp. 207–10, and Aslar Susser, "The Palestine Liberation Organization," pp. 342–44, and "Jordan," pp. 675–99, all in *The Middle East Contemporary Survey*, vol. 6.

39. David Ignatius, "Jordan's Hussein Welcomes Some of PLO, but Fears Further Instability to Region," *The Wall Street Journal*, August 10, 1982, p. 30.

40. Official text of the Reagan peace proposals, compliments of the United States Information Service in Tel-Aviv.

41. Ignatius, "Jordan's Hussein Welcomes Some of PLO," *The Wall Street Journal*, August 10, 1982, p. 30.

42. *The Washington Post*, June 17, 1982.

43. Consultations both in Washington and between administration emissaries and other concerned or sympathetic parties are traced in Aaron S. Klieman, "Origins and Assumptions of the Reagan Middle East Initiative," *Crossroads* 10 (Spring 1983): 5–29.

44. U.P.I. report, "Andropov in Meeting with Arabs, Assails U.S. Plan for Middle East," *International Herald Tribune*, December 4–5, 1982, p. 2.

45. PNC (Palestine National Congress) members' comments reported in "P.L.O. Calls Reagan's Proposal Unacceptable," *The New York Times*, February 22, 1983.

46. Quotes by Arafat taken from an interview with him that appeared in "The Desirable, the Possible, the Acceptable," *Middle East* no. 108 (May 1983): 23.

47. Reported in the *International Herald Tribune*, September 6, 1982.

48. Fouad Ajami, "A Cautious Monarch Amid the Passions of Palestine," *International Herald Tribune*, February 23, 1983, p. 5.

49. The claim that Hussein received American pledges appears in the *International Herald Tribune*, March 31, 1983.

50. Text of government communiqué reprinted in the series of Middle East documents printed by the Foreign Broadcast Information Service, "Cabinet Issues Communique on Talks with PLO," vol. 11 (FBIS), April 11, 1983, pp. F1–F7.

8

SAUDI ARABIA'S KING KHALED AND KING FAHD

David Pollock

GENERAL BACKGROUND

The modern kingdom of Saudi Arabia was exactly half a century old when Israel invaded Lebanon in 1982. Throughout the entire period of its existence, both the authoritarian internal political structure and the basic, pro-Western foreign policy orientation of the monarchy were preserved remarkably intact, despite two generations of upheaval in the surrounding area. Common to both internal and external Saudi policies during this entire period—and responsible in part for the large measure of stability and continuity in the kingdom's political life— was an important overlay of Islamic outlook and practice. Still, in the foreign policy arena, Islam has tended to influence actual policy only on the margins or in the public presentation of the Saudi position.[1]

Much more important in practice has been the constant if generally low-key struggle of Saudi leaders to maintain the kingdom's security against the perceived twin evils of Zionism and Communism. More specifically, the major task was to resist the potentially destabilizing consequences that might result from Soviet and radical (leftist, pro-Soviet, or socially revolutionary) Arab "exploitation" of the unresolved Arab-Israeli conflict. From 1956 through 1970, Nasser's brand of pan-Arabism was the primary threat of this type. More recently, after a relatively brief spell of enhanced Saudi influence and an overall sense of security in the mid–1970s, a whole complex of related new concerns has arisen at home, in the war-torn Gulf, and in the Arab-Israeli arena. These concerns have become an added focus of Saudi attention and apprehension.

The stage for Saudi Arabia's emergence as a regional power was set by the fateful decision of King Feisal to participate in the politically motivated oil

The views expressed in this chapter are purely the author's personal views and are not necessarily those of USIA or any other government agency.

embargo of 1973, and to go along with the concomitant OPEC (Organization of Petroleum Exporting Countries) pressures for ever-higher oil prices. These steps gave Saudi Arabia a respite from nationalist agitation and even a claim to some leadership in the Arab world, but they also entangled the country much more deeply in the turbulent politics of the region and threatened to unleash social forces that could ultimately elude the kingdom's control. To be sure, the monarchy survived Feisal's assassination in 1975, and even prospered for a time by continuing his comparatively ambitious foreign and domestic policies. However, by the late 1970s and early 1980s—in other words, by the time of the Lebanon war—a succession of crises had jeopardized Saudi ability to maintain a leadership role. These crises included, in rapid succession, Sadat's "defection" from Arab ranks; the Islamic revolution in (and threat of its export from) Iran; renewed problems of instability in the Yemens and on the Horn of Africa, in Saudi Arabia's "backyard"; the Soviet invasion of Afghanistan; the outbreak, intensification, and increasingly unfavorable course of the Iran-Iraq war; the continuing inability of the United States to deal effectively, as the Saudis viewed things, with most of these crises; and, finally, the beginning of the international "oil glut" that gradually reduced the kingdom's ability to maneuver among all these issues.[2]

Fundamentals of Saudi Foreign Policy

The essential problem of Saudi foreign policy has been an imbalance in the resources of power at its command; simply put, the kingdom lacks the advantages of a large and loyal population and military establishment in an area increasingly in turmoil. Massive petrodollar subsidies to Egypt, Syria, Iraq, North Yemen, Jordan, the PLO (Palestine Liberation Organization), and other regional contenders (despite, or in a few cases actually because of, the antipathy of some of these "clients" toward each other) have afforded the Saudis some leverage or at least protection in this context. However, oil wealth has at the same time made them the envy and the target of political pressures from more aggressive regimes.[3] Increasingly, the dictates of geography, of spreading regional conflicts, of modern mass communications even in a tightly controlled society, and to some extent also of Islamic and Arab nationalist ideologies—along with some of the earlier choices made by Saudi Arabia's own leaders—have drawn the kingdom deeper into this unstable Mideast vortex. This has occurred even as the Saudis have perforce maintained their Western and particularly U.S. protective connections of last resort.

In attempting to manage these cross-pressures, Saudi Arabia has been neither the omnipotent behind-the-scenes player that many observers claimed to discern in the mid–1970s, nor the "pitiful, helpless giant" that was "virtually enthralled to Syria" that other analysts claimed to see a decade later.[4] Rather, as is so often the case in the Middle East, the truth lies somewhere in between. All during this period, the favored Saudi strategy has been one of avoiding impossible choices by promoting an Arab consensus that the kingdom could live with—on more or less favorable terms, and with varying but always partial measures of success and failure. The favored vehicles for implementing this strategy have included a series of pan-Arab meetings at or just below the summit level; the new forum provided by the Gulf Cooperation Council (GCC) since 1981; a consultative grouping of the Saudis and their five smaller, neighboring, and conservative oil-rich monarchies; and always, in keeping with the Saudi style, a succession of discreet bilateral contacts with both Arab and other interlocutors. The other side of Saudi Arabia's search for consensus has been eternal vigilance against the possibility of an effective but hostile Arab coalition. However, this possibility has been exaggerated by some outside observers, for the depth and breadth of inter-Arab divisions makes a united anti-Saudi front a most unlikely prospect.[5]

Insofar as Lebanon and broader Arab-Israeli issues are concerned, the long-term Saudi strategy has been one of reliance on Washington to pursue a regional settlement on acceptable terms. The hope was that this would defuse the conflict and the variety of indirect threats it posed to Saudi security. In the short term, however, the Saudi leadership has typically taken refuge behind the search for an Arab consensus on these issues. Moreover, Riyadh has mortgaged its long-term goal to the more immediate task.

Thus, in part because it was able to obtain Syrian approval, Saudi Arabia offered indirect political and financial support for Kissinger's step-by-step Arab-Israeli disengagement diplomacy in the wake of the October War (1973–75). The Saudis did likewise for the early Carter administration's effort to reconvene a Geneva conference with the PLO's blessing, which was aimed at a comprehensive Arab-Israeli peace. However, after the September 1978 Camp David accords, in the face of Arab and now also Iranian objections and pressures, Riyadh abruptly abandoned Crown Prince Fahd's last-ditch effort to maintain policy coordination with Washington. Instead, the Saudis reluctantly subscribed to the new Arab consensus, consecrated at the first and second Baghdad summits. This consensus condemned Camp David and the resulting Egyptian-Israeli peace treaty, and vowed to ostracize the "traitorous" Sadat regime.[6]

In all the years since, the Saudis have continued to defer to an essentially negative Arab consensus on Arab-Israeli issues, while fitfully attempting to push that consensus toward acceptance of a negotiated settlement of the festering Arab-Israeli dispute. In the meantime, Riyadh has largely confined its efforts to interceding with Washington to restrain the Israelis during moments of crisis, and to mediating missions aimed at repairing Syria's badly frayed relations with all the other Arab actors in this desultory drama: Jordan, the PLO, and, more distantly, Iraq. Of course, ever since the outbreak of the Iran-Iraq war in September 1980, and even more so since the invaded Iranians began to turn the tide back to their favor a year later, Saudi attention has understandably been concentrated on other dangers much closer to home. At the same time, on Arab-Israeli issues, the Saudis continue to point to the resolution they successfully promoted at the second Fez Arab summit in September 1982, in the immediate aftermath of the war in Lebanon. That resolution endorses both an independent PLO state and security guarantees for all the other states in the region—implicitly including Israel, so Saudi spokesmen say in private conversation.

In pursuing this characteristically ambiguous policy, the leading—in fact, practically the only—national actors on the Saudi side have of course been the senior princes of the ruling Saud dynasty, with the king generally holding the responsibility for achieving a working agreement among rival royal family factions and tactical policy orientations. In this sense, the Saudis' search for consensus abroad has been paralleled by their continual search for a foreign policy consensus at home.

Saudi Leading National Actors, and Social and Political System

A full discussion of the Saudi political system is obviously beyond the scope of this essay; in fact, even a detailed analysis of what is conventionally labeled a country's "foreign policy establishment" is largely irrelevant here. This is not just a matter of scope and focus, but of the reality of Saudi policy making, so far as it can be understood from the outside. Especially on critical foreign policy issues, the organizations, bureaucratic bargains, standard operating procedures, interest groups, and the like, that may be pertinent elsewhere, are simply not significant in Saudi Arabia—or at least much less significant than in other, more democratic or more institutionalized states. Rather, in this unusual case, a bit of unavoidable oversimplification actually captures the essense of the matter: Saudi foreign policy is what the royal family says it is.

In emphasizing the autocratic character of the Saudi system, some analysts go on to argue that it inevitably gives individual leaders a more than usually decisive role.[7] To be sure, middle-class Saudi technocrats have so far remained remarkably apolitical; even cabinet-level commoners (emphatically including the redoubtable former oil minister Shaykh Ahmad Zaki al-Yamani), let alone working-level bureaucrats, may be and actually have been ignored, overridden, or even threatened with dismissal almost at will by the royal family. Even the *ulema*, the official Islamic clergy, can routinely be coopted, divided, or mobilized to legitimate a royal decision that is already a *fait accompli*, or perhaps to disregard it if necessary.[8] To this extent, then, individual Saudi leaders are nearly free from the normal procedural and policy constraints of governance.

All this is not to say that the king has a completely free hand. That is precluded by the sheer size of the royal family, composed as it is of some 4,000 adult males and several score of senior princes with key positions in the government or the military, or considerable informal influence. The family is thus almost literally a class by itself, and its contending factions, personal rivalries, and policy differences must be adroitly managed in order to arrive at the requisite degree of policy consensus.[9] The process by which this is accomplished remains rather mysterious, nothwithstanding some recent heroic research efforts; and it is, almost by its very nature, difficult to generalize about.[10] In this essay, reference will be made as appropriate to the dynamics of this problem only as it impinged upon Saudi policy in Lebanon, bearing in mind two things: that this is probably the crucial internal dimension of Saudi leadership, or lack thereof, in the international arena; and that information about it is notoriously unreliable or incomplete.

In addition, there is one other feature of the Saudi system that merits brief mention here. Precisely to the extent that this system can be an effective vehicle for forceful individual leadership in foreign policy (assuming family politics are properly managed), it can also be undermined or at least threatened by external pressures for a more "progressive" or even a more "Islamic" political structure and policy orientation. In other words, foreign affairs can affect Saudi domestic politics, and not just vice versa; Saudi leaders must be acutely aware of the internal implications of whatever foreign policy course they choose to pursue. Any policy departure, in particular, that could provoke charges abroad (and potential echoes at home) that Saudi rulers were insufficiently Islamic or Arab nationalist—or overly pro-United States—would have to be very carefully considered, to say the least. This tension created by the "built-in" structural preconditions for both individual initiative and systemic vulnerability helps to define the royal margin for maneuver in international affairs.

Finally, one last general comment about internal aspects of Saudi international leadership is in order. A recent and well-regarded analysis of Saudi Arabia's "ceaseless quest for security" argues that a large part of the blame for the country's straitened circumstances and reduced leadership role lately must be laid at the door of a decline in the quality, and therefore also the unity, of Saudi leadership since the death of King Feisal.[11] It is probably correct to note that neither of his two successors to the throne exhibited the same imposing personal presence, even if that much-abused epithet "charismatic" is patently incongruous when applied to Faisal's dour countenance. However, the question of how much of Saudi Arabia's recent partial eclipse as a leading regional power is due to personal factors, and how much to external circumstances—or, to put it differently, which of these problems came first—is obviously a complicated and subtle one.

I will suspend judgment on this question until after an examination of the leadership of Faisal's successors on Lebanese issues. Suffice it for now to note that the full measure of Faisal's success awaited external events over which he had little or no control: Nasser's crushing defeat by Israel in 1967, his untimely death three years later, and the global oil shortage that soon followed. Khaled and Fahd, by contrast, had the misfortune to ascend the Saudi throne just as a much less favorable constellation of outside forces—a revolution in Iran, and before too long a worldwide oil glut—was in the ascendant. With these comments in mind, we can proceed to a more detailed look at the personal leadership of these last two Saudi kings in the unstable environment they inherited from their illustrious predecessor.

THE LEADER AS A PERSON

The analysis of Saudi leadership during the 1982 crisis in Lebanon is complicated by two factors: first, King Khaled died and was succeeded by his half-brother Fahd in mid-June, at the very height of the Lebanese war; and second, more fundamentally, very little is known about the invariably secretive Saudi decision-making process during this or any other crisis, or even about the personal characteristics of various Saudi leaders. In somewhat different ways, Khaled and Fahd shared a commitment to personal leadership of the unique Islamic-dynastic legacy they were bequeathed by their father, King Abdul Aziz Ibn Saud. They also shared a commitment to the preservation of this apparently anachronistic organism through selective adaptation to changing circumstances and political winds. Their mechanisms of informal consultation and consensus building within the royal family, virtually to the exclusion of outsiders where critical matters of foreign policy were concerned, were likewise broadly similar.

There were also conspicuous differences in the personal background and operational style of the two kings. Khaled was more retiring, more frail of health, more traditional, and more isolated from affairs of state. Fahd, by contrast, had long been groomed for an active political role in a succession of important ministries and diplomatic missions. He was more ambitious, energetic, and outspoken than Khaled; he was also much more attuned, as a matter both of national policy preference and of personal predilection, to economic and technological modernization, to U.S. connection, and to Western ways (including, for example, an occasional attraction to gambling). As crown prince under Khaled, Fahd was widely assumed, with some justice, to be the real power behind the throne.

Biographical Background on King Khaled

Khaled ibn Abd al-Aziz, whose fate it was to preside over the first stages of Saudi policy in the Lebanese war, was 63 years old and in frail health when he assumed the throne upon the assassination of his half-brother, King Faisal, in March 1975. Khaled's right of succession was virtually assured, since he had been designated crown prince a decade earlier in the course of the intensive royal family consultations surrounding Faisal's replacement of Saud as king. Nevertheless, Khaled was widely believed to have neither the temperament nor the training to be more than a figurehead monarch. Most observers assumed, based in part on Khaled's almost entirely passive performance as crown prince, that even as king he would continue to reign rather than rule. The reasons for this widespread (although, as we shall see, somewhat flawed) assumption related both to Khaled's personality and to his earlier, and very scanty, political career.[12]

Contrary to popular impression, Khaled's past was not totally devoid of political or diplomatic experience. As a young man in his 20s and 30s, Khaled had been personally involved in several diplomatic episodes on behalf of the fledgling Saudi state. He led an official reconciliation mission to Yemen in 1935, and he was reportedly a favorite travelling companion of the future king Feisal on the latter's frequent diplomatic missions, including the founding conference of the United Nations in San Francisco a decade later. In addition to the United States and Britain, Khaled visited Germany at least once during this period; according to one account, he actually dined with Hitler just after the latter's diplomatic triumph at Munich in 1938. However, after these fleeting forays into the international arena, Khaled seemed to lose whatever interest he may have had in politics, preferring to concentrate on more tranquil and traditional domestic pursuits.

After an apparent lapse of almost 20 years, Khaled was once again brought into royal-family high politics when the crisis over the split between King Saud and Crown Prince Faisal came to a head in 1964. Despite his apolitical temperament which was conservative almost to the point of passivity, when the choice became unavoidable, Khaled is reported to have thrown his support quietly behind Faisal, the eventual winner in this internal power struggle. Perhaps this was because Faisal promised to be a more stable and effective leader; perhaps it was also because of the close personal relations these two half-brothers enjoyed. The typically scanty data do not permit a confident interpretation of Khaled's motives, or even confident assertions about his decisions and their role in this affair.

Once Saud was finally deposed and Faisal formally installed as king, Khaled, who was a respected senior prince in a different line of descent from Abd al-Aziz, a timely supporter of the new monarch, and yet a relatively apolitical figure widely acceptable both within the Saudi family and among the traditional tribal leaders, was prevailed upon to accept the position of crown prince and designated successor to the throne. Khaled seems to have done so only with great reluctance and after an interval of several months, upon entreaties not just from Faisal himself but also from Khaled's own sole full brother Muhammed and from veteran family adviser Rashad Pharaon. Also included were promises from all that he would still be free to devote his time to his beloved desert pursuits of riding, falconry, and informal family and tribal councils. It appears that those promises were kept, for during the ensuing decade of Faisal's successful reign, there is no record that Crown Prince Khaled was more than marginally involved in any Saudi affairs of state. His medical need to undergo major heart surgery in 1972 made it seem even less likely that he would ever take an active leadership role.

Thus, when Khaled unexpectedly succeeded to the throne upon Faisal's assassination three years later, he was something of an unknown quantity but presumed to be destined for figurehead status, while his younger half-brother, the much more politically active and experienced Fahd, took over as crown prince. In fact, Fahd quickly assumed a leadership role in the kingdom's foreign policy, at times supported and at times parried by other senior princes, with Khaled tending to intervene only when the absence of family consensus on a critical issue made his deciding voice essential. Nevertheless, Khaled's own role was more than merely symbolic, which makes a closer look at his governing style necessary here.

In general, Khaled was inclined to delegate responsibility, not only for foreign policy but for domestic affairs as well. Consequently, for example, the various ministers and provincial governors were allowed greater latitude than had been the case in Faisal's day to manage their respective jurisdictions and even to offer certain policy initiatives for limited public discussion. As king, Khaled continued to focus on the ritual and social functions of his office, including the large-scale weekly *majlis* with representative ulema, tribal leaders, and ordinary citizens, rather than on the formulation or implementation of detailed government programs. To the extent that he did preside over truly political matters, these tended to be directly related to immediate family issues like the apportionment of royal perquisites (including real estate) among the many senior princes or to relations with the traditional tribal sector of Saudi society. Significantly, Khaled's personal role during the 1979 Mecca uprising—probably the gravest internal crisis to confront the Saudi regime in the past two decades—was by all accounts not a very large one.

Nevertheless, there were some important matters of state in which Khaled's direct personal intervention during his brief reign appears to have made a significant difference. For example, his approval reportedly shifted Saudi policy toward more stringent application of the Islamic *hudud* (criminal penalties), in line with the post–Iranian revolution climate in the region. Those penalties were now occasionally applied even to non-Muslim miscreants, U.S. citizens included—crossing what one well-placed observer has aptly called the "flogging threshold" for foreigners. More important still, Khaled's increasing personal dislike for Sadat helped tip the balance against continued Saudi cooperation with the Egyptian leader's ever more idiosyncratic diplomacy.[13] Khaled also made a few well-timed symbolic visits to some sensitive destinations: for example, in late 1975 to Damascus, to cement closer Saudi-Syrian relations; and in 1980 to the restive Shiite communities of Saudi Arabia's own Eastern Province, to manifest royal determination to manage that area better in the wake of local riots and religious demonstrations.

On Lebanese issues in particular, Khaled's reign began on a rather auspicious note. His succession to the throne upon Feisal's assassination took place just before Lebanon erupted into civil war, followed a year later by Syria's massive military intervention in that country. Once the Saudis sorted out the details of their succession process, they successfully engaged in what one astute analyst has labeled "an unaccustomed display of Saudi political and financial muscle" in managing the inter-Arab implications of the ongoing Lebanese crisis.[14] At a couple of Arab summits held in quick succession in the fall of 1976, Saudi Arabia took the lead in reconciling Egypt and Syria, the price being pan-Arab recognition of the latter's special role in Lebanon. This was, in the words of another authority on the subject, "the crucible in which the post-Feisal Saudi leadership was tempered," at least for a time.[15] Significantly, the Saudi-sponsored reconciliation between Cairo and Damascus did not outlast the next major twist in Sadat's diplomacy, namely, his sensational trip to Jerusalem barely one year after making up with Syrian President Hafez al-Assad in Riyadh.

Four years later, during the next crisis over the Syrian presence in Lebanon, Saudi Arabia again offered discreet but effective support for a negotiated resolution (or at least deferral) of the immediate issues at hand. This time the Saudis backed a U.S. effort to defuse a looming Syrian-Israeli confrontation sparked by new Syrian antiaircraft missile deployments inside Lebanon, coupled with an all-but-official August 1981 cease-fire agreement between Israel and the PLO military command headquartered in Beirut. This time, the Saudis helped secure no more than a short-lived postponement of what turned out to be a much more serious confrontation in Lebanon, the one that erupted when Israel invaded that country in full force in June of 1982.

While Khaled himself presided over Saudi strategy on Lebanese issues, the leading private diplomatic conduit for consulations with Syria was probably Prince Abdallah, the influential commander of the Saudi national guard and second in line for the throne after Crown Prince Fahd. Abdallah was loosely tied to Syria by birth (his mother hailed from the northern Shammar tribes with historical connections across the border), and more closely tied to Syrian President Assad's own family by marriage; he shared with the Syrian leader a certain Arab nationalist inclination, including a wariness of too close a U.S. connection; and he was also reputedly close, in both personal and policy terms, to Khaled.

It was Crown Prince Fahd, however, who took the lead in mapping out the main lines of Saudi Arabia's diplomatic approach, whether in 1976 or in 1981. In so doing, he strove to maintain the relatively assertive Saudi role in the inter-Arab and Arab-Israeli arenas that Feisal had had the foresight to initiate a decade earlier. Furthermore, it was Fahd who, by an ironic turn of fate, was in the midst of his own transition to kingship just as the next major Lebanese crisis was underway in the summer of 1982.

Biographical Background on King Fahd

Fahd ibn Abd al-Aziz, though almost ten years Khaled's junior, was a much more experienced political leader when he ascended the Saudi throne upon the latter's death in June 1982. For three decades, Fahd had served ably in a variety of increasingly important high-level government posts: as minister of education in the 1950s, as minister of the interior in the 1960s, and then as second deputy prime minister (and, in practice, chief executive officer of the Saudi government under King Feisal) through the eventful first half of the 1970s. Even if Fahd was passed over for succession to the kingship, becoming crown prince and first deputy prime minister instead, when Feisal fell victim to an assassin's bullets in 1975, there were reasonable grounds for expecting that Fahd was being groomed during this long period of apprenticeship for eventual assumption of supreme Saudi leadership.[16]

This expectation stemmed in part from Fahd's family position as one of the seven Sudairi senior princes, the powerful clan of full brothers who were sons of King Abd al-Aziz by Hassa bint Ahmad al-Sudairi, all of whom had long held important political or commercial roles in the country (or both), while maintaining a high degree of loyalty to each other as well. In part, too, the expectation that Fahd would one day be king derived from the demonstrated (and generally justified) confidence that the royal family as a whole—with some dissenters—had placed in him throughout his successful political career, capped by his status and activist profile as crown prince under the ailing King Khaled. In that capacity, Fahd tried and often managed to exercise a dominant voice in Saudi foreign and oil policy, while delegating authority (more so than had been the practice during Faisal's day) in other areas to other senior government figures. In addition, anticipation of Fahd's succession to the throne derived from widespread and accurate (if incomplete) perceptions of his own high level of personal ambition.

However, if Fahd was ambitious, he was also (to judge from the admittedly incomplete evidence of his behavior over the years) a bit moody, inclined on occasion to absent himself in protest or simply withdraw from the fray if he did not get his way. He had not shied away from controversy in his earlier years, championing "progressive" innovations like television and women's education as part of his attachment to economic development and technological modernization. Even so, Fahd seemed to become more cautious the closer he came to achieving his ultimate ambition (and the more, presumably, he needed to ensure that there would not be any last-minute hitches in his quest for the kingship). An important example of this proclivity had occurred in the first half of 1979. Fahd found himself in a minority within the higher family councils in his persistent advocacy of a pro-U.S. and even pro-Egyptian line, despite the controversial Camp David accords. He therefore went on vacation for several months to nurse his grudge, his health, and a new young bride all at once.[17]

Later, as king, Fahd exhibited a similar tendency to avoid political showdowns. Possibly stymied on some issues by rival cliques within the royal family, and most likely apprehensive about his own lack of strong religious credentials in an increasingly unpredictable regional Islamic climate, Fahd adopted a cautious, low-profile approach to royal rule. He has hardly ever taken decisive initiatives; in this connection, it is noteworthy that the Arab-Israeli peace plan that bears his name was announced before his accession to the throne. He rarely presides in person over the weekly meeting of the Council of Ministers, preferring to leave that task (as the precedent Fahd himself established suggests, but does not dictate) to the crown prince and first deputy prime minister—and Fahd's own alleged rival, Prince Abdullah.

Fahd has likewise been loath to punish poor performance or corruption within the Saudi establishment. With a couple of notable exceptions, officials derelict in their duties or otherwise in disfavor have not been dismissed; instead, some of their responsibilities have been quietly transferred elsewhere in the bureaucracy. Finally, the king has so far remained remarkably tolerant of instances of nepotism or family favoritism egregious even by local standards, especially where his own immediate family is concerned. One of his young sons, Faisal, was picked over other, arguably more qualified candidates to head a youth and welfare agency. Another of Fahd's sons, Muhammad, was very handsomely rewarded for a huge international business deal in telecommunications, even at the risk of tension with a rival claimant from within the royal family—his namesake, the elderly and irascible Prince Muhammad.[18] The pattern for Fahd has thus been one of insistence on relatively minor matters of personal or immediate family concern, coupled with neglect, circumspection, and enforced collegiality in the larger dimensions of political leadership.

Fahd's political caution has been reinforced by another personality trait, namely, ambivalence about hard work and a predilection toward what might kindly be called a comfortable lifestyle. Before his ascension to the throne, according to one gossipy but basically credible account, Fahd was inclined to extremes in this respect, alternating between periods of intense, "workaholic" activity on the one hand, and periods of rather prolonged relaxation or even seclusion and lethargy on the other.[19] For a time in 1974–75, soon after the oil bonanza that transformed the kingdom's fortunes, Fahd was apparently much taken with the resulting "good life," eating and smoking too much, putting in only perfunctory appearances at royal family working sessions, and even indulging in a couple of known excursions to casinos in London or Monte Carlo and some extravagant journeys in the company of high-flying Saudi businessman Adnan Kashoggi. Fahd was supposedly called to account by King Feisal shortly before the latter's untimely death and advised to channel his energies into more productive (and less sacrilegious) directions, which is what Fahd indeed proceeded to do.

Once on the throne, Fahd reverted, within reason, to a taste for personal luxury that Feisal would probably not have countenanced, and a routine that one perceptive outside observer has frankly described as "self-indulgent."[20] To some extent, his health may be a factor here; while Fahd appears to be in reasonably good shape, he is known to have suffered from back problems and from diabetes complicated by a tendency toward excess weight. In addition, as one sympathetic Saudi observer suggested, the king may feel that, having successfully led his controversial crusade to modernize his country's economy, technology, and educational system, and having safely steered the monarchy through some very troubled international waters, he needs or at least deserves to rest on his laurels for a bit.

On foreign policy issues, Fahd's personal preferences reportedly run toward extensive cooperation with the United States. He is more inclined that way than some conservative elder princes, or some of the more fiercely nationalist younger ones already active in high-level Saudi politics. During the late 1970s, Washington could count on Fahd's friendly voice in Riyadh. This was true across a broad spectrum of issues: on oil (relatively stable prices, high production levels, and even acquiescence in the plan for a U.S. strategic petroleum reserve); on regional strategy, in particular the U.S.-Saudi primary arms sales connection; and on Arab-Israeli diplomacy, in particular the Carter administration's proposal for a renewed Geneva peace conference, and even its subsequent involvement in mediating Sadat's unprecedented direct approach toward negotiations with Israel.[21] However, in a harbinger of things to come, Fahd was unwilling or unable to insist on continued close Saudi cooperation with the United States (at least not on all these issues) in the face of the new strains in this relationship created by the tumultuous events of early 1979: the separate Egyptian-Israeli peace treaty, the second Baghdad Arab summit conference that rejected this "betrayal," the Islamic revolution in Iran, and Saudi Arabia's own resulting loss of leverage over international oil prices.

What matters most in this connection is that both Fahd and Khaled turned out upon accession to the kingship to be quite different from what their respective personal histories and reputations might have suggested. Far from being a mere figurehead, Khaled proved to be an important arbiter—precisely because he was so "neutral"—of royal family (and therefore national policy) disputes. On at least one important occasion, in early 1979, he even acted directly and almost publicly at Fahd's expense in tipping the balance decisively against continued Saudi cooperation with Egyptian-U.S. diplomacy in the Arab-Israeli peace process.

On the other hand, the supposedly activist Fahd turned out to be a much more cautious, even passive king than many had anticipated. Indeed, he failed to follow up effectively or consistently on any of the initiatives, either foreign or domestic, that he had launched shortly before or soon after assuming the throne (for example, the "Fahd plan" for Arab-Israeli peace; or the proposals for internal consultative councils and Islamic *ijtihad*, that is, innovative interpretation). In a similar vein, as already noted, Fahd has been disinclined to take the lead in cracking down on some of the lucrative and arguably irregular business dealings of royal family members.

These opposite "surprises" regarding the last two Saudi kings derived, in part, merely from comparisons with unrealistic expectations entertained by outsiders. Attempts by both men to compensate (or overcompensate) for perceived weaknesses or flaws in their personal character and endowments may have played a part as well. Nonetheless, the "blossoming" of King Khaled and the "disappointing" leadership performance of King Fahd also derived partly from the dynamics of royal family interaction that successively encouraged or constrained their leadership roles.

LEADER–FOLLOWER RELATIONS

In the special Saudi context, particularly where the linkage between national leadership and foreign policy is concerned, relations between the leader and the masses, the religious establishment (ulema), and even the growing technocratic and commercial elite and middle class are of little import. Admittedly, both Khaled and Fahd have delegated more responsibility to national and even to local government bodies than was the case in Feisal's day, but both, especially Fahd, have occasionally chosen to reassert royal prerogatives: for example, in forcing the ouster of the popular and scholarly minister of health, Ghazi al-Qusaibi; or in overruling the minister of petroleum, Ahmad Zaki al-Yamani, on critical issues of oil policy in an increasingly difficult economic environment. Indeed, as already noted, the key leadership roles, formal and (primarily) informal structures of power, patterns of recruitment to and rivalry for leadership, and, to a great extent, sources of authority and political influence all derive mainly from the interaction of individuals and informal cliques within the royal family.[22]

Although the general outlines of this interaction can be inferred with some confidence, the specific internal discussions and individual leadership roles regarding particular policy issues can only be surmised. As Sir James Craig, a scholarly Arabist and former British ambassador to the kingdom, has aptly put it,

the circle which makes the big decisions in Saudi Arabia is a closed community. Neither . . . I, nor anyone outside the circle, knows who says what in the debate, or why, or who carries weight. The press cannot help at all, and the dispatches of ambassadors very little. Any discussion, therefore, of the formation of high Saudi policy is bound to be largely guesswork.[23]

Here again a certain irony is apparent in a comparison between Khaled and Fahd. The former had only one full brother to rely on in internal politics, and a rather isolated one at that. He had few other such ties beyond an affinity with some of the remaining tribes enjoying marital or historical links with the house of Saud, yet it was just this absence of identification with one of the major competing Saudi royal factions that made Khaled a less partisan and therefore more effective arbiter, if not leader.

Fahd, by contrast, presumably benefited from his status as one of the powerful "Sudairi Seven" (more properly, the al-Fahd) senior princes—who include the ministers of defense and interior and two (or at times more) important provincial governors. However, this allegiance (or at least connection) has aroused significant countervailing royal family pressures, and so has probably contributed to Fahd's newfound need to temper his ambitions. Here the key figure is probably Crown Prince Abdallah, who is from a different maternal line of descent. He appears to represent a more "conservative" wing of the Saudi establishment—one that also, paradoxically, gets some support from the "third-generation" grandsons of Abdul Aziz. These include senior, well-educated, highly placed, and in some cases more outspokenly "nationalist" Saudi princes, notably Minister of Foreign Affairs Prince Saud al-Feisal.

Thus, Khaled and Fahd have both been constrained, in different ways, by the necessity of finding a family consensus in what is less an absolute monarchy than a collegial dynasty. The imposing presence of their predecessor Feisal has eluded them both, depriving them of the nearly undisputed following inside the royal family which is essential for controversial initiatives. Neither is there any evidence that either man has attempted to transcend this limitation by cultivating a following outside the family framework. Beyond this internal constraint on their freedom to act, both Khaled and Fahd have had to confront the limits of Saudi national power and resources in their efforts to shape a more secure international environment.

LEADER–LEADER RELATIONS

Saudi leaders have enjoyed an extensive, high-level, and close—though not always cooperative—network of contacts with other Arab and international leaders.[24] A useful if sometimes stormy working relationship with President Assad of Syria was cultivated by the royal family (interestingly enough, with neither Khaled nor Fahd but rather Prince Abdullah taking the lead), in which large-scale Saudi subsidies and discreet consultations with diverse political elements provided some limited leverage over Syrian policies—or at least some insurance against Syrian-instigated subversion. A roughly parallel set of contacts, this time with Fahd himself reportedly playing a leading role, existed with PLO leader Yasser Arafat.

A different network of discreet contacts and economic interdependence links Saudi and U.S. leaders. In fact, one recurring Saudi tactic has been an effort to mediate between Damascus and Washington on a variety of divisive issues, including Lebanon. High-level contacts with Egypt, however, were largely soured if not totally severed after the rather desperate Saudi decision (in which Fahd had been compelled to acquiesce) to boycott the Camp David "betrayal" by Sadat. Saudi relations with Israeli and, in almost equal measure, Soviet leaders were of course indirect at best, and generally were mutually suspicious or downright hostile. Inside Lebanon itself, the Saudi leadership developed contacts not just with the nominal president but also with assorted sectarian and factional leaders—in particular, the Maronite-Phalange leader, Bashir Gemayel.[25] It is thus not so remarkable that, during the dark days of the siege of Beirut, the latter was invited to the Islamic bastion of Saudi Arabia for high-level (albeit ultimately unproductive) consultations aimed at a compromise solution for the problematic PLO presence in Lebanon.

The pursuit of top-level, behind-the-scenes contacts with foreign leaders once a crisis has crystallized is characteristic of the Saudi diplomatic style. In that pursuit, perhaps the most striking Saudi misperception is that of potentially unlimited U.S. influence on Israel, an exaggeration of reality that has nevertheless often been the misguided object of Saudi importunings. In their relations with Arab leaders, on the other hand, the Saudis have most often demonstrated a keenly accurate perception of conflicting interests and an appropriately cynical posture of hedging their bets. Within that framework, the judgment of Saudi leaders has usually been that their own interests are best served by mediating inter-Arab differences rather than taking sides, and by trying to nudge the Arab mainstream in a favorable direction while taking care not to stray too far from its course themselves.

THE SPECIFIC SITUATION

King Khaled lived through the first week of the 1982 Lebanese war. In the first heat of the crisis, the Saudi posture was predictably and undoubtedly genuinely outraged, at least on the rhetorical level. Privately, Saudi efforts were directed toward mobilizing cautious pressure on all sides to accept a cease-fire, thereby defusing the conflict and deflecting possible counterpressures on Riyadh to take a more active and exposed position. On this last point, at least, the Saudis were successful. There is no evidence, though, that the king himself took a leading part in this effort; nor is there any sign that the succession to Fahd meant a change or even a major pause in Saudi policy, which (like that of all other Arab bystanders) was already relatively aloof from the carnage underway on Lebanese soil.[26]

When this first phase of the war was followed by a protracted Israeli siege of Beirut rather than a calming of the storm, the newly installed King Fahd faced the prospect of mounting inter-Arab and perhaps even domestic pressure to intervene in some fashion. Fahd responded with a series of moves that were much more in line with the cautious Saudi tradition than with the activist personal image he enjoyed. First, he moved to align his country with an emerging pan-Arab consensus, while taking care to keep any such steps below the summit level at which pressures for immediate or drastic action might have been irresistible. Second, Fahd activated his "back channel" of contacts with Reagan and other U.S. leaders, hoping—with some success, as it turned out—to contribute to U.S. pressure on Israel to desist. Third, and most important, Fahd gradually and discreetly facilitated the evolution of an Arab consensus on the "compromise" of evacuating the PLO from Beirut, making sure to keep open channels of communication with all sides, and to screen his essentially defensive policy with defiant rhetoric in the process.

As a tactical performance, this typically "diffident leadership" must be judged a success, but neither Khaled (not surprisingly), nor Fahd (more surprisingly), dared to go beyond this toward a persistent effort to change the international agenda or move toward resolution of underlying issues. In this crucial dimension of leadership, the Saudi kings clearly preferred a cautious, short-term, risk-avoidance strategy—one of mediating and perhaps subtly managing a multilateral

Arab consensus, coupled with carefully limited collaboration with the United States—over a strategy seeking to assert a position of personal or national preeminence in an all-too-typical Mideast crisis environment.

The Background of Saudi Policy in Lebanon

In general, the rather distant crises in Lebanon have not been an urgent Saudi concern, certainly not in comparison with other flare-ups much closer to home in the past few years. Precisely for that reason, Lebanese issues lent themselves well to the Saudi penchant for discreet application of ''riyalpolitik,'' that is, diplomacy backed by financial inducements and pressures on the contending Arab parties—minus some of the risks of such a policy applied on issues of more immediate moment. Indirectly, Lebanese crises raised inter-Arab issues of importance to Riyadh; and, on a more emotional level, the spectacle of carnage in that country aroused concern about a number of causes that many Saudis cared about. The resulting temptation to become at least peripherally involved in Lebanon has therefore periodically proved to be more than Saudi leaders would or could resist.

Saudi Arabian involvement in Lebanese ''crisis management'' can be dated from the first phase of that country's civil war, in 1975–76. At that time, the internal Lebanese struggle that pitted a conservative, mostly Maronite Christian establishment against a mostly Moslem, leftist-PLO coalition erupted into open warfare. However, even then a bewildering array of other opposing sects, factions, and assorted armed militias was already actively engaged on all sides. Riyadh had quietly cultivated contacts and clients among several different elements of Lebanon's increasingly fractious mosaic, both Moslem and Christian, whose major common denominator and claim on Saudi sympathy and support was their generally traditional and relatively moderate nature. However, Lebanon did not become an important concern for the Saudis until its internal strife got entangled with outside Arab (particularly Syrian) intervention.

In the first half of 1976, Syrian troops intervened across the border. First, they supported moderate Moslem demands; but then, when the Moslem-leftist-PLO coalition held out for more, the Syrians moved decisively in favor of the Maronite Phalangist forces. This remarkable reversal was intended to stabilize the Lebanese military picture, and then to assert Syrian influence as the arbiter of that country's destiny. It was pursued relentlessly in the face of vociferous Arab (and more low-key Soviet) opposition.

For Saudi Arabia, the entire situation posed potential dangers of polarizing inter-Arab politics, jeopardizing Riyadh's pursuit of a ''consensus'' Arab-Israeli settlement and, more immediately, forcing the Saudis to choose sides—something they were usually loathe to do. The Saudis soon managed to mediate the immediate inter-Arab dispute, but not to keep an Arab consensus on Arab-Israeli diplomacy. Instead, Saudi efforts after Sadat's unexpected November 1977 trip to Israel were increasingly confined to short-term crisis management in Lebanon, as opposed to more ambitious efforts to coordinate the Arab side of an overall Arab-Israeli settlement. In this vein, the Saudis added their voice to the chorus of pressures on Washington to compel an Israeli pullback after Israel's first large-scale incursion into Lebanon, in the spring of 1978. Three years later, as already noted, Riyadh helped mediate a temporary end to the Syrian-Israeli "missile crisis" and to PLO-Israeli hostilities across the Lebanese border.

Throughout these episodes, the hallmark of Saudi diplomacy in Lebanon was close consultation with Syria. By mid–1982, the Saudis were disenchanted with Syria's rejectionism abroad and repression of the Moslem Brotherhood at home. Still, when a new and much more serious Lebanese crisis erupted that summer, Riyadh resumed its favored role as mediator between Damascus and Washington.

Saudi Policy during the War

In the months leading up to Israel's invasion, and for about a week after the invasion was already underway, the PLO expected the Saudis to mediate a rapid and effective U.S.-sponsored cease-fire, saving the Palestinian organization from military defeat and scoring some additional political points at the same time.[27] This expectation was based in large part on Saudi success in doing just that during the preceding August. This time, the PLO was to be sorely disappointed—even if bitter experience had taught the Palestinians not to expect concrete combat assistance from any Arab leader, whether Saudi or Syrian.[28]

The Saudis did issue rapid demarches to Washington, demanding that it press the Israelis for a cease-fire. In so doing, the Saudis hoped both to protect the Syrians, who had already suffered a humiliating military defeat, and to prevent an escalation or widening of the conflict to the point where the Saudis could be more directly implicated against their better judgment. These Saudi efforts may have contributed to the acceptance of a Syrian-Israeli cease-fire within a week of fighting—but the contribution cannot have been more than marginal, since both belligerents (obviously for their own reasons) wanted the cease-fire in any case. More important, the cease-fire did not apply to Israel's continuing assault on the PLO, which now looked ever more expectantly to Riyadh for a diplomatic rescue mission. Just then, the political situation in Riyadh itself was briefly complicated by the death of King Khaled on June 13, 1982, and the immediate ascension of King Fahd to the throne.

On that very day, the Israelis reached the outskirts of Beirut and first presented their demand that the PLO evacuate the city. Many of that organization's leaders continued to look to Riyadh for the kind of diplomatic intercession with Washington that would enable them to resist Israel's demand, or at least to improve the terms for PLO withdrawal. From the perspective of the new Saudi leader, the top priorities at this juncture remained unchanged: to defuse the crisis by helping to arrange a PLO withdrawal, while holding Israeli forces at bay. This was a delicate combination calculated to end the fighting, reduce the pan-Arab sense of crisis and outrage, and preempt external or internal pressures for a more drastic and risky Saudi reaction against either Israel or the United States, thereby protecting their own vital U.S. connection. With the Iran-Iraq war still simmering—indeed, just then reaching a rapid boil and threatening to spill over into the Gulf—the Saudis could ill afford overtly hostile gestures against the United States, their protector of last resort.

Fortunately, the overall diplomatic disarray in the Arab world, so often lamented by Saudi leaders, had the virtue of mitigating the prospect of coordinated pressures on Riyadh to "unleash the oil weapon" in response to this latest example of "American-supported Israeli aggression." In any case, the oil "weapon" had been blunted by the evident approach of an international glut of petroleum supplies. As a result, such Saudi saber rattling—the only kind in which Riyadh could reasonably indulge—would have been less credible than heretofore.

The problem was that Riyadh's two immediate objectives were partly contradictory, in that a diminution of Israeli military pressure might also diminish PLO anxiety to evacuate Beirut. Apparently, the Saudis strove to balance this equation by discreetly resisting PLO efforts to insist on some political quid pro quo for an evacuation, and lobbying for U.S. restraint of Israel at the same time. Saudi leaders soon became heavily involved in behind-the-scenes consultations to that end with U.S. officials—to the extent that the Saudis were implicated, at least in part, in the chain of events that led U.S. Secretary of State Alexander Haig to resign three weeks into the Lebanon war.

This surprising sequence can be dated from June 16, when the newly installed King Fahd conferred with U.S. Vice President George Bush in the Saudi capital. Fahd warned the visiting Bush that U.S.-Saudi relations would be jeopardized if the battle for Beirut continued to escalate. Bush reportedly responded by revealing a private Israeli commitment not to occupy the city. The Saudis soon went public with a gratuitous but appropriately defiant warning to Israel to stay out of the Lebanese capital. They followed up a week later with an urgent request for President Reagan's intervention to stop a massive Israeli bombardment of Beirut. Once again, some U.S. officials promised a favorable response. This time, however, Haig argued forcefully that such a show of restraint would only delay the desired goal by alleviating the pressures on the PLO, and he threatened to resign in protest. Coming as it did after a period of accumulated, high-level internal political tension in Washington, Haig's bluff (if such it was) was unexpectedly called by Ronald Reagan. Not only was his resignation accepted, but a suitable U.S. warning to Israel was issued shortly thereafter.[29] Israeli assaults on Beirut then dwindled dramatically for several weeks.[30]

When the Israeli attacks resumed in force in late July, they provoked a new series of ever more explicit, direct, and ultimately effective admonitory messages—on August 1, 5, and 12, 1982—from Fahd to Reagan, and then from Reagan to Begin, urging that the costly fighting be ended.[31] The final, ferocious Israeli bombardment of the city, one of many that inflicted heavy civilian casualties, was viewed by the Saudis and others as particularly outrageous, since agreement on all the major and nearly all the minor points of a detailed PLO evacuation plan had already been achieved. However, the Saudis could still take some credit for the marginal change in U.S. policy (and policy-makers) described above, even if it temporarily rendered PLO agreement on an evacuation all the more elusive.

Having demonstrated the importance of their U.S. connection, the Saudis now adopted a more activist posture. They hosted a special Arab League committee meeting (including a rather remarkable appearance by Lebanese Phalangist leader Bashir Gemayel) in their summer capital of Ta'if, at which the various delegates began to explore the possibilities and limits of a PLO withdrawal from Beirut. No agreement was reached, partly because the PLO was still trying to forestall a total, unconditional evacuation in the face of Phalangist insistence on exactly that. In part, the deadlock at this stage can be laid at the door of the Syrians, who were determined to recoup some of their damaged political stature by ostentatiously refusing to host any of the PLO evacuees and thus participate in a "defeatist" denouement—although Damascus clearly had no better alternative to offer. Despite Saudi failure to persuade the Syrians just yet, the high-level dialogue between the two Arab countries continued. Eventually, that dialogue did yield some results.

Equally important at this stage of the diplomatic game, if not more so, was a behind-the-scenes Saudi effort to deflect (or "sabotage," in the words of one scholar sympathetic to the PLO) a joint French-Egyptian initiative.[32] This effort would have linked a negotiated cease-fire and disengagement in Lebanon with progress toward resolution of some of the underlying regional issues, particularly that of mutual Palestinian-Israeli recognition and acceptance of self-determination for both sides. The Franco-Egyptian initiative, promoted both at the United Nations and in coordinated, high-level private contacts with PLO leaders by Paris and Cairo, was on its face fully in line with long-standing declaratory Saudi policy. Nevertheless, the Saudis viewed the Franco-Egyptian approach as excessively ambitious and inopportune. It would have entangled their effort to secure an end to the crisis (even at the expense of the PLO's presence in Beirut) with impossibly difficult political conditions. Moreover, as the Saudis quickly discovered, the United States was unalterably opposed to such "distractions" (or to anything that might salvage the PLO's political stature). That alone must have been enough to convince most Saudi leaders that any effort to reap some political capital from the Lebanese crisis was not just unrealistic but dangerously dilatory as well.

As a result, high-level Saudi representatives, in their capacity as the leading intermediaries between U.S. and PLO officials, did their best to discourage both parties from contemplating any form of cooperation with this Franco-Egyptian "trial balloon." The United States, of course, needed little in the way of discouragement. PLO officials, on the other hand, were successively confused and deeply disappointed by this "obstructionist" Saudi position. However, by then, the Saudis were intent on doing what they could to end the fighting as quickly as possible, to dispel the spectre of internal or inter-Arab political turmoil and tension in Arab U.S. relations. They would, if necessary, jettison any excess political baggage that might burden a simple cease-fire and evacuation arrangement.

By mid-July 1982, as the Israeli siege of Beirut continued, the specific focus of Saudi diplomacy centered on a visit to Washington by Foreign Minister Prince Saud al-Faisal, accompanied by his Syrian counterpart and PLO leader Khaled al-Hassan. Saud attempted to move a bit beyond the main Saudi policy line of brokering an immediate and almost unconditional PLO withdrawal. He did this by introducing broader political conditions (or at least a broader political context) into the discussions. When even this high-level delegation emerged from their meetings with U.S. officials essentially empty-handed, the full extent of Saudi failure became apparent. As Rashid Khalidi has aptly summarized the situation:

It seems to have been the utter failure of Arab efforts during July to change the U.S. position—worse, tacit Arab acceptance of that position—which brought the PLO to decide that there was little point in holding out further.[33]

The only remaining question then, at least in the short term, was that of obtaining final agreement on the mechanics of the PLO withdrawal from Beirut.

The role of Prince Saud in this diplomatic demarche deserves closer examination. He was supposedly a leader of the "third generation," more nationalist and less pro–U.S. elite in the Saudi foreign policy establishment. From all appearances, Saud was indeed a key figure in this episode of Saudi crisis diplomacy, closely in touch both with his fellow delegation members from Syria and the PLO on the one hand, and with his contacts at the highest U.S. executive and Congressional levels on the other. Specifically, Saud reportedly tried to convince the PLO to comply at this desperate juncture with the perennial U.S. demand that it accept UN Resolution 242 of 1967, and thereby "qualify" as a negotiating partner in the quest for an Arab-Israeli diplomatic settlement. The immediate issue of Beirut would thus have been linked with the larger, longer-term issues in conflict, possibly to the advantage both of Saudis and of the PLO itself. However, Saud was unable to obtain any U.S. guarantees regarding eventual Palestinian self-determination or other rewards for this painful diplomatic concession, or even regarding the prospect of a matching Israeli withdrawal from Lebanon.

What is most striking about Saud's performance in this little drama is that, his reputation to the contrary notwithstanding, he showed little sign of willingness to risk a defiant attitude toward an unyielding U.S. position. According to one account, Saud may not even have raised the PLO's own 11-point counterproposal concerning the scope and safeguards for its withdrawal from Beirut—let alone its demand for a political quid pro quo—in his meetings with President Reagan and with the new U.S. Secretary of State, George Shultz. The most he was able to accomplish was to obtain U.S. agreement to consider some marginal modifications of the plan for total and "apolitical" PLO evacuation that had already been presented by U.S. Special Envoy Philip Habib.[34]

In this connection, one should add another observation about the role of this crisis of individual Saudi leaders besides the king. Conspicuously absent from the recorded consultations with foreign leaders was a large role for Abdallah, despite his obviously relevant experience and connections with Syrian leaders. His low profile might have been related to the fact that Syria was plainly in retreat during this period—although the secretive style of Saudi leadership decision making renders such inferences hazardous at best. Assuming that Abdallah was indeed comparatively quiescent, that might have given Fahd more latitude to act, yet there is no evidence that the king availed himself greatly of this opportunity, if indeed it ever arose.

While the Saudis were able to obtain some demonstrative if short-lived displays of restraint in the military arena, they were clearly unable to secure political compensation for the forced withdrawal of the PLO from the Lebanese capital. The failure of the July delegation to Washington was repeated when the Saudis hosted another meeting of the Arab League ministerial committee, this time in Jeddah, at the end of the month. The committee endorsed a new, six-point PLO evacuation plan, one that pointedly omitted any overtly political conditions and merely specified certain safeguards for the departing Palestinian fighters and the civilians they would leave behind in Beirut.[35] When even this proved unacceptable to Israel and the United States, the Saudis, like the other Arab governments and the PLO itself, had little choice but to convey their more or less grudging acceptance of the still more restrictive plan originally offered through the mediation of U.S. Special Envoy Habib. The last particulars were agreed upon two weeks later, on August 12, 1982; and the last PLO guerrillas, accompanied by their leader, Yasser Arafat, were gone from Beirut by the end of that month.

All during the preceding month, as Israel's air and ground assaults on Beirut increased in ferocity, PLO spokesmen could only decry the "paralysis" and impotence of other Arab leaders, issue vain appeals for a Saudi oil embargo against the United States, and ultimately condemn the "cowardice and treachery" of their fellow Arabs far afield. Arafat himself remained relatively cautious in his public statements on this painful subject; but his deputy Salah Khalaf (alias Abu Iyyad) was considerably more explicit and accusatory.[36] Even so, as Israel's military pressure continued unabated and the PLO found itself ever more alone, Arafat was compelled to rely in part on the good offices of the Saudis to help arrange as safe (and as face-saving) an exit from Beirut as was possible under the circumstances. By the time the evacuation agreement was finally put together, PLO leaders had reverted to a public posture of gratitude toward the Saudis for their unspecified assistance to the Palestinians in their hour of greatest need.[37]

With the PLO evacuation smoothly underway (indeed, it was the only maneuver during this entire sorry episode that actually proceeded ahead of schedule), the limited direct Saudi role in the 1982 Lebanese crisis came nearly to an end.

Arafat appeared again in Saudi Arabia, this time as an honored guest at an Islamic conference, where he characteristically described his organization's forced retreat as a sign of Israeli and U.S. weakness.[38]

A more realistic prescription for the postcrisis Arab-Israeli arena was offered shortly thereafter by U.S. President Reagan, in a new peace plan calling for Palestinian self-government in association with Jordan rather than the PLO. The Saudis greeted the plan with cautious interest, but deferred as usual to another Arab summit that was meeting (not by coincidence) just then in Fez.[39] In what may well have been the high-watermark if not the "last hurrah" for Saudi influence on Arab-Israeli diplomacy since Faisal's death, the summit approved a modified version of the plan authored by Crown Prince (now King) Fahd that had been rejected a year earlier. Significantly however, this version was newly diluted with some concessions to the Arab radicals, like the stipulation for a UN guarantee (instead of a peace settlement) establishing an independent, PLO-led Palestinian state.

Even this relatively promising diplomatic development was quickly derailed by a new succession of bloody incidents in Beirut: the assassination of the newly elected president, Bashir Gemayel; the entry of Israeli troops into the city; and the massacre they permitted of Palestinians in the Sabra and Shatila refugee camps. The Saudis (along with the rest of the world, including many Israelis) reacted with new expressions of outrage, probably made particularly poignant in the Saudi case by a sense of betrayal by the United States of promises to safeguard the civilian Palestinians left behind in the Lebanese capital. However, there was little that King Fahd could do except vent his outrage, vainly appeal once more for the elusive goal of Arab unity, and call the United States to account for failing to keep its past commitments. Gradually, behind the scenes, Fahd accommodated himself to the reality of a resurgence of Syrian power, if need be at the expense of Saudi support for U.S. policy in Lebanon.[40]

In retrospect, the events of September 1982 marked the beginning of the end of Israel's grand political strategy for Lebanon, and of a new and ill-fated U.S. intervention in that country (from late 1982 through early 1984). They also paved the way for a reassertion of Syrian influence there. For the Saudis, as the record of the last three years makes clear, the Lebanese denouement can only have reinforced their growing disinclination to take an exposed leadership position on Arab-Israeli issues, especially in conjunction with the United States. It is against this background of widely shared disappointment that one can attempt a very brief concluding (and all-too-literally appropriate) "post mortem" on the Lebanese crisis, as seen through Saudi eyes.

CONCLUSION

Saudi Arabia has lately had only limited influence in Lebanon, but then Lebanon is only of limited Saudi concern. Indeed, for a country whose reputation has been far in excess of its resources, Saudi Arabia could take some satisfaction from its role in the immediate Lebanese crisis of 1982. It emerged from the events of that summer not only unscathed but temporarily enhanced in pan-Arab prestige, if only by Syrian default. By late August 1982, in fact, Arafat was once again praising Saudi solidarity with his cause, notwithstanding the ''cowardly betrayal'' his own lieutenants had denounced just a few short weeks before.

As a matter of individual leadership, however, neither Khaled nor Fahd evinced striking qualities during this period. Both personal and political factors played a part in producing this outcome. For Fahd, especially, it was not so much the immediate wartime crisis as the follow-up leadership role—or lack thereof—that was so disappointing. The internal divisions and external distractions that have afflicted his tenure as king were perhaps less in evidence during the heat of the Lebanese crisis, but they surfaced soon thereafter; and they stood in the way of an effective Saudi effort to use the postcrisis situation to either national or personal political advantage.

In this respect, the fate of the ''Fahd plan'' for a comprehensive Arab-Israeli settlement, tabled by the Saud king just before and again just after the Lebanese war, is most instructive. After the earlier, more successful behind-the-scenes Saudi effort to mediate a tactical agreement in Lebanon in the summer of 1981, Fahd had launched his plan, only to back down in the face of Syrian protests at the first Fez summit in November of that year. The following September, with Syria weakened by the war and more beholden to Saudi support, a slightly watered down version of his plan was in fact approved by the all-important Arab consensus at a second summit in Fez; and yet, when Syria soon regained its strength while neither Israel nor the United States proved receptive, Fahd failed to follow through on this proposal. Instead, he devoted the limited attention he could divert from more pressing dangers in the Gulf to overseeing, in a rather distant way, gradual Saudi attempts to mediate the conflicts dividing Syria from Jordan, Iraq, and the PLO. As of early 1986, only the first of these conflicts, that between Syria and Jordan, appeared amenable to the limited ameliorative effect that Saudi good offices could produce. As for Saudi leadership on larger and even more divisive issues of Arab-Israeli relations, that appeared to be little more than a distant hope or, more precisely, a memory.

Thus, the 1982 Lebanese crisis revealed a pattern of Saudi behavior that continues to hold true: when open conflict erupts, Riyadh will work quietly to nudge the Arab mainstream toward a tactical position that will avoid active confrontation with the United States. Otherwise, it will concentrate on fitful efforts to repair the badly frayed fabric of inter-Arab politics, reluctant as the Saudis are to be forced into choosing sides. As for personal leadership, the new, supposedly more activist king who took over at the height of the 1982 crisis has proved to be hardly more forceful in foreign affairs than his ailing predecessor. Indeed, when Arab consensus threatens to be elusive, and any Saudi position correspondingly controversial, King Fahd has typically chosen to avoid risking his personal prestige or position, preferring to send other less visible princes to represent the kingdom publicly in his stead.

It is in this crucial sense that one might compare Fahd's leadership unfavorably to Feisal's. Not only did Feisal take greater personal charge of a more assertive national policy earlier during the 1973 wartime crisis; he also managed to maintain the momentum of Saudi foreign and domestic policy (despite some opposition at home and abroad) once the crisis was over, during the year-and-a-half that was left of his life. Under Fahd, Saudi Arabia quickly dissipated whatever advantages might have accrued from its indirect role in the 1982 Lebanese war.

Thus, to the extent that one can generalize from one example, two propositions are suggested by this case study: First, autocratic systems do not necessarily produce powerful individual leaders. Second, neither strong leaders nor favorable circumstances are sufficient by themselves to ensure effective international leadership—although both factors are probably necessary.

Today, four years after the 1982 Lebanese crisis, the prolonged confrontation with an avowedly Islamic challenge from Iran, the lingering spectre of seriously divided counsels at home, and the intervening years of unaccustomed economic austerity (at least as compared with earlier expectations) have all taken their toll on Saudi Arabia. The kingdom is compelled to conserve what remains of its wealth, legitimacy, and foreign friendships even more carefully than before. The king himself is constrained, for both personal and political reasons, to act accordingly and keep his profile low. In short, the Saudi national role on the world stage can be characterized as leadership only in the most limited sense. Furthermore, as this study has suggested, personal leadership of truly international dimensions has been removed from the royal chambers in Riyadh.

NOTES

1. See especially James P. Piscatori, "Islamic Values and National Interest: The Foreign Policy of Saudi Arabia," in *Islam in Foreign Policy*, ed. Adeed Dawisha (Cambridge: Cambridge University Press, 1983), pp. 33–53.

2. For a useful summary of Saudi foreign policy concerns, see William B. Quandt, *Saudi Arabia in the 1980s: Foreign Policy, Security, and Oil* (Washington, D.C.: The Brookings Institution, 1981), ch. 1.

3. See, for example, Bahgat Korany, "Defending the Faith: The Foreign Policy of Saudi Arabia," in *The Foreign Policies of Arab States*, ed. Bahgat Korany and Ali E. Hillal Dessouki (Boulder, Colo: Westview Press, 1984), pp. 241–82, esp. p. 275.

4. See, for example, Adeed Dawisha, "Saudi Foreign Policy," in *Orbis*, Spring 1979, esp. p. 129; Rod McLaurin and Lewis Snider, *Middle East Foreign Policies: Issues and Processes* (New York: Praeger, 1983), ch. 6; cf. Nadav Safran, *Saudi Arabia: The Ceaseless Quest for Security* (Cambridge: Harvard University Press, 1985), esp. pp. 233, 324, 453.

5. McLaurin and Snider, *Middle East Foreign Policies*, pp. 222–24.

6. See Bernard Reich, David Pollock, and Sally Ann Baynard, "The Iranian Revolution: Implications for the Middle East," in *Economic Implications of the Revolution in Iran*, ed. U.S. Congress, Joint Economic Committee (Washington, D.C.: U.S. Government Printing Office, 1979).

7. See, for example, McLaurin and Snider, *Middle East Foreign Policies*, pp. 200–01; Quandt, *Saudi Arabia*, p. 87.

8. For two views of the role of the *ulema* in Saudi politics, see Alexander Bligh, "The Saudi Religious Elite (Ulama) as a Participant in the Political System of the Kingdom," *International Journal of Middle East Studies* 17, no. 1 (February 1985); 37–50; and Joseph A. Kechichian, "The Role of the Ulama in the Politics of an Islamic State: The Case of Saudi Arabia," *International Journal of Middle East Studies* 18, no. 1 (February 1986); 53–71.

9. See, for example, Korany, "Defending the Faith," p. 257; Quandt, *Saudi Arabia*, p. 83.

10. Gary Samore, "Royal Family Politics in Saudi Arabia," Ph.D. diss., Harvard University, 1984.

11. Safran, *Saudi Arabia*, passim.

12. For biographical and political background on King Khaled, see Robert Lacey, *The Kingdom* (New York: Harcourt Brace Jovanovich, 1981), pp. 360–61, 432–33; David Holden and Robert John, *The House of Saud*, pp. 384–85, 418–19, 464–65, 506, 512, 522; Korany, "Defending the Faith," pp. 259–60; Richard F. Nyrop, ed., *Saudi Arabia: A Country Study* (Washington, D.C.: U.S. Government Printing Office, 1984), pp. 44, 52.

13. On Khaled's personal dislike for Sadat, see Quandt, *Saudi Arabia*, p. 31 n. 9.

14. Ibid., p. 112.

15. For Saudi policy in Lebanon during the critical 1975–76 period, see M. Graeme Bannerman, "Saudi Arabia," in *Lebanon in Crisis: Participants and Issues*, ed. P. Edward Haley and Lewis W. Snider (Syracuse: Syracuse University Press, 1979), pp. 113–32, esp. p. 132.

16. For biographical and political background on King Fahd, see Holden and John, *House of Saud*, pp. 386, 396, 420, 497, 500–504; Lacey, *Kingdom*, pp. 438–44; *The Middle East* (London), July 1982, p. 12; Nyrop, *Saudi Arabia*, pp. 212, 226–27, 233.

17. Safran, *Saudi Arabia*, pp. 226–27, 311–13; Holden and John, *House of Saud*, pp. 500–507.

18. Lacey, *Kingdom*, pp. 441–42; Holden and John, *House of Saud*, pp. 412–14.

19. Holden and John, *House of Saud*, pp. 386, 420.

20. Joseph Kraft, "Letter from Saudi Arabia," *The New Yorker*, July 4, 1983, p. 53; see also Holden and John, *House of Saud*, p. 461.

21. Safran, *Saudi Arabia*, chs. 12 and 16; Quandt, *Saudi Arabia*, p. 80; Holden and John, *House of Saud*, pp. 454, 492, 502–4.

22. On the various personal and policy "cliques" within the Saudi royal family and their relations with bureaucratic and technocratic figures, see, for example, John A. Shaw and David E. Long, *Saudi Arabian Modernization: The Impact of Change on Stability*, Washington Paper no. 89, (Washington, D.C.: Georgetown University Center for Strategic and International Studies/Praeger Publishers, 1982), pp. 60–62; Holden and John, *House of Saud*, pp. 390, 415–16, 452–53, 459–60, 528; Nyrop, *Saudi Arabia*, pp. 224–25, 228–31; Quandt, *Saudi Arabia*, pp. 83–87, 108–10, 122; Kraft, "Letter," pp. 441–42; John K. Cooley, "Iran, the Palestinians and the Gulf," *Foreign Affairs*, Summer 1979; and "Correspondence," *Foreign Affairs*, Fall 1979, pp. 181–84; Korany, "Defending the Faith," p. 260.

23. James Craig, "Saudi Arabia: The Pivotal Kingdom" (review of Safran, *Saudi Arabia*), *The Washington Post Book World*, Dec. 29, 1985, p. 5.

24. See, for example, Quandt, *Saudi Arabia*, p. 24; Holden and John, *House of Saud*, pp. 423–26.

25. Bannerman, "Saudi Arabia"; Holden and John, *House of Saud*, pp. 439–40.

26. For the outlines of Saudi policy during the 1982 Lebanese war, see Rashid Khalidi, *Under Siege: P.L.O. Decisionmaking During the 1982 War* (New York: Columbia University Press, 1986), passim; Safran, *Saudi Arabia*, pp. 341–51. For a balanced outline of the broader Lebanese context, see Itamar Rabinovich, *The War for Lebanon, 1970–1983* (Ithaca: Cornell University Press, 1984).

27. Khalidi, *Under Siege*, pp. 38, 40.

28. Ibid., pp. 73–74.

29. Safran, *Saudi Arabia*, pp. 346–47.

30. For a statement by King Fahd implying satisfaction—short-lived, as it turned out—with U.S. pressure on Israel during this interlude, see *Al-Sharq Al-Awsat* (London), July 14, 1982.

31. For Saudi reports about two of these messages, see Foreign Broadcast Information Service, *Daily Report: Middle East and Africa* (hereafter *FBIS-MEA*), Aug. 2 and 13, 1982.

32. Khalidi, *Under Siege*, ch. 4.

33. Ibid., p. 92.

34. Ibid., pp. 154–63.

35. *FBIS-MEA*, July 29 and 30, 1982.

36. See, for example, *FBIS-MEA*, June 21, July 2 and 29, and August 2, 1982.

37. See, for example, statement by PLO leader Khalid Al-Hassan to the Saudi newspaper *Al-Madinah*, trans. in *FBIS-MEA*, September 1, 1982.

38. Broadcast of Arafat address to the World Muslim League meeting in Saudi Arabia (as heard).

39. *FBIS-MEA*, September 2, 3, 8, 9, 1982.

40. For analyses of the Fahd plan "fiasco" and subsequent developments, see Safran, *Saudi Arabia*, pp. 332–41; Joseph Kostiner, "The Saudi Arabian Kingdom," in *Middle East Contemporary Survey*, vol. 7, ed. Colin Legum and Haim Shaked, 1982/83, pp. 744–67.

9

THE SOVIET UNION'S
LEONID BREZHNEV

Dina Rome Spechler

According to the almost unanimous opinion of scholars and journalists, when Israel invaded Lebanon in June 1982, Leonid Brezhnev and the Soviet leadership did their utmost to avoid becoming involved. They delayed as long as possible before even making a public statement about the Israeli action and rejected repeated Arab pleas to intervene.[1] The Kremlin leaders rendered only the most timid and vague warnings to Israel and the United States, provided no military aid during the course of the fighting, and failed to take "even cosmetic steps to aid [their] allies." Rather, they stood on the sidelines and allowed their friends to be militarily devastated.[2] So passive and ineffective were they throughout the crisis that they exercised almost no influence on events.[3] The USSR, one expert concluded, had become "a superpower in eclipse."[4] Its behavior thus contrasted sharply with its conduct in the previous Arab-Israeli war in October 1973, and constituted a radical break with the interventionist approach to Third World conflicts that it had displayed throughout the 1970s.[5]

The alleged passivity and ineffectiveness of Brezhnev and his colleagues has been explained as a consequence of two sets of developments. On the one hand, it is argued, changes in the Middle East in the years after the October War had substantially reduced the USSR's ability to exert influence there and significantly diminished its eagerness to remain involved, both in the region as a whole and in the Arab-Israeli conflict in particular.[6] At the same time, the ability of the Soviet leadership to take decisive and forceful action in world affairs had declined sharply since the end of the 1970s. This decline is attributed to Brezhnev's physical deterioration, which is widely believed to have virtually incapacitated

This chapter is based on a paper prepared for presentation at the annual meeting of the American Political Science Association, August 28–31, 1986. A shorter, somewhat different version was published in *Studies in Comparative Communism* (Summer 1987).

The author thanks Paul Richardson of Indiana University for his expert research assistance.

him near the end of his life. "A feeble invalid," kept alive by sophisticated drugs and medical techniques during his last years in power, he is said to have been able to work only a few hours a week.[7] In this condition, he was unable to maintain control over the government apparatus and Politburo.[8] Thus by the summer of 1982, so the argument goes, there was no single dominant figure on the Soviet political scene, no one capable of exerting effective leadership. Preoccupied with the impending succession, the Kremlin sought above all to avoid unnecessary risks, commitments, or involvement abroad.[9]

The assertion that there were significant differences between Soviet behavior in 1982 and 1973 is not incorrect. The Kremlin's crisis diplomacy in Lebanon was more cautious, its involvement in the conflict more limited. Similarly, the explanations offered for these differences are a partly accurate description of the regional and domestic situation confronting the Politburo in the summer of 1982. The obstacles to the expansion of Soviet influence in the Middle East were, indeed, greater than they had been a decade before. In part as a result of these changes, and in part owing to the Soviets' own responses to them, the position of the USSR in the Middle East had deteriorated substantially in the previous decade, especially after 1979. It is also the case that Brezhnev's health had manifestly worsened after 1974, and was probably quite poor at the time of the invasion.

However, there are serious problems both with this account of the conduct of the Kremlin leadership during the crisis and with the explanations given for it. The contrast between Soviet behavior in 1982 and 1973 is greatly exaggerated. In fact, Moscow was extremely active during the invasion, both diplomatically and militarily, and its intervention was highly effective. Indeed, the USSR succeeded either in inducing all the important parties in the conflict to heed its wishes or, when they refused to do so, in undermining their actions and plans.

To the extent that the Soviet leaders were more restrained and their assistance to their allies was more limited in 1982 than in 1973, this was not due to diminished interest in the Middle East. Although the Soviets had encountered major problems in their efforts to expand their influence in the region, they were no less eager to do so. On the contrary, precisely at those moments when they perceived themselves to have suffered the most serious setbacks—following their expulsion from Egypt in 1972, the successful completion of the U.S.-sponsored Israeli-Egyptian and Israeli-Syrian disengagement negotiations in 1974, the signing of the Camp David agreement in 1978, the invasion of Afghanistan in 1979, and the outbreak of the Iran-Iraq war in 1980—they noticeably stepped up their efforts to cement their relationships with those regional actors who were most ideologically attractive, such as Syria, or which could offer them a unique entrée into Middle East diplomacy, such as the PLO (Palestine Liberation Organization).[10] Thus, throughout the decade prior to 1982 and especially after 1979, they had steadily intensified their efforts to woo both Syria and the PLO, gradually increasing their involvement with and commitment to both.

Moreover, if Brezhnev had been ill for several years (and, indeed, he had apparently suffered a stroke in April 1982), the state of his health had fluctuated markedly; he was not always disabled, and was clearly very deeply involved in and highly active during the Lebanese crisis. Indeed, it may be argued that he had more impact on the Middle East policy of the regime during the crisis than at any time in the previous ten years.

To understand both the nature and limits of Soviet involvement in the crisis, and Brezhnev's impact on Soviet behavior at the time, one must know something about the attitudes and objectives of the leaders and elite groups whose views were influential in the formulation of Soviet global and Middle East policy prior to the war. This chapter will therefore present a brief account of the dynamics of foreign-policy decision making in the USSR as they affected Soviet policy toward the Middle East and the Arab-Israeli conflict in the crucial period 1967–82. It will then examine Soviet conduct during the invasion and the results of the USSR's intervention, paying particular attention to Brezhnev's role in shaping and implementing Soviet policy during the crisis. Finally, the discussion will draw on and extend the analysis of the dynamics of Soviet policy making to offer an explanation of the limits of Soviet involvement—the steps not taken in 1982.

BREZHNEV AND SOVIET MIDDLE EAST POLICY PRIOR TO THE CRISIS

1967 to 1973

During his first years in power, Brezhnev seems to have shared the general Politburo consensus that the objective of Soviet policy toward the Middle East should be the reduction and eventual elimination of the United States' presence and influence in the region.[11] However, the general secretary appears to have been deeply shaken by the outbreak of war between Israel and its Arab neighbors in June 1967. Surprised and shocked by the difficulty both superpowers experienced in restraining their respective allies, he began to fear that in a future conflict both might find it necessary to intervene. Thus, a new war in the Middle East could "bring the whole world to the brink of catastrophe."[12] Brezhnev became convinced that the primary aim of Soviet policy must be to avert such a catastrophe—to prevent a military confrontation between the superpowers. He concluded that the USSR must cooperate with the United States both to bring about a lasting solution to the Arab-Israeli dispute and to insure that while the effort to achieve such a solution was underway there would be no further resort to force by either side.[13] Moscow could and would continue to compete with Washington for influence in the Middle East, as elsewhere in the Third World, but it could not allow that competition to threaten world peace.[14]

Two assumptions underlay Brezhnev's thinking. One was that resolution of the Arab-Israeli conflict would not reduce but would rather enhance Soviet influence in the Middle East so long as three conditions were met: The USSR must play a major role in the negotiations, the agreement arrived at must meet the fundamental interests of the Arabs, and the Soviet Union must be accorded a major role in guaranteeing it. Brezhnev also assumed that the U.S. leadership concurred in the necessity and urgency of working with the USSR to eliminate "hotbeds of tension" in the Middle East and elsewhere.[15]

These assumptions were by no means shared by all influential elites in the USSR. Both high-ranking military leaders, such as Defense Minister Andrei Grechko and head of the Navy Admiral Sergei Gorshkov, and many ideologues in the Party apparatus, such as Party Secretary Mikhail Suslov and head of the Moscow Party organization Nikolai Egorychev, argued that the fundamental opposition between the interests of the Soviet Union and those of the United States rendered a settlement in the Middle East both impossible and undesirable. It was illusory, they contended, to think of restraining U.S.-Soviet competition, and any attempt to do so would gravely harm the USSR. Highest priority must continue to be accorded the expansion of Moscow's political influence and strategic presence in the Middle East (and the Third World generally) and the effort to expel the United States from the region.[16] This meant that the USSR should give the Arabs the fullest possible support, and provide them with—even encourage them to use—whatever means they thought necessary to achieve their goals.[17] The Soviets must not try to curb their ambitions or compel them to accept unpalatable compromises; on the contrary, they must be prepared to intervene directly and, if necessary, confront the United States on the Arabs' behalf.[18]

The disagreement between Brezhnev—who increasingly came to see the United States not merely as an adversary but also as a potential partner in the preservation of global peace—and the leaders and elites who regarded the United States as an unqualified and unalterable antagonist, surfaced almost immediately after the Six-Day War.[19] The Politburo had split on the question of whether Premier Aleksei Kosygin should meet with President Lyndon Johnson in June 1967 to attempt to reach agreement on terms for a Middle East settlement. Suslov reportedly attacked the plan, but Brezhnev's defense of it was decisive.[20]

From then on, until full-scale war again broke out between the Arabs and Israel in October 1973, there was a constant clash within the Soviet leadership between these two contending views of U.S.-Soviet relations, of the role the Soviet Union should play in the Middle East, and of the kinds of behavior on the part of the Arabs that the USSR should support. Whenever escalation of the conflict or an increase in the USSR's commitment to its allies was considered, Brezhnev was opposed, while influential ideologues and military officers were in favor.[21] This clash resulted in what amounted to a dual, often contradictory, policy: repeated efforts to work out an agreement with the United States, intense diplomatic pressure on the Arabs to accept the formulae devised, yet steadily increasing military backing for Egypt and Syria despite their rejection of these formulae.[22]

Although the general secretary did not always prevail, for a period of almost six years he was able to see to it that critical rules of restraint were adhered to in the supply of arms. During that period, despite repeated Arab pleas and warnings of a rupture in relations with the USSR, the Soviets refrained from providing their friends with the weapons they considered essential for launching an attack on Israel.[23] Brezhnev was therefore able to insure that the war he dreaded would not come about.[24]

Early in 1973, however, a decision was made to provide Egypt and Syria with planes and missiles capable of striking the Israeli interior. This reversal of previous policy was undertaken with the knowledge that war would almost certainly result. The new course was bitterly opposed by the general secretary. It represented a major victory for those forces in the Soviet leadership that upheld the primacy of competition with the United States rather than the avoidance of confrontation and development of cooperation with it.[25]

1973 to 1982

This victory reflected a crucial shift in the balance of power among the holders of these contending viewpoints. As a consequence, the USSR's quest for political influence and military presence in the Third World was greatly intensified; the frequency, scale, and geographical scope of Soviet intervention in Third World conflicts increased markedly; and Soviet military commitments—both to regimes involved in protracted conflicts and to "national liberation" movements—escalated sharply.[26]

Brezhnev appears to have opposed this new tendency toward increased military involvement in regional conflicts and aggressive competition with the United States in the Third World.[27] He does not seem to have objected to closer ties with Syria and the PLO. However, he continued to be deeply concerned about the possibility of a U.S.–Soviet confrontation.[28] He therefore wished to avoid commitments that could involve the USSR in war, and levels or types of assistance that would encourage the Arabs or provoke the Israelis to initiate violence. The general secretary continued to promote the idea of U.S.-Soviet cooperation to arrange a political solution, on the one hand denouncing Henry Kissinger's "shuttle diplomacy" and the subsequent Camp David accords because they excluded the Soviets, and on the other hand insisting that Syria and the PLO agree to participate in a superpower-sponsored international peace conference.[29] He tried to moderate the behavior of both allies, repeatedly telling their leaders they must accept the principle of Israel's right to exist.[30] He personally demanded that Syria withdraw its troops from Lebanon when its 1976 invasion raised the threat of war with Israel.[31] It was probably Brezhnev who was primarily responsible for repeated Soviet efforts to persuade the PLO to abandon the use of terror and substitute political for armed struggle.[32] The Party chief likewise appears to have opposed both Syria's request for weapons that would give it strategic parity with Israel and the PLO's pleas for a modern arsenal.[33] He remained convinced of the need for mutual restraint on the part of both superpowers, even proposing a code of conduct to which they should adhere throughout the Third World.[34]

However, in the years after the October War, it became even more difficult for Brezhnev to "sell" his belief in the importance of restraint to the rest of the Soviet leadership and elite. For one thing, supplying weapons to the Arabs had become much more lucrative.[35] Second, as a result of the apparent success of the new policy of massive force projection and greater support for Third World allies, the prestige and influence of the advocates of that policy grew steadily, making it harder to counter their arguments.[36] U.S. behavior during and after the October War only reinforced their claim that the United States was not interested in superpower cooperation and that Soviet restraint would not be reciprocated.[37] Indeed, to many in the elite it began to seem that only by arming the more hard-line elements opposed to negotiating with Israel could the USSR demonstrate to the United States that Moscow's cooperation was indispensable for an agreement to be obtained.[38] Most important, the more the United States seemed to be succeeding in its drive to evict the Soviets from the region—the more the Soviet position deteriorated—the more necessary it seemed for the Soviets to cultivate whatever allies they could in whatever way they could. It appears to have been widely believed in the political establishment that the USSR had to provide the military aid and diplomatic backing its friends desired, or it would lose the precarious political and strategic foothold it had retained after Egypt's "desertion."[39]

Thus, Soviet involvement with and commitment to Syria and the PLO increased dramatically after 1973. Syria in particular was wooed assiduously. Its armed forces were rebuilt quickly, the Soviet military presence in the country was greatly enhanced, and Syria was given explicit assurances that the USSR would come to its aid if it were the victim of aggression.[40] The PLO, too, received steadily increasing political, diplomatic, and military support. The USSR became a vocal champion of the Palestinian cause, backing their demand for an independent state, defending their right to return to their homeland, and calling for East Jerusalem to be restored to them. Offices of the PLO were opened in Moscow, training centers for its guerrillas were set up in many Soviet and Soviet-Bloc cities, and it was provided with extensive supplies of weapons and ammunition.[41]

The year 1978 marked an important juncture in Soviet relations with both Syria and the PLO. In that year the first of a series of developments occurred which were perceived as major setbacks by those in the Soviet leadership who viewed the United States as an unmitigatable antagonist and the Middle East as a crucial arena for combating U.S. influence and power. The strategy of this group had been to attempt to use the Arab-Israeli conflict as a device with which to unify the Arab world around the USSR in opposition to the United States.[42] The Camp David accords, signed in September 1978, appeared to strike a devastating blow against that strategy. Those accords and the Egyptian-Israeli Peace Treaty that followed in March 1979 were seen as a tremendous success for U.S.

diplomacy. They proved that the United States could induce Israel to return Arab territory and, in effect, to recognize Arab rights. Thus they seemed to validate and render irreversible Sadat's switch of allegiance between the superpowers and posed a grave threat that others—even the USSR's closest allies—might follow Egypt's lead.

There now seemed to be a greater need than ever before to demonstrate the value of the USSR as an ally. This need appeared to be even more acute after the Soviet invasion of Afghanistan in December 1979, a move that deeply antagonized the entire Moslem world and sparked a U.S. drive to persuade its members to endorse a "strategic consensus" aimed against the USSR. The outbreak of the Iran-Iraq war in September 1980 further aggravated the situation. It seemed to shatter the last remnants of Arab unity remaining in the wake of Camp David, and Soviet efforts to sustain a position of neutrality in the conflict aroused the resentment of nearly everyone in the region.[43]

These events, ominously perceived as they were by influential Soviet leaders and elites, had a major impact on the Kremlin's policy toward Syria and the PLO. Soviet links with both allies were noticeably intensified, and Moscow became much more receptive to their requests. In 1979–80 there was a sharp increase in the weapons provided to Syria.[44] The Treaty of Friendship, signed in October 1980, guaranteed Soviet cooperation to remove any threat to Syrian peace or security; this was a much stronger pledge of military support than had been provided by the USSR in any previous treaty with a Third World country.[45]

That the Soviets were prepared to stand by their promise was indicated the following year, when Assad responded to a Phalangist attack on Syrian troop transports near the Lebanese town of Zahle by installing SAM–6 missiles south of the city and moving others close to his border with Lebanon. Ater the Israelis threatened to attack the missiles, the USSR demonstrated its willingness to defend Syrian territory by sending advisers to assist in the operation of the batteries on the Syrian side. The chief of staff of the Soviet armed forces reportedly flew to Damascus and helped draw up a plan for joint military action in case Syria were endangered, and 53 Soviet ships were dispatched to the Mediterranean to participate in amphibious landing exercises on the Syrian coast.[46] Finally, early in 1982, the Soviets made a highly significant new commitment to Syria, agreeing in principle to Assad's long-standing request for "strategic parity," that is, for weapons that would make that country alone the military equal of Israel.[47]

Although to a significantly lesser degree, the PLO similarly benefited from the heightened concern in the Soviet leadership to maintain Moscow's Middle East position. Immediately after the Camp David talks, the USSR agreed to assist Arafat's campaign to win international recognition for the PLO by formally affirming that it was the sole legitimate representative of the Palestinian people. Full diplomatic recognition was accorded by the Kremlin in October 1981.[48] In the intervening years, there was a marked escalation of military support. Soviet military experts helped the PLO fortify its position in Lebanon, assisting in the construction of an elaborate network of underground bases and supply depots underneath the major cities along the coast. These depots were stocked with vast amounts of ammunition and weaponry. On Soviet insistence, PLO cadres were trained to function not merely as terrorists or guerrillas, but as a regular army.[49] The volume and nature of the arms shipments and the scale and variety of the training after 1978 suggest that the Palestinians were being prepared not merely to defend themselves, but to attack or perhaps even to seize and occupy positions in northern Israel.[50]

Thus, by mid–1982, the Kremlin had established very strong political and military ties with its two principal allies in the region. Probably in large part as a result of Brezhnev's restraining influence, these commitments were not as broad as those allies wished. The Treaty of Friendship and Cooperation with Syria did not spell out precisely what sort of cooperation the Soviets would provide if that country's security were threatened. Neither, in practice, were the Syrians allowed to determine when a threat entitling them to Soviet aid had in fact arisen.[51] Moreover, when the Syrians asked to upgrade the treaty into a "strategic cooperation" agreement of the sort the United States concluded with Israel at the end of 1981, they were repeatedly refused.[52] Such an agreement, it was feared, would obligate the USSR not only to defend Syria itself, but also to guarantee its position in Lebanon and to provide it with top-of-the-line weapons that might tempt it to undertake an offensive against Israel.[53] The PLO received much less advanced weapons in far smaller quantities than Syria.[54] These curbs on the ambitions and capabilities of the Syrians and Palestinians were an important factor in averting a major Arab-Israeli war for almost a decade. However, Brezhnev was unable to prevent his colleagues from providing a degree of military backing to both allies that enabled and encouraged them to engage in activities that the Israelis found threatening and that ultimately resulted in their invasion of Lebanon.[55]

BREZHNEV AND THE SOVIET RESPONSE TO THE CRISIS IN LEBANON

The USSR's behavior during the crisis reflected the persistent elite and leadership differences in perspectives and priorities that had characterized the formulation of Soviet foreign policy in the previous decade and a half. Brezhnev articulated the viewpoint of those who feared a U.S.-Soviet confrontation; these people wanted first and foremost to see the Arab-Israeli conflict controlled and resolved, or had come to doubt the wisdom of deeper involvement. There were others, however, notably military officials and ideologues, who were primarily concerned with expanding Soviet influence in the region and countering that of the United States. They therefore emphasized the need for strong backing for Syria, the PLO, or both.

At the same time, Moscow's actions can be seen as a response to an evolving situation, with each new phase of the crisis presenting a different set of problems and threats, which in turn generated different concerns on the part of the individuals involved in the determination of Soviet policy. It is therefore useful to analyze Soviet reactions in terms of the four stages in which the crisis unfolded for Brezhnev and the Kremlin leadership.

Stage I (June 6–June 11, 1982)

The Israeli invasion of Lebanon did not initially alarm the Soviet leadership. The real crisis came only on the fourth day (June 9). As a result of heavy fighting near the strategic Beirut-Damascus highway, the IDF (Israeli Defense Forces) captured important vantage positions overlooking the road. They also initiated a fierce assault on the missile screen near Zahle, which the Syrians had erected in 1981 to protect their forces in the Bekaa Valley. It appeared that the Israelis were attempting to break through into eastern Lebanon and open up an invasion route into Syria.[56] Reports apparently even reached Moscow that Damascus was under attack.[57] Full-scale war between Israel and Syria seemed about to break out, which led the entire Soviet leadership to concur in the view that such a war had to be prevented.

It was of little comfort that the "strategic alliance" that the United States concluded with Israel in 1981 had subsequently been suspended.[58] Brezhnev assumed that the Americans were prepared to uphold that alliance whenever the need arose. He undoubtedly remembered the strong U.S. reaction to his suggestion in October 1973 that Soviet forces might be sent to enforce the cease-fire between Egypt and Israel. If Henry Kissinger had been prepared to call a worldwide nuclear alert to obstruct Soviet efforts to implement an arrangement he himself had desired and negotiated, what would Ronald Reagan, viewed as far more reckless and anti-Soviet, be prepared to do if the USSR sent troops to fight the United States's closest ally in the region?

The Soviet leadership's chief concern in this stage of the crisis was therefore to halt the fighting between Israel and Syria. Its efforts to achieve this became progressively more intense as the situation deteriorated and the likelihood of war increased. Its first step was to call on the UN Security Council to arrange a cease-fire and take responsibility for resolving the dispute. This was the least risky and, from Brezhnev's point of view, the most desirable approach to the crisis: it could have led to UN-sponsored peace talks, which would have brought the USSR back into Middle East diplomacy.[59]

When the United States vetoed the Soviet-backed resolution, Moscow called on the Arab states to use their collective oil "weapon" to induce the Americans to force Israel to halt.[60] This course was probably most attractive to those in the leadership who were hoping to restore Arab unity in opposition not merely to Israel, but to the United States as well. When this too failed, and when Syria itself appeared to be in danger, Brezhnev appealed directly to Reagan to stop the Israeli advance. Sending a message over the hot line to Washington, the Soviet leader avoided threatening language that might provoke the U.S. president, but reportedly warned him that "a most serious situation had been created, which contained the possibility of wider hostilities.''[61] At the same time, Moscow reportedly told the Syrians that it expected them to accept a cease-fire if one were proffered.[62]

These diplomatic moves were accompanied by a series of signals to the United States and Israel of Soviet determination to aid Syria if its security were threatened. Five warships were added to the USSR's fleet in the eastern Mediterranean, permission was requested from Turkey for transport of arms by air over its territory, massive quantities of military equipment were quickly (and visibly) stockpiled at airports in the southern part of the USSR, and two airborne divisions were placed on alert.[63]

Whether Brezhnev would, in fact, have agreed to a direct intervention, and whether, if he had not, his position would have prevailed, will never be known. His warning to Reagan, reinforced as it was by adroit crisis signalling, had precisely the effect he desired. Within hours of receiving the message, the U.S. President informed the Israeli prime minister that the United States was firmly opposed to expansion of the war with Syria. Citing Brezhnev's words, Reagan told Begin that there was a distinct possibility of Soviet intervention and asked for a cease-fire between Israeli and Syrian troops within four hours. A refusal by Israel to agree to a cease-fire, he declared, would threaten world peace and cause great tensions in U.S.-Israeli relations.

Persuaded that both the United States and the USSR were serious, Begin summoned his cabinet in the early hours of the morning of June 10, and procured from his reluctant ministers an agreement to let the United States negotiate an immediate cessation of hostilities.[64] The cease-fire went into effect on June 11. While it subsequently broke down on a number of occasions, Israel was henceforth greatly restrained by its uncertainty as to what the United States and the USSR might do if the fighting escalated. Brezhnev's letter thus played a crucial role in preventing not only a full-scale war between Israel and Syria, but possibly also a superpower collision in the Middle East.

Stage II (June 11–July 6, 1982)

Temporarily reassured that Israel would not carry the war into Syrian territory or provoke a massive response from Assad by challenging his control over eastern Lebanon, the Kremlin decision-makers now faced a very different threat as the results of the first six days of fighting became known. In ground clashes, the Syrians had lost hundreds of tanks, including T–72s, which the Soviets had advertised as the most sophisticated in the world.[65] The Israelis, in these encounters, had lost only a small number of tanks and not a single plane.[66]

As reports of these losses reached Moscow, along with bitter Syrian criticisms of the weapons they had received, Soviet military leaders were confronted with a very serious problem. At stake in Lebanon was not only the USSR's credibility as a supplier of arms to the Arab and other Third World countries, but even the credibility of the air defense system and combat forces of the Warsaw Pact (which relied heavily on SAM–6 missiles and T–72 tanks).[67] Moreover, in the opinion of some in the military and the Party apparatus, it was imperative that major steps be taken so that the Soviets might maintain their alliance with a disillusioned and humiliated Syria.[68]

The Soviet leaders responded to these challenges as they had to the dangers of the first stage of the war, with alacrity. They sent to Syria, along with an entourage of advisers, the first deputy commander-in-chief of the Soviet Air Defense Force. Arriving on June 13, General Evgenii Iurasov personally inspected the SAM sites in the Bekaa and delivered a promise from his superiors to replace all Syrian losses and upgrade and modernize Syrian equipment.[69] Moscow immediately initiated an airlift to implement this commitment, and on a daily basis began steadily and rapidly to replenish Syria's armed forces with new tanks, high-performance aircraft, and improved air defenses.[70]

The scale of these deliveries was much smaller than that of the Soviet resupply effort in the 1973 war, but Syria's losses were also much smaller. More significantly, this one was conducted much more quietly and with less fanfare than in 1973.[71] Clearly, Brezhnev sought to avoid provoking the United States unnecessarily, as had happened in the well-publicized 1973 operation.[72]

As a result of the Kremlin's willingness and ability to provide new and better weapons as soon as the need became apparent, the credibility gap it faced, if not fully closed, was at least reduced to manageable proportions.[73] The Syrians were sufficiently mollified to announce that relations with the USSR were "excellent in all fields."[74] At the same time, U.S. Secretary of State Alexander Haig described Soviet behavior as "encouragingly cautious."[75] All factions in the leadership thus had reason to be satisfied.

To insure that the IDF exercised the necessary caution vis-à-vis Soviet facilities and personnel, the Kremlin sent a note to Begin via the Finnish embassy in Tel Aviv reminding him that the Soviet embassy was "in the vicinity of Israeli troops." This was followed by a telegram through the same channel, with an explicit request to refrain from hitting the embassy.[76] Since the Israelis were eager to avoid provoking the Soviets, these messages, although devoid of any threat of military or political action, proved to be sufficient. The IDF was careful to direct its fire away from the Soviet compound.

It was far more difficult (as well as far more important in Brezhnev's eyes) to control the conflict between Israel and Syria. It soon became apparent that so much was at stake for both that neither would yield easily to superpower efforts at restraint. Indeed, the first clash between the two, at the outskirts of Beirut, occurred precisely at the time the cease-fire took effect in eastern Lebanon. At noon on June 11, in the midst of an assault on Syrian troops deployed at a critical junction that controlled access to Beirut from the east and south, the Israelis called on their adversaries to lay down their arms. They refused, and the fighting went on for many hours until the IDF had captured the junction. By the next day (June 12), it was clear to Soviet observers that the Israelis were bent on pressing forward into the capital, and in so doing were making no effort to withhold their fire from Syrian forces in and around Beirut. It was also clear that the Syrians were prepared to fight tenaciously to maintain their position in the city.[77]

Alarmed by the fragility of the truce, Brezhnev sent a second message to President Reagan, warning him of the dangers of spreading violence if the cease-fire were not reestablished and extended to all parties to the conflict.[78] Worded like his earlier message to arouse concern without providing provocation, it too appears to have had the desired effect. U.S. efforts to induce all parties to halt their hostilities were intensified. State Department officials worked throughout the night and into the morning, and by midday on June 13 were able to announce that an agreement involving not only Israel and Syria, but also the PLO, had been arranged.[79]

There was a limit to what the United States could accomplish, however. Later in the day, with the Israeli government apparently unaware of what its forces were doing, IDF units pushed forward to meet Phalangist troops outside Beirut and then proceeded to enter the city. The first step in the escalatory scenario that Moscow feared had been executed: the Lebanese capital had been encircled, and the Syrian forces there cut off.[80] The Soviet leaders concluded that stronger language and more direct pressure were needed to make Tel Aviv aware of the perils of its course. An official government statement issued on June 14 bluntly reminded "those who are making Israel's policy today" that the Middle East "is a region situated in direct proximity to the southern borders of the Soviet Union" and thus "events there cannot help but affect the interests of the USSR." Probably owing to Brezhnev's concern for caution, the statement employed a carefully crafted formulation that seemed to threaten direct involvement without actually committing the Kremlin to it. "The Soviet Union," Israel and its supporters were warned, "is on the Arabs' side not just in words but in deeds."[81]

This statement appears to have had an impact both on the United States and on Israel, although it is hard to say precisely how much influence it exerted. Certainly the attitude of the Reagan administration toward Israel's actions began to harden very perceptibly after the Kremlin warning was issued. When Begin arrived in the United States two days later (on June 16), Reagan's aides informed him that the President might cancel their scheduled meeting unless the cease-fire were implemented immediately.[82] Although the strain in U.S.-Arab relations caused by Israel's move into Beirut was probably the chief reason for the U.S. response, the threat of Soviet intervention was probably a factor as well. Similarly, the five-day lull in the intensity of the fighting after June 14 can be explained primarily by Israel's reluctance to antagonize the United States any further and to incur the casualties that would result from an assault on the Lebanese capital. However, concern over the Soviet response to such a move probably also played a role in its hesitation.

Moscow's warning did not, however, ultimately deter Israel from renewing hostilities with the Syrians. Contemptuous of his government's caution, Israeli Defense Minister Ariel Sharon was determined to strengthen his troops' hold in

Beirut. He resolved to push the Syrians back from the mountain ridge above the city and to take the crucial Beirut-Damascus Highway, thereby preventing the Syrians from reaching their forces in the capital. Major clashes between the two sides were thus resumed on June 19 and 20.[83]

These Israeli moves led the Syrians to announce that their consent to a cessation of hostilities was "strictly conditioned" on an immediate withdrawal of Israeli troops from Lebanese territory. Moreover, this announcement was accompanied by a renewed call for a "strategic alliance" with the USSR; that is, for Soviet support in repelling not only direct threats to Syrian security but also indirect threats, such as the challenge Israel was mounting to Syria's control of Lebanon.[84]

There were apparently some in the Soviet leadership who believed Moscow should provide such support. An account of the press conference at which the appeal was articulated (by Syrian Information Minister Ahmad Iskander) was published after a two-day delay in *Pravda*.[85] However, probably because the Syrian statement also expressed considerable gratitude to the USSR and did not seem to imply a rupture in relations if the request were again refused, Brezhnev appears to have prevailed. Assad received a letter from him on June 23 that reportedly assured the Syrians that while they "would not fight alone" if Israel attacked their own territory directly, the USSR's commitment would not be extended beyond the borders of Syria.[86]

Soviet refusal to provide the requested backing helps to explain why the Syrians decided to withdraw from the field of battle on June 25, leaving the vital segment of the Beirut-Damascus road to the east of the city in Israeli hands.[87] This defeat was a very significant one for Syria: henceforth it would be unable to reach Beirut. There were many reports that Assad himself flew to Moscow at this time, probably to render one last plea for help in Lebanon.[88] However, Brezhnev appears to have given him no encouragement, telling him that the USSR wanted the cease-fire restored without conditions.

With simultaneous parallel pressure being exerted on Israel by the United States, the general secretary was at last able to achieve his objective.[89] There were no further significant Israeli-Syrian encounters in or around Beirut. Apparently as a result of Soviet insistence, the Syrians did not attempt to open the highway to the capital. They did not mount any other major military challenge to Israel in order to preserve their position in Lebanon, and eventually they agreed to withdraw their forces from Beirut. Implicit Soviet cooperation with the United States thus succeeded once again in controlling the crisis in Lebanon and preventing its escalation into a superpower confrontation.

Stage III (July 6–August 31, 1982)

While Brezhnev had welcomed U.S. efforts to negotiate, extend, and sustain a cease-fire, he was deeply opposed to any U.S. role in enforcing the arrangements made unless the Soviets were given an equivalent part to play. A consistent advocate of joint superpower efforts to "eliminate the hotbed of tension" in the

Middle East, he objected as strongly as did his colleagues to actions by the United States that would improve its political and strategic position in the region at the expense of the USSR. He was therefore infuriated when President Reagan effectively repudiated collaboration with the Soviet Union by announcing on July 6 that the United States was prepared to send its troops to Beirut to oversee the evacuation of the PLO and police the cease-fire. The "multinational" force in which the United States would participate would not, it was clear, include the USSR.

This announcement, which marked the beginning of the third phase of the crisis for the Soviet leadership, created a difficult dilemma for the general secretary. He regarded the unilateral injection of U.S. soldiers into a region abutting the border of the USSR as inimical to Soviet interests, but it was not clear what he could do to prevent such a move without bringing on the confrontation he had labored so hard to avoid.

By means of still another message to Reagan, Brezhnev tried to warn him that the Kremlin would not view such a step with equanimity. Again avoiding an explicit threat of retaliatory action, he told the U.S. president that if U.S. troops were sent, "the USSR would construct its policies taking this fact into account."[90] A similar warning appeared to have been sufficient to keep the United States out of Iran after the fall of the shah in November 1978.[91] It was worth trying again. The Soviet leader reinforced the message with an interview in *Pravda* reiterating the USSR's "categorical" opposition to the appearance of U.S. forces on Lebanese soil and offering a constructive compromise: the Soviet Union would support instead the use of UN forces to supervise a PLO withdrawal.[92]

Once again the Politburo backed its diplomacy with signals of its seriousness and its ultimate willingness to use instruments of force to defend its interests. It made public for the first time the airlift to Syria.[93] It sent the chief of staff of the Soviet armed forces to Damascus with a second team of military experts—this time several hundred of them—to discuss and implement Syria's needs.[94] Most important, it noticeably stepped up the pace, scale, and technological sophistication of the weapons deliveries to Syria and introduced into the Bekaa a new generation of surface-to-air missiles, SAM–8 and –9s, with Soviet crews to man them.[95]

When these steps failed and the United States went ahead with the deployment of marines to Beirut, the Soviet leaders reacted angrily. It was apparently in response to that deployment that they decided to increase substantially their military commitment to Syria once the war was over. They agreed to provide their ally with a state-of-the-art integrated air-defense system which had never before been deployed outside the Warsaw Pact.[96] The promised system included extra-long-range SAM–5 surface-to-air missiles, new horizon-scanning radars, highly advanced electronic jammers, and a sophisticated command, control, and communications network linked to the Soviets' own air defense headquarters in Moscow.[97] Requiring an additional 1,000 to 1,500 Soviet military personnel (advisers and crews) to be stationed in Syria, the new systems would constitute a response in kind to the American move. U.S. troops were placed close to the Soviet border; Soviet missiles and missile crews would be placed in positions to threaten carrier-based aircraft from the 6th Fleet and NATO forces in Turkey.[98]

While this decision was probably advocated by those in the Party and the military who had consistently urged a purely competitive approach to the United States, and who thus attached great importance to the alliance with Syria, it may also have been acceptable to Brezhnev. It is true that the general secretary was undoubtedly concerned by the presence of a large number of Soviet combat troops in so volatile an area. Moreover, because the new air defense system would go a long way toward neutralizing the critical advantage in airpower that the Israelis had always enjoyed over the Syrians, it would bring Assad close to his goal of achieving strategic parity with Israel and might thus tempt him to go to war.[99] On the other hand, the command, control, and communications system to be installed along with the new missiles and the Soviet crews manning them would give the USSR considerably more information about and control over Syrian military activity than it had hitherto possessed.[100] Moscow's ability to restrain its ally would thus be greatly enhanced.

The Soviet leaders did not succeed in deterring the introduction of U.S. forces into a region they considered vitally sensitive: their own ''backyard.'' However, their increased commitment to Syria would later embolden Assad to reject and undermine the Lebanese settlement that the United States worked so hard (and so visibly) to negotiate. They were thus able to deal a major defeat to U.S. diplomacy.[101] Moreover, the presence of Soviet combat troops actively engaged in the defense of Syrian territory created a situation so dangerous that it played a major role in turning U.S. public opinion against the continued stationing of U.S. soldiers in Lebanon. In the end, the Soviet leaders did succeed in attaining what—because of U.S. behavior—had become their common objective: insuring that the Lebanese crisis would not lead to an increase in U.S. prestige or power in the region.

Stage IV (September 1–September 20, 1982)

Although Politburo members were probably in agreement on the need to prevent a U.S. gain in the Middle East at the USSR's expense, Brezhnev's primary goal was not merely the negative one of undermining American influence. Since the beginning of the war, he had wanted above all to exploit the outbreak of violence to effect changes, both in the region and in the international system, that would prevent the occurrence of future Third World crises with a potential for superpower confrontation. He had thus hoped to persuade the important regional and extraregional actors of the need and urgency for both a peaceful solution to the Arab-Israeli conflict (with a Soviet role in arranging and guaranteeing such a solution) and an East-West agreement to control and deescalate competition in the Third World.

Brezhnev also saw that the Lebanon war provided an excellent opportunity for the USSR to move in this direction. The more moderate Arabs were both angered by the U.S. role in encouraging the invasion and relieved by Soviet restraint. They were therefore more receptive to Kremlin overtures than they had been for nearly a decade. In Israel, skepticism regarding the need for the operation the army had undertaken and reports of heavy casualties had heightened the eagerness for peace among broad segments of the population.

Thus, since the beginning of the war, the general secretary had pursued his objectives of exploiting the crisis to press for peace, broadening Soviet ties in the Arab world, and creating a more moderate image of the USSR in the region. The first Soviet statement on the invasion, a TASS bulletin on June 7, emphasized that events in Lebanon demonstrated the urgent need for a comprehensive solution of the Arab-Israeli conflict.[102] As soon as the situation seemed under control, King Hussein of Jordan was invited to Moscow to "become acquainted with the country" and discuss ways of resolving the dispute.[103] Brezhnev took time out to send a message to Saudi Arabia's new ruler, King Fahd, congratulating him on his recent coronation and underlining Soviet eagerness to develop and enhance cooperation between the two countries.[104] The Party chief also sent warm wishes to Egypt's President Mubarak on the 30th anniversary of the July 23 Revolution, and saw to it that Egypt was kept informed of Soviet views on the crisis.[105] Moreover, Brezhnev used his *Pravda* interview to revive his proposal for an international conference to achieve a settlement; he emphasized the USSR's readiness to cooperate with "*everyone* who wished to work for peace in the Middle East," and stressed (probably in answer to the objections of both Soviet and Arab hard-liners) that "*even in Israel* more and more people [were] coming to realize the futility of force to solve the problems of the area."[106]

The quest for a permanent settlement in the Middle East, along with moderation of East-West competition in the Third World generally, now became the main focus of Brezhner's activity. The issuance of a comprehensive U.S. plan for peace in the Middle East on September 1 posed a new challenge that the Soviet leader had to meet in order to seize the diplomatic initiative from the United States and insure a Soviet role in the peace process. The announcement of the "Reagan Plan" thus marked the beginning of the fourth and final stage of the crisis as seen from the Kremlin.[107]

The publication eight days later of a significantly different Arab League plan made a timely response from the USSR all the more imperative.[108] Brezhnev could not afford to lose this unique opportunity to point out the moderation and reasonableness of Soviet policy. In contrast with Washington, whose plan had already been denounced as reflecting Israeli concerns on every crucial point, Moscow would demonstrate its willingness to take into account the legitimate interests of all parties to the conflict.[109] Likewise, the forthcoming visit by the Premier of South Yemen, Ali Nasser Mohammed, offered an ideal context in which to present a Soviet plan for peace. The presence of the PDRY leader when the plan was articulated would seem to apply endorsement of it by one of the most militant Arab states. The appearance of such backing could help win acceptance of the USSR's position by its other allies in the Middle East, who had never been enthusiastic about a political settlement. That, in turn, could generate broader international support for the Soviet proposal.

The "Brezhnev Plan" was therefore set forth in a speech in honor of Premier Mohammed on September 15. Although very similar to the Fez statement, Brezhnev's proposals were much more explicit with regard to Israel's right to exist and the necessity of ending the state of war and establishing peace between Israel and the Arabs. "It is impossible to ensure the security of some states while trampling on the security of others," the Soviet leader warned. Specifically mentioning the Palestinians, Brezhnev told them that if they wanted a state of their own, they must be prepared to commit themselves to solve any disputes with Israel by peaceful means, through negotiations. The general secretary also made clear not only that the UN Security Council (of which the USSR was a permanent member) must guarantee the settlement, but also that its terms must be worked out in an international conference in which all interested parties would be allowed to participate.[110]

As if to underscore his belief that no settlement, however comprehensive, could be permanent so long as East-West competition in the Third World continued unabated, the Soviet leader ended his last speech dealing with Lebanon with a final statement of the need for superpower cooperation to insure that such competition remained peaceful. In an address welcoming Indian Prime Minister Indira Gandhi to Moscow on September 20, he urged that NATO and the Warsaw Pact agree to refrain from providing military guarantees to the countries of Asia, Africa, and Latin America. Such concrete actions, he admonished both his Kremlin colleagues and the Western powers, are required "to stop mankind from slipping into nuclear catastrophe."[111]

Brezhnev's "peace offensive" had little direct impact on the United States. Its effect in the Middle East was noticeable, however. Both the peace plan and the diplomatic overtures which preceded it considerably strengthened moderate Arab support for Soviet policy. In the long run, they helped to lay the groundwork for subsequent Soviet reconciliation with Egypt and the establishment of relations with Oman and the United Arab Emirates. More immediately, they turned Jordan's King Hussein into a forceful advocate of a Soviet role in arranging a settlement. Brezhnev's insistence on Arab acceptance of and peaceful coexistence with the Jewish state, articulated with greater emphasis and firmness than ever before, likewise helped to make an international conference with Soviet participation more acceptable to many Israelis. Eventually, this new Arab and Israeli support for the idea would even induce President Reagan to go along with it.

THE LIMITS OF SOVIET INVOLVEMENT

In view of the readiness and ability of the Soviet leadership to become deeply involved in the crisis, both diplomatically and militarily, it is puzzling that

Moscow's actions in support of the PLO were extremely limited. Its treatment of its Palestinian friends contrasted markedly with its behavior vis-à-vis Syria. It not only ignored the PLO's frantic appeals for aid and bitter Arab criticisms of the USSR's unwillingness to provide it, but even refused repeated requests to use stronger language on behalf of the organization in dealing with Washington and Tel Aviv.[112]

The PLO received no direct Soviet military support, even symbolic. It was told almost immediately after the invasion began that the USSR would send no troops or advisers to assist it, and this message was reiterated after its fighters were surrounded and besieged in Beirut.[113] Even when supplies could no longer reach the PLO forces from Syria, the Soviets apparently undertook no resupply operation of their own.[114] They employed only mild diplomatic pressure in an effort to persuade the Israelis to cease their attacks on the Palestinians and—what is even more striking—made no mention of support for the PLO per se in their official pronouncements and communications during the crisis.[115] It is this behavior and the Arab criticisms of it which created the erroneous impression of Soviet passivity during the war.

It is clear that neither lack of interest in retaining political influence and strategic presence in the Middle East nor political paralysis engendered by the incapacitation of the Party chief can explain the Soviet leaders' refusal to assist an ally to whom they had rendered substantial, steadily increasing support for nearly a decade. What, then, does account for their behavior?

THE POLICY DEBATE

There were two options open to the Kremlin leaders had they wished to provide more extensive help to the PLO: One was to send the organization sufficient aid to defeat and repel the IDF and force it to leave Lebanon. Short of that, the Soviets could have attempted to deter the Israelis, first from continuing their advance on PLO strongholds, and later from maintaining their siege and bombardment of Beirut.

Given that Brezhnev's primary objectives in the crisis were to avoid a superpower confrontation, broaden Soviet ties in the region, and lay the groundwork for a resolution of the Arab-Israeli conflict, it is virtually certain that the general secretary opposed the first option and highly likely that he rejected the second as well. Because of the vast discrepancy in the size, equipment, and skill of the two sides' forces, a truly massive intervention by Soviet troops would have been necessary to enable the Palestinians to defeat their foes.[116] The risks in undertaking such an operation against a close ally of the United States were obvious, especially in view of the assumption in Moscow that the United States endorsed the Israeli move against the PLO. Moreover, there were few in the Arab world who desired or would have approved such a step. The moderate regimes that Brezhnev wished to cultivate were very strongly opposed to the influx of Soviet troops into the region, and even some of the most radical leaders, such as Khaddafi, shared that sentiment.[117]

An attempt to deter the Israelis through a demonstration of Soviet support for the PLO, while somewhat less dangerous, would also have entailed substantial risks. The use of any Soviet ground or airborne troops (even a small number) in such an endeavor would have been highly provocative to the United States, as would the provision of Soviet combat ships and sailors to challenge the blockade of the Lebanese capital. Even a resupply operation (which the Israelis might have tried to block) or threats of possible Soviet involvement might have initiated an escalatory process that could have had disastrous consequences.

Brezhnev was probably also persuaded that the USSR stood to lose relatively little if the PLO were defeated. We have seen that in the decision regarding aid to Syria during the war, the performance of the USSR's advanced weaponry and its credibility as an alliance partner were at issue. This was not the case with the question of whether to help the PLO, which had received few modern arms and no formal pledges of assistance if attacked. Syria was one of Moscow's oldest and most loyal (although by no means docile) friends among the Third World states. It had good socialist credentials and valuable strategic assets, which it had placed at Moscow's disposal.[118] The PLO was merely a political movement, whose chances of obtaining its own territory and controlling strategic assets were unclear, and whose ties to the conservative Moslem states suggested a probable domestic policy orientation (if it were to come to power) which would allow only minimal Soviet influence.

Most important for Brezhnev, the weakness of the moderates in the PLO had resulted in its repeated rejection of what was the centerpiece of the Soviet leader's Middle Eastern policy: the quest for a political settlement of the Arab-Israeli conflict based on a division of Palestine between Arabs and Jews.[119] There was, therefore, no reason why Brezhnev should have wanted to take significant risks on behalf of the PLO. Indeed, it is not impossible that he actually desired its defeat as a means of convincing it to abandon armed struggle and accept a territorial compromise.[120] Certainly he would have seen little reason to help defend its presence in Lebanon, which he appears to have consistently opposed.[121]

Not everyone who played an important role in the decision process during the crisis seems to have shared Brezhnev's views. Certain ideologues, probably led by the highly influential first deputy director of the Party Central Committee's International Department, Vadim Zagladin, appear to have argued for more tangible aid to the PLO. Their views were widely expressed in the Soviet media, suggesting that they had strong backing at a very high level. Moreover, because of the centrality of the International Department in the formulation of Soviet foreign policy, especially toward the national liberation movement and the Third World, these opinions were undoubtedly given serious consideration both by the Politburo as a whole and by that portion of it that was most actively involved in dealing with the crisis.[122]

The case made by these ideologues for more active assistance to the PLO rested on several interrelated arguments. The first was that the survival of the PLO was essential to the survival of the movement it led. Arafat's organization had become the "banner and mobilizing center of the Palestinian resistance." If one were able to eliminate the PLO as a political and military factor in the Middle East, one would succeed in "bringing the Palestinian people to their knees."[123]

Second, the proponents of more tangible support for the PLO maintained that the Palestinian Resistance Movement (PRM) was the most radical or "progressive" portion of the national liberation movement in the Middle East as a whole. This meant that the fate of the PRM was of "key significance," not only for the larger movement, but for the social (and hence political) development of the entire region.[124] In other words, the Palestinian movement was the key to the victory of socialism throughout the Middle East; its defeat would be a very serious defeat for socialism.

If that alone were not sufficient reason to intervene to save the PLO, these ideologues argued, it was important to understand who was trying to destroy it, and why. It was not Israel which was primarily responsible for the war in Lebanon. That war was "part of the current strategy of imperialism," that is, part of a far-reaching U.S. design. Washington supported this invasion because it saw it as the beginning of "a global offensive against the liberation forces in the Third World"—an offensive that "Washington politicians [had] long been calling for." The motive behind this offensive was the expansion of U.S. hegemony in the Third World, by means of the territorial aggrandizement of U.S. allies (or stooges). Thus, Tel Aviv's plans of creating a "greater Israel from the Nile to the Euphrates" were part of Washington's plans "to recarve the map of the Middle East according to [its] own ideas."[125]

According to this perspective, Washington regarded Israel as "its own Near East policeman, carrying out the will of American hegemonism." It was attempting "to consolidate through the hands of the Israeli gendarme American imperialism's rule in the Middle East."[126] The reason why this ambition was so dangerous and had to be thwarted was that if it were realized, the United States would transform the Middle East not only into a source of energy for the West, but also into an "important military-political staging ground," presumably for expansion into other areas of the Third World.[127] Moreover, in the end, it was not only the developing countries that would be the targets of U.S. aggression. "It is clear that all this is aimed against the military balance that has emerged in the world," that is, "against the socialist countries." In other words, not only the future of socialism in the Third World, but the security of the USSR and the Soviet Bloc was being threatened.[128]

What, according to these ideologues, should the USSR do in response to this situation? First, the Kremlin decision-makers must realize that "the struggle against the Palestinians [was] the most important part of the American plan." The Palestinians were the chief obstacle to the implementation of this strategy. Second, those in charge of Soviet policy could not assume that this imperialist offensive would "pass of its own accord" if the socialist countries did nothing to counter it. "It will not pass of its own accord." Whether or not "the imperialist wave" is rebuffed "depends on us." To those who argued (as many Soviet commentators and presumably policy-makers did) that the USSR should not do what the Arab states were themselves unwilling to do, these ideologues responded, "We cannot answer for others, but we can for ourselves." As for Brezhnev's fear that Soviet intervention would lead to war with the United States, that contention was unwarranted. If the USSR acted immediately, not waiting for imperialism to substantially alter the global "equilibrium of forces" in its favor, that equilibrium would be sufficient to prevent war. It was "a guarantee that we can advance," that is, assist the forces of national liberation, "and not allow imperialism to realize its [hegemonial] plans."[129]

These arguments did not go unanswered. One of Brezhnev's advisers, Middle East expert Aleksandr Bovin, was given the task of replying.[130] He did so, on at least four occasions during the crisis, by attempting to dissociate the United States from Israel's actions. He insisted that, in fact, Washington opposed "Begin's excessive bellicosity."[131] Brezhnev himself, while conceding that Israel had received U.S. backing (a concession necessary to the argument that the Middle East crisis could be resolved only by means of superpower cooperation), did not emphasize the point, and did not attribute to Washington a grand design aimed at the Third World or the Soviet Union. Rather, he portrayed the United States as sufficiently involved in Lebanon to justify Soviet caution, but not so deeply or with such aggressive intent as to require a dangerous Soviet initiative in response.[132]

The existence of these differing views, regarding the desirability of greater Soviet involvement on behalf of the PLO, explains the contradictory signals emitted by the Kremlin concerning Arab intervention to aid the PLO. A constant theme in the Soviet press was the need for the Arabs to stand behind their Palestinian brothers. Occasionally they were implicitly encouraged to use force, and in one instance a TASS commentary indicated that the USSR would support such an operation "not simply [with] vague assurances or words," but with "timely and effective aid."[133] Brezhnev, however, avoided all reference to Arab military intervention, opposing any action that could escalate the conflict. (What he asked of the Arabs was to formulate a unified position on terms for settling the Arab-Israeli dispute so as to assure the Palestinians their rights.)[134] Moreover, when Khaddafi appealed to Assad to send his troops into battle, the Libyan leader received a message from Moscow within a few hours telling him not to get the USSR involved.[135]

THE OUTCOME OF THE DEBATE

On all previous occasions in which influential Soviet elites debated whether or not to increase their country's involvement in the Arab-Israeli conflict (that is, in 1968, 1970, and 1973), the interventionist position ultimately prevailed,

Brezhnev's policy of restraint was rejected, and the Arabs received the assistance they requested. It was likewise the interventionist position (and not Brezhnev's views) that dominated Soviet policy making toward the Middle East (and the Third World generally) in the years after 1973. Why, then, did the interventionists' arguments fail to carry the day with regard to the PLO in the summer of 1982? Why was Brezhnev's policy adopted in this instance?

The prolonged, unprecedentedly large-scale Soviet engagement in Afghanistan appears to have triggered (or greatly reinforced and accelerated) a widespread reconsideration of the utility of military intervention outside the Soviet Bloc.[136] Even in those segments of the elite in which there had previously been the most enthusiasm about the expansion of Soviet influence in the Third World and the greatest readiness to use force to establish a global presence, there was a growing perception that the benefits of such activity were often less or less lasting than anticipated, and the costs and risks were higher.

Third World groups had been notably resistant to Soviet political control, even when Soviet arms had brought them to power and kept them there. In a number of key cases in which very extensive military support had been provided, Soviet allies had proved ungrateful, unreliable, and disloyal, refusing to provide requested military facilities or withdrawing access to them and repudiating the treaties of friendship that had guaranteed them. Moreover, military success had often been elusive, and the Soviets had found themselves involved in numerous protracted conflicts around the globe.[137] This had begun to limit the options open to the Kremlin in crisis situations such as that which had recently arisen in Poland, in which vital Soviet interests were clearly at stake. Most important, it had become clear that the United States would not remain passive while the frequency and scale of Soviet interventions markedly increased. The major military buildup (both nuclear and conventional) that the United States had undertaken after 1979, the establishment of the U.S. Rapid Deployment Force and a network of bases to support it, and the pursuit of an anti–Soviet ''strategic consensus'' in the Middle East were seen in Moscow as, at least in part, a response to Soviet actions in the Third World.[138]

In this new international situation, in which the United States was widely perceived as being on the offensive, many more people in high positions had begun to share Brezhnev's belief in the need for caution.[139] President Reagan's virulently anti-Communist rhetoric had engendered particular alarm.[140] More and more widely it had begun to be argued that the danger of war was increasing and that the USSR must therefore take great care not only to avoid a superpower confrontation, but also to prevent any further deterioration in U.S.-Soviet relations.[141] Indeed, at the highest levels it had begun to be emphasized that Moscow must act in such a way as to make it possible to revive detente.[142] As one commentator put it, the Kremlin should administer a ''local anesthetic'' to regional conflicts to protect the ''living tissue'' of U.S.-Soviet relations.[143]

In addition to the international situation, developments at home were leading many to place greater emphasis on good relations with the United States. At the end of the 1970s and beginning of the 1980s, Soviet leaders and members of the elite had begun to be very concerned about the performance of the economy. By the summer of 1982, they had come to attach great importance to assuring and increasing regular shipments of U.S. grain, reviving U.S. exports of technology, and resuming negotiations to curb the costly strategic arms race. Progress in all of these areas had been blocked by the United States in response to direct or indirect use of force by the USSR, and discussions with Washington on all these subjects had reached a critical juncture just as the Lebanese crisis erupted.[144]

Given the changes in attitude that had occurred in Moscow in the preceding three years, the case for intervening on behalf of the PLO would have to have been made much more strongly than would have been necessary previously. However, the strongest, most influential supporters of the national liberation movement and the most enthusiastic Politburo advocates of an interventionist policy were no longer available to argue this case. The militantly anti-Western Aleksandr Shelepin had been removed from that body in 1975.[145] Defense Minister Grechko, a vigorous proponent of military assistance to the ''people's liberation struggle,'' who had urged forcible resistance to ''imperialist aggression'' anywhere on the globe, had died in 1976.[146]

Most significant was the death of Party Secretary Suslov in January 1982. Not only had Suslov been the leadership's most ardent champion of the national liberation movement generally, he also appears to have been a firm backer of the PLO.[147] At the same time, he was extraordinarily powerful—regarded by some as the preeminent figure on the Politburo.[148] It was he, above all, who could and probably would have argued effectively for rescuing the PLO.

With Suslov's passing, moreover, Foreign Minister Andrei Gromyko had become the most authoritative voice on foreign policy issues.[149] A major architect of détente, he was reputed never to have given reports on the Third World more than a glance. Certainly he was second only to Brezhnev in his concern to avoid a superpower confrontation, his belief in the importance of improving U.S.–Soviet relations, and his lack of enthusiasm for military involvement in national liberation struggles.[150]

Not only had the balance of opinion in the Politburo shifted toward greater caution, it appears that many of those elites who still favored military backing for national liberation groups in general did not press for greater assistance to the PLO in the summer of 1982. The ideologues in the Party seem to have been divided. While some did urge very strongly that more be done to aid the Palestinian fighters, there is reason to believe that many others remained silent. Most likely this was owing to their discomfort with the sociopolitical character of the PLO. They viewed it as a bourgeois nationalist organization which not only would be extremely unlikely ever to establish a socialist society, but could not even be relied upon to remain an ally of the Soviet Bloc—much less to promote social revolution in the region as a whole.[151]

It is not unlikely that the long-time head of the International Department,

Boris Ponomarëv, was among those ideologues who distrusted the PLO. He had opposed Khrushchev's initiative in establishing close relations with nationalist leaders like Nasser and Sukarno, arguing that this was contrary to Soviet ideology and inimical to the advancement of Communism in the Third World.[152] Very probably, he was not much more enthusiastic about his colleagues' support for Arafat.[153]

It also appears likely that key figures in the military were reluctant to intervene on behalf of the PLO. It was not so much that they were indifferent to the fate of the organization they had trained and supplied for so many years (even though the PLO could do little in the short run to enhance the USSR's strategic presence in the Third World, the military seems to have been highly supportive of the organization and Moscow's links with it).[154] Rather, the leaders of the Soviet armed forces were probably swayed by their appraisal of the difficulties and risks inherent in the kind of rescue operation they would have had to mount.

The military must have ruled out very quickly any small-scale use of force intended simply to demonstrate support for the Soviet ally.[155] In the absence of a massive intervention by the Arab states, such a demonstration would have no military value. On the other hand, direct intervention on the scale that would have been necessary to repel the IDF would have posed extremely serious operational and logistical problems. The Soviet armed forces had never been sent to wage a major war against a regular army in an area not contiguous with the Soviet border; indeed, they were neither trained nor equipped to conduct such an operation. Soviet airborne divisions had not been designed for prolonged combat without substantial and rapid backup. Intended for very limited functions, such as the seizure of key road junctions, railroad centers, bridges or ports, or the capture of bridgeheads or airfields to facilitate the deployment of a larger ground force, they were too lightly armed to withstand large-scale air or armored attacks.[156] The special airborne battalions that had recently been assigned the artillery, armor, and engineering equipment necessary for major combat, were not available in sufficient numbers to take on the IDF.

The situation in Lebanon, moreover, presented particularly great difficulties for the deployment and supply of either airborne or ground forces. Tyre, the only Lebanese port familiar to the Soviets and the place where they had previously made all direct deliveries of weapons to the PLO, was encircled on the first day of the war. A Soviet airborne brigade or division could not have been dispatched and deployed quickly enough to prevent the Israelis from taking the Beirut airport, even if no effort had been made to interfere with the operation. Timely deployment of a fully equipped mechanized or armored division together with air brigade and support forces, which would have been necessary to overcome Israeli resistance, was even more out of the question.[157]

Even if Soviet forces could somehow have been brought to the battlefield and been adequately supplied, they would have been at a considerable disadvantage vis-à-vis the Israelis. They did not know the terrain and were unaccustomed to the very hot, dry climate. They would have had no sanctuaries from which to operate, and at least initially, their opponent would have enjoyed overwhelming air superiority.[158]

Most important, Soviet military leaders must surely have been reluctant to take on a superbly trained, battle-tested enemy, whose weapons and tactics were far more sophisticated than those of any opponent the USSR and its allies had previously encountered in the Third World. This was especially true in light of the disappointing performance of Soviet weapons when pitted against that enemy. The fact that the Red Army was already engaged in a major war in Afghanistan, and might be called upon at any moment for active duty in Poland, must likewise have made full-scale intervention to save the PLO seem inadvisable, even to those who had actively promoted assistance to that organization and overseen the creation of its military infrastructure in Lebanon. The possibility of counterinvolvement by the United States, however remote in the eyes of the generals, must surely have reinforced their disinclination to commit their troops.[159]

In sum, although certain ideologues with very high-level backing argued for much more to be done to assist the Palestinian fighters, the leadership was less convinced than in the past of the benefits accruing to military intervention and more concerned about its dangers and costs. The absence of strong pressure from powerful individuals or influential and united elite groups thus left Brezhnev free to pursue with regard to the PLO the policy of restraint he had advocated for the Middle East as a whole since June 1967.

CONCLUSION

The response of Brezhnev and the Soviet leadership to the Israeli invasion of Lebanon was far from passive and ineffective. The USSR hardly behaved like a superpower in eclipse. At those moments during the crisis when it was perceived that important Soviet interests were at stake—that is, when the survival of the Syrian regime appeared to be endangered, when the credibility of Soviet weapons and commitments might plausibly have been challenged, and when the military–political balance of power and influence in the Middle East seemed about to be altered in favor of the United States—the Kremlin leaders moved quickly to prevent these developments from materializing or to limit their impact. The coercive diplomacy they employed included not only warnings and threats, but also the use of force, both indirect (the airlift of weapons) and direct (the deployment of ships, missiles, and missile crews). Although the USSR avoided unnecessary risks—carefully formulating their threats in general terms, giving only scant publicity to their assistance, timing their deployments so as to minimize the danger that their forces would become involved in the fighting, and notifying their allies of the limits of their support—their actions were extremely effective. The danger to Syria was quickly eliminated, the USSR's credibility as an ally was sustained, and the United States's unilateral diplomacy was undermined.

To the extent that the Soviet leaders declined to become even more deeply involved, this was not due either to their lack of interest in the Middle East or to Brezhnev's incapacitation. Their behavior in support of Syria and in response to the deployment of the U.S. marines indicated the strength of their interest in sustaining their political-strategic presence in the region. Brezhnev was highly active during the crisis, communicating with all the major participants. He personally conducted most of the Kremlin's diplomacy and clearly had a major role in determining the tone, content, and timing of Moscow's moves.

Refusal to undertake the unprecedentedly large intervention that would have been needed to rescue the PLO reflected a growing climate of skepticism among Soviet elites regarding the wisdom of military involvement in regional conflicts, a new international and domestic situation that made such involvement seem more dangerous and more costly, and changes in the composition of the top leadership that removed its most ardent interventionists. Also important were the nature of the client to be aided and the great difficulty and risk involved in providing the PLO with effective support. All these factors combined to allow Brezhnev's counsel of restraint to prevail, enabling the general secretary to have a greater influence on Soviet policy than at any time in the previous decade. The behavior that resulted, while by no means a radical break with the interventionism of that decade, represented both a more cautious and a more selective approach to competition with the United States in the Third World.

NOTES

1. Dan Bavly and Eliahu Salpeter, *Fire in Beirut* (Briarcliff Manor, New York: Stein and Day, 1984), pp. 112–15; Robert O. Freedman, "The Soviet Union, Syria, and the Crisis in Lebanon," *The Middle East Annual*, ed. David H. Partington (Boston: G. K. Hall, 1984), pp. 118–19.

2. Dmitri Simes, "Moscow's Middle East," *New York Times*, Nov. 10, 1982, p. 31; Robert O. Freedman, "Moscow, Damascus and the Lebanese Crisis of 1982–1984," paper presented to meeting of the American Political Science Association, August, 1984, p. 9 (subsequently published in *The Middle East Review* 27 [Fall, 1984]) p.26; Galia Golan, "The Soviet Union and the Israeli Action in Lebanon," *International Affairs* (London), 59 (Winter, 1982): 12–13; U.S. Congress, House, *The Soviet Union in the Third World, 1980–85: An Imperial Burden or Political Asset?* Report prepared for the Committee on Foreign Affairs by the Congressional Research Service, Library of Congress, 99th Congress, 1st sess., 1985 (Washington, DC: Government Printing Office, 1985), pp. 176, 178.

3. Simes, "Moscow's Middle East"; Freedman, "Moscow, Damascus," p. 9; Karen Dawisha, "The USSR in the Middle East: Superpower in Eclipse?" *Foreign Affairs* 61 (Winter 1982/83): 438; Harry Gelman, *The Brezhnev Politburo and the Decline of Detente* (Ithaca: Cornell University Press, 1984), p. 23; Howard Spier, *From the Sidelines—The USSR and the Lebanese Crisis*, Research Report No. 18 (London: Institute of Jewish Affairs, 1982), p. 1.

4. Dawisha, "USSR in the Middle East," p. 438.

5. Ibid.; Freedman, "Moscow, Damascus," p. 9; Golan, "Israeli Action," p. 12; Bavly and Salpeter, *Fire in Beirut*, p. 114; Jonathan Steele, *Soviet Power: The Kremlin's*

Foreign Policy—Brezhnev to Andropov (New York: Simon and Schuster, 1983), p. 179; Blema Steinberg, "The Superpowers and the Arab-Israeli Conflict: Impact of the War in Lebanon," *Middle East Focus* 5 (Nov. 1982): 6; John F. Burns, "Moscow Scowls and Bears It," *New York Times*, July 4, 1982, Section 4, p. 2.

6. See Dawisha, "USSR in the Middle East," pp. 444–49; Amnon Sella, *The Soviet Attitude Towards the War in Lebanon—Mid 1982*, Research Report No. 47 (Jerusalem: The Soviet and East European Research Centre, Hebrew University, 1982), pp. 3–4, 8; Spier, "From the Sidelines," p. 2; Freedman ("Moscow, Damascus," pp. 2–3) also discusses the emergence of obstacles to the expansion of Soviet influence.

7. Arkady N. Shevchenko, *Breaking with Moscow* (New York: Alfred A. Knopf, 1985), p. 304.

8. "Changes in Soviet Leadership Suggest Weakening of Brezhnev Group," Radio Liberty Research Report No. 221/82 (May 28, 1982), pp. 4–5.

9. Dawisha, "USSR in the Middle East," p. 450; Gelman, *The Brezhnev Politburo*, pp. 174–84; Steele, *Soviet Power*, pp. 8–9; U.S. Congress, House, *The Soviet Union in the Third World*, p. 178.

10. See Alvin Rubinstein, "The Soviet Union's Imperial Policy in the Middle East," *Middle East Review* 15 (Fall/Winter, 1982–83); 19; also Galia Golan, "The Soviet Union and the Palestinian Issue," paper presented to the Third World Congress, International Association for the Advancement of Slavic Studies, October 1985, p. 4.

11. See Erwin Weit, *At the Red Summit: Interpreter behind the Iron Curtain* (New York: Macmillan, 1973), p. 139.

12. Brezhnev's remarks, quoted in Mohamed Heikal, *The Road to Ramadan* (New York: Quadrangle/New York Times Book Co., 1975), p. 48.

13. See Dina Rome Spechler, *Domestic Influences on Soviet Foreign Policy* (Washington, D.C.: University Press of America, 1978), pp. 15, 17, 21. Cf. Henry Kissinger, *Years of Upheaval* (Boston: Little, Brown, 1982), p. 234.

14. See Brezhnev's speech on the 50th anniversary of the USSR (*Pravda*, Dec. 22, 1972).

15. See Spechler, *Domestic Influences*, pp. 18, 21–22, 37, 65.

16. Ibid., pp. 15, 37–39, 48, 60, 67–68; Ilana Kass, *Soviet Involvement in the Middle East: Policy Formulation, 1966–1973* (Boulder: Westview, 1978), pp. 210–11, 220–22; and Christian Duevel, "The Political Credo of N. G. Yegorychev," Radio Liberty Research Paper, no. 17 (1967), pp. 6–7.

17. See Lieutenant-General Saad el-Shazly, *The Crossing of the Suez* (San Francisco: American Mideast Research, 1980), pp. 161–62; also Mohamed Heikal, *The Sphinx and the Commissar* (New York: Harper and Row, 1978), p. 253; Spechler, *Domestic Influences*, pp. 68–69; Kass, *Soviet Involvement*, pp. 163–64.

18. See Heikal, *Sphinx*, pp. 28, 194; see also John R. Thomas, "Soviet Foreign Policy and the Military," *Survey* 17 (Summer 1971); 147.

19. See Spechler, *Domestic Influences*, pp. 64, 67; Duevel, "Yegorychev," Foreward and pp. 7–8; also Alvin Z. Rubinstein, *Red Star on the Nile* (Princeton: Princeton University Press, 1977), p. 17n.22; and Thomas, "Soviet Foreign Policy," p. 147.

20. Heikal, *Sphinx*, pp. 188–89.

21. See Spechler, "The USSR and Third World Conflicts: Domestic Debate and Soviet Policy in the Middle East, 1967–1973," *World Politics* 38 (April 1986): 450–53; Kass, *Soviet Involvement*, pp. 157–63, 207–11.

22. See Spechler, "USSR and Third World Conflicts," p. 445; G. Breslauer, "Soviet

Policy in the Middle East, 1967–1972,'' in *Managing U.S.-Soviet Rivalry*, ed. Alexander George (Boulder: Westview, 1983), pp. 65–106; Heikal, *Sphinx*, pp. 186–87, 193–95, 216–17, 22; Shazly, *Crossing of the Suez*, pp. 161–62; Anwar el-Sadat, *In Search of Identity: An Autobiography* (New York: Harper and Row, 1977), pp. 196–97; John D. Glassman, *Arms for the Arabs* (Baltimore: Johns Hopkins, 1975), pp. 65–124.

23. See Spechler, "USSR and Third World Conflicts," pp. 437–38; Glassman, *Arms*, pp. 108–10.

24. See Heikal, *Road*, pp. 158–59.

25. See Spechler, "USSR and Third World Conflicts," pp. 438–39, 443–44, 455, 457; also Spechler, "Soviet Policy in the Middle East: The Crucial Change," in *Superpower Involvement in the Middle East*, ed. Paul Marantz and Blema Steinberg (Boulder: Westview, 1985), p. 136.

26. See Spechler, "USSR and Third World Conflicts," pp. 454, 456–58. Cf. Gelman, *The Brezhnev Politburo*, pp. 25, 164.

27. See Spechler, "USSR and Third World Conflicts," pp. 459–60.

28. See *Pravda*, May 23, 1981.

29. See *Pravda*, April 12, 1974, September 28, 1974; Galia Golan, *The Soviet Union and the Palestine Liberation Organization* (New York: Praeger, 1980), pp. 129–34.

30. See *Pravda*, April 12, May 31, and June 15, 1974; April 27, 1975, and April 19, 1977; Golan, *The Soviet Union and the PLO*, p. 74

31. See Kemal Junblat, *I Speak for Lebanon* (Westport, Conn.: Hill, 1982), p. 17; Golan, *The Soviet Union and the PLO*, pp. 184–85.

32. On those efforts see Golan, *The Soviet Union and the PLO*, pp. 210–27; Golan, "The Soviet Union and the Palestinian Issue," pp. 5–6.

33. See *Pravda*, October 7, 1978; Ned Temke, "Soviets, Syrians At Odds Over Mideast Diplomacy," *Christian Science Monitor*, Nov. 30, 1978, p. 4; also R. Israeli, ed., *The PLO in Lebanon: Selected Documents* (London: Weidenfeld and Nicolson, 1983), pp. 43, 48; Golan, "Israeli Action," p. 9.

34. *Pravda*, April 28, 1981.

35. See Spechler, "USSR and Third World Conflicts," p. 455; Rubinstein, *Red Star*, p. 242; also Mary Kaldor, "Economic Aspects of Arms Supply Policies to the Middle East," in *Great Power Intervention in the Middle East*, ed. Milton Leitenberg and Gabriel Sheffer (New York: Pergamon, 1979), p. 225; U.S. Congress, House, *The Soviet Union in the Third World*, pp. 180–82; Cynthia Roberts, "Soviet Arms-Transfer Policy and the Decision to Upgrade Syrian Air Defenses," *Survival* 25 (July 1983); 159.

36. Gelman, *The Brezhnev Politburo*, pp. 46–49, 59–60.

37. See Ibid., pp. 148–51, 155–56, 161–62, 252 n.80; Spechler, "Domestic Debate," pp. 459–60; Steele, *Soviet Power*, p. 63.

38. Cf. Golan, *Yom Kippur and After*, p. 215.

39. Ibid., p. 214.

40. Robert Harkavy, "Strategic Access, Bases, and Arms Transfers: The Major Powers' Evolving Geopolitical Competition in the Middle East," in *Great Power Intervention in the Middle East*, ed. Milton Leitenberg and Gabriel Sheffer (New York: Pergamon, 1979), p. 173; Golan, *Yom Kippur and After*, pp. 169, 211–13; *An Nahar Arab Report and Memo* 6 (January 25, 1982): 5.

41. Golan, "The Soviet Union and the Palestinian Issue," pp. 14–15; Israeli, *The PLO in Lebanon*, pp. 74–167, 269, 293; Lieutenant Colonel David Eshel, *The Lebanon War, 1982* (Hod Hasharon, Israel: Eshel Dramit, Ltd., 1983), pp. 26–27.

42. Cf. Freedman, "Moscow, Damascus," p. 3.

43. Cf. Freedman, "Moscow, Damascus," pp. 5–8; and Freedman, "The Soviet Union, Syria," pp. 10–12.

44. Freedman, "The Soviet Union, Syria," pp. 9, 11.

45. See Karen Dawisha, "Soviet Decision-Making in the Middle East: The 1973 October War and the 1980 Gulf War," *International Affairs* (London) 57 (Winter 1980/1981): 59.

46. Ze'ev Schiff and Ehud Ya'ari, *Israel's Lebanon War* (New York: Simon and Schuster, 1984), p. 34; Beirut Voice of Lebanon, May 12, 1981 (*FBIS:MEA*, May 12, 1981, p. 114).

47. See Thomas L. Friedman, "Israel and Syria Believed to Face Risk of Conflict," *New York Times*, May 18, 1986, pp. 1, 8; see also "Damascus Moves Closer to Moscow," *An-Nahar Arab Report and Memo*, 6 (January 25, 1982): 5; Ghassan Beshara, "Syria: Towards an Arab Summit," *Monday Morning* (Beirut) 11 (January 25, 1982): 58–59.

48. Golan, "The Soviet Union and the Palestinian Issue," p. 15; *Pravda*, Oct. 21, 1981.

49. Eshel, *Lebanon War*, p. 49; Mark Heller, Dov Tamari, and Zeev Eytan, *The Middle East Military Balance, 1983* (Tel Aviv: Jaffee Center for Strategic Studies, Tel Aviv University, 1983), pp. 265–66; Golan, "The Soviet Union and the Palestinian Issue," pp. 6–7.

50. Cf. David Shipler, "Israelis Say PLO Can Leave Carrying Weapons," *New York Times*, June 30, 1982, pp. A1, A10; see also Kuwait News Agency, February 5, 1982 (*FBIS:MEA*, February 5, 1982, p. A1); Voice of Palestine, February 2, 1982 (*FBIS:MEA*, February 2, 1982, p. A3); Israeli, *The PLO in Lebanon*, pp. 206–12; Schiff and Ya'ari, *Lebanon War*, p. 83.

51. See Robert Rand, "The USSR and the Crisis over the Syrian Missiles in Lebanon: An Analysis and Chronological Survey," Radio Liberty Research Bulletin, RL 227/83 (June 3, 1981), pp. 2, 6; Robert Rand, "Moscow, Damascus, and the Crisis in Lebanon," Radio Liberty Research Bulletin, RL 239/82 (June 10, 1982), pp. 1–2.

52. Robert Rand, "Syria Presses For Strategic Alliance With Moscow; PLO Criticizes Soviet Response to Invasion of Lebanon," Radio Liberty Research Bulletin, RL 257/82 (June 23, 1982), p. 102; U.S. Congress, House, *The Soviet Union in the Third World*, p. 179.

53. "Damascus Moves Closer to Moscow," *An-Nahar Arab Report and Memo*, 6 (January 25, 1982): 5; Craig Oliphant, "The Performance of Soviet Weapons in Lebanon," Radio Liberty Research Bulletin, RL 68/83 (February 7, 1983), p. 4.

54. Kuwait News Agency, February 5, 1982 (*FBIS:MEA*, February 5, 1982, p. A1); Voice of Palestine, February 2, 1982 (*FBIS:MEA*, February 2, 1982, p. A3).

55. See Beshara, "Towards an Arab Summit," pp. 58–59; Kuwait News Agency, February 1, 1982 (*FBIS:MEA*, February 2, 1982, pp. A2-A3).

56. On Israel's moves and their military significance, see Eshel, *Lebanon War*, pp. 35, 37–38, 40, 71; Henry Tanner, "Syria's Cease Fire: War Too Perilous," *New York Times*, June 13, 1982, p. 12; John Bulloch, *Final Conflict: The War in Lebanon* (London: Century Publishers, 1983), p. 195.

57. Radio Moscow, June 10, 1982, cited in Nicolas Spulber, "Israel's War in Lebanon through the Soviet Looking Glass," *Middle East Review* 15 (Spring/Summer, 1983): 23.

58. Cf. Gromyko's assertion in January 1982, that "only hopeless political simpletons

could be deceived by the performance staged over the 'suspension' of that agreement" (*Pravda*, January 16, 1982).

59. Robert Rand, "Soviet Policy in the Middle East and the Crisis in Lebanon," Radio Liberty Research Bulletin, RL 237/82 (June 10, 1982), p. 1.

60. "Radio Peace and Progress in Arabic," June 8, 1982, cited in Golan, "Israeli Action," p. 14.

61. Alexander Haig, *Caveat* (New York: Macmillan, 1984), p. 339; Shipler, "Israelis Say."

62. Robert Rand, "Moscow Issues Blunt Warning to Israel Over Lebanon," Radio Liberty Research Bulletin, RL 244/82 (June 15, 1982), p. 2.

63. Golan, "Israeli Action," p. 8; Dawisha, "USSR in the Middle East," p. 439; Schiff and Ya'ari, *Lebanon War*, p. 168.

64. Haig, *Caveat*, p. 340; Shipler, "Israelis Say"; Bulloch, *Final Conflict*, p. 195; Itamar Rabinovich, "The War in Lebanon," *Middle East Contemporary Survey* 6 (New York: Holmes and Meier, 1984): 117; Schiff and Ya'ari *Lebanon War*, p. 16.

65. Heller, et al., *Military Balance, 1983*, pp. 234–35; Oliphant, "Soviet Weapons in Lebanon," Radio Liberty Research Bulletin, RL 68/83, p. 2; *The Military Balance, 1982–1983* (London: The International Institute for Strategic Studies, 1982), p. 62; Bavly and Salpeter, *Fire in Beirut*, p. 116; Schiff and Ya'ari, *Lebanon War*, p. 179.

66. Oliphant, "Soviet Weapons in Lebanon," Radio Liberty Research Bulletin, RL 68/83, p. 2; Seth Carus, "Military Lessons of the 1982 Israel-Syria Conflict," in *The Lessons of Recent Wars in the Third World*, I, ed. Robert E. Harkavy and Stephanie G. Neuman (Lexington: Lexington Books, 1985), p. 263.

67. Roberts, "Soviet Arms Transfer Policy," p. 157; Rand, "Moscow, Damascus, and the Crisis in Lebanon," Radio Liberty Research Bulletin, RL 239/82, p. 2; Bavly and Salpeter, *Fire in Beirut*, p. 117.

68. Mark Heller, Dov Tamari and Zeev Eytan, ed., *The Middle East Military Balance, 1984* (Boulder: Westview, 1985), p. 30.

69. Damascus Domestic Service, June 13, 1982 (*FBIS:USSR*, June 16, 1982, p. H1); Drew Middleton, "Mideast War: Things Soviets Learned in '82," *New York Times*, January 2, 1983, p. 13; Heller et al., *Military Balance, 1984*, p. 30.

70. Dawisha, "USSR in the Middle East," p. 439; Robert Rand and Robert Lyle, "The United States Assesses Brezhnev's Message to Reagan about the Situation in Lebanon," Radio Liberty Research Bulletin, RL 279/82 (July 9, 1982), pp. 2–3; Roberts, "Soviet Arms Transfer Policy," p. 156.

71. See Gromyko's comment on the subject, *Pravda*, June 23, 1982.

72. Interview with Vadim Zagladin, first deputy chairman of the International Department, *La Republica*, October 27, 1982 (*FBIS:USSR*, November 2, 1982, p. G3).

73. See Edward N. Luttwak, "Gauging Soviet Arms," *New York Times*, December 31, 1982, p. 19; Oliphant, "Soviet Weapons in Lebanon," Radio Liberty Research Bulletin, RL 68/83, pp. 1–6.

74. Robert Rand, "Soviet Policy Towards Lebanon: The View From the Arab World and Iran," Radio Liberty Research Bulletin, RL 288/82 (July 15, 1982), p. 2.

75. "Interview on 'This Week With David Brinkley,' " June 13, 1982, *Department of State Bulletin*, July 1982, p. 56.

76. *Jewish Chronicle* (London), June 25, 1982 (report on comments made by Begin during visit to the U.S.), cited in Spier, *From the Sidelines*, p. 5; Shipler, "Israelis Say" (citing Knesset speech by Begin).

77. Schiff and Ya'ari, *Lebanon War*, pp. 185–86, 188, 191–92.

78. Interview with Alexander Haig, *Department of State Bulletin*, July 1982, p. 56.

79. Ibid.

80. Schiff and Ya'ari, *Lebanon War*, pp. 186–88, 192–93; Haig, *Caveat*, p. 341.

81. *Pravda*, June 15, 1982.

82. Schiff and Ya'ari, *Lebanon War*, p. 202.

83. Ibid., p. 203.

84. Damascus Domestic Service, June 20, 1982 (*FBIS:MEA*, June 21, 1982, p. H1).

85. *Pravda*, June 22, 1982.

86. Bavly and Salpeter, *Fire in Beirut*, p. 115; Dawisha, "USSR in the Middle East," p. 440.

87. Schiff and Ya'ari, *Lebanon War*, p. 204.

88. "Syrians Are Rumored Holding Soviet Talks," *New York Times*, June 19, 1982, p. 5.

89. On U.S. pressure on Israel at the same time see Haig, *Caveat*, pp. 346–47; Schiff and Ya'ari, *Lebanon War*, p. 205.

90. *Pravda*, July 9, 1982.

91. See Rand and Lyle, "The United States Assesses Brezhnev's Message to Reagan about the Situation in Lebanon," p. 2.

92. *Pravda*, July 21, 1982.

93. TASS, July 8, 1982 (FBIS:USSR, July 8, 1982, p. H12).

94. See Roberts, "Soviet Arms-Transfer Policy," p. 156; and Bavly and Salpeter, *Fire in Beirut*, p. 117.

95. Haig, *Caveat*, p. 351; Roberts, "Soviet Arms Transfer Policy," p. 156; Oliphant, "Soviet Weapons in Lebanon," Radio Liberty Research Bulletin, RL 68/83, p. 5.

96. Roberts, "Soviet Arms-Transfer Policy," pp. 154, 156–57 (citing U.S. intelligence sources).

97. Ibid.; Heller et al., *Military Balance, 1984*, p. 30.

98. Roberts, "Soviet Arms-Transfer Policy," p. 154; and Daniel Pipes, "Syria: The Cuba of the Middle East," *Commentary* 82 (July, 1986): 17.

99. U.S. Congress, House, *The Soviet Union in the Third World*, p. 181 n. 13; Friedman, "Israel and Syria," pp. 1, 8; Leslie Gelb, "Israelis Say They Fear Syria Might Seek War," *New York Times*, July 20, 1986, p. 3.

100. Pipes, "Syria," p. 17; U.S. Congress, House, *The Soviet Union in the Third World*, p. 181; see also R. W. Apple, Jr., "Formidable Missiles Put in Place at Russian Bases in Western Syria," *New York Times*, May 16, 1983, p. 6.

101. Cf. Itamar Rabinovich, Speech to Glickman-Galinson Symposium, Lipinsky Institute for Middle East Studies, San Diego State University, reported in San Diego *Jewish Press Heritage*, June 28, 1985, p. 17.

102. TASS, June 7, 1982 (in *Pravda*, June 8, 1982).

103. *Pravda*, June 27, 1982.

104. SPA (Riyadh), June 27, 1982 (*FBIS:MEA*, June 18, 1982, p. C5).

105. See Middle East News Agency, July 22, 1982 (*FBIS:MEA*, July 23, 1982, p. D1); Radio Cairo Domestic Service, Aug. 5, 1982 (*FBIS:MEA*, August 6, 1982, p. D2).

106. *Pravda*, July 21, 1982 (italics mine).

107. See *The New York Times*, Sept. 2, 1982.

108. *AP* September 9, 1982.

109. For Arab criticisms of the U.S. plan, see Damascus Domestic Service, Radio

Monte Carlo, *Akhbar Al-Khalij* (Bahrain), Al-Wahdah (Abu Dhabi), September 2–3, 1982 (*FBIS:MEA*, September 3, 1982, pp. A1, A2, C1, C4, C5, H7, H8).

110. *Pravda*, Sept. 16, 1982.

111. *Pravda*, Sept. 21, 1982.

112. Appeals for Aid: Voice of Palestine, June 7, 1982 (*FBIS:MEA*, June 8, 1982, p. A2); June 9, 1982 (*FBIS:MEA*, June 9, 1982, p. ii); June 10, 1982 (*FBIS:MEA*, June 10, 1982, p. A3); Robin Wright, "The PLO Strives to Preserve Its Dignity and Underwrite Its Future," *Sunday Times* (London), July 4, 1982, p. 9; Reuters, June 26, 1982; AFP (Paris), July 15, 1982 (*FBIS:MEA*, July 16, 1982, p. A3). The strongest criticism was voiced by Libyan leader Muammar Khadaffi (JANA [Tripoli], June 26, 1982 (*FBIS:MEA*, June 26, 1982, pp. Q2-Q3).

113. See WAFA, June 9, 1982, cited in Golan, "Israeli Action," p. 11; Dusko Doder, "Soviets Said to Reject Increase in Military Involvement in Lebanon," *Washington Post*, July 6, 1982, p. A14 (citing Arab diplomats in Moscow).

114. By 1982, all Soviet military aid to the PLO was being channeled through Syria (Eshel, *The Lebanon War*, p. 26).

115. See, for example, Brezhnev's letters to Reagan, *Pravda*. July 9, and August 3, 1982. Cf. Dawisha, "USSR in the Middle East," p. 441.

116. According to an Israeli expert on the Soviet military, 15 divisions (more than the number of soldiers then deployed in Afghanistan) would have been required. See Sella, *War in Lebanon*, p. 23.

117. Heller, *Military Balance, 1983*, p. 331.

118. Golan, "Syria and the Soviet Union Since the Yom Kippur War," *Orbis* 21 (Winter, 1978), p. 777; Pipes, "Syria," p. 17.

119. Golan, "Soviet Union and the Palestinian Issue," pp. 10–13.

120. Cf. Dawisha, "USSR in the Middle East," p. 449.

121. See Golan, "Soviet Union and the Palestinian Issue," pp. 13–14, on Soviet opposition to the PLO presence in Lebanon.

122. On the importance of the International Department, see Robert N. Kitrinos, "The International Department of the CPSU," *Problems of Communism* 33 (September-October, 1984): 50–51, 60, 62.

123. Pavel Demchenko, "Stop the Aggression," *Pravda*, June 10, 1982.

124. Vadim Zagladin, Interview on Prague Radio, July 30, 1982 (*FBIS:USSR*, Aug. 4, 1982, p. CC9); V. Kudriavtsev, "Time of Severe Trials in the Middle East," *Izvestiia*, July 5, 1982, p. 3.

125. Zagladin, Interview on Prague Radio, pp. CC8, CC10; Dmitry Volsky, "Tragedy Without Epilogue," *New Times*, 35 (1982): 10; Yurii Kornilov, Moscow Domestic Service, June 8, 1982 (*FBIS:USSR*, June 9, 1982, p. H4).

126. Pavel Demchenko, "Crusade by Washington and Tel Aviv," *Sel'skaia zhizn'*, June 26, 1982 (*FBIS:USSR* July 7, 1982, p. H5); TASS, commentary by Greorgiy (*sic*) Kuvaldin, June 27, 1982 (*FBIS:USSR*, June 28, 1982, p. H4).

127. Kudriavtsev, "Severe Trials," p. 2; Demchenko, "Aggression," p. 5.

128. Demchenko, "Crusade"; Volsky, "Tragedy," p. 10; Zagladin, Interview on Prague Radio, p. CC9.

129. Zagladin, Interview on Prague Radio, pp. CC9, CC10, CC11.

130. On Bovin's role as a personal adviser to the general secretary see Gelman, *The Brezhnev Politburo*, pp. 91–92, 215; as *Izvestiia*'s Middle East expert, see Mikhail Agur-

sky, "Contradictions in Soviet Middle East Policy," *The Soviet Union and the Middle East* (Jerusalem), Supplement 2, 1982, pp. 4–5.

131. A. Bovin, "Dead End Street," *Izvestiia*, June 10, 1982; Moscow Domestic Television, June 8, 1982 (*FBIS:USSR*, June 10, 1982, p. H3). See also Bovin on Moscow Radio, June 20, 1982 (cited in Golan, "Israeli Action," p. 16) and on Soviet television, July 31, 1982 (*FBIS:USSR*, Aug. 2, 1982, p. CC5), and Igor' Beliaev, *Literaturnaia gazeta*, July 7, 1982 (cited in Golan, "Israeli Action," p. 16).

132. *Pravda*, July 21, 1982.

133. TASS, July 1, 1982 (*FBIS:USSR*, July 2, 1982, pp. H3, H4).

134. *Pravda*, July 21, 1982.

135. *Al-Mussawar* (Cairo), quoting the PLO representative in Cairo (cited in Golan, "Israeli Action," p. 7 n.2).

136. Cf. Golan, "The Soviet Union and the Palestinian Issue," p. 23; Elizabeth Kridl Valkenier, "Revolutionary Change in the Third World: Recent Soviet Assessments," *World Politics* 38 (April 1986): 432–33.

137. On the effect of this experience on the Soviet military's appraisal of the utility of force in the Third World, see Mark Katz, *The Third World in Soviet Military Thought* (Baltimore: Johns Hopkins, 1982), pp. 95–96.

138. See K. Brutents, Interview with *As-Safir* (Beirut), January 26, 1982 (*FBIS:USSR*, Jan. 29, 1982, p. H2); Zagladin, Interview, pp. CC10, CC11.

139. See Karen Brutents, Deputy Director of the International Department, Interview with *Al-Watan*, April 25, 1982 (*FBIS:USSR*, May 7, 1982, pp. H3, H4). Rostislav Ulianovskii, Deputy Director of the International Department, cited in Valkenier, "Revolutionary Change," p. 421.

140. Two particularly strong doses of that rhetoric, delivered by Reagan in speeches to the British Parliament and the UN Disarmament Session on June 1982, may have had an impact on Soviet behavior during the crises. See *New York Times*, June 9 and June 18, 1982.

141. "Report by K. U. Chernenko at the Ceremonial Meeting in Moscow Dedicated to the 111th Anniversary of the Birth of V. I. Lenin," *Pravda*, April 23, 1981; Katz, *Soviet Military Thought*, p. 97.

142. This was a major theme in the articles and speeches of Politburo members before and during the 26th Party Congress: Kunaev (*FBIS:USSR*, Feb. 18, 1981, p. R3), Ustinov (*FBIS:USSR*, Feb. 23, 1981, pp. V4-V5), Shcherbitskii (*FBIS:USSR*, Feb. 25, 1981, p. R2), Grishin (*FBIS:USSR*, Feb. 26, 1981, Supplement, p. 44), and Romanov (*FBIS:USSR*, Feb. 27, 1981, Supplement, p. 38).

143. Fédor Burlatskii, quoted in "Soviet-American Competition in the Third World: Moscow's Evolving Views on a 'Code of Conduct,' " *FBIS*, Analysis Report FB–83–10002, January 17, 1983 (cited in Francis Fukuyama, *Moscow's Post-Brezhnev Reassessment of the Third World* [Santa Monica: RAND, 1986], pp. 24–25).

144. See U.S. Department of State, *American Foreign Policy Current Documents, 1982* (Washington, D.C.: Government Printing Office, 1985), pp. 656–57, 660, 664.

145. On Shelepin's views see Spechler, *Domestic Influences*, pp. 15–16, 67–68; Kass, *Soviet Involvement*, p. 219; and Gelman, *The Brezhnev Politburo*, pp. 83, 87–88.

146. See *Pravda*, April 3, 1971; *Voprosy istorii KPSS*, (May 1974), p. 39.

147. See "Arafat Sends Condolences on Suslov's Death," Voice of Palestine, Jan. 27, 1982 (*FBIS:MEA*, Feb. 2, 1982, p. A3); also see Philip D. Stewart, Roger A. Blough, and James Warhola, "Conflict and Consensus in Soviet Foreign Policy: A Study of

Politburo Attitudes,'' paper presented at annual meeting of the International Political Psychological Association, Washington, D.C., June 25–27, 1982, p. 35; Gelman, *The Brezhnev Politburo*, pp. 87–88; Bulloch, *Final Conflict*, p. 195.

148. Cf. Simon Head, ''Brezhnev and After,'' *New York Review of Books*, March 4, 1982, p. 38; Gelman, *The Brezhnev Politburo*, pp. 87–88

149. Kitrinos, ''International Department of the CPSU,'' p. 60; Shevchenko, *Breaking with Moscow*, pp. 149–50.

150. Shevchenko, *Breaking with Moscow*, pp. 149–52; Stewart et al., ''Politburo Attitudes,'' pp. 29, 35.

151. Golan attributes this attitude to the Soviet leadership as a whole. (''The Soviet Union and the Palestinian Issue,'' pp. 10–13, 16; ''Israeli Action,'' pp. 10–11.) It was undoubtedly ideologues who were most concerned about such matters.

152. Stewart et al., ''Politburo Attitudes,'' p. 35; Kitrinos, ''International Department of the CPSU,'' pp. 65–66.

153. While Ponomarëv met with the head of the Syrian Communist Party, Khalid Bagdash, when he came to Moscow in mid-July 1982, members of the PLO Executive Committee who arrived in mid-August were able to speak only with the First Deputy Chairman and a Deputy Chairman of the I.D.

154. See, for example, the enthusiastic article that appeared in the army newspaper, *Krasnaia zvezda* (Red Star) on the eve of the invasion (May 21, 1982), p. 3.

155. That explains why the PLO was immediately informed that the USSR would send no troops or advisers. (See note 113 above.)

156. Cf. Sella, *War in Lebanon*, p. 14.

157. See Heller et al., *Military Balance, 1983*, pp. 330–31.

158. Cf. Heller et al., *Military Balance, 1983*, p. 331; Freedman, ''The Soviet Union, Syria,'' pp. 24–25.

159. See Zagladin, Interview with *La Republica*, p. G3.

10

THE UNITED STATES'S
RONALD REAGAN

Betty Glad

INTRODUCTION

The United States has been concerned with developments in the Middle East since the end of World War II. Four major objectives have been sought: the minimization of Soviet influence in the area, the guarantee of Israel's security, the uninterrupted flow of oil from the Persian Gulf region to the West, and the promotion of regional peace and stability—to avert possible wars between U.S. allies as well as the establishment of new radical regimes friendly with the USSR. The way in which the U.S. government has weighted these various concerns has depended to a great extent on the "ideas, the attitudes, and the experiences of the 'people at the top.' "[1]

With the election of Ronald Reagan as President in the fall of 1980, the United States began to emphasize the first three concerns, putting projects for mediating conflicts between Middle Eastern states on the back burner. Reagan's emphasis on the Soviet threat led the United States to back Israel's policies in Lebanon in the summer of 1982 and to get bogged down in political terrain it did not fully understand. A feeling of anti-Communism that saw the USSR as the source of most of the conflict in the world would blind the administration to indigenous political conflicts and to the sensibilities of moderate Arab leaders in the area. Confusing signals and an inability to get Israel to coordinate strategies, even tactically, got in the way of the effective pursuit of the immediate policy goals that both countries shared in Lebanon. Where the United States and Israeli policies diverged—that is, on the issue of the autonomy of the West Bank—the Reagan administration never went beyond mere talk. It was unwilling to commit its political capital to attempt some resolution of that difficult issue. This approach was a function of Reagan's political history, his personality, his worldview, and the organizational arrangements he used to process information and make decisions. In his efforts, he would have to work within a domestic political climate that supported the special tie to Israel and a renewed commitment to U.S. strength abroad while eschewing costly U.S. military involvements in conflicts that did not clearly involve the USSR.

Ronald Reagan won the U.S. presidency in 1980, taking approximately 51 percent of the popular vote. Because he won 489 votes to Jimmy Carter's 49 in the electoral college and brought Republican control to the U.S. Senate for the first time since 1954, his election was widely perceived as a landslide. The peculiarities of the electoral college and the distribution of Jimmy Carter's 41 percent of the vote (Anderson took 7 percent) led to this result. The most conservative candidate to be elected president in over 50 years, his popular following at the beginning of his term was somewhat lower than that of his predecessors upon taking office.[2] Opinion polls, moreover, showed that U.S. citizens had made no major switch to the Right by November 1980; their vote was simply one of no confidence in the Carter regime.[3]

Unlike most presidents, Reagan did not come into office after a long apprenticeship in politics, law, or the military.[4] He first won national attention as a contract actor at Warner Brothers from 1938 to 1942. Called up in April 1942 as a reserve second lieutenant in the cavalry, he was transferred to the motion picture unit of the Army Air Force, where for the rest of the war he turned out training films for the services and other material designed to boost morale on the homefront. After the war, his movie career floundered on a succession of mostly grade B movies and he negotiated a deal with Warner Brothers which took him off his exclusive contract. As his movie career faded, he came to play an important role in Hollywood politics, lining up with Jack Warner, Walt Disney, and other studio heads who were dedicated to keeping Communists out of the industry. When the leftist Conference of Studio Unions went on strike in 1946 in a battle for control of the set designers, Reagan helped lead the Screen Actors Guild into an alliance with the more conservative International Alliance of Theatrical Employees. In 1947, when the House Un-American Activities Committee sent a subcommittee to begin a new investigation on communism in the film industry, Reagan was a "friendly" but not hysterical witness. As president of the Screen Actors Guild, Reagan backed a referendum that prohibited Communists from becoming members of the guild, and required new members to declare that they were not and never had been members of the Communist party. Publicly opposed to unofficial blacklists, Reagan privately cooperated with the FBI, giving them the names of colleagues he thought might be Communists.

With the advent of television, Reagan's acting career took on new life. From 1954 to 1962, he was host and sometimes star of the General Electric (GE) dramatic series. He also became increasingly interested in national politics. Visiting GE plants around the country for several weeks each year as part of the company's Employee and Community Relations Program, he started telling people about how he had met the threat of international Communism in Hollywood. He gradually moved from the mainstream Democratic philosophy he had espoused in his earlier career to opposing almost every social welfare program enacted during the New Deal and thereafter.[5] His political views won the national spotlight in 1966 when he made a fund-raising speech for Barry Goldwater that raised over half a million dollars. After viewing the show, several wealthy businessmen in Los Angeles convinced him that he should run for governor of California. Presenting himself as a "citizen politician," Reagan turned his amateur status into an asset. He beat the incumbent Democrat, Edmund G. Brown, by over one million votes.

Reagan's record as governor of California was much more centrist than his campaign rhetoric suggested it might be. His first year was marred by incompetence and bad relations with the members of the state legislature and the press.[6] Over time, however, Reagan learned how to woo and bargain with the leaders of the senate and the assembly to obtain some of his programs and to win a more favorable mass media response. He got a major tax bill through the legislature later in his first term in office and he passed a welfare reform bill in his second term. This tilt toward the center, however, was more a reflection of his need to accommodate a Democratic-controlled legislature to accomplish his major objectives than a shift in his basic political ideology. His aide Lyn Nofziger noted at the time that "he's as ideological as he can afford to be and still get something. He's not going to go down in flames for its own sake."[7]

Reagan's first two bids for the Republican nomination for president were unsuccessful. A short-lived impromptu campaign against front-runner Richard Nixon for the nomination in 1968 fizzled. In the 1976 Republican primaries, however, he almost took the nomination away from the incumbent Jerry Ford— an attempt not often made in U.S. politics.[8] In the 1980 campaign, he was the front-runner after the New Hampshire primaries and was able both to dominate the party platform and to unify the party at the Republican National Convention. He came to the presidency with the Republican party solidly behind him.

STYLE

Reagan's experience with movies would serve him well in the presidency. His style is well suited to politics in the television era. He moves gracefully, stands tall and erect, smiles easily, and has a spontaneous wit. A former bodyguard, Arthur Van Court, took thousands of photographs of Reagan during his career; he claimed he did not have one that showed Reagan with a frown or awkward posture.[9] Indeed, as Reagan noted in *Where's the Rest of Me?*, an actor has advantages over others in knowing how he looks. "We don't know how we look from behind, from the sides, talking, standing, moving normally through a room. It's quite a jolt."[10]

Most of his oral presentations show the polish of a professional actor. Reagan memorizes lines for conversation and speeches, and once he has found a felicitous phrase or a good anecdote, he repeats it almost verbatim in a variety of settings. His 1964 speech for Goldwater put him into the national limelight. In 1968, he outperformed Senator Robert Kennedy in an internationally televised program that dealt with U.S. foreign policy and the Vietnam War.[11] During the North Carolina primary in 1976, he rescued his campaign with an election-eve television appeal.[12] As president, he won support for his controversial budget in 1981 after making his case over national television.[13] His skill at the quip gives him time on the evening news shows, where 30 seconds is a long exposure. Above all, he knows how to take advantage of publicity opportunities.

Unlike many high achievers, Reagan is not a workaholic. When he took office, the president's national security briefing was moved from 7:30 A.M. to 9:30 A.M. His preparation for press conferences was casually handled, until his gaffes began to draw critical press attention.[14] On the campaign or the presidential trail, his personal appearances are rationed to give him the best television coverage and the widest audiences. An aide recognized some time ago that "the most effective thing we can do is put him on television whenever we can."[15]

Reagan has suffered little political fallout from his relatively short work hours because he delegates a great deal of responsibility. The system developed for foreign-policy decision making is outlined below. Suffice it to say at this point that Reagan does not like conflict around him. If a debate between his advisers gets tense, Reagan introduces a tone of levity in the discussion to relax tensions. Reagan makes the final decisions easily. He doesn't let the minutiae bother him, and he doesn't worry over the big decisions until it is time to make them.[16]

His pragmatic strain was already evident in his governorship of California, as we have seen. He gradually learned how to deal with political journalists and other politicians, and to compromise on his programs when necessary. His bargaining style was aptly summarized by one biographer: "He would boldly announce a controversial program, quietly modify it in the face of criticism and then hail the compromise as a complete victory."[17] As president, he would show the same capacity.

WORLDVIEW

Reagan's domestic philosophy is a throwback to late-nineteenth-century Social Darwinism. He dreamt of a United States unfettered by laws restricting the efforts of individual entrepreneurs to compete and rise to the top. Business is the major positive force in society and the source of all progress. Government's proper role should be to provide order, security, and defense. It should have little or no role in promoting equality of opportunity or in redistributing income. Social protest movements he views with suspicion. As he said in 1968, "history is strangely barren of any record of advances made by collective action." By contrast, "the road from the swamp to the stars is studded with names of individuals who achieved fulfillment and lifted mankind another rung."[18]

Reagan's foreign policy views would evolve somewhat toward the end of his second term in office. At the time of the Israeli intervention in Israel, however, he saw world politics as a battle between the forces of good and evil. The United

States is the highest embodiment of the good that individuals have known. Its wars have all been noble, and today it stands as "the only island of freedom that is left in the world."[19] The USSR, by way of contrast, he viewed as the embodiment of evil. "The only morality they recognize is what will further their cause, meaning they reserve unto themselves the right to commit any crime, to lie, to cheat," he declared in his first press conference as president.[20] In his speech before the British Parliament on June 8, 1982, he called for a plan that would promote democracy throughout the world and leave "Marxism on the ash heap of history."[21] Speaking to the UN Disarmament Conference on June 17, 1982, Reagan accused the USSR of deception in policy matters and cited its record of tyranny.[22] Even after his meeting with Mikhail Gorbachev in late 1985, Reagan showed this same mind-set. In an interview with Barbara Walters on March 24, 1986, Reagan affirmed that he had not changed his views about the evil intent of the USSR.[23]

The Communists, according to Reagan, had no real desire to relax tensions between themselves and the United States. Accommodation with them is appeasement. "The spectre our well-meaning liberal friends refuse to face is that their policy of accommodation is appeasement, and appeasement does not give you a choice between peace and war, only between fight or surrender."[24] Détente, he suggested in 1977, "may actually have improved the climate for Soviet promotion of proxy wars and skirmishes."[25] In his October 1, 1981, news conference he charged that the Soviet Union believes that nuclear war is winnable.[26]

For Reagan, the battle between the forces of Communism and those of liberty was the only one of importance in the contemporary world. Conflicts that stem from other causes he has difficulty understanding. In 1980, he could not understand the civil war in Lebanon. "After all, they're Lebanese."[27] He even has problems understanding those U.S. citizens who do not heed his battle call. Supporters of the nuclear weapons freeze movement, he suggested on October 10, 1982, are dupes of the Communists. The movement "is inspired not by the sincere honest people who want peace, but by those who want the weakening of America and so are manipulating many honest and sincere people."[28]

Reagan's worldview is accompanied by a certitude that his view is the correct one. Pragmatic in the sense that he will settle for some of what he wants rather than lose it all, he is ideological in that he never questions the precepts outlined here. For him, there are no ambiguities about the nature of the enemy that deserve further exploration, no moral dilemmas, and no questions about the facts that support his theories. "For many years now," he said in 1968, "you and I have been shushed like children and told that there are no simple answers. . . . Well, the truth is, there are simple answers. There just aren't easy ones."[29] As Stuart Spencer says, "I see less change in him than in any political figure I have ever known. He has a set of values, and everything stems from those values."[30] Laurence Barrett noted that Reagan has a "turn of mind that resists ambiguity the way an immune system rejects alien substances."[31]

The cognitive process described here is often based on deeper needs in the personality structure. As Else Frenkel-Brunswick has suggested, cognitive rigidity is often a defense against the immobilization that could result from a close encounter with ambivalence and ambiguity. Reagan's personality suggests this may be so with him.[32]

PERSONALITY

There are not "two Ronald Reagans," Nancy Reagan says firmly.[33] Most Reagan associates agree that Ronald Reagan is as pleasant, thoughtful and courteous to his family and friends as he is to those he meets in public. He is a considerate boss "who hates to impose on anyone . . . and never reprimands," says William Clark.[34] Unlike some politicians, if Ronald Reagan is "onstage" there is no conscious hypocrisy about it.

The other side of the coin is that Reagan displays a certain detachment from both the settings in which he finds himself and his emotions. Seldom does he show great joy or anger—or indulge in a full belly laugh. He is easily bored when the details of policies or tactics are discussed. In his relations with others there is a guarded quality. His initial standoffishness with state legislators in California has been noted. With one or two exceptions, Reagan is not close to his subordinates.[35] Except for Paul Laxalt, the Republican senator from Nevada, and one or two others, Reagan does not seem to need much companionship.[36] Except for his wife, Nancy, he is even something of a loner in respect to his family.[37] His son Mike and daughter Maureen (children from his first wife, actress Jane Wyman) learned that he was running for governor from the newspapers.[38]

The roots of this detachment can be traced to Reagan's childhood.[39] Generally, when a child feels vulnerable and is determined to overcome those feelings to prove himself through accomplishment, he has to detach himself from seeing and feeling the disturbing things around him.[40]

In Reagan's case, there was much to feel vulnerable about. His father, Jack, was a charmer, but he provided a nomadic life for his wife Nellie and his two sons, Neil and Ronald. A shoe salesman, he moved his family from Tampico (where Ronald was born) to Chicago and then back to Galesburg, Monmouth, Tampico, and Dixon in West Illinois. From 1922 to 1933, the family lived in five different rented houses in Dixon.[41] Once, during the Depression, the family lived in the bedroom of a house they sublet to others.[42] As Reagan recalls, "Our family didn't exactly come from the wrong side of the tracks but we were certainly always within sound of the train whistles."[43] Moreover, Jack showed little interest in his sons. He seldom saw their football games, and he sometimes showed a punitive side when he thought Ronald might be losing a physical fight.[44]

Most important, Jack was an alcoholic. Ronald came home from school at age 11 to find his father dead drunk on the front porch, his arms spread out as if he were crucified.[45] On top of this, Ronald had extremely poor eyesight as a child and was slight of build. When his mother fitted him out with huge, black-rimmed spectacles, he saw the world more clearly, but he hated the glasses.[46] He was, as he later recalled, "always the last chosen for a side in any game."[47]

Young Reagan dealt with these problems by overcoming them. His mother— a proud, religious, and vivacious woman who adhered to middle-class values despite everything—showed him the way. Thus, Ronald Reagan joined her Christian Church (Disciples of Christ) rather than his father's Catholic church, adopted her interest in acting and was a "good" boy—gentle, polite, and re-sponsible—someone she could be proud of. Neil later recalled with a smile, "I don't think he [Ronald] ever saw the inside of a poolroom."[48]

His masculine model was not his father, but the conventional hero: the football star—the competitor who overcomes great odds. Certain sports, he discovered— such as hockey and football—did not depend so much on good vision.[49] Nor did his size deter him from football scrimmage in high school. "Somehow, instinctively, I knew that I'd grow up someday."[50] His competitive spirit, good looks, affable personality, and fine physique (he shot up to his movie star height when he was about fourteen) brought him the early success that would confirm his instinct. In high school, he made the football team and was class president, yearbook editor, and a star in several plays. At nearby Eureka College, he was captain of the swim team and president of his fraternity (TKE), the Booster Club, and the entire student body. He also was second lead in several theatrical performances.[51]

Early career successes reaffirmed his view that anyone who really tried could make it. Graduating from college in the depression, he quickly found work as a sportscaster at WOC in Davenport and later at WHO in Des Moines. On a spring training trip with the Chicago Cubs, he impressed Max Arnow of Warner Brothers in his first screen test and won a contract with the studio.[52] A series of grade B films ensued, leading to stardom in such films as *Knute Rockne* and *King's Row*. His marriage to starlet Jane Wyman in 1940 led to stories in *Photoplay* and *Silver Screen* extolling their perfect marriage.[53]

To achieve these things, Reagan no doubt detached himself from the disturbing currents in his immediate personal environment, as well as in his own psyche. Even as a boy he was following Eddie Foy's admonitions: "Sing pretty, act pretty, pretty things they enjoy."[54] Thus he would feel no resentment toward his father's drinking. His mother had taught him that alcoholism was a sickness that could not be helped.[55] He did not realize his family was poor; and in high school he preferred playing heroes to villains.[56] His best friend in high school, the son of the family that owned the local cement factory, felt he never really knew what Reagan's inner feelings were.[57] Later, in 1947, when Jane Wyman told him she wanted to divorce him, he seemed to be surprised by her decision. As he wrote in *Where's the Rest of Me?*, "I suppose there had been warning signs, if only I hadn't been so busy."[58] Potential conflict arising between the values acquired from his mother and those obtained from his masculine hero role model was not dealt with consciously, although in *Where's the Rest of Me?* he mentions his puzzlement about "a personality schizo-split between sports and stage."[59]

This detachment, however, would be dysfunctional in some ways for Reagan as a political leader and administrator. He finds it difficult to discipline his staff and to show anger to political intimates in well-modulated ways. He has a problem with the subtleties of conflict, as his second wife, Nancy Davis, once suggested: "He doesn't understand undercurrents. He can't function when there is tension and people aren't getting along."[60]

Oftentimes others handled these problems for him. As governor of California he left it to Mike Deaver, then his assistant chief of staff, to tell department heads when they had acted inappropriately or needed to shape up. Nancy has played the heavy for him, both before he gained the presidency and after. Her later role in pushing Reagan to dismiss his chief of staff, Donald Regan, after the Iran-contra affair became public, would be widely noted in the popular press.[61]

Eventually, he may blow up and take things into his own hands. But by this time, the situation has generally disintegrated beyond repair. During the 1980 campaign, for example, Reagan silently watched John Sears fire one old Reagan hand after another, with no regard for his or Nancy's feelings. Finally, when Sears moved to get rid of Ed Meese—the last old Reagan hand in the upper echelons of the campaign staff—Reagan exploded. In a stormy meeting in a Massachusetts hotel room one night, from 10 P.M. to 4 A.M., Reagan got so angry that one observer thought he might actually strike Sears. "You did in Mike Deaver," he raged. "But by God, you're not going to get Ed Meese." Reagan waited until the New Hampshire primaries were over and then fired Sears.[62]

Nonetheless, Reagan can show anger and sustained aggression in relation to those outside his own group or circle if he sees them as "evil" in some way. When he perceived the leftists in Hollywood as trying to take over the film industry, he went after them with vigor and commitment.[63] As governor during the student demonstrations at Berkeley, Reagan called a regent who opposed him "a lying son-of-a-bitch" and pushed another regent who tried to restrain the two from a physical fight.[64] His fantasy of how he would deal with Leonid I. Brezhnev is indicative of this tendency. He told his son, Mike, after his loss to Ford in 1976, that the thing that upset him was losing the opportunity to say "nyet" in a face-to-face encounter with Brezhnev.[65] Indeed, Reagan's feelings about Communists suggest that he has some deeper animosity against them. On a fight during the 1980 campaign, Reagan recounted his earlier anti-Communist activities to Laurence Barrett of *Time*—speaking of how he had discovered first hand the Communists' cynicism, brutality, immorality, and cold-bloodedness in their attempt to gain control of the film industry. With bitterness, he noted that they could destroy careers, "and they did," in an "effort directed by Moscow."[66]

POLITICAL AND INSTITUTIONAL CONSTRAINTS

As president, Reagan quickly moved to win "the establishment" over to his cause. He met Katherine Graham, the publisher of the *Washington Post*, at a party thrown by columnist George Will, and later at her home he met a cross section of Washington influentials—senators, journalists, interest group leaders, liberals, and conservatives. He and his wife wooed these movers at subsequent social events in and out of the White House.

Yet, if Reagan had any proclivities for turning toward the mainline politics of the Washington establishment, he was constrained by the values and interests of those in his core coalition. Reagan had come to the forefront of the Republican party with the backing of Christian fundamentalists and other groups of the New Right in his party.[67] His biggest financial backers were mainly conservative Republican businessmen from the Southwest. If Reagan went too far in compromising their values, he would be called to account by them. Indeed, even the minor concessions he made in his first few months in office caused problems with them. In July 1981, Richard A. Viguerie's *Conservative Digest* devoted a special issue to Reagan, warning him that his "mandate for change" was being subverted by persons in his personnel operations.[68]

The president faced other constraints in Congress. The opposition Democrats controlled the House and the Senate was led by Republicans who were independent of the president. In the Senate Foreign Relations Committee, Jesse Helms of North Carolina scrutinized Reagan's foreign policy appointments for ideological purity and succeeded in holding up some of Haig's State Department appointments for months. On the other side, moderates and liberals shot down the appointment of Ernest Lefever as assistant secretary of state for human rights because he seemed to have little commitment to that concept. Both houses of Congress monitored Reagan's military commitments in the Middle East, using the War Powers Resolution passed in 1973 in an effort to avoid involvement that could lead the United States into another Vietnam.

On Middle East matters, Reagan had to operate between two kinds of domestic interest groups. Most influential was the American Israel Public Affairs Committee (AIPAC), the umbrella organization that represents many diverse Jewish groups in the United States and is devoted to the protection of Israel's interests.[69] Its strength is partly based on the concentration of Jewish voters (though comprising only 2.7 percent of the population) in New York, California, New Jersey, and Florida—states politically important because of their weight in the electoral college and the Democratic primaries. AIPAC's strength is also based on the proclivity of the American Jewish community to contribute to political campaigns. Approximately 50 percent of all Democratic party funds comes from the Jewish community.[70] Equally important, AIPAC's goals have broad support in the U.S. political culture. Leaders of both political parties have had sentimental ties to Israel based on their own religious roots in the Judeo-Christian tradition, and Israel is viewed as a key strategic asset, with a central role to play in containing the USSR in the Middle East—a perception strengthened by Israel's extraordinary military performance in the 1967 war.[71] Elite opinions are buttressed by popular attitudes. Most public opinion polls since 1948 have shown that U.S. citizens favor Israel over its Arab neighbors by a four-to-one ratio.[72] In recent years neoconservatives (who hail Israel as the bastion of anti-Communism in the Middle East) and Christian fundamentalists (who see Israel as performing a biblical role in the last days before the final holocaust) have become especially strong Israeli supporters.[73]

Less influential was the pro-Arab lobby. In the early 1980s, corporate interests selling to Saudi Arabia, U.S. Arabs, Middle East experts in the State Department, and Defense were pushing Caspar Weinberger and others in the bureaucracy to promote pro-Arab policies. Unlike AIPAC, however, the pro-Arab lobby has no broader base from which to build support. Arabs who have emigrated to the United States are mostly Christian, and their attitudes toward the dominant Moslem Arabs in the Middle East often have not been supportive.[74] Moreover, U.S. elites have little real understanding of Arab culture and Moslem religion. Americans generally tend to see the Arab world in the grip of an Islamic fundamentalism that is essentially an irrational fanaticism directed against the Judeo-Christian cultural tradition.[75]

Within the government, the military establishment was willing to sustain U.S. military operations abroad only if the United States went out to win and had full public support. The military had responded to the Vietnam experience by vowing to never undertake war again without the full support of the U.S. people.[76] The U.S. public, however, was not inclined to give that support. True, humiliation over the Iranian hostage crisis rankled, and there was a readiness to increase defense spending and show muscle in a way that would increase national pride, but there was still considerable opposition to the actual deployment of U.S. troops overseas in ways that could lead to another Vietnam.

STAFF ORGANIZATION AND INFORMATION PROCESSING

Not inclined to play an active role in either choosing top aides or defining their relationship to one another, Reagan initially selected two men to organize his staff. Edwin Meese, the conservative Californian who as Reagan's chief of staff in Sacramento had worked out the decision-making system Reagan used as governor, was named chief policy adviser. James Baker of Texas, a moderate and pragmatic Republican, was made chief of staff. Michael Deaver, another former Reagan aide, would oversee the travel arrangements of the president and first lady, preside over the presidential schedule, oversee political relations with groups outside the White House, and choose Nancy Reagan's staff. Richard Allen, the new National Security Council adviser, would report to the president through Meese. His office was designed to play a less central role in advising the president and coordinating foreign policy operations throughout the government.

Alexander Haig, the new secretary of state, wanted to become the president's "vicar" in the area of foreign policy making. However, his draft memo outlining a centralized role for the secretary of state over foreign policy was never really considered; and his request for a weekly meeting with the president went unanswered.[77] Caspar Weinberger, the new secretary of defense, was personally close to Reagan and had the easy personal access to the president that Haig lacked.[78] William J. Casey, the new director of the Central Intelligence Agency, had status as a full member of the cabinet, offering recommendations to the president on a wide range of policy issues.[79] Jeane Kirkpatrick, the U.S. ambassador to the United Nations and a neoconservative university professor with her own political following, would have direct access to Reagan.

None of the top staff aides had prior experience in foreign affairs. Of those with cabinet status, only Haig had an extensive foreign policy background.[80] All of them, however, had been chosen after going through a screening process that guaranteed that they shared Reagan's basic views regarding the nature of Communism and the need for the United States to achieve military superiority.[81] Haig and Weinberger saw the USSR as the source of most of the evil in the world. Allen at the National Security Council was such a hard-liner that he even bored Reagan, and the briefings he conducted for the president were soon discontinued.[82] Kirkpatrick shared Reagan's suspicion of détente, and with her distinctions between authoritarian and totalitarian regimes, provided an intellectual rationale for supporting anti-Communist dictatorships of the Right.[83] Indeed, 24 high-level members of the Reagan administration belonged to the 50-member Committee on the Present Danger, formed a few years earlier to alert the United States to the Communist menace.[84]

The decision-making process at the highest level was influenced by Reagan's personality and his idea that the amateur politician is best at defining political goals.[85] For information on specific topics, Reagan depended on one- or two-page minimemos, modeled after legal briefs. Everyone in attendance at decision-making meetings was encouraged to comment on a variety of issues, not just on matters within his or her area of responsibility. The president's own ideological predispositions served as a framework within which the debate would take place. Out of this discussion, it was assumed, some consensus would emerge. Reagan would approve the decision on the spot or at a subsequent time. Basically the approach was deductive rather than inductive; the truth was derived from abstract precepts about the nature of the world and the role the United States should play.[86]

There were problems with the particular arrangements his aides worked out. Meese, who in 1981 tried to coordinate all policy, had over-reached himself. At times the process was so tightly centralized among top advisers on the staff that no one with pertinent expertise was involved in decision making. On other occasions, the system was so anarchic that department heads and top aides would debate each other in the newspapers for weeks at a time. By October 1981, key administrative officials were talking to legislators and representatives of the media in an attempt to build up pressure for changing the structure and the process.[87]

Moreover, Reagan's failure to clearly define roles and responsibilities contributed to conflict between the key players. Haig had open, running battles with Allen, Weinberger, and Kirkpatrick. When William Clark, another former chief of staff for Reagan during his governorship, replaced Allen as national security adviser in January 1982, the situation did not improve. Clark had far more power as national security adviser than had Allen as well as an access to the president which Haig lacked, and required that all overseas trips, as well as instruction for all special diplomatic envoys, be cleared with him.[88] Indeed, relations between Haig and Clark had deteriorated so much by the time of Reagan's trip to Europe in June 1982 that the two got into a shouting match over protocol in front of aides.

For the president, personally, the system also presented problems. Reagan was often misinformed on important matters.[89] At a press conference in June 1981, for example, he fumbled a question on the surface-to-air missiles the Syrians had placed in Lebanon, calling them offensive weapons. His inattention to detail sometimes created the impression that aides were performing his job. When two Libyan planes were shot down over the Gulf of Sidra in 1981, Meese decided when the epsiode should be announced, called all the members of the National Security Council, informed Vice President Bush, and then called the president at 4:24 the next morning. Newspaper coverage of the event suggested that the president may have delegated too much power to his subordinates.[90]

FOREIGN POLICIES

Reagan's top foreign policy objective, in accord with the Republican party platform of 1980, was to restore U.S. superiority vis-à-vis the USSR in the world. National Security Council Document 32, adopted in May 1982 after close consultation between the Pentagon, the National Security Council, and the president, called for an armed force buildup that would enable the United States to prevail in either a prolonged conventional war or a nuclear war, should deterrence fail.[91] Suggestions for summit meetings and arms limitation agreements were brushed aside the first several months Reagan was in office.[92]

Basically, Reagan saw the Soviet Union as the chief source of conflict in the Middle East and he thought it was necessary to build positions of strength against them there. They should know that "if they made a reckless move [in the Middle East], they would be risking confrontation with the U.S."[93] Later, he would fall in with Haig's view that the civil war in Lebanon was the result of Soviet meddling via its support of Syria and the PLO (Palestine Liberation Organization) rather than forces indigenous to the area.

To meet this threat in the Middle East, Reagan's policy was to create an alliance against the USSR. To this end he aimed at increasing the military capabilities of friendly Arab regimes. Thus, in the spring of 1981, the president approved proposals to resume exporting arms to Pakistan and to export AWACS electronic surveillance aircraft and F–15s (already agreed to by Carter) to Saudi Arabia. He personally wooed several Arab heads of state and diplomats during his first two years in office. Meeting with Arab ambassadors in June 1981 to discuss the bombing of Iraq by the Israelis, Reagan expressed shock and disappointment at the methods used by Israel, and he went through the motions of reprimanding Israel by temporarily suspending a shipment of military planes.[94] Later that summer, Reagan and Anwar Sadat agreed that it was necessary for "U.S.-Egyptian collaboration to vigorously resist Soviet inspired aggression."[95] The new Egyptian president, Hosni Mubarak, met with Reagan in February 1982, and the two agreed to strengthen their economic ties.[96] Signals from these Arab leaders that they saw Israel as the threat and that they put Palestinian autonomy near the top of their political agendas, however, were ignored.

Israel would be made the centerpiece of the administration's alliance against the USSR. Reagan had long been friendly to Israel. As a candidate for the Republican presidential nomination in 1976, he had held up the dramatic Israeli rescue of hostages at Entebbe as an example of the way "America used to act."[97] During the presidential campaign in 1979, he wrote in the *Washington Post* that the fall of Iran had increased Israel's value "as perhaps the only remaining strategic asset in the region."[98] In his most important campaign speech on Israel, he suggested that he would not constrain Israel as prior administrations had, criticized Carter's sale of F–15s to Saudi Arabia, expressed skepticism about the Camp David process and stated that a U.S.-promoted peace plan in the Middle East should not try to "force" any Middle East settlement on the Israelis.[99] With Menachem Begin as prime minister, Reagan had another reason for remaining close to Israel. The prime minister was tough and conservative—the kind of man Reagan liked. The Israeli government also seemed to agree with Reagan's foreign policy objective to make Israel the centerpiece of its anti-Soviet consensus in the Middle East. A memorandum of understanding was signed with the Begin government in September 1981, in which the two countries agreed to cooperate to counter any threat to peace from the USSR or Soviet-controlled forces. This cooperation included joint maneuvers and stockpiling of militarily relevant supplies.

This friendship, however, was sorely tested in the first few months of the Reagan administration, as the Begin government initiated several unilateral moves to find permanent solutions to its security problems. When Israeli-piloted U.S. jets took out a nuclear reactor near Baghdad on June 5, 1981, the United States responded with a temporary freeze on F–16 fighters to Israel. When Menachem Begin, after his meeting with Reagan in September 1981, seemed to be directly intruding in the U.S. policy process by expressing his strong opposition to the U.S. sale of AWACS to Saudi Arabia before the House and Senate Foreign Relations Committee, Haig was sent on a special trip to meet with Begin for an explanation.[100] When the Begin government pushed through the Knesset its plan to annex the Golan Heights during the height of the Polish crisis, the United States suspended the memorandum of mutual security concluded 17 days earlier. Begin responded with a tirade against the United States. "Are we a banana republic," he queried. "Are we fourteen-year-olds, who if we misbehave, we get our wrists slapped?"[101] It was an extraordinary statement to be aimed at the government that had provided Israel with most of its arms for several decades. "Boy," Reagan was heard to remark on occasion, "that guy makes it hard for you to be his friend."[102]

Yet, the Israelis did let the United States know beforehand that they were going to undertake the war against Lebanon. At Anwar Sadat's funeral in October 1981, Begin told Haig that Israel was planning a move into Lebanon that would not bring Syria into the conflict.[103] The following May, Begin sent an oral warning to Washington that it might become "imperative and inevitable" for Israel to remove the PLO threat.[104] Later that month, General Ariel Sharon outlined to a roomful of State Department officials in Washington two plans for an Israeli invasion—one to pacify Southern Lebanon, the other to remake the political map of Lebanon to strengthen the Christian Phalange.[105]

The United States's response to these signals was ambivalent. At Sadat's funeral, Haig told Begin that Israel would be alone if it undertook any such action, but that one could not deny their right of self-defense.[106] In early 1982, Reagan wrote several letters to Begin stating U.S. opposition to any invasion. When Sharon outlined Israel's two invasion plans at the Department of State in late May, Haig claims to have condemned the invasion in the "plainest possible language."[107] According to other accounts, however, Haig suggested that the United States would not object to a quick, neutralizing operation to deal with the PLO. Certainly Sharon thought he received a green light for an invasion of Lebanon.[108] Another discussion between Haig and the new Israeli ambassador in Washington reinforced that view. Haig's subsequent letter to Begin outlining the U.S. opposition to any invasion was sufficiently mild that it was read in Israel as a diplomatic maneuver—a mere expression of U.S. reservations designed to protect itself diplomatically should the operation backfire.[109]

U.S. actions, moreover, suggested that Israel risked no rupture in its relations with the United States should such an invasion be undertaken. Despite rhetorical slaps at the Israelis whenever they undertook unilateral acts of questionable legality, the United States usually pulled back from any strong statements or serious punishments. On January 20, 1982, for example, the United States vetoed a compromise UN Security Council resolution calling for the punishment of Israel for annexing the Golan Heights. After the bombing of the nuclear plant in Iraq, the United States opposed attempts to apply sanctions against Israel. When Israel bombed PLO sites on the Lebanese coast on April 25, 1982, the United States simply deplored all cease-fire violations—violence against the Israelis as well as the violence of Israel's air strike. Throughout this period, U.S. arms sales to Israel increased from 24,700,000 in 1980 to 148,000,000 in 1981, to 217,600,000 in 1982.[110]

THE INVASION AND THE U.S. RESPONSE

The Israeli invasion of Lebanon began on June 6, 1982, while Reagan was at the Versailles economic conference. One armored column thrust up the coastal road and two pushed inland, while the air force and navy pounded Palestinian positions along the coast. Despite Begin's earlier suggestions that a war between Israel and Lebanon would not involve Syria, Israeli and Syrian jets clashed in the air and Israeli planes took out 17 of the 19 ground-to-air missile batteries in the Bekaa Valley. When Israeli troops reached the outskirts of Beirut on June 10, they began exchanging fire with 2,500 Syrian forces sent to Lebanon as a peace-keeping force in 1975 by the Arab League.

By early July, the Israelis were making it clear that removing the PLO from West Beirut was necessary if a bloodbath in Beirut was to be avoided. The Israelis torqued up the pressure on July 3, cutting off electricity, water, medicine, and food supplies going into the Moslem part of the city. On July 22, Israel initiated seven straight days of bombing and shelling. On July 29, after a two-day truce, Israel escalated the attacks on Palestinians in West Beirut. On August 1, Israeli ship artillery and war-planes bombarded PLO positions and residential areas of West Beirut for 14 hours. A short cease-fire was ended at about midnight on August 3 when Israeli tanks and armored infantry crossed the "Green Line" in a multipronged attack into West Beirut. Arafat rallied his people to fight to the death and the Israelis gained little ground. Fierce air attacks beginning on August 9 were climaxed by a massive 11-hour raid over Beirut on August 12—the most massive attack since the invasion began.

Given Reagan's proclivities for delegating responsibilities, the chief architects of the U.S. response to the Israeli invasion would be his top political aides. Of these, Secretary of State Haig, through sheer determination, was the dominant force until his removal from office in early July. As Haig saw it, Syria's Soviet-made MIGs and antiaircraft batteries in the opening days of the war and Syria's poor overall performance on the battlefield promised to undermine the influence of both Syria and the USSR in the Middle East. Furthermore, with the PLO out of Lebanon, wonderful things would happen. Lebanon would become an independent country again and would sign a peace agreement with Israel. International terrorism, of which the PLO was a major source, would be weakened, and order would be restored in the Middle East and other parts of the world. Saudi Arabia would feel less inhibited in the Middle East peace process and a secure Israel would be more likely to make concessions.[111]

Given this assessment, Haig's strategy was to provide the diplomatic means by which the PLO could be induced to leave Lebanon. Tough action against Israel, he warned, would be counterproductive, encouraging the PLO to hold on in West Beirut. So with the support of Kirkpatrick and the president, he muted U.S. critiques of Israel. On June 26, for example, the United States alone voted against a UN Security Council resolution which called for Israel to pull back ten kilometers from Beirut and for Palestinian forces in Beirut to withdraw to existing camps.[112] A U.S. delegate to the United Nations explained that the proposal had been opposed because it did not eliminate armed Palestinian elements in Beirut and elsewhere.

The brunt of the negotiations for the removal of the PLO, however, fell on the shoulders of a professional diplomat and special Middle East negotiator, Philip Habib. On his way back to the Middle East when the war broke out, he made a short detour to Versailles to meet President Reagan, then went on to Jerusalem and then Damascus in an attempt to bring about a cease-fire between Syria and Israel. His instructions were to reestablish an effective government in Lebanon, arrange for the withdrawal of the PLO and all foreign troops, and secure a safe northern border for Israel.[113]

These tasks were made more difficult by those he was trying to serve. The United States refused to deal directly with the PLO, and Habib had to communicate with them through representatives of the Lebanese government. The Israeli rolling military assaults made it necessary for him to negotiate one cease-fire after another. As he complained to Begin on one occasion about the creeping truce, "It has legs or something."[114] At times, Israeli military moves made it difficult for him even to talk to Lebanese political leaders. When the bombardment of West Beirut on June 25 almost led to the collapse of the recently formed National Salvation Council and the Lebanese cabinet, an agitated Habib called to Haig to report that Israeli military actions were destroying hope for an agreement.[115] Without a Lebanese government, he said, there would be no one to negotiate with the PLO.[116] When Lebanese Prime Minister Shafik al-Wazan refused to cross Israeli military lines around the presidential palace in early July, Habib demanded their removal.[117]

Despite these difficulties, there was an apparent breakthrough in early July. On July 4, the PLO signed an agreement with the government of Lebanon that it would leave Lebanon, and at the Arab League meeting in Saudi Arabia, the Syrians agreed to receive PLO leaders and followers and to accept a phased withdrawal from Lebanon. Haig had visions of a total withdrawal by July 9.[118] The logjam had been broken by Reagan's decision to let U.S. Marines join in a multinational peace-keeping force which would guarantee the withdrawal of all parties from Beirut, thereby giving the PLO a way to withdraw with grace. Habib had forwarded a Lebanese initiative along these lines in late June and Haig sold the proposal to a reluctant Caspar Weinberger and then to the President.[119]

On July 5, Haig was asked to give up all his foreign policy responsibilities. The next day, the package Haig thought he had put together began to fall apart. A leak in the Israeli press to the effect that the United States would send troops to Israel was confirmed by Reagan, and Leonid Brezhnev of the USSR sent the United States a note saying that the USSR would "build its policy in due consideration of this fact."[120] A new shipment of arms and Soviet advisers flew into Syria, and the Syrian government announced it could not accept the PLO and reneged on its agreement to withdraw from Lebanon.

Up to this point in time, Haig had pushed his policies against strong opposition from most of the other presidential advisers. The crisis management team, under Vice President George Bush's direction, reported directly to Clark and the president, bypassing the Department of State.[121] Their recommendation, immediately after the Israeli invasion, that the United States vote for a United Nations resolution threatening sanctions against Israel was reversed only when Haig, casually informed of the decision at a dinner at Windsor Palace, went to the president personally. Haig's instructions to Habib the weekend after the president returned to the United States were forwarded despite Clark's insistence that he should wait until a Monday meeting in the White House and despite Reagan's own insistence on that delay when Haig called him at Camp David. (The president apparently had not even seen the instructions at the time Haig placed his call, though they had been data-faxed to him.)[122]

Then, in a top-level meeting at the White House shortly before Begin's scheduled visit with Reagan on June 21, it was Haig against everyone else. He argued that Begin not be publicly put on the spot in his forthcoming meeting with the president, while Weinberger and Clark argued that a business-as-usual response would undermine U.S. credibility with moderate Arab regimes already perceiving the United States as having given Israel implicit backing for the invasion.[123] Begin had insulted the president too, several aides felt, with his half-truths in a letter of June 6 to Reagan suggesting that Israel would move only 40 kilometers into Lebanon, and by ignoring Reagan's initial requests for a cease-fire.[124]

Behind the scenes, Haig encouraged Begin and Sharon in the very policies that created so many problems for others in the administration. His signals before the invasion suggesting that the United States would not oppose a quick and clean Israeli invasion of Lebanon have been noted. In late June, at a time when Reagan and other top decision-makers were concerned with showing Israel the extent of U.S. displeasure with Israeli go-it-alone policies, Haig reinforced Begin's truculence. Just before Begin's meeting with Reagan at the White House, for example, Haig had advised him "to hold out for what you want!" At the conclusion of the meeting, according to one account, Haig sent Begin a thumbs-up sign.[125]

There were several problems in Haig's policies. The unconditional commitment to Israel's attempts to drive the PLO out of Lebanon placed the United States in an awkward position in which its own mediation efforts were undermined by Israeli military moves. The identification of the United States with Israeli military policies in the area could have undermined U.S. relations with moderate Arab regimes, and made it more difficult for the United States to persuade them to accept contingents of the PLO driven out of Lebanon. In broader terms, the administration's anti-USSR alliance in the Middle East, which depended on the cooperation of Arab nations as well as Israel, was called into question by the close alliance with Israel.

Once the United States had committed itself to Israel's goal of driving the PLO out of Lebanon, however, the even-handed approach was counterproductive. Haig's strategy of keeping the pressure on the PLO was imperiled by Vice President George Bush and Defense Secretary Caspar Weinberger at the funeral of King Khaled of Saudi Arabia. They told the new king, Ibn Abdul Aziz al Saud Fahd, that the United States would not let the Israelis enter West Beirut. National Security adviser Clark told the Saudi ambassador in Washington the same thing.[126] Subsequently, on June 24, White House press spokesman Larry Speakes told the press, inaccurately it seems, that Begin had promised Reagan in their meeting the previous Monday that Israel would go no further into West Beirut.[127] These signals, Haig would later claim, led the PLO to play for more time.[128]

With Haig's departure, Reagan put some distance between the United States and Israel. In mid-July, the president wrote a letter to Begin saying the United States might have to deal directly with the PLO. Ambassador Samuel Lewis personally delivered the letter to Begin, who was especially quiet upon receiving this threat.[129] By July 27, Reagan had decided on an indefinite suspension of the delivery of cluster-bomb artillery shells to Israel.[130] During this period, the Arabs were wooed at the highest level. Reagan, in a letter to King Fahd of Saudi Arabia in mid-July, solicited help in finding a haven for the PLO evacuees.[131] By late July, there was a payoff. The Arab League for the first time presented a plan in which the Arab world took responsibility for receiving members of the PLO who would be ousted from Lebanon, and the PLO sent Habib a detailed plan for the evacuation of 6,000 guerrillas from West Beirut to these countries.[132]

The escalation of Israeli assaults on West Beirut in early August, just as these major diplomatic breakthroughs were occurring, enraged President Reagan. In a highly publicized meeting with Israeli Foreign Minister Itzhak Shamir on August 2, the president insisted that the United States could not "accept a situation of constantly escalating violence" and called for a complete withdrawal by all fighting forces in and around Beirut so that Habib could continue his mediation efforts.[133] On the morning of August 4, after Israeli tanks crossed the Green Line, Reagan sent a sharp letter to "Mr. Begin" (rather than the usual "Dear Menachem") calling the Israeli move disproportionate and suggesting grave consequences if Israel penetrated further into West Beirut.

Still, the president's responses were hedged. Threats of possible sanctions were excised from the draft of the "Dear Mr. Begin" letter, at the suggestion of Ambassador Samuel Lewis,[134] and on August 6, the United States vetoed a Soviet-sponsored, French-supported UN Security Council resolution calling for a boycott on military aid to Israel.[135]

But then, on August 12, the day of massive Israeli bombings of West Beirut, Reagan sent a strong message to Begin via Ambassador Lewis threatening to call off the Habib peace mission. Reagan himself called the prime minister on the telephone—he wanted Begin to feel his outrage. After an hour of trying to get through, during which time Reagan received a call from King Fahd demanding that the White House take some action, the connection was made. "I want it [the bombing] stopped, and I want it stopped now," Reagan demanded. Begin called back 20 minutes later to say that the cease-fire was in effect once again. (Actually, Reagan had not caused the back-down despite appearances. Sharon had exceeded his authority and the Israeli cabinet had already agreed to end the barrage prior to Reagan's phone call.)[136]

In the five days that followed the cease-fire of August 12, Philip Habib hammered out the few remaining details on the PLO withdrawal, and the evacuation of the PLO by sea and land to South Yemen, Algeria, Tunisia, and Syria took place between August 21 and 27.[137]

With this crisis apparently resolved, the Reagan administration belatedly moved to deal with the problem of self-government in the "occupied territories." On September 1, Reagan interrupted his vacation in California to enter the NBC studios in Burbank to present his first comprehensive Middle East plan. The new political circumstances created by the Israeli invasion, he said, made a new start more feasible. The military losses of the PLO had not ended the desire of the Palestinian people for a just solution to the PLO's claims, nor was Israeli preeminence in the area sufficient to achieve a just and lasting peace. An autonomous Palestinian entity in a federation with Jordan should be created. He also suggested that Israel give up much of the territory captured since 1967 and that Jewish settlements in the Gaza Strip and on the West Bank immediately be frozen. The Arab world, in turn, would recognize the legitimacy of Israel's border and its existence as a nation.[138] Reagan had bought Haig's idea that the Israeli invasion offered new opportunities for negotiation. The PLO, with its political and military options dwindling, was apt to be in a more compliant mood. The USSR, in the throes of a leadership transition, was not inclined to take risky moves. Syria had been weakened by its military defeat at the hands of Israel.

The plan, the result of several weeks of work by Middle East experts in the State Department, bet on Jordanian and Saudi support. Assistant Secretary Nicholas Veliotes, the top-ranking Middle East expert in the State Department, had gone to Jordan in late August before the plan was made public and had received assurance that Jordan would support the plan within hours of its announcement.[139] There were also indications from other Arab regimes that they would support Jordan's effort to be named the negotiating authority for the Palestinians.[140] If it were backed by the Arab League, Jordan could move forward with genuine proposals for a settlement. Public opinion in Israel would push either the Begin government or a more adaptive, successor Labour party government to negotiate seriously.

The Reagan proposal enhanced the president's image as a possible peacemaker, both at home and in the Arab world. But it did not accomplish much on the diplomatic front. At Fez, Morocco, on September 9, 1982, Arab League leaders found the proposal a useful beginning. However, they reaffirmed their earlier insistence on the PLO as the sole legitimate representative of the Palestinian people.[141] Israel rejected the Reagan initiative outright, and the cabinet hastily approved of eight new Jewish settlements on the West Bank. Begin wrote Reagan that he would oppose with total dedication an autonomous Palestinian entity in the West Bank. With these rejections, the president would let things drift. Not until December 1982 would he try to get the peace process off the ground.[142]

The public debate over Reagan's Middle East plans was eclipsed by the Israeli return to West Beirut in early September, the subsequent assassination of Lebanese President-elect Bashir Gemayel, and the massacres in the PLO camps at Sabra and Shatila.[143] Responding to these events, the United States called for an Israeli pullback and voted for a UN Security Council resolution condemning "the criminal massacre of Palestinian civilians in Beirut."[144] Reagan said, "I was horrified to learn this morning of the Palestinian [massacre] which had taken place in Beirut."[145] Most importantly, Reagan decided to send U.S. troops back into Lebanon, escalating their goal to aid the Lebanese government in reasserting its authority over all its territory.[146] At his September 28 news conference, Reagan said the United States would stay in Lebanon until all foreign troops were withdrawn and until "such time as Lebanon says they have the situation well in hand."[147] This was an enormous commitment given the nature of Lebanese politics, and it threatened to pull the United States into the Lebanese civil war.

FOREIGN POLICY DETERMINANTS

Reagan's personality and his decision-making style, as this earlier analysis suggests, had an important impact on his policies toward the Middle East. His apparent dislike of hard work and detail meant that he did not try to be his own secretary of state, as Roosevelt and other presidents have done at times. But neither did he delegate major responsibility for foreign policy to one strong and experienced individual, as Harding, Truman, and Nixon had done. Instead, he loosely delegated power to several like-minded actors—a situation conducive to political and turf battles.

Reagan's dislike of controversy and his difficulty in standing up to those in his immediate environment, moreover, left conflicts simmering. This is evident in the difficulties he had in firing Alexander Haig. The secretary of state had directly challenged his authority and his confrontational style made Reagan uncomfortable. But the president, in a meeting on June 14, simply admonished the secretary of state for his insubordination in sending Habib instructions the previous Saturday. It was Haig who confronted the president—telling him that he (Haig) could not continue for four more years if the necessary steps were not taken to make U.S. foreign policy coherent. The best time for his departure, Haig suggested, would be after the November elections. However, the president did nothing for ten days, and only after some prodding from Haig did the two men finally meet again. Clearly uncomfortable, Reagan listened to Haig's chronicle of the contradictory signals that had plagued his foreign policy efforts.[148] The next morning—after a meeting in which Baker, Clark, and Deaver urged him to get rid of Haig—Reagan drafted a letter accepting a resignation Haig had not yet presented. As Reagan told his advisers, "I just don't want to get in any more of these things about who's right and who's wrong."[149] In their meeting later that day, Reagan simply handed Haig the letter.[150] He had difficulty in saying directly that he no longer needed Haig's services.

When an arrangement for Haig to continue to conduct foreign affairs until George Schultz could take over failed, Reagan had Schultz call Haig to say he should quit immediately. When Haig insisted that he had to hear the decision from the president himself, Reagan called. However, he could not say outright that he no longer needed Haig's services. "Al, George Schultz tells me he's had a discussion with you," Reagan said. "I just wanted to tell you that what he told you had my approval."[151] Very little more was said.

Reagan had similar problems dealing with Begin. Haig and many others in the State Department advised him that any attempt to pressure Begin would be counterproductive, and there certainly was evidence that Begin could dig in when directly confronted. Hearing that the president might not receive him on his visit to the United Nations in June 1981, Begin sent angry instructions back to Jerusalem telling his cabinet that they should do whatever was best for Israeli security. Following Reagan's Middle East proposals on September 1, Begin, in an angry speech in the Knesset, declared that Judea and Samaria (the biblical names for the West Bank) would be for the Jewish people to "the end of time."[152] As Sol Linowitz, Jimmy Carter's Middle East negotiator pointed out, a get-tough attitude generally is not the way to move Begin:

He will become even more adamant about his assertions if he feels that threats are being used and pressure applied in order to get him to give way. If we take that approach, he may become more intractable, and, what is more, the Israeli nation may rally around him with a passion.[153]

Nevertheless, part of Reagan's problem in dealing with Begin stemmed from his difficulty in being direct and clear with Begin before the conflict between the United States and Israel came to a head. Begin was a man who prided himself on being frank and sticking to his commitments. He had informed the United States that Israel would probably invade Lebanon; and on several occasions he told Haig and Reagan personally that Israel would never give up the occupied territories. Nonetheless, Reagan and his aides did not listen seriously to what Begin had to say. Reagan, for example, claimed in late June that the United States had no advance warning about the invasion. Later, Reagan had difficulties in expressing the growing White House resentment concerning the unilateral aspects of Israeli policies. In his meeting with Begin on June 21, for example, Reagan condemned the Israeli invasion, and afterwards administration officials stressed that Reagan had been forceful with him. However, Reagan read his comments from cards, which made the protest look pro forma, and a White House statement issued after the meeting seemed to back Israeli policies in Lebanon.[154] Certainly Begin did not feel chastised. Warned by Sol Linowitz before his meeting that he would have a difficult time, he afterwards told Linowitz through an intermediary that Linowitz had been wrong: Everything had gone just fine.[155]

Later, in early September, when Israeli troops returned to West Beirut, Reagan excused their behavior. "I am sure what led them to move in was an attack by some leftist militia forces," he said in an offhand comment. Clear talks about U.S.-Israeli policy differences probably would not have eradicated policy differences, but they could have cleared the air.

Ideological factors also played an important role in wedding the United States to Israeli policies. Reagan's anti-Communism provided a framework that guided the selection of his key advisers and placed boundaries on the policy choices they would consider. But to view the Soviet Union as the source of all the difficulties throughout the world does not describe how it might threaten a particular region of the world and how that threat should be countered. Reagan's ideology was so abstract that it provided little guidance regarding specific foreign policy choices. On top of this, the president had little specific knowledge about the Middle East. (One aide recalls Reagan measuring points in Israel and Lebanon with his finger and exclaiming, "Gosh, they really are close.")[156]

The specific form Reagan's anti-Communist policy took in the Middle East, thus depended to a great extent on his advisers. Divided over the extent to which the alliance against the USSR should be based on an identification with Israeli interests as opposed to a more even-handed policy between that country and the moderate Arab regimes, they presented Reagan with divergent opinions in the early phases of the war, and their conflicts sometimes surfaced, muddying the policy waters.

Through sheer forcefulness as well as his ability to identify the Israeli cause with the anti-Communist policy goal, however, Haig was able to dominate policy for some time. Certainly the extent of the U.S. commitment to Israeli military policies in Lebanon up through early July was his doing. The rationale was given later in his memoirs. The specific obstacle to peace in Lebanon, Haig wrote, has been "the presence of two foreign armies, the Syrian peacekeeping force and the military arms of the Palestinian Liberation Organization."[157] The civil conflict there had its origins in the PLO's creation of a state within a state and the Soviet Union's support of Syria and her "oft-time agent, the PLO."[158] The dangerous forces loose in the area, associated with "the advance of Soviet influence in the Middle East," could best be checked by a show of U.S. resolve. "Few in the Middle East," he said, "failed to make the connection between the decline in American strength and the rise in tension and disorder."[159]

Information that would have challenged this view—that the major destabilizing force in the Middle East was the USSR—did not get through to the president. Experts in the Bureau of Near East and South Asian Affairs in the Department of State saw a somewhat more complex reality, and were well aware of the indigenous roots of conflict in Lebanon and the Middle East. The U.S. ambassadors in Lebanon, Syria, and Jordan were doing some first-class reporting on local conflicts and sensibilities.[160] Their reports, however, were screened through

Haig at the State Department. Middle East experts in the Defense Department had some impact on Weinberger, and he would sometimes take their views to National Security Council meetings. However, as one of those experts noted, Weinberger's views never seemed to be acted upon.[161]

Even after Haig's departure from office, however, the administration continued to tilt in the Israeli direction. The president's Middle East Peace proposals suggested he wished to pursue a more even-handed policy, but, as we have seen, the whole process was never pursued with any real fervor. A more vigorous and politically determined president might have pursued the peace process with more vigor, at least for a short time in 1982. Elite and broader public opinion would have permitted stronger pressure on Israel for approximately four months after the invasion. Editorial opinion in U.S. newspapers was more critical of Israel than before.[162] Members of Congress showed their frustration. Indeed, Democrat Joseph Biden of Delaware got into a shouting match with Begin in a meeting with the Senate Foreign Relations Committee on June 21, 1982. Paul Tsongas, a Democrat from Massachusetts, said afterward that he had never seen such an angry session with a foreign head of state.[163] Clement Zablocki and Charles Percy, chairmen of the committees dealing with foreign relations in the House and Senate, respectively, were both critical of Israeli policies.[164] There was even public criticism of Israeli policy by U.S. Jews. Shortly after the invasion, several Jewish intellectuals signed advertisements in the *San Francisco Chronicle* saying, "Menachem Begin does not speak for us."[165] After Begin's brusque rejection of Reagan's peace plan, Bnai Brith praised Reagan's call for Palestinian self-government.[166] Following the massacre at the Sabra and Shatila camps, a *Newsweek* poll showed a majority of U.S. Jews felt Israel had to share some of the responsibility for the massacre.[167]

The U.S. public, too, was more critical of Israel than it had been in the past. The *Newsweek* poll showed that for the first time in years, U.S. citizens were almost evenly divided in their sympathies for Israel and the Arab states (32 percent to 28 percent).[168] Meg Greenfield of *Newsweek* saw in these reactions a "turning away from an unnatural relationship in which Israel's friends and many indifferent to its concerns, were wary of ever criticizing, questioning, or resisting its policies."[169]

Reagan, however, was not inclined to run any domestic political risks for the sake of a Middle East peace plan. In late August, for example, administration officials met with 40 U.S. Jewish leaders to reassure them that no sanctions against Israel were being considered.[170] Later, the administration would find that AIPAC's political activities would constrain their policy choices. In late November, 1982, for example, Congress insisted on appropriating more funds for Israel than President Reagan wanted, despite the lobbying efforts of Bush, Shultz, and Weinberger.[171] Contributions to the opponents of Israeli critics in the 1982 elections by pro-Israeli political action committees (PAC's) had quieted Israel's critics in Congress. Paul Findley, a Republican member of the House Committee on Foreign Affairs, who had on several occasions urged the United States to deal with the PLO, was defeated by Richard Durbin, to whom 31 pro-Israeli PAC's had contributed $103,325. Clement Zablocki faced a serious challenge when 14 pro-Israel PAC's contributed $13,350 to his opponent.[172]

The reluctance by Congress and the public to get involved militarily anywhere abroad also had an impact on the Reagan policy. When the president first announced he would send troops to Lebanon, several congressmen registered their concern and said the president would have to consult Congress.[173] Reagan reluctantly informed Congress on August 25, the day the U.S. Marines first landed in Lebanon, that this action was "consistent with," but not "under" or "pursuant to" the War Powers Resolution. The premature pullout of these troops on September 10, 15 days before their official mission would have ended, temporarily quelled potential controversy over their use. When the president sent the marines back into Lebanon on September 29, due to his open-ended and ill-defined objectives, a confrontation with Congress was inevitable. When the marines were still in Lebanon a year later and exchanging gunfire in Syrian-held territory, Reagan finally had to recognize his duty to inform Congress under the War Powers Resolution and negotiate a specific cutoff date in exchange for explicit statutory authority to extend their presence in Lebanon.

CONCLUSION

The extent to which the Reagan administration identified its goals with Israel's policies in the Middle East was criticized by several Middle East experts at the height of the Lebanese crisis. We can no longer "play the postman role" to Israel, said former Under Secretary of State Joseph Sisco.[174] However, as this analysis shows, Reagan and his aides followed Israeli policies because they saw the invasion of Lebanon as opening up new strategic opportunities. Ideologically inclined to see the Soviets as the source of all disturbances in the area and the PLO and the Syrians as simply their surrogates, the Reagan administration could not refrain from taking advantage of early Israeli military victories.

The implementation of that policy was greatly influenced by Reagan's personality and decision-making style. The president's dislike of detail and of conflict among his political intimates led to policy and turf battles which the president had no taste for controlling and which undermined his policies. The extent to which he surrounded himself by like-minded persons and sought their conformity to his basic worldview cut him off from experts in the lower echelons of government who understood the indigenous nature of much of the conflict in Lebanon and the Middle East, and could have warned him of the dangers of his policies. The president's desire to help the Gemayal government establish its authority over all of Lebanon was beyond his power to achieve in any circumstance, but Reagan's concession to congressional opinion meant that the U.S.

Marines sent would be limited in number and placed under instructions not to use their arms except in self-defense.

The administration during these four months might have opted for a more even-handed approach to Israel and moderate Arab regimes in the area, and it could have used political muscle to win support for the president's own Middle East proposals. Both elite and public opinion had tilted away from Israel after the invasion and the abrupt rejection of Reagan's Middle East peace proposals. Later, the very influential AIPAC would make those options less viable in terms of domestic politics. Basically, the notion that the Israeli invasion offered grand new strategic opportunities for the U.S. to achieve its anti-Soviet, anti-radical goals, proved chimerical. As Middle East expert William Quandt said of that whole idea at the height of the crisis, "That's not the Middle East I know. There are some new elements in the picture, but the Middle East is extraordinarily complicated. It will take some unusually skillful playing of our hand to take any advantage from it."[175]

NOTES

1. Steven Spiegel, *The Other Arab-Israeli Conflict* (Chicago: University of Chicago Press, 1985), p. 390.

2. *The Gallup Report*, 186 (1981): 2–3.

3. Betty Glad, "How Jimmy Carter Lost the Election of 1980," William Howard Taft University Lecture, University of Cincinnati, 1981.

4. Details from Reagan's early life given in this section, unless noted otherwise, are from Betty Glad, "What Politics Does for Ronald Reagan," paper presented at the annual meeting of the International Society of Political Psychology, Frankfurt, 1981.

5. Ibid.

6. Bill Boyarsky, *Ronald Reagan: His Life and Rise to the Presidency* (New York: Random House, 1981), pp. 111–12; Lou Cannon, *Reagan*, (New York: The Putnam Publishing Group, 1982), pp. 119–38.

7. Glad, "What Politics Does for Ronald Reagan," p. 50.

8. Betty Glad, "The 1976 Elections," in *History of American Presidential Elections*, ed. Arthur Schlesinger, Jr. (New York: Chelsea House, 1986), 5, pp. 94–99.

9. Boyarsky, *Ronald Reagan*, p. 5.

10. Ronald Reagan with R. G. Hubler, *Where's the Rest of Me?* (New York: Duell Sloan and Pierce, 1965), p. 79.

11. Boyarsky, *Ronald Reagan*, p. 19.

12. Glad, "The 1976 Elections," p. 95.

13. Fred Greenstein, *The Reagan Presidency: An Early Assessment* (Baltimore: Johns Hopkins University Press, 1983), p. 174.

14. Laurence I. Barrett, *Gambling with History* (Garden City, N.Y.: Doubleday, 1983), p. 25; and "Nine Hours inside the Oval Office," *U.S. News & World Report* (July 6, 1981): pp. 14–20.

15. Boyarsky, *Ronald Reagan*, p. 103.

16. Glad, "What Politics Does for Ronald Reagan."

17. Boyarsky, *Ronald Reagan*, p. 124.

18. Ronald Reagan, *The Creative Society: Some Comments on Problems Facing America* (New York: Devin-Adair, 1968), p. 121; for details of Reagan's world view,

see Betty Glad, "Black and White Thinking: Ronald Reagan's Approach to Foreign Policy," *Political Psychology* 4, no. 1 (Spring 1983): pp. 33ff.

19. Reagan, *The Creative Society*, p. 84.

20. Ronald Reagan, *Public Papers of the Presidents of the United States: Ronald Reagan, 1981* (Washington: GPO, 1983), p. 57. All references to this multivolume source cited hereafter as *Public Papers: 1981* or *Public Papers: 1982*.

21. Reagan, *Public Papers: 1982*, p. 747.

22. Ibid., p. 786.

23. Barbara Walters, "Interview with Ronald Reagan," American Broadcasting Company, March 24, 1986.

24. Reagan, *Where's the Rest of Me?*, p. 311.

25. Ronald Reagan, "Human Rights and Soviet Challenges," *Los Angeles Times*, June 23, 1977, p. 17.

26. Reagan, *Public Papers: 1981*, p. 871.

27. *Middle East Policy Survey* no. 4 (February 29, 1980), cited in Spiegel, *The Other Arab-Israeli Conflict*, p. 400.

28. *United Press International*, October 10, 1982.

29. Reagan, *The Creative Society*, pp. 7–8.

30. Quoted in Glad, "What Politics Does for Ronald Reagan."

31. Barrett, *Gambling with History*, p. 24.

32. This is not to suggest that no cognitive changes take place in rigid individuals. Belatedly, after receiving overwhelming evidence that certain categorizations are inaccurate, they may change their minds. E. Frendel-Brunswik, "Intolerance of Ambiguity as an Emotional and Perceptual Personality Variability," *Journal of Personality* 18, no. 10 (1949/1950): pp. 108ff.

33. "Ronald Reagan up Close," *Newsweek* (July 21, 1980): 25–26.

34. Lou Cannon, *Ronnie and Jessie: A Political Odyssey* (Garden City, New York: Doubleday, 1969), p. 164.

35. "Meet the Real Ronald Reagan," *Time* (October 20, 1980).

36. Steven V. Robert, "Reagan's First Friend," *New York Times Magazine*, March 21, 1982.

37. "Meet the Real Ronald Reagan" and "Keeping It in the Family," *Time*, (October 20, 1980): pp. 27, 28.

38. *Newsweek*, July 21, 1980.

39. Betty Glad, "Black and White Thinking," pp. 35ff.

40. Karen Horney, *The Neurotic Personality of Our Time* (New York: W. W. Norton, 1937), pp. 46–60, 98–99.

41. Dwight Younger, *Reagan's Dixon* (Dixon: The Official Dixon Press, 1980), pp. 4–5.

42. Helen Kennedy Lawton, interview with author, Dixon, Ill., March 27, 1983.

43. Reagan, *Where's the Rest of Me?* p. 40.

44. Ibid., p. 8.

45. Ibid., pp. 7–8.

46. Ibid., p. 19.

47. Ibid., p. 18.

48. Joel Kotkin and Paul Grabowicz, "Dutch Reagan, All-American: A Documentary History of the Growing Boy from Dixon, Illinois," *Esquire* (August, 1980): 26.

49. Reagan, *Where's the Rest of Me?* pp. 18–19.

50. Ibid., p. 19.

51. Glad, "What Politics Does for Ronald Reagan."

52. Reagan, *Where's the Rest of Me?*, p. 74.

53. Cannon, *Ronnie and Jessie*, pp. 60–61.

54. Reagan, *Where's the Rest of Me?* p. 38.

55. Ibid., p. 8.

56. Ibid., p. 38.

57. Carl Buckner, interview with author, Dixon, Ill., March 28, 1983.

58. Reagan, *Where's the Rest of Me?* p. 201.

59. Ibid., p. 38.

60. "Ronald Reagan Up Close," *Newsweek* (July 21, 1980): 50.

61. "Meet the Real Ronald Reagan," *Time* (October 20, 1980): 22; "A First Lady of Priorities and Properties," *Time* (January 5, 1981): 25; Elizabeth Mehren and Betty Cuniberti, "First Lady Taking Over a Political Role," *Los Angeles Times*, March 4, 1987, pp. 1, 14, 15.

62. "Ronald Reagan Up Close," p. 50.

63. Betty Glad, "Reagan's Midlife Crisis and the Turn to the Right," paper presented at the annual meeting of the International Society of Political Psychology, San Francisco, 1987.

64. "Ronald Reagan Up Close," p. 46.

65. Ibid., p. 53.

66. Barrett, *Gambling with History*, pp. 57–58.

67. Glad, "The 1976 Elections," pp. 95–99.

68. Quoted in Barrett, *Gambling with History*, p. 61.

69. For background on AIPAC see Edward Tivan, *The Lobby: Jewish Political Power and American Foreign Policy* (New York: Simon and Schuster, 1987), pp. 162–180; David K. Shipler, "On Middle East Policy, a Major Influence," *New York Times*, July 6, 1987, pp. A1, A4; Robert Pear and Richard L. Berke, "Pro-Israel Group Asserts Quiet Might as it Rallies Supporters in Congress," *New York Times*, July 7, 1987, p. A8.

70. For campaign contributions and the Jewish vote, see Ben Bradlee, "Competing for the Jewish Vote," *Boston Globe Magazine*, April 29, 1984; Charlotte Salkowski, "America's Israeli Aid Budget Grows," *Christian Science Monitor*, November 30, 1983, p. 1; Stephen D. Issacs, *Jews and American Politics* (Garden City, New York: Doubleday, 1977), p. 119.

71. Bernard Reich, "United States Middle East Policy in the Carter and Reagan Administrations," *Australian Outlook* 38, August 1984, pp. 77–78.

72. Howard C. Nielson, "Examining U.S. Perceptions and Attitudes Towards the Middle East," *American-Arab Affairs*, Fall, 1984, p. 10.

73. Tivnan, *The Lobby*, pp. 181–83.

74. Thomas C. Sorenson, "U.S. Foreign Policy and the Middle East: Origins and Limitations," *Journal of Arab Affairs*, October 1982, pp. 1–28; Spiegel, *The Other Arab-Israeli Conflict*, (vol. 2), p. 398.

75. Sorensen, "U.S. Foreign Policy and The Middle East," pp. 1–28.

76. Richard Halloran, "Reagan as Military Commander," *New York Times Magazine*, January 15, 1984, p. 25ff.

77. Alexander M. Haig, *Caveat: Realism, Reagan and Foreign Policy*, (New York: MacMillan, 1984), pp. 53–55, 74, 85, 92.

78. Leslie H. Gelb, "Foreign Policy System Criticized by U.S. Aides," *New York Times Magazine*, October 18, 1981, p. 1.

79. Ibid., pp. 1, A8.

80. For background on top aides see "The Power Brokers Around the President," *US News & World Report* (February 9, 1981): 19–22.

81. Greenstein, *The Reagan Presidency*, pp. 171–72; Gregory Black, "Foreign Policy Making in the Reagan Administration: An Analysis and Critique of the New Cold Warriors," unpublished paper, University of Illinois-Urbana, 1981.

82. Gelb, "Foreign Policy System Criticized," p. A8.

83. Jeane J. Kirkpatrick, *The Reagan Phenomenon and Other Speeches of Foreign Policy* (Washington, D.C.: American Enterprise Institute for Public Policy Research, 1983), pp. 30–31.

84. Gregory Black, "Foreign Policy Making in the Reagan Administration."

85. Glad, "What Politics Does for Ronald Reagan."

86. Glad, "What Politics Does for Ronald Reagan"; Greenstein, *The Reagan Presidency*, pp. 171, 179–80.

87. Gelb, "Foreign Policy System Criticized," p. A8.

88. Barrett, *Gambling With History*, pp. 239–40, 244–45, 331; Gelb, "Foreign Policy System Criticized," p. A8.

89. Barrett, *Gambling With History*, p. 24.

90. Ibid., pp. 95–96.

91. Richard Halloran, "Reagan as Military Commander," *New York Times Magazine*, January 15, 1984, pp. 58–59.

92. Reagan, *Public Papers: 1981*, pp. 152–53, 194–95.

93. *Facts on File*, 1981, p. 59.

94. Bernard Gwertzman, "U.S. Citing Possible Violation of Arms Agreement, Suspends Shipment of 4 Jets to Israel," *New York Times*, June 11, 1981, p. 1; Steven R. Weisman, "Reagan Voices Regrets to Arabs, but Assures Israel on Ties," *New York Times*, June 12, 1981, p. 8.

95. Bernard Gwertzman, "Sadat Assured Over U.S. Role in the Mideast," *New York Times*, August 7, 1981, p. 1.

96. "Visit of Egyptian President Mubarak," and "Statement of Principle," *State Department Bulletin*, April 1982, pp. 77–79.

97. Spiegel, *The Other Arab-Israeli Conflict*, p. 406.

98. Ronald Reagan, "Recognizing the Israeli Asset," *The Washington Post*, August 15, 1979, p. A25.

99. Barrett, *Gambling With History*, pp. 264–65.

100. Haig, *Caveat*, pp. 187–88.

101. David K. Shipler, "Begin Contends U.S. Policies Treat Israel Like A 'Vassal,' " *New York Times*, December 21, 1981, p. 1.

102. Barrett, *Gambling with History*, p. 271.

103. Haig, *Caveat*, p. 326.

104. Ibid., p. 330.

105. Ibid., p. 335.

106. Ibid., pp. 326–27.

107. Ibid., p. 335.

108. For views that Haig had approved some sort of Israeli operation, see Ze'ev Schiff and Ehud Yáari, *Israel's Lebanon War* (New York: Simon & Schuster, 1984), p. 74;

Avner Yaniv, *Dilemmas of Security* (New York: Oxford University Press, 1987) p. 139. For Sharon's interpretation of this meeting, see Spiegel, *The Other Arab-Israeli Conflict*, p. 414.

109. Spiegel, *The Other Arab-Israeli Conflict*, p. 414; Schiff and Ya'ari, *Israel's Lebanon War*, p. 75.

110. Concerning arms shipments, see Yaniv, *Dilemmas of Security*, p. 138. For U.S. position at the United Nations see Kirkpatrick, *The Reagan Phenomenon*, p. 119.

111. "When Push Comes To Shove," *Time* (August 16, 1982): 8–16.

112. Bernard D. Nossiter, "U.N. Lebanon Plan Is Vetoed by U.S.," *New York Times*, June 27, 1982, p. 1.

113. Haig, *Caveat*, p. 392.

114. "The Fragile Truce in Lebanon," *Newsweek* (June 28, 1982): 29.

115. Haig, *Caveat*, p. 346.

116. Ibid.

117. "A Fortress Under Heavy Fire," *Time* (July 19, 1982): 16.

118. Haig, *Caveat*, p. 350.

119. "The Crucial Decision," *Newsweek* (July 19, 1982): 19.

120. For text of Brezhnev statement from TASS, see *New York Times*, July 9, 1982, p. 6.

121. Haig, *Caveat*, p. 306.

122. Ibid., pp. 310–11; 338–39.

123. *Facts on File*, 1982, p. 458.

124. "Risks and Opportunities," *Time* (June 28, 1982): 12. For Begin and Sharon's differing views on the nature of the invasion before it began, and their cooperation afterwards, see Yaniv, *Dilemmas of Security*, pp. 101–2, 110, 119.

125. Schiff and Ya'ari, *Israel's Lebanon War*, p. 30.

126. Spiegel, *The Other Arab-Israeli Conflict*, p. 415.

127. Haig, *Caveat*, pp. 343, 346.

128. Ibid., p. 344.

129. "A Fortress Under Heavy Fire," *Time*, July 19, 1982, p. 11.

130. Judith Miller, "U.S. Bars Cluster Shells for Israel Indefinitely," *New York Times*, July 28, 1982, p. 16.

131. For story on Reagan's letter to Fahd, see *New York Times*, July 15, 1982, p. 1.

132. "Talking Under the Gun," *Time*, August 9, 1982, p. 22.

133. Reagan, *Public Papers: 1982*, p. 997.

134. "When Push Comes to Shove," *Time* (August 16, 1982): 10–13.

135. Bernard D. Nossiter, "US Vetoes U.N. Resolution Seeking Israeli Arms Cutoff," *New York Times*, August 7, 1982, p. 1.

136. Bernard Weinraub, "Reagan Demands End to Attacks in a Blunt Telephone Call to Begin," *New York Times*, August 13, 1982, p. 1; "Menachem, Shalom," *Time* (August 23, 1982): 28–30.

137. James F. Clarity, "Syrian-Led Forces Quit West Beirut," *New York Times*, August 28, 1982, p. 1; and Leslie H. Gelb, "US Mideast Policy Is at a Crossroads," *New York Times*, September 21, 1982, p. 1.

138. Ronald Reagan, "A New Opportunity for Peace in the Middle East," *State Department Bulletin*, September 1982, pp. 23–25.

139. Spiegel, *The Other Arab-Israeli Conflict*, p. 419.

140. Ibid., p. 420.

141. Reich, "U.S. Middle East Policy," p. 76.

142. William B. Quandt, "Reagan's Lebanon Policy: Trial and Error," *The Middle East Journal*, Spring 1984.

143. Colin Campbell, "Israel Drives on West Beirut to Prevent Guerilla Gains After Staying of Gemayel," *New York Times*, September 16, 1982, p. 1; Thomas L. Friedman, "Christian Militiamen Accused of a Massacre in Beirut Camps," *New York Times*, September 19, 1982, p. 1.

144. Reagan, *Public Papers, 1982*, p. 1181.

145. Ibid., p. 1181.

146. Ibid., pp. 1187–90.

147. Ibid., pp. 1226–29.

148. Haig, *Caveat*, pp. 311–12.

149. "The Shakeup at State," *Time* (July 5, 1982): 8–14.

150. Haig, *Caveat*, p. 315.

151. Ibid., p. 351.

152. "A Defiant No to Reagan," *Time* (September 20, 1982): 28.

153. "You Have to Level with Begin," *Time* (June 28, 1982): 18.

154. Haig, *Caveat*, p. 344; Reagan, *Public Papers: 1982*, p. 799; "The Shakeup at State," *Time* (July 5, 1982): 11.

155. Barrett, *Gambling with History*, p. 283.

156. Reagan quotes from "A Growing Sense of Betrayal," *Time* (October 4, 1982): 26.

157. Haig, *Caveat*, p. 318. Haig may also have contributed to Begin's misinterpretation of the mood in Washington. In a cordial meeting in New York prior to Begin's visit with Reagan, Haig had confided that he had battles within the administration regarding his policies but would carry the day in the end. See Barrett, *Gambling with History*, pp. 281–82.

158. Haig, *Caveat*, pp. 319–20.

159. Ibid., p. 169.

160. Ben Fitzgerald, interview with author, Urbana, Ill., November 6, 1985.

161. Ibid.

162. Sorenson, "U.S. Foreign Policy and the Middle East."

163. "When Push Comes to Shove," *Time* (August 6, 1982): 13.

164. Bernard Gwertzman, "Mood is 'Angry' as Begin Meets Panel of Senate," *New York Times*, June 23, 1982, p. 1; Haig, *Caveat*, p. 345.

165. "Lebanon Splits U.S. Jews," *Newsweek* (July 12, 1982): 32.

166. "Breaking a Long Silence," *Time* (September 20, 1982): 37.

167. "Newsweek Poll: Israel Loses Ground," *Newsweek* (October 4, 1982): 23.

168. Ibid.

169. Quoted in Sorenson, "U.S. Foreign Policy and the Middle East."

170. "When Push Comes to Shove," *Time* (August 16, 1982): 13.

171. Cheryl Rubenberg, "The Conduct of U.S. Foreign Policy in the Middle East in the 1983–84 Presidential Election Season," *American-Arab Affairs* (Summer 1984): 22–45.

172. Ibid.

173. For congressional concern over use of American forces in Lebanon see *New York Times* (July 7, 1982): 1.

174. "Send in the Marines," *Newsweek* (July 19, 1982): 15.

175. "Looking for a Way Out," *Newsweek* (July 19, 1982): 19.

11

COMMENTARY: THE LEADER VERSUS THE ACADEMIC ANALYST

Saadia Touval

INTRODUCTION

It is intriguing to speculate about the diplomacy of the 1982 Lebanon war, especially with the benefit of hindsight. The toll of human suffering exacted by the war makes one wonder whether more skillful negotiations could have achieved a better outcome for all concerned.

Refusal to believe that the bloody course of the Lebanon war was inevitable is reflected in the questions that the editors of this volume have addressed to the contributors, and in their general hypothesis. They ask: "How might the negotiations (or lack thereof) during the 1982 period in question have been handled differently by one or more of the leaders involved? What opportunities did they miss?"[1] Further, the editors hypothesize: "Opportunity for the containment, management, and reduction of international conflict through negotiation will be significantly enhanced by the availability of information on the role, history, style, beliefs, policies and situations that characterize or confront each pertinent national leader."[2]

These formulations reflect the concerns of the outside analyst, not of the leaders who are the subject of this book. Since this chapter will discuss the above questions from both perspectives, it is necessary to clarify the difference between the two.

The student of negotiation is concerned with opportunities to reduce or manage the conflict. On the other hand, discussion of the leaders' perspectives is premised on their given power-political goals, as described in the leadership chapters of this book. Clearly, the leading actors were not necessarily concerned with the reduction of conflict. They were out to win. They sought to avoid defeat, and

The author thanks the Center for International Affairs at Harvard University for its generous support.

they tried to deny victory to their adversaries. This is not to say that the parties were averse to conflict reduction or resolution. Indeed, some of them engaged in efforts to prevent the war or achieve a cease-fire. However, to the extent that they were interested in conflict reduction, they pursued this objective not as an end in itself, but as a means to achieve their competitive power-political goals while denying gains to their rivals.

This chapter is primarily concerned with the question of whether the leaders, given their goals and perspectives, could have used better information—had it been available—to avoid the war or to reduce their losses by agreeing earlier to a cease-fire. If, with the benefit of hindsight, the analysis shows that they could have made different decisions based on better information, then I shall try to answer the question of why they did not do so. I shall examine these questions with respect to the two major wars fought between June and August 1982: the Israel-PLO (Palestine Liberation Organization) war, and the Israel-Syrian war; and I shall discuss both the warring parties and the various diplomatic intervenors.

In the concluding section, I shall discuss some lessons for the outside analyst, not bound by the leaders' goals, who seeks ways to reduce or resolve international conflicts.

THE WARRING PARTIES

The Israel–PLO War

Begin's Perspective. Menachem Begin's main goal in launching the war was to destroy the territorial base that the PLO had established in Lebanon. Additional objectives that he probably hoped to attain were the destruction of Syrian anti-aircraft missiles, the weakening of Syrian influence in Lebanon, and the establishment of a pro-Israeli, Maronite-dominated government in that country.[3]

The objective of destroying the PLO base in Lebanon stemmed mainly from Begin's perception of the organization and its goals. The demonstrated ability of the PLO to harass northern Israel by rocket attacks was, of course, an immediate concern, because it made normal life in that part of the country impossible. However, this problem could have been dealt with both by a more limited military operation and by diplomacy, such as the cease-fire mediated by Philip Habib in 1981. What made these solutions appear insufficient to Begin was his belief that the PLO's real aim was the destruction of Israel. Begin was probably aware that since the mid–1970s PLO policy statements had been more ambiguous and indeed were interpreted by many experts to mean that it was prepared to accept, at least temporarily, a Palestinian state in the West Bank and Gaza (instead of all of Palestine), and to coexist with Israel.[4] That Begin dismissed this view, continuing to adhere to a more liberal interpretation of PLO statements, can be attributed to his belief system which, as described by Ofira Seliktar, is a product of his personality, background, and environment.[5]

Given Begin's perception of the PLO as bent on the destruction of Israel, a negotiated solution of the conflict was impossible. However, there remains the question of whether, with the benefit of hindsight, Begin might have acted differently. It is obvious that in launching the war, Begin miscalculated. First, Israeli casualties were probably much higher than Begin had anticipated. Second, the economic cost was ruinous. Third, the domestic political cost to the Likud and Begin personally was unexpectedly high, and contributed to Begin's decision to retire from politics. Finally, Begin must have been disillusioned by the unreliability of the Maronite allies, and by Israel's inability to establish a friendly and stable Lebanese government.

Begin's miscalculation must be attributed mainly to his personality. Although one of his characteristics was an interest in detail, in this episode another character trait prevailed: deference to military heroes. There was enough information and advice available for Begin to foresee the obstacles to the attainment of his objectives and the high cost that the war would exact from Israel. However, because of Begin's ideological commitment and interpersonal dynamics, he apparently felt more comfortable with the advice he received from Minister of Defense Ariel Sharon and General Rafael Eitan, the chief of staff, rather than the counsel of Mordechai Zippori (a member of Begin's own Herut party) and other experts from within the defense establishment.[6]

It is impossible to determine if Begin, had he established the course and consequences of the war more accurately, would have acted differently. It is certainly plausible that he would have launched a more limited military operation. In any event, a negotiated resolution of the conflict between Israel and the PLO would have remained outside the realm of possibility.

There is then the question of whether, once the war was launched, better information could have brought about an earlier cease-fire. Given Begin's view of the PLO, it is unlikely that he would have accepted less than Israel finally obtained: the evacuation of the PLO from Beirut. With the benefit of hindsight, it is probable that Begin would have pursued the military pressure on the PLO even more vigorously because, as it turned out, the repeated suspension of the Israeli military pressure (at the insistence of the United States) encouraged Arafat to try to hold out for better terms. Thus, the war was extended and the casualties on all sides were greater.

Arafat's Perspective. According to Rashid Khalidi, Yasser Arafat's goals have changed over the years. His initial objective was the "dismantling" of Israel, but in the mid–1970s he redefined his goals and has aimed since then at the creation of a Palestinian state in the West Bank and Gaza Strip. This implies that he accepted the idea of a Palestinian state alongside Israel, rather than in its place. Officially this is referred to as the "provisional program," the old objective of the dismantling of Israel now being called a "dream." Arafat also redefined the means by which he would pursue the PLO's goal. Reference to armed struggle as the "sole means of regaining Palestine" was replaced by a two-track—military and diplomatic—struggle. This required an independent PLO base in Lebanon, and it brought Arafat into conflict not only with Israel, but also with the Maronite presidents of Lebanon, who wished to preserve their authority over all parts of their country, and with President Hafez al-Assad of Syria, who wanted to extend his influence over the PLO.[7]

Arafat could have foreseen that his policy would lead to war. He could not have doubted that the PLO's military harassment of Israel was bound to lead to a major Israeli drive against PLO forces. He also knew that his efforts to create and maintain an independent base in Lebanon and his alliance with the Lebanese Moslems were bound to provoke the Maronites to fight him and to cooperate with Israel against their common enemy.

If all this was foreseeable, why did Arafat pursue policies that would lead to war? One explanation is that his self-image and ideological commitment prevented him from suspending the armed struggle against Israel. Another explanation is that he hoped that pressure by the great powers and Arab states would deter Israel from acting against his forces. If he mistakenly thought that sufficiently heavy pressure could be applied, then it was not for the lack of information about the attitudes and policies of Assad (who was eager for his downfall), the other Arab leaders (who did not wish to risk a clash with Israel), and the superpowers; but because he misunderstood the environment in which he operated. If this was the case, then the misunderstanding was induced in part by the wide international support that the PLO had received since the mid–1970s. It may also have been caused by his tendency to surround himself with associates who were reluctant to provide him with information and advice that they knew would be painful.[8]

A somewhat different explanation of Arafat's failure to avoid the war is that his policy was directed not only at Israel, but also at his constituents and political rivals. He may have felt that he had to persist in harassing Israel in order to assure his political survival, since any restraint on his part would have diminished his popularity and weakened his ability to continue to lead the PLO.

Once his forces were encircled in Beirut, Arafat could have reached a cease-fire earlier than he did, saving his forces and Beirut's civilian population many casualties. It seems that he did not do so for internal political reasons. As early as June 11, the proposal for a cease-fire provoked a bitter debate within the PLO as George Habash and Nayef Hawatmeh, the leaders of the Popular Front for the Liberation of Palestine and the Democratic Front respectively, as well as some leaders of Arafat's own Fateh, strongly opposed a cease-fire. In view of the internal opposition within the PLO to the acceptance of Israel's demand for PLO evacuation from Beirut, Arafat attempted to obtain political concessions in return for a withdrawal. Several weeks were thus spent in efforts to have a joint French-Egyptian proposal linking evacuation to the recognition of the Palestinian right to self-determination adopted by the Security Council. After these efforts failed, the acceptance of the Habib evacuation plan was delayed by another week or two while an Arab League delegation visited Washington in another effort to obtain political concessions for the PLO in return for withdrawal. Only after these efforts failed as well, and Israel resumed heavy bombardment, did Arafat finally agree to evacuate without receiving any concessions in return. According to Khalidi, Arafat did not expect these efforts to succeed. Nevertheless, to placate his opponents, he delayed the acceptance of the cease-fire terms.[9]

Thus, throughout the Lebanon war, both in his failure to forestall the Israeli attack and in his delaying the PLO's withdrawal, Arafat acted in spite of information that indicated his policy would be very costly to the PLO. Arafat decided as he did because he gave higher priority to internal Palestinian politics, upon which his political survival depended, than to military considerations which, whatever their impact, would not determine the leadership of the PLO.

The Syrian-Israeli War

Although Syria and Israel regarded each other as enemies, it seems that in 1982 neither country wanted a war. Therefore, the important questions are: Why did the war erupt, and could it have been prevented?

Assad's Perspective. Assad adheres to the ideology of the ruling Baath party, which aims at Arab unity and socialism. In turn, Zionism and colonialism are viewed as the Arabs' principal enemies. According to Margaret Hermann, Assad aspires to establish a "Greater Syria," consisting of Syria, Lebanon, Jordan, and Israel. He has a "devil image" of Israel, and believes that since Syria and Israel both want the same land, they "have a basic conflict of interest."[10] Of immediate concern for Assad are the recovery of the Golan Heights, which Syria lost to Israel in the 1967 war, and the situation in Lebanon.

Assad's goal in Lebanon was to preserve Syria's predominant influence there. This required preventing any of the rival Lebanese communities from prevailing, forestalling or undermining any alliance between the Maronites and Israel, and denying Israel a political or military presence in Lebanon. Both in the context of Syria's Lebanese policy and its wider Arab concerns, Syria also sought to establish its influence over the PLO and constrain that organization's independence and freedom of action. In pursuit of these goals, Assad intervened militarily in Lebanon, and also engaged in active diplomacy in order to try to shape the internal situation so that Syria could control the course of events.[11]

These aims notwithstanding, Assad, reputedly a pragmatist, did not want a war. The signals that Syria sent in the early part of 1982, when Israel's intentions were widely and openly discussed, as well as Syria's behavior during the first three days of the fighting between Israel and the PLO (before Israel took on the Syrian forces), indicate that Assad sought to avoid a direct confrontation. He probably thought that Syria was not yet sufficiently strong, and wanted to avoid defeat.[12]

Why, then, did Assad place antiaircraft missiles in Lebanon near the Syrian-Lebanese border, knowing full well that Israel would regard this act as a violation of the "Red Line" understanding (by which Israel tacitly agreed to Syrian intervention in Lebanon in return for certain limitations on the scope of this intervention) and would probably proceed to remove this threat? A likely explanation is that he felt compelled to do so by the circumstances in which he found himself. Both Assad and Begin were maneuvered into a confrontation by Bashir Gemayal's attack on Syrian forces at Zahle in the Spring of 1981, an attack generally believed to have been designed to draw Israel into a clash with Syria. When Syria used helicopters against the Phalangists, which Israel regarded as a violation of the Red Line agreement, Israel came to the Phalangists' rescue by shooting down a Syrian helicopter. In response to the involvement of the Israeli air force, Assad felt obliged to deploy the missiles.[13] He felt he had to do so for internal reasons. Failure to provide protection to his army would have probably provoked strong criticism from the military, and might have endangered his regime.

Begin and the Syrian War. As for Begin, it appears that his deference to the views of Sharon and Eitan led him to abandon his preference for avoiding a war with Syria. His statements that Israel wished to avoid a war with Syria were probably sincere, but after the war against the PLO started, he and the cabinet were advised by Sharon and Eitan that a successful operation would require action against the Syrian forces in Lebanon. Having failed to evaluate the initial plan, he again refrained from examining the assertions of the military and imposing his own authority. Unlike Assad, however, Begin's concurrence with Sharon and Eitan was not prompted by fear of losing vital support for his regime. Rather, he went along because of certain character traits that made him defer to a military opinion.[14]

Thus Syria and Israel engaged in the 1982 war despite the reluctance of both their national leaders. Of course, each leader and his followers perceived the other side as implacably hostile, and believed that their basic values and goals were incompatible. However, both also shared an immediate interest—the weakening of the PLO. The outbreak of the Syrian-Israeli war must therefore be attributed to two main causes. One was Begin's personality, which caused him to disregard the warnings of experts against entering into a commitment to the Maronites. He also ignored the obvious geostrategic fact that Lebanon is vital to Syria's security but not to Israel's. The second main cause of the war was Assad's internal vulnerability and his decision to give priority to protecting himself against possible criticism from the military even at the risk of a disastrous confrontation with Israel.

THE DIPLOMATIC INTERVENORS

The leaders of Jordan, Egypt, and Saudi Arabia, as well as the leaders of the two superpowers, intervened diplomatically in the conflict with the ostensible purpose of preventing, limiting, or stopping the fighting. Examination of their goals and actions will show that it was competition for power and influence, much more than any aversion to war, that motivated their peace-making interventions. There remains, however, the question of whether these leaders could have acted more effectively to prevent the war, or shorten it once fighting had started.

The Arab Leaders

Jordan's King Hussein was the least active of the three Arab leaders. Perceiving a potential threat to Jordan's independence from domination by Israel, Syria, or the PLO, his interest lay in the weakening of these three adversaries. Continued fighting between them thus had no direct negative effect on Jordanian interests. There was some risk that the turmoil would spread, however, and it is for this reason that Hussein welcomed a cease-fire, though he did not himself actively pursue it.[15]

Egypt's President Hosni Mubarak was much more active. As Kenneth Dana Greenwald observes, Egypt felt greatly embarassed by Israel's invasion of Lebanon because of the recent peace treaty it had concluded with Israel. To many Arabs, including many Egyptians, it appeared that Egypt's withdrawal from the common Arab front encouraged Israel to risk launching the war. Thus, the Israeli invasion of Lebanon confronted Mubarak with a double challenge: to ward off domestic criticism of the peace with Israel, and to overcome the increased criticism of Egypt's separate peace in the Arab world so as to achieve his main foreign policy goal—the readmission of Egypt into the Arab political community. The advantage that Mubarak derived from the weakening of his Syrian adversary, as well as the predicament of the PLO, did not suffice to compensate for the embarrassment caused by the Israeli action.[16]

However, this embarrassment also afforded an opportunity. The crisis enabled Mubarak to demonstrate both to his domestic opponents and the Arab world that Egypt was a loyal and valuable member of the Arab community. As Greenwald observes, he succeeded in this enterprise while at the same time fashioning a policy that maintained U.S. support for his regime, and preserved Egypt's peace with Israel. The policy consisted of denouncing Israel and reversing the normalization process called for by the peace treaty, emphazing Arab solidarity, and taking certain diplomatic initiatives to end the war on terms more favorable to the PLO than those offered by Israel.[17]

Besides calling on Israel to withdraw from Lebanon and recognize the PLO, and appealing to Bashir Gemayal to abandon his alliance with Israel and cooperate with the PLO, Mubarak also appealed to the United States to urge Israeli withdrawal and to support the Palestinian demand for self-determination. These gestures were supplemented with a diplomatic initiative, undertaken jointly with France and in consultation with the PLO. This initiative was designed to bring about a UN Security Council resolution calling for mutual PLO and Israeli withdrawal ''with dignity,'' Palestinian self-determination, and the preservation of Lebanon's independence.[18]

Although the Egyptian-French initiative failed, Mubarak succeeded in improving Egypt's image in the Arab world. Arafat, in his moment of need, responded by suppressing his criticism of Egypt's peace with Israel and facilitating Egypt's rehabilitation as a loyal member of the Arab community. Ironically, despite the failure of Mubarak's peace-making efforts, his larger political goals were successfully advanced.[19]

Mubarak was probably aware that he could realize some of his goals even while failing as a peace-maker. Surely he would have gained even more had he been able to rescue the PLO from its predicament and enabled it either to stay in Beirut or to withdraw on more favorable terms. In theory, Mubarak could have tried to mediate between Israel and the PLO. Had he tried and failed, however, he would have been worse off because the mediation attempt would have required him to moderate his verbal attacks on Israel. Thus, he would have drawn heavy criticism from the Arab world. He did not try to mediate, probably because he felt that Egypt had insufficient leverage with Israel and because the threat of freezing the normalization process might have failed to deflect Israel from its policy toward the PLO.

Trying to influence U.S. policy and promoting a Security Council resolution was a less risky course to pursue. Success would have been very advantageous for Mubarak. Had he been able to demonstrate that his influence in Washington made it possible for him to rescue the PLO, Mubarak would have greatly enhanced his standing in the Arab world and might have helped to justify among Arab elites his collaboration with the United States. However, failure did not hurt him.

The Saudi leaders also pursued very active diplomacy. Their actions during the crisis were in line with the traditional Saudi policy of seeking to reduce regional conflicts that could pose a threat to the security and stability of the Saudi state. Saudi leaders have believed that their interests are best served by keeping open lines of contact with radical leaders and by "mediating inter-Arab differences rather than taking sides."[20] Over the years, Saudi leaders have sought to mediate between the various factions in Lebanon, and between Syria and Egypt over Syria's intervention in Lebanon. They have also helped U.S. mediation efforts to reduce the Arab-Israel conflict, notably in 1973–74; following Assad's introduction of antiaircraft missiles into Lebanon in 1981; and in effecting a cease-fire between the PLO and Israel in July 1981.[21]

The Saudis saw the Lebanon war as threatening their interests because of its potential to heighten inter-Arab tensions, rekindle the Arab-Israeli dispute, and complicate their own relations with the United States. The immediate Saudi reaction was to urge the United States to pressure Israel into a rapid cease-fire. The Saudis engaged themselves in mediating between the United States, Syria, and the PLO to bring this about.[22]

David Pollock is probably right in his observation that, while the Saudis contributed to the speedy arrangement of the Syrian-Israel cease-fire, "the contribution cannot have been more than marginal, since both belligerents (obviously for their own reasons) wanted the cease-fire in any case."[23] However, their involvement in the effort to negotiate PLO withdrawal from Beirut was very significant, despite the mixed results. The Saudis made a notable contribution to the emergence of Arab consensus in support of PLO evacuation from Beirut, but their mediation between the PLO and the United States on this matter, while it ultimately helped produce an agreement, also had the unintended effect of delaying the evacuation, prolonging the crisis, and thus increasing the number of casualties. Why did Saudi involvement have these unintended consequences?

Some of the reasons for the delay have already been mentioned: Arafat's expectation that international pressure would force Israel to relax its hold, and his intraorganizational need to demonstrate his toughness. Pollock suggests that an additional factor may have been Saudi misjudgment about the degree of U.S. influence on Israeli policy, leading the Saudis to expect more from the United States than it could deliver, and thus prolonging the negotiations. The Saudis simultaneously pursued two contradictory goals, seeking both to diminish Israel's military pressure on the PLO and hasten the PLO's acceptance of the Israeli terms. However, the Saudis' success in moving the United States to pressure Israel into suspending its military operations also encouraged the PLO to hope that this delay might work to their advantage. The Saudis reportedly worked against the Egyptian-French initiative at the United Nations because they believed it would not succeed and would only delay the inevitable. Perhaps, in classic Saudi style, they were too circumspect about explaining their estimate of the situation to the PLO, thus contributing to the PLO's misapprehension of the situation they were in.[24]

Viewed from another perspective, the relative inefficiency of the Saudi mediation process was not detrimental to their policy objectives. True, they wanted the cease-fire and evacuation to take place swiftly, in order to minimize the risk of political complication, escalation, or other events that might have endangered their security. However, the purpose of Saudi mediation was also to demonstrate their attentiveness to PLO needs, and to demonstrate to the PLO the usefulness of the Saudi connection for communicating with the United States. A prolonged negotiation, even one which did not bring the PLO the terms it wished for, still served this purpose. Had the Saudis explained their assessment of the situation to the PLO more directly, and had they insisted that the PLO accept the terms of the evacuation without further delay, they would have performed their mediating mission more efficiently. However, this would have undermined one of the purposes of their intervention—fostering and nurturing good relations with the PLO. They would have even risked blame for the PLO's eviction from Beirut. Since the Saudi goal was not the conduct of an efficient mediation service but rather producing political consequences that would help protect the Saudi state from radicals, there was no real reason for them to pursue their peacemaking efforts differently than they actually did.

It is more difficult to respond to the question of why the Saudi leaders did not make a greater effort to prevent the war in the first place. They could have tried harder to persuade Arafat, as well as his critics, to moderate the PLO's military activities; they could have attempted to influence Assad to withdraw the missiles, and they could have pressed the United States to clarify its opposition to Israel's prepublicized attack. Possibly they did not do so because they were preoccupied with other concerns, especially their campaign to obtain congressional approval for the sale of the AWACS aircraft. King Khaled's personality and passivity, as described by Pollock, may have been another reason. In any event, the Saudi failure can be ascribed to a lack of information, to an overload of the decision-making system, and to the personality and character of the Saudi leaders.

The Superpower Leaders

In seeking to contain the Lebanon conflict and achieve a cease-fire, Ronald Reagan and Leonid Brezhnev faced a choice between a unilateral policy, pursued within the context of a competitive strategy, and a joint effort, pursued within the context of a cooperative strategy. Inevitably their choices were embedded in the context of their global policies.

Reagan and Brezhnev operated within a framework that crystallized after World War II, in which the two superpowers viewed themselves as engaged in a global competition for primacy. This resulted in their evaluation of most international issues, including those pertaining to the Middle East, in terms of their impact on overall Soviet-U.S. competition.

The superpowers realized that the situation in the Middle East imposed on them a mixture of conflicting and cooperative interests. On the one hand, they were engaged in a competition. On the other, they shared a common interest in avoiding direct military confrontation. Their competitive interests required supporting local allies in their conflict with adversaries. Common interests required an active policy of containing and managing regional conflicts and restraining their allies lest they drag their superpower patrons into a direct military confrontation. This mixture of competitive and common interests has often produced policy dilemmas, as witnessed by the policies of the superpowers in the Middle East since 1967.[25]

When the Lebanon war erupted in June 1982, tendencies toward cooperation were at a low ebb. The period was one of increased Soviet-U.S. tensions, following the successful expansion of Soviet influence in Angola, South Yemen, and Ethiopia; the Soviet invasion of Afghanistan; and the imposition of martial law in Poland. Soviet concern over potential U.S. gains as a result of the Egyptian-Israeli peace treaty led them to strengthen relations with their Middle Eastern allies, Syria and the PLO. Strengthening these relations required increased military and diplomatic support rather than exerting pressure on them to moderate. In the United States, too, the dominant mood was competitive. As noted by Betty Glad, President Reagan's approach to foreign affairs was shaped by his view of the Soviet Union as the embodiment of evil. Both he and Secretary of State Alexander Haig believed that Soviet policies engendered conflict in the

Middle East, and that Soviet encouragement of Syria and the PLO contributed significantly to the turmoil in Lebanon.[26]

A joint cooperative effort might have been effective had the principal objective of the superpowers been the reduction of the conflict, but the dominant mood in both Moscow and Washington was competitive, resulting in unilateral approaches to conflict management.

Brezhnev. Dina Rome Spechler's analysis of Brezhnev suggests that he could have done more to prevent the war. According to Spechler, the interventionists lost much of their influence in the two to three years before the war.[27] Therefore, we can attribute the continuing Soviet encouragement of Syria and the PLO before the war at least in part to Brezhnev's reluctance to undertake an abrupt policy shift toward these two allies, especially in light of increased tension in Soviet-U.S. relations.

Once fighting erupted, the Soviets sought to prevent escalation into a full-scale Syrian-Israeli war. They were probably concerned that Israel would prevail, thus endangering the friendly Baathist regime in Damascus and possibly generating a demand for Soviet military intervention.[28] Given these concerns, an effective response on the part of the Soviets was remarkably slow in developing. They could not have expected their appeal to the UN Security Council to produce an immediate and effective cease-fire. Their call on the Arab oil producers to threaten another oil embargo in order to induce the United States to pressure Israel to halt its advance also was unlikely to produce an immediate and effective cease-fire. To be sure, Brezhnev's message to Reagan warning him about the possibility of the spread of hostilities may have had some effect on U.S. attitudes, but the Soviet moves were mainly of a confrontational nature; they initiated no serious diplomatic maneuvers to bring about a negotiated cease-fire. The cease-fire that finally resulted can be attributed mainly to U.S. efforts, with the Soviets only in a supporting role, advising the Syrians that they expected them to accept a cease-fire if one were proffered.[29]

Soviet response to Israeli pressure on the PLO was somewhat more effective. The USSR issued strongly worded warnings to Israel and the United States, which may have had some effect on Israeli and U.S. policies. Moreover, by not promising assistance to the PLO, it probably influenced the internal debate within that organization toward the acceptance of evacuation. At the same time, the Soviets restrained Syria by making clear to them that their own commitment would not extend beyond the Syrian border. Thus, the Soviet Union contributed to the containment of the war and to the removal of the PLO from Beirut.[30]

Given Soviet goals in the Middle East, given the fact that they broke diplomatic relations with Israel and had little diplomatic influence there, and given the background of Soviet-U.S. relations at the time and the internal debates within the Soviet Union—given all these things, it is difficult to see what the Soviet Union could have done to prevent the war or bring about an earlier cease-fire.

Reagan. The most active and effective of the diplomatic intervenors was the United States. It was largely through U.S. efforts that war between Syria and

Israel was averted in the spring of 1981 and that the cease-fire between the PLO and Israel was arranged in July 1981. Nevertheless, there remains the question of whether more effective U.S. action could have helped avert or at least shorten the war in 1982. In addressing these questions we must again take U.S. goals into account.

These goals were essentially the same in 1982 as they had been under previous administrations: to maintain and even expand U.S. influence, to reduce Soviet influence, to support Israel's security, and to ensure the uninterrupted flow of oil.[31] The difference between Reagan's policy and those of previous administrations lay in the means used to achieve these ends. This shift was brought about by the combination of altered circumstances and the change in leadership.

In the 1970s, the United States competed with the Soviets mainly by demonstrating that Soviet arms would not win Israeli concessions for the Arabs and would not enable the radicals to undermine pro-Western regimes. Concessions from Israel would be obtainable only through cooperation with the United States. Also, one of the chief instruments for denying Soviet opportunity to expand its influence was U.S. mediation of local conflicts.

By the time Reagan assumed office, circumstances had changed. The Soviets resumed their expansionist policies and strengthened their relations with Syria and the PLO. Reagan and his advisers believed that the new Soviet drive must be countered with a show of resolve and demonstrations of U.S. strength. At the same time, the tactic of demonstrating to the Arabs that cooperation with the United States could lead to Israeli concessions became more problematic, since Israel was much more firm on the remaining issues of withdrawal from the West Bank, Gaza, and the Golan, than it was regarding Sinai. Thus the possibilities for expanding U.S. through peace-making—while simulataneously reducing Soviet influence—were much more limited than had been in earlier periods.

Given U.S. goals, could the United States have prevented the war? It seems that U.S. officials, aware of Israel's intention of striking against the PLO and the likelihood of an ensuing clash with Syria, tried to prevent the war. U.S. efforts began in the spring of 1981, when Syria placed its antiaircraft missiles in Lebanon. After first postponing an air strike against the missiles because of bad weather, Israel suspended action against the missiles when the United States sent Ambassador Philip Habib to the area in an attempt to defuse the crisis. While he failed to bring about the withdrawal of the missiles, subsequent U.S. efforts in this area were linked to a more far-reaching effort to reduce the tension between the PLO and Israel.[32]

These efforts all failed. They had virtually no chance of success because they were not pursued vigorously, and because they were not lent the weight and prestige of the secretary of state and the president (both of whom had played major roles in previous successful crisis management diplomacy in the Middle East). The absence of such backing can be attributed more to the president's personality than to his worldview or policy objectives. The preoccupation of top

U.S. officials with other pressing issues—first the Polish crisis and its aftermath, then the Falkland-Malvinas conflict—also contributed to the inability of the Reagan administration to pursue diplomatic efforts in the Middle East more vigorously.

Having failed to prevent the war, could the United States have speeded up the cease-fire? Probably it could have, had it been able to speak with a single voice. Alexander Haig was almost certainly right in blaming the contradictory signals emanating from Washington for the delays in the cease-fire. On several occasions, when agreement on PLO evacuation seemed near, reports of U.S. pressure on Israel to refrain from moving against PLO strongholds in Beirut appear to have contributed to delays as the PLO tried to improve on the terms that it was previously inclined to accept.[33] In other words, the delays were caused not by the absence of information, but by the way the PLO leadership interpreted debates within the U.S. administration.

While these perceptions can be attributed in some measure to the belief systems and wishful thinking of PLO leaders, clearly the incoherence of the Reagan administration's policy must share the blame. While some members of the administration, notably Secretary of State Haig, sympathized with Israel's problem and hoped that an Israeli victory would be a setback for the Soviet Union, others were more concerned about avoiding the impression that the United States sided with Israel. While there is nothing unusual about differences of opinion within the administration, the incoherent policies that it produced must be attributed to President Reagan's personality and "management style." It is not that Reagan failed to provide leadership. He did lead, by setting the general tone of confronting the Soviet Union and its allies. The problem is that the direction he provided was not specific enough to address the details of policy and tactics. In addition, Reagan was reluctant to make a clear choice when confronted with different policy proposals.

CONCLUSION: LESSONS FOR THE STUDENT OF NEGOTIATION

As the foregoing discussion indicates, the various leaders failed to act effectively to avoid the war or shorten it for several reasons. Lack of information was only one of them. Other reasons were the requirements of domestic politics and political survival, and perhaps also physical and mental infirmities, but the most important reason was the leaders' goals. Both the substance of these goals and their rigidity can be traced to the leaders' background and personality, as described in the leadership profile chapters of this book. Both help to explain why they failed to avert the war, and after it erupted, why they were incapable of shortening it.

With respect to both Begin and Arafat, a case can be made that had they been better informed they would have acted differently. While Begin would not have sought a negotiated solution to the conflict with the PLO, he might have launched a more limited operation, designed only to remove the PLO from Southern Lebanon and destroy the Syrian missiles. It is possible that he would have refrained from authorizing the more far-reaching objectives of dislodging the PLO from Beirut, of attempting to establish a friendly Lebanese government through a close alliance with the Maronites, and of engaging in a land war with the Syrian army. However, Begin's policies stemmed not from a lack of information, but rather from his rejection of the information and advice that was offered to him. This, in turn, was the product of a rigid belief system that rejected dissonant information, as well as personal and political preference for the advice of Ariel Sharon over that of other military experts.[34]

Arafat's inability to avert the war was also not simply a matter of poor information. He must have known that Israel would regard the PLO's presence in Lebanon as menacing, and would probably try at some point to destroy his base there. However, he was unable to refrain from provoking Israel; both before July 1981, and on a few occasions thereafter, Arafat authorized artillery and rocket attacks on northern Israel, while the PLO continued its other military activities against Israel as well as a build-up of its military capability in Southern Lebanon. In Arafat's case, too, the problem was largely that both his self-image and his perception of the PLO could not accommodate the suspension of military activity against Israel that would have been necessary in order to avert war. Subsequent delay in the acceptance of the Habib evacuation plan can be attributed in large measure to the information that was available: criticism of the war in Israel, widespread support for the Palestinian cause among many governments, and diplomatic efforts through a French-Egyptian initiative at the United Nations and through Arab League representatives in Washington to obtain political concessions for the PLO in return for the withdrawal. As in the case of Begin, Arafat's misinterpretation of this information also stemmed from his beliefs and ideology, as well as his choice of advisers.

Another factor that prevented leaders from acting to avoid the war or to shorten it was the priority they assigned to their domestic political requirements. Assad felt he could not remove the missiles, and Arafat felt he could not accept the terms of the evacuation. Obviously both leaders attached high priority to their political survival, and feared that compromise or flexibility in their struggle against Israel might undermine their standing with key groups among their constituents.

The intervention of third parties contributed to the attainment of the cease-fire and evacuation agreements. To some extent this contribution consisted of information; information about what various actors said they would do under certain contingencies, as well as information about the availability of certain options (cease-fire and the terms for the PLO evacuation from Beirut) that would have enabled the principal contenders to avoid the painful consequences of other choices. However, it is difficult to distinguish between the third parties' role of conveying information and their role of actually structuring the situation: telling the parties what they will do in certain contingencies, exerting pressure, and offering incentives and assurances. Third parties did not affect the principal actors' basic goals in the conflict, nor did they have a noticeable impact on the basic beliefs of Begin, Assad, and Arafat, from which their political goals derive.

The foregoing discussion highlights an important difference between the perspectives of the negotiating actor and the student of negotiation; it stems from their respective goals. For the student of negotiation, the goal is the management, reduction, or resolution of conflict through negotiation. The student of negotiation seeks to devise a process that will enable the actors to cooperate, and will enable all to gain or at least minimize their loss. For the actor or leader, including a leader who seeks to mediate an international conflict, goals are defined in competitive terms.[35] Goals relate to the leader's political survival and to his relative standing as compared to those of his rivals and adversaries. The search for an integrative solution that leaves everybody better off is alien to this frame of mind.

Students of negotiation are likely to view the Lebanon war as a Prisoner's Dilemma in which the actors chose non-cooperative strategies and thus lost more than they would have had they cooperated. According to this view, all the actors' concerns and interests are incorporated into a single game, played between the main antagonists. The leaders, on the other hand, see themselves as playing different games simultaneously, on different chessboards.[36] They play against their enemies, against their domestic competitors, and even against friends and allies at home and abroad. They recognize that the games are interdependent, that their fortunes in one are likely to affect their standing in others. Unlike students of negotiation who abstract values, and seek to maximize them on a single scale, the national leader tends to keep the games separate, and to rank them according to priorities.

For Begin, the top priorities were expulsion of the PLO from Lebanon and elimination of Syrian antiaircraft missiles. For Arafat and Assad, "the essential domino," whose collapse they feared most, was the domestic one.[37] However much they wished to deny Begin any achievements and to minimize their own losses in a military contest, they nevertheless assigned even higher priority to their own political survival.

Students of negotiation will tend to regard the war and its outcome as a costly and inefficient way of pursuing national interests. For the principal antagonists, the outcome is not as clear cut. Arafat and Assad survived politically. While defeat in a war against Israel would have undermined their domestic standing, both Arafat and Assad were nevertheless correct in estimating that it was less risky to fight and lose than to yield or compromise with Israel. Arafat's leadership was challenged after the war, but the challenge arose not because he lost the war but because of his alleged moderation.

Begin's breakdown and withdrawal from public life can be attributed in large measure to the war in Lebanon. He withdrew not because of political pressures, however, but because of mental anguish. The death of his wife contributed significantly to his collapse. Even so, he could still claim to have achieved two of his principal goals in the war: expulsion of the PLO from Beirut and Southern Lebanon, and elimination of the Syrian missiles.

All this points to the limited effects of ''better information.'' Opportunity for the containment, management, and reduction of the 1982 conflict in Lebanon through negotiation could have been enhanced by the availability of better information on the role, history, style, beliefs, policies, and situations that characterized or confronted each pertinent national leader—but only marginally so. As we saw, abundant information was available to the leaders. However, some of it was disregarded, some was misinterpreted, and some was used for advancing other goals—protecting their domestic political standing and maneuvering for advantage over external adversaries. The contribution of such information to the containment, management, and reduction of conflict would have been greater if the leaders had shared the goal of the student of negotiation, namely of devising a process enabling the leaders to cooperate in a manner that minimizes everybody's loss and maximizes their gains. However, as this book demonstrates, the leaders were motivated by ''realist'' goals, seeking to improve their standing relative to other actors.

The critical obstacle to conflict reduction through negotiation was not information or the inability to devise an integrative solution, but the goals of the principal actors—goals that emerged from deeply engrained belief systems. Conflict resolution would be far easier if belief systems were flexible and able to adjust to new information, and if leaders defined their goals in terms of absolute rather than relative gain (or loss). The difficulty exists because belief systems tend to be rigid rather than flexible; because they are the products of culture, socialization, and conditioning; and because they produce a disposition to view politics as a competitive contest.

Unfortunately, this is a somewhat pessimistic conclusion. The prospects for the reduction or resolution of the Arab-Israeli conflict would be obviously greater if the ability to devise more efficient negotiation processes and invent more attractive integrative solutions depended mainly on better information. However, if the reduction or resolution of the conflict depends on a change of belief systems, then the task ahead is infinitely more difficult.

NOTES

Unless otherwise noted, references are to this volume.

1. Prospectus for the contributors.

2. Barbara Kellerman, p. 4.

3. Ofira Seliktar, pp. 42–44.

4. For such an interpretation, see Rashid Khalidi, pp. 51–52. For detailed accounts of the complexity and ambiguity of the PLO's policy, see Helena Cobban, *The Palestinian Liberation Organization* (Cambridge: Cambridge University Press, 1984); Alain Gresh, *The PLO: The Struggle Within* (London: Zed Books, 1985); and Shaul Mishal, *The PLO Under Arafat* (New Haven: Yale University Press, 1986).

5. On Begin's conceptual rigidity, see Seliktar, p. 38.

6. Seliktar, p. 45; Ze'ev Schiff and Ehud Ya'ari, *Israel's Lebanon War* (New York: Simon and Schuster, 1984), pp. 24–61.

7. Khalidi, pp. 51–52, 54, 59.

8. Khalidi, p. 56.

9. Khalidi, pp. 62–65.

10. Margaret G. Hermann, pp. 71, 73–74.

11. Hermann, pp. 73–74, 79, 82, 83, 85–86; David M. Rosen, pp. 21–22.

12. Hermann, pp. 74–75, 90.

13. Schiff and Ya'ari, *Israel's Lebanon War*, pp. 31–35. On the "Red Line" understanding, see Yair Evron, *War and Intervention in Lebanon: The Israeli-Syrian Deterrence Dialogue* (Baltimore: The Johns Hopkins University Press, 1987).

14. Seliktar, p. 45. For a reconstruction of Israeli decisions, see Schiff and Ya'ari, *Israel's Lebanon War*, pp. 151–56.

15. Aaron S. Klieman, pp. 129, 130–31.

16. Kenneth Dana Greenwald, pp. 96, 104–6.

17. Greenwald, pp. 107–9.

18. Greenwald, pp. 108–9.

19. Greenwald, pp. 110, 111.

20. David Pollock, pp. 145, 146.

21. Pollock, pp. 151, 156, 158.

22. Pollock, pp. 158–59.

23. Pollock, p. 156.

24. Pollock, pp. 156–60.

25. Dina Rome Spechler, pp. 168–73. See also George W. Breslauer, "Soviet Policy in the Middle East, 1967–1972: Unalterable Antagonism or Collaborative Competition?" and Alexander George, "The Arab-Israeli War of October 1973: Origins and Impact," both in *Managing U.S.-Soviet Rivalry*, ed. Alexander L. George (Boulder, Colorado: Westview Press, 1983), pp. 65–105 and 139–54, respectively.

26. Betty Glad, pp. 203–4, 210.

27. Spechler, pp. 187–88.

28. Spechler, pp. 174.

29. Spechler, p. 175.

30. Spechler, pp. 176–78; Khalidi, p. 50.

31. Glad, p. 200.

32. Alexander M. Haig, Jr., *Caveat* (New York: Macmillan, 1984), pp. 330–35.

33. Haig, *Caveat*, pp. 344–52.

34. For a stimulating theoretical discussion on how beliefs affect information processing and decision making by leaders engaged in international bargaining, see Glenn H. Snyder and Paul Diesing, *Conflict Among Nations* (Princeton: Princeton University Press, 1977), pp. 282–418.

35. For a discussion of international mediation within a "realist" power-politics framework, see I. W. Zartman and Saadia Touval, "International Mediation and Power Politics," *Journal of Social Issues* 41, no. 2 (1985): 27–45. The framework is applied to mediation in the Arab-Israeli conflict in Saadia Touval, *The Peace Brokers* (Princeton: Princeton University Press, 1982).

36. For a stimulating discussion of simultaneous games, see Robert D. Putnam, "Di-

plomacy and Domestic Politics: The Logic of Two-Level Games,'' *International Organization* (forthcoming).

37. The phrase is borrowed from Leslie H. Gelb, ''The Essential Domino: American Politics and Vietnam,'' *Foreign Affairs* 50 (April 1972): 459–75.

12

COMMENTARY: ON NEGOTIATING THE NON-NEGOTIABLE

Morton Deutsch

This chapter is divided into three main sections. The first uses the discussion of a case of marital conflict to articulate a framework for thinking about negotiating the non-negotiable. For various parties involved in the Arab-Israeli conflict, many of the issues seem non-negotiable, and it may be helpful to consider the general conditions that are relevant to determining whether negotiations are apt to take place and to succeed. The second considers the Lebanese war of 1982 and why constructive negotiations were not a likely outcome. The final section addresses the question of what could be done, under present circumstances, to promote constructive negotiations.

A FRAMEWORK FOR THINKING ABOUT NEGOTIATING THE NON-NEGOTIABLE

As a psychologist, I have had the opportunity to do therapeutic work with couples who have been involved in bitter conflicts over issues that they considered non-negotiable. I will briefly describe a young couple who were involved in what I have elsewhere characterized as a "malignant process" of dealing with their conflicts.[1]

The malignancy of their process of dealing with their conflicts was reflected in the tendency for them to escalate a dispute about almost any specific issue (for example, a household chore or their child's bedtime) into a power struggle in which each spouse felt that his or her self-esteem or core identity was at stake. The malignant process resulted in (as well as resulted from) justified mutual suspicion; correctly perceived mutual hostility; a win–lose orientation to conflicts; a tendency for each to act toward the other in a way that would lead the other to respond in a way that would, in turn, confirm the former's worst suspicion of the latter; an inability to understand and empathize with the other's needs and vulnerabilities; and a reluctance—based on stubborn pride, nursed grudges, and fear of humiliation—to initiate or respond to a positive generous action to break out of the escalating vicious cycle in which they were entrapped.

Many couples involved in such malignant conflicts do not seek help: they continue to abuse one another, sometimes violently, or they break up. The couple that I worked with sought help for several reasons. On the one hand, their conflicts were becoming physically violent: this frightened them and it also ran counter to their strongly held intellectual values regarding violence. On the other hand, there were strong constraints making it difficult for them to separate. They felt they would be considerably worse off economically, their child would suffer, and they had mutually congenial intellectual, esthetic, sexual, and recreational interests which would be difficult for them to engage in together if separated. As is often the case in such matters, it was the woman—being less ashamed to admit the need for help—who took the initative to seek the assistance of a skilled third party.

Developing a Readiness to Negotiate

Before I turn to a discussion of the negotiation of a non-negotiable issue, let me briefly discuss the steps involved in getting the couple to the point where they were ready to negotiate. There were two major interrelated steps, each of which involved many substeps. The first entailed helping each spouse to recognize that the present situation of a bitter, stalemated conflict no longer served his or her real interests. The second step involved aiding the couple to become aware of the possibility that each of them could be better off than they currently were if they recognized their conflict as a joint problem, which required creative, joint efforts in order to improve their individual situations. The two steps do not follow one another in neat order: Progress in either step facilitates progress in the other.

Irrational Deterrents to Negotiation

There are many reasons why otherwise intelligent and sane individuals may persist in behaviors that perpetuate a destructive conflict harmful to their rational interests. Some of the common reasons are:

1. It enables one to blame one's own inadequacies, difficulties, and problems on the other so that one can avoid confronting the necessity of changing oneself. Thus, in the couple I treated, the wife perceived herself to be a victim, and felt that her failure to achieve her professional goals was due to her husband's unfair treatment of her as exemplified by his unwillingness to share responsibilities for the household and child care. Blaming her husband provided her with a means of avoiding her own apprehensions about whether she personally had the abilities and courage to fulfill her aspirations. Similarly, the husband who provoked continuous criticism from his wife for his domineering, imperial behavior employed her criticisms to justify his emotional withdrawal, thus enabling him to avoid dealing with his anxieties about personal

intimacy and emotional closeness. Even though the wife's accusations concerning her husband's behavior were largely correct, as were the husband's toward her, each had an investment in maintaining the other's noxious behavior because of the defensive self-justifications such behavior provided.

2. It enables one to maintain and enjoy skills, attitudes, roles, resources, and investments that one has developed and built up during the course of one's history. The wife's role as "victim" and the husband's role as "unappreciated emperor" had long histories. Each had well-honed skills and attitudes in relation to their respective roles that made their roles very familiar and natural to enact in times of stress. Less familiar roles, in which one's skills and attitudes are not well developed, are often avoided because of the fear of attempting the unknown. Analogous to similar social institutions, these personality "institutions" also seek out opportunities for exercise and self-justification, and in so doing help to maintain and perpetuate themselves.

3. It enables one to have a sense of excitement, purpose, coherence, and unity which is otherwise lacking in one's life. Some people feel aimless, dissatisfied, at odds with themselves, bored, unfocused, and unenergetic. Conflict, especially if it has dangerous undertones, can serve to counteract these feelings: it can give a heightened sense of purpose as well as unity, and can also be energizing as one mobilizes oneself for struggle against the other. For depressed people who lack self-esteem, conflict can be an addictive stimulant which is sought out to mask an underlying depression.

4. It enables one to obtain support and approval from interested third parties. Friends and relatives on each side may buttress the opposing positions of the conflicting parties with moral, material, and ideological support. For the conflicting parties to change their positions and behaviors may entail the dangers of loss of esteem, rejection, and even attack from others who are vitally significant to them.

How does a therapist help the conflicting parties overcome such deterrents to recognizing that their bitter, stalemated conflict no longer serves their real interests? The general answer, which is quite often difficult to implement in practice, is to help each of the conflicting parties change in such a way that the conflict no longer is maintained by conditions in the parties that are extrinsic to the conflict. In essence, this entails helping each of the conflicting parties to achieve the self-esteem and self-image that would make them no longer need the destructive conflict process as a defense against their sense of personal inadequacy, their fear of taking on new and unfamiliar roles, their feeling of purposelessness and boredom, and their fears of rejection and attack if they act independently of others. Fortunately the strength of the irrational factors binding the conflicting parties to a destructive conflict process is often considerably weaker than the motivation arising from the real havoc and distress resulting from the conflict. Emphasis on this reality, if combined with a sense of hope that the situation can be changed for the better, provides a good basis for negotiation.

Conditions That Foster the Recognition of the Conflict as a Joint Problem Requiring Joint Efforts

What are the conditions that are likely to help conflicting parties become aware of the possibility that each of them could be better off than they currently are if they recognize that their conflict is a joint problem that requires creative, joint efforts in order to improve the individual situations? A number of such conditions are listed below:

1. Crucial to this awareness is the recognition that one cannot impose a solution which may be acceptable or satisfactory to oneself upon the other. In other words, there is recognition that a satisfactory solution for oneself requires the other's agreement and this is unlikely unless the other is also satisfied with the solution. Such recognition implies an awareness that a mutually acceptable agreement will require at least a minimal degree of cooperation.

2. To believe that the other is ready to engage in a joint problem-solving effort, one must believe that the other has also recognized that he or she cannot impose a solution— that is, the other has also recognized that a solution has to be mutually acceptable.

3. The conflicting parties must have some hope that a mutually acceptable agreement can be found. This hope may rest upon their own perception of the outlines of a possible fair settlement or it may be based on their confidence in the expertise of third parties, or even on a generalized optimism.

4. The conflicting parties must have confidence that if a mutually acceptable agreement is concluded, both will abide by it or that violations will be detected before the losses to the self and the gains to the other become intolerable. If the other is viewed as unstable, lacking self-control, or untrustworthy, it will be difficult to have confidence in the viability of an agreement unless one has confidence in third parties who are willing and able to guarantee the integrity of the agreement.

The foregoing conditions for establishing a basis for initiating the joint work necessary in serious negotiation are much easier to develop when the conflicting parties are part of a strong community in which there are well-developed norms, procedures, professionals, and institutions which encourage and facilitate problem-solving negotiations. This is more apt to be the case in interpersonal conflicts than in conflicts between ethnic groups or nations that do not perceive themselves as members of a common community. When the encouragements to negotiation do not exist as a result of belonging to a common community, the availability of helpful, skilled, prestigious, and powerful third parties who will use their influence to foster problem-solving negotiations between the conflicting parties becomes especially important.

Negotiating the Non-Negotiable

Issues that seem vitally important to a person, such as one's identity, security, self-esteem, or reputation, often are experienced as non-negotiable. Thus, consider the husband and wife who viewed themselves in a conflict over a non-negotiable issue. The wife who worked (and wanted to do so) wanted the husband to share equally in the household and child-care responsibilities; she considered equality between the genders to be one of her core personal values. The husband wanted a traditional marriage with a traditional division of responsibilities, in which he would have primary responsibility for income-producing work outside the home while his wife would have primary responsibility for the work related to the household and child care. The husband considered household work and child care as inconsistent with his deeply rooted image of adult masculinity. The conflict seemed non-negotiable to the couple—for the wife it would be a betrayal of her feminist values to accept her husband's terms; for the husband, it would be a violation of his sense of adult masculinity to become deeply involved in housework and child care.

However, this non-negotiable conflict became negotiable when, with the help of the therapist, the husband and wife were able to listen to and really understand each other's feelings and the ways in which their respective life experiences had led them to the views they each held. Understanding the other's positions fully and the feelings and experiences which were behind them made them each feel less hurt and humiliated by the other's position and more ready to seek solutions that would accommodate the interests of both. They realized that with their joint incomes they could afford to pay for household and child-care help, which would enable the wife to be considerably less burdened by these responsibilities without increasing the husband's chores in these areas: of course, doing so lessened the amount of money they had available for other purposes.

This solution was not a perfect one for either party. The wife and husband, each would have preferred that the other share their own view of what a marriage should be like. However, their deeper understanding of the other's position made them feel less humiliated and threatened by it and less defensive toward the other. It also enabled them to negotiate a mutually acceptable agreement that lessened the tensions between them despite their continuing differences in basic perspectives.

The general conclusions that I draw from this and other experiences with a ''non-negotiable'' issue is that most such issues are negotiable even though the underlying basic differences between the conflicting parties may not be reconcilable. The issues become negotiable when the conflicting parties learn to listen, understand, and empathize with the other party's position, interests, and feelings, providing they are also able to communicate to the other their understanding and empathy. Even though understanding and empathy do not imply agreement with the other's views, they indicate an openness and responsiveness which reduces hostility and defensiveness and which also allows the other to be more open and responsive. Such understanding and empathy help the conflicting parties to reduce their feelings that their self-esteem, security, or identity will be threatened and endangered by recognizing that the other's feelings and interests, as well as one's own, deserve consideration in dealing with the issues in conflict.

"Non-negotiable" issues also become negotiable when the conflicting parties can be shown that their vital interests will be protected or enhanced by negotiation. As R. Fisher and W. Ury have stressed, it is helpful for negotiators to learn the difference between "positions" and "interests."[2] The positions of the conflicting parties may be irreconcilable, but their interests may be concordant. Helping parties in conflict to be fully in touch with their long-term interests may enable them to see beyond their non-negotiable positions to their congruent interests. An atmosphere of mutual understanding and empathy fosters the conditions that permit conflicting parties to get beyond their initial rigid, unnegotiable positions to their underlying interests.

THE LEBANESE WAR OF 1982 AND THE POSSIBILITIES OF CONSTRUCTIVE CONFLICT RESOLUTION IN THE ARAB-ISRAELI CONFLICTS

In the previous section of the chapter, I have utilized a case of marital conflict to illustrate some thoughts related to the conditions affecting the readiness to negotiate and some notions relevant to negotiating the non-negotiable. Although the Arab-Israeli conflicts are vastly more complex, multilateral, and difficult than the case I have used for illustrative purposes, I believe the ideas contained in the discussion of the simpler situation are applicable to the more complex one. From my perspective as a "conflict resolver," the two key process issues in resolving the Arab-Israeli conflicts are: (1) creating the conditions in which the various parties to the conflicts are ready to engage in creative, joint problem-solving efforts as part of a negotiation to resolve their disputes, and (2) helping the disputants to negotiate the substantive concerns that they consider to be non-negotiable.

I have no special knowledge or expertise relating to the Middle East or to the nations and their leaders which are discussed in the various chapters of this book, so the discussion that follows is speculative, and draws heavily on material presented by the authors of the earlier chapters. From this material, it seems evident to me that before the onset of the 1982 war in Lebanon, none of the national leaders or the peoples directly involved felt that conditions were ready for joint problem-solving negotiations on the Israeli-Jordanian-Palestinian-Syrian complex of problems. The lack of readiness to negotiate reflected internal political and psychological deterrents to negotiation, a distrust of the other sides with whom one would be involved in negotiations, and beliefs that one might improve one's position in future negotiations through unilateral actions in Lebanon. The weakness of Lebanon—resulting from its bitter internal strife—had left it prey to the alien purposes of the PLO (Palestine Liberation Organization), Syria, and Israel.

The disastrous 1982 invasion of Lebanon by Israel, the chapter by Ofira Seliktar indicates, had as its maximalist objectives the strengthening of the Maronite government in Lebanon, the weakening of Syrian influence, and the denial of a territorial base to the Palestinian resistance led by the PLO. Presumably, the attainment of these objectives would have enormously strengthened Israel's strategic position in future negotiations on the Israeli-Jordanian-Palestinian-Syrian complex of problems. Hopefully, from Menachem Begin's perspective, it would have insured a non-aggressive Lebanon, decapitated the Yasser Arafat-PLO leadership of the movement for an independent Palestinian nation, encouraged King Hussein to assume control over a binational Jordanian-Palestinian state, and isolated rejectionist Hafez al-Assad. These maximalist objectives were consistent with the ''New Zionism'' and the ''idealistic'' approach that Seliktar indicates characterized the approach of Begin and his colleagues to foreign policy thinking. As Betty Glad's chapter suggests, these objectives were also not inconsistent with the views of a key part of the Ronald Reagan administration. However, in retrospect, it is obvious that these objectives were inconsistent with reality.

It is also apparent that important elements of the Begin government and the Reagan administration were, from the beginning, strongly opposed to the maximalist objectives that Ariel Sharon, the Israeli Defense Minister, ardently advocated before and during the invasion and pursued relentlessly throughout. Why did the realism of the opponents of the maximal objectives, who were probably sufficiently powerful politically to do so, not block the pursuit of these objectives? The chapters by Seliktar and Glad make it clear how intragovernmental organization and decision-making procedures that were inadequate and unclear, combined with weak leadership by Begin and Reagan, enabled those who favored the maximalist objectives to pursue these objectives.

As Seliktar indicates, there is little reason to doubt that Begin's flawed leadership during the Lebanon invasion reflected both enduring and temporary features of his personality. Many of his enduring personality characteristics predisposed him toward the ''New Zionism,'' an activist foreign policy, contempt for the Arabs, and a win–lose orientation toward conflict which would have made him sympathetic to the maximalist objectives advocated by Sharon. On the other hand, other enduring personality characteristics such as his intelligence, realism, and strong impulse control would have raised doubts about their feasibility and might well have led him to restrain Sharon. However, his psychological depression at the time of the invasion of Lebanon seems to have been sufficiently intense for him to have withdrawn into himself so much that he no longer maintained adequate knowledge or effective control of the actions of the officials in his government. The unreflective impulse of his ''New Zionist'' government was ''maximalist''; it would have necessitated Begin's strong impulse control, intelligence, and realism being effectively employed to restrain this impulse.

Similarly, Glad's discussion of Reagan's personality indicates how his enduring personality characteristics and style of leadership resulted in actions and inactions that gave the impression that, at the minimum, the U.S. government was acquiescing in the Israeli actions and not restraining their invasion of Lebanon. As Glad points out, Reagan was ideologically inclined to see the Soviets as the source of all disturbances in the Mideast, and the PLO and the Syrians as their surrogates; hence, he was not unhappy with the initial Israeli military victories. However, among his key advisers there was considerable conflict over the Israeli invasion. Secretary of State Alexander Haig apparently thought that the Israeli invasion offered grand new strategic opportunities for the United States to achieve its anti-Soviet and antiterrorist goals, as well as to facilitate a Middle East peace based on new power alignments. Others saw the maximalist objectives of the Israelis as unrealistic, as alienating of the Arab world, and as being destructive of U.S. interests. However, as Glad points out, Reagan's dislike of detail and his difficulty in confronting conflict among his political intimates led to policy and turf battles which he had no taste for controlling. This led to a considerable incoherence of policy in which the U.S. government was perceived by the Arabs and Israelis alike as implicitly endorsing Israeli actions because it did not act consistently and strongly to restrain the Israelis: something which was within its power.

The results of the Israeli invasion of Lebanon were a disaster for almost all the parties directly or indirectly involved. For Israel, there were the large number of casualties, an enormous economic drain, an increased political rancor in Israel, the intensified hostility of almost all groups in Lebanon, the further alienation of Egypt and Hosni Mubarak, and the tarnishing of its reputation and loss of much public sympathy in the United States and among other supporters in the West. For Lebanon, there were the enormous destruction and casualties as well as the further demonstration of the impotence of its central government. For the United States, its credibility in the Arab world was decreased and its relations with Israel were significantly strained. The PLO was very much weakened by its severe military losses, the loss of its military base in Lebanon, the dispersion of its fighting force to a number of different countries, the internal conflicts among its component units, and the Syrian attempt to gain control over the PLO. The Arab nations lost credibility because of their lack of effective intervention and support for the PLO. Similarly, the Soviet Union also lost credibility because of its lack of effective action in support of the PLO and because of the poor performance of the military equipment it had provided to Syria. The Palestinians in Lebanon suffered severe casualties and abuse, and lost much of the protection provided by the PLO, while the Palestinians in the West Bank and Gaza felt that their prospects of achieving an autonomous national state had been lessened because of the decreased strength of the PLO.

The only gainers seemed to be the leaders of Syria, Egypt, and Jordan: Assad, Mubarak, and Hussein. Assad's power was enhanced by Lebanon's increased dependence upon Syria, by his increased control over important components of the PLO, and by the increased quality and quantity of military supplies provided by the Soviets in an attempt to rebuild its military image in the Mideast. Mubarak increased his acceptance in the Arab world, decreased some of the internal dissent in Egypt, and helped Egypt to resume some of its former leadership role by his denunciation of Israel and by his support of the PLO. Hussein's importance as a potential negotiator and spokesman for the Palestinians increased as the PLO's strength was weakened.

From this situation of disaster for so many of the leading actors in the Mideast, with its vivid human tragedies, it was theoretically possible that the follies of their orientations and behaviors in relation to the Arab-Israeli conflict would become so salient that they would undergo a fundamental change and reexamine their underlying assumption about how they should act in relation to their conflicts. Unfortunately, instead of the occurrence of a "conversion" phenomenon with the creation of new opportunities for constructive negotiation, a more typical "dissonance reduction" phenomenon seems to have occurred, in which the key leaders defensively dug into their previously held positions and tried to justify them even more.

For a conversion phenomenon to have occurred as a consequence of the mutually disastrous and tragic experiences associated with the invasion of Lebanon, several conditions that were not existent would have had to be present. First of all, it would have required cooperation between the United States and the Soviet Union to establish a framework for constructive negotiation and for each country to place the necessary persuasive pressure on its friends in the Mideast to engage in such negotiation. As I indicated in the first section, when the encouragements to negotiation do not exist as a result of the conflicting parties belonging to a strong common community, powerful third parties will have to use their influence if problem-solving negotiations are to occur between embittered adversaries. However, the intense antagonism between the two superpowers during the first term of the Reagan administration would have made such cooperation impossible. Beyond that, the initial incoherence of the Reagan administration's policy in the Middle East and the recent Soviet invasion of Afghanistan would have made effective cooperation impossible.

Secondly, it would have required Begin's government to adopt a new understanding, a more generous attitude, and less defensiveness toward the legitimate aspirations of the Palestinians and their leader, Yasser Arafat. This would have taken strong, daring, imaginative leadership by Begin, but this was not possible given his psychological condition during this period. Moreover, Begin's personal attitudes toward the PLO, his religious convictions, and his new Zionist ideology would not have predisposed him to such an initiative. Third, the weakened PLO, with Arafat's leadership under strong challenge from Syrian-supported factions, was not in a position to take a more open, accepting stance toward Israel's existence as a nation without the risk of being further torn apart by internal dissension. Fourth, Assad of Syria would have had to negotiate from a position that would not be as strong as he expected it would be in the future. He believed that the relative balance of power between Syria and Israel was shifting away from Israel and that, similarly, his relative power among the Arab nations was also increasing; furthermore, Assad believed that he would be in a better position to achieve his objectives of a Greater Syria if he waited. Finally, given the populist outrage throughout the Arab world at the Israeli invasion, it would have taken unusually courageous and far-sighted leadership for the "moderate" Arab leaders such as Hussein and King Fahd to propose or even support direct negotiations with Israel about many issues that are considered non-negotiable in the Arab world. However, as the chapters on Hussein and Fahd indicate, neither of these leaders has the personal boldness or sense of invulnerability that would enable them to follow in Anwar Sadat's footsteps.

For these and many other reasons, I suggest that the summer of 1982 and the following period were not times in which there was any readiness in any of the major actors (except possibly Egypt) to negotiate constructively about the issues involved in the Arab-Israeli conflicts, and it would have been impossible to create the conditions under which the conflicting parties would have actually attempted to negotiate the non-negotiable. Have things changed sufficiently since 1982 to permit more positive possibilities? I shall address this question in the remaining section of this chapter.

WHAT CAN BE DONE NOW?

The situation has changed in many respects from the circumstances around the time of the 1982 war in Lebanon. I select two changes for emphasis because I believe that they bear strongly on the likelihood that constructive negotiations can be initiated and conducted. First of all, I believe that a number of factors have contributed to the increased recognition by the leading actors in the multiple Arab-Israeli conflicts that they cannot impose a solution which is acceptable or satisfactory only to them upon their adversary.[3] Secondly, changes within the Soviet Union and the United States, and in their relations with one another, provide new possibilities for developing a constructive context for negotiations.

The increased recognition that one cannot impose a solution upon one's adversary is reflected in the Fez Declaration of the Arab League Summit Conference on September 9, 1982, which implicitly endorsed the UN Security Council's resolutions that affirm "the sovereignty, territorial integrity, and political independence of every State in the area and their right to live in peace within secure and recognized boundaries free from threats or acts of force" (UN Resolution 242). As the chapter on King Fahd indicates, the Fez Declaration represented a Saudi initiative; the watered-down quality of the declaration reflected the indecisive, weak quality of Fahd's leadership. It is also reflected in the Jordanian-Palestinian agreement between King Hussein and Chairman Arafat of February 11, 1985. Further, as Margaret Hermann points out in her chapter on Assad, Assad tacitly recognized Israel as early as May 1984, when he signed a disengagement treaty with Israel, and he has clearly adhered to the terms of the treaty since then. Additionally, Kenneth Dana Greenwald's chapter on Mubarak indicates that Mubarak has maintained Sadat's policy of peace with Israel despite the severe strains placed on the relations between Israel and Egypt caused by the Israeli invasion of Lebanon. Finally, the multiple and severe costs of Israel's military adventurism in Lebanon have made it politically unfeasible for Israel's leaders to employ Israel's military power other than for well-defined defensive purposes; strong opposition within Israel as well as from Israel's supporters in the United States would be expected.

This change of viewpoint comes from several sources. The repeated Arab-Israeli wars, none of which have enabled the parties involved to achieve their maximalist objectives or even to achieve gains that would not be subject to future challenge, have led the conflicting parties to reduce their aspirations and to have more realistic objectives vis-à-vis one another. Although not pleased by it, most of the Arab leaders have come to accept the idea that Israel will continue to exist as a nation: they are only in the beginning stages of coming to terms with the practical implications of this idea.[4] Similarly, most Israelis have come to accept the view that the Palestinian aspirations for autonomy and nationhood cannot be ignored and denied forever: they too are only in the early stages of coming to terms with the practical implications of this recognition.

Since 1982, the economic situation of all of the nations in the Middle East has worsened considerably. For Israel, this has been largely due to the costly consequences of the Lebanon invasion and occupation, while the oil glut has severely affected the Arab nations. The worsened situation has two important possible consequences. It may make leaders such as Assad, Mubarak, and Yitzhak Shamir even more prudent and less likely to engage in costly military adventurism, and it creates more unrest among the nations' populations. To the extent that the leaders seek to address the domestic economic problems underlying the unrest, they will be less apt to think they have the resources necessary to impose their will on their external adversary. On the other hand, if they feel unable to cope successfully with their domestic economic problems, they may attempt to channel the internal unrest toward the external "devil" as a means of redirecting it away from themselves. Thus, the current economic adversity in the Middle East represents an opportunity if the leaders in these nations can be helped to cope with their domestic economic problems, and a danger if they are not so helped.

Another factor contributing to the growing acceptance of the fact that neither the Arabs nor the Israelis can impose their solutions on the other is the recognition that the superpowers will not allow this to happen. The United States will not allow Israel to be dismembered nor, as Dina Rome Spechler's chapter indicates, will the Soviet Union allow Syria to be overwhelmed by Israel. These realities serve to limit and constrain the military options available to the opposing sides.

Despite the growing awareness that the Arab-Israeli conflicts cannot be resolved by military force and the increasing recognition that the continuing military jousting is debilitating to the economies and to the national well-being of the various nations involved, it is evident that there is considerable resistance to participating in serious negotiations within each of the parties to the conflicts— Israel, Syria, Jordan, Egypt, Lebanon, the Palestinians (and the PLO). I suspect that the political and psychological deterrents to serious negotiations within each nation, and within the bloc of Arab nations, are sufficiently strong at the present time to make it unlikely that a creative initiative which could overcome the obstacles to negotiations would come from any of the leaders in the Middle East.[5] Such an initiative and pressure apparently must come from outside, as I suggested in part I, if the barriers to problem-solving negotiations are to be overcome.

A joint initiative by the Soviet Union and the United States, supported by the other Western nations, is most apt to create the conditions for fruitful negotiations. A framework for such a joint initiative has been outlined by Nadav Safran in *The Wall Street Journal*. He proposes that the following two steps be undertaken in rapid succession:

First, U.S. and the Soviet Union would simultaneously announce parallel moves: The U.S.S.R. would restore diplomatic relations with Israel and indicate ... that it would allow large-scale Jewish emigration. . . . Simultaneously, the U.S. would announce its acceptance of the latest Palestine Liberation Organization "peace proposals," which envisaged acceptance of Resolution 242 the moment the U.S. acknowledged the right of the Palestinians to self-determination ... and open a diplomatic dialogue with the PLO. . . .

In an immediate second step, Washington and Moscow would cause the United Nations secretary-general to issue an invitation to all the parties to the Arab-Israeli conflict to rendezvous at Geneva at a designated prompt date for a peace conference. . . . Once the conditions long insisted upon by the parties have been essentially met by the first step, nonattendance would carry its own penalty of isolation and superpower ire. No agreement on procedure would be negotiated in advance; procedure would be the first and only substantive item on the agenda. The only other requisite, adherence to 242, would have been secured by the first step. A peace conference can thus be envisaged to take place within a month of the first step.

The Soviet move would compensate Israel for the American move and diminish its resistance to it. It is useful to recall that Shimon Peres has already agreed to an international conference and has intimated that a PLO that accepted Resolution 242 would "no longer be PLO." ... The U.S. move would compensate the Arab side for the Soviet move and clear the way for PLO participation alongside Jordan in the peace process. The U.S. move would ... [also] have an excellent chance of gaining endorsement by the great majority of Arab countries, and thus generate enormous pressure on Syria, too, to adhere to it or at least to subscribe to the second step.[6]

Is such a joint initiative by the United States and the Soviet Union feasible? On the one hand, the political leaders of both superpowers undoubtedly recognize that one of the greatest perils that they face is the risk of getting involved in a direct military confrontation with one another through the escalation of conflict between nations in the Middle East to whom each of the superpowers has strong commitments (for example, Israel and Syria). This shared recognition of danger can provide the basis for a joint initiative of the kind described above. On the other hand, the superpowers have been rivals for influence in the Middle East, and much of their rivalry has been expressed through the supplying of weapons to the conflicting parties, feeding a dangerous arms race in this area. In pursuing the U.S.-Soviet rivalry, the Soviet Union has curried favor with the Arabs by breaking diplomatic relations with Israel and by ostracizing that country, while the United States has attempted to limit Soviet influence by excluding it from involvement in Arab-Israeli peace negotiations. My hunch is that each of the superpowers is beginning to recognize how self-defeating their strategies have been. By ostracizing Israel, the Soviet Union has cut itself off from playing any effective role in promoting peace in the Middle East; and by "freezing" the Soviet Union out of any constructive role in peace negotiations, the United States has inadvertently encouraged them to play the role of "spoiler" to any Arab-Israeli peace negotiations.

A joint initiative such as the one proposed by Nadav Safran seems desirable because it would not only lessen the likelihood that a war between the superpowers might arise out of the conflicts in the Middle East, but also because it would enhance the interests of both superpowers.[7] Such an initiative would implicitly recognize the legitimacy of the Soviet interest in the Middle East, something very much sought after by that country, and it would at the same time place the USSR under strong pressure to give up the "spoiler" role, something clearly in the interests of the United States. A joint initiative of this sort would have to be preceded by quiet diplomacy between the two superpowers to detail the terms of the joint initiative. Undoubtedly, it would require considerable preparatory work, as well as diplomatic skill, for such an initiative to be developed successfully.

Could such an initiative set the stage for constructive negotiations about the Arab-Israeli conflicts? It could if the proposal were phrased in such a way that it successfully addressed the basic anxieties of the Israelis and the Arabs. There is considerable reason to believe that the basic anxieties of the Jewish people in Israel center around the images of the Nazi Holocaust and their history of centuries of rejection and traumatic persecution.[8] Given these anxieties, it is not surprising that security and acceptance have become overriding objectives of Israel, nor is it surprising that being "strong" and "tough" have come to be viewed as national virtues. There is also reason to believe that the basic anxieties of the Arab people center around being humiliated and treated as inferiors, and about being dominated and exploited by intruders. It is easy to understand the Arab preoccupation with self-determination, the occupation of its territories, and its proud refusal to be treated as a defeated party.

The joint initiative proposed by Safran could start the process of addressing the anxieties of both the Israelis and the Arabs. The restoration of relations with the USSR, the resumption of more regular Jewish emigration from the Soviet Union, and the PLO acceptance of the UN Resolution 242 would reduce some of Israel's apprehensions. The United States acknowledgement of the right of self-determination for the Palestinians and its opening of a diplomatic dialogue with the PLO, following its acceptance of Resolution 242, would meet some of the Arab concerns.

Once this process has been started, informal dialogues between influential representatives (rather than the top leaders) of the Israelis and the various Arab groups would be encouraged in order to prepare them and their constituents for constructive, realistic negotiations about the issues in conflict. At this informal stage of prenegotiations, it would be very useful to have impartial discussion facilitators available to help the conflicting parties deal successfully with the difficulties that are apt to rise in such meetings.[9] Such informal meetings would not only precede the conference proposed by Safran but would continue during and subsequent to such a conference. They would provide an opportunity to test out proposals, for each of the conflicting parties to communicate their views and feelings fully to the other, for possible agreements to be developed, and to work out some of the underlying emotional concerns that might stand in the way of agreement.

If the Arabs and Israelis were enabled to listen to and really understand each other's feelings and how their respective experiences have led to the views each side holds, they would become more able to seek solutions that would accommodate the interests of both. This would be true even for issues that are considered to be non-negotiable. As I have stated earlier, non-negotiable issues become negotiable (even though underlying basic differences may not be reconciliable) when the conflicting parties learn to listen, understand, and empathize with each other's position, interests, and feelings, providing they are also able to communicate their understanding and empathy.

A joint initiative such as proposed by Safran seems desirable, but is it likely? As I started to write this paper early in November 1986 (before the Iran arms scandal became known), I believed it was a possible but not probable initiative. I thought that there would be more resistance to it within the Reagan than the Gorbachev administration. The ultra-conservatives believe that it is neither desirable nor feasible to try to engage in constructive cooperation with the Soviet Union on the problems in the Mideast, and they would be able to immobilize colleagues who were less ideologically committed to an adversarial relation with the Soviet Union. The complexity of the issues involved would make it highly unlikely that Reagan (as depicted by Glad) would take a strong leadership position implementing the proposed Safran initiative, even were it brought to his attention. Such an initiative might have had more chance of acceptance by Israel when Shimon Peres was Prime Minister than under Shamir, who was opposed to the Camp David accord.

After the arms control debacle in Iceland and the scandal over the arms deal with Iran, the Reagan administration's foreign policy, at the time of this writing (January 1987), seems to be in disarray. The administration's arms deal with Iran has impaired its credibility with the leaders of the Arab nations and made its policy seem duplicitous or incoherent. Under such conditions, it is rather unlikely that the Reagan administration will take any major new initiatives in the Middle East. Nevertheless, it is not altogether impossible that under the pressure to have some dramatic accomplishment in foreign policy to compensate for its recent debacles, the Reagan administration might be open to new ideas.

To sum up this discussion, to establish the conditions necessary for "negotiating the non-negotiable'' between parties involved in an embittered conflict usually requires help from influential, prestigious third-parties. The required assistance is of two kinds: (1) help in getting the parties to communicate effectively (2) help in getting them involved in a constructive problem-solving process. Such help is initially directed toward addressing the basic anxieties of the conflicting parties. By so doing, one enables them to listen, understand, and empathize with one another sufficiently that they are ready to seek solutions that would also accommodate the interests of the opposing side. The second function required is assisting the parties to identify or create potential agreements that would be responsive to the interests of each of the parties involved. The two kinds of help are mutually supportive. To the extent that the parties can see the possibility of a mutually satisfying agreement, they will be more able to listen to one another in an understanding, empathic manner, and, of course, the converse is true too.

The current situation in the Middle East is, I believe, potentially conducive to serious negotiations about the Arab-Israeli conflicts. Despite this potential, there is sufficient resistance within each of the parties involved in the conflicts to require the intervention of third parties before serious negotiations are likely to begin. If the United States and the Soviet Union could, as influential third parties, mount a joint initiative such as the one described above, it would have a good chance of starting a constructive process of negotiation. Unfortunately, at the time of this writing, it does not seem likely that such an initiative will be undertaken in the near future. It would take strong, highly skilled, active leadership by the United States to foster the complex, creative negotiations required in the Middle East. Such a leadership capability in foreign affairs has not been evident so far in the Reagan administration.

NOTES

1. See Morton Deutsch, *Distributive Justice: A Social-Psychological Perspective* (New Haven: Yale University Press, 1985), ch. 17.

2. See R. Fisher and W. Ury, *Getting to YES: Negotiating Agreement without Giving In* (Boston: Houghton Mifflin, 1981).

3. I exempt from this generalization only the leaders of Libya and Iran, who have messianic visions that may have little to do with current or foreseeable realities.

4. See H. H. Saunders, *The Other Walls: The Politics of the Arab-Israeli Peace Process* (Washington, D.C.: American Enterprise Institute for Public Policy Research, 1985), for further discussion of current Arab views.

5. My hunch is that Assad of Syria is in the best (but very unlikely) position of any of the leaders in the Mideast to break through the impasse between Israel and the Arab nations with a bold Sadat-like initiative. However, the initiative would have to be preceded by secret negotiations with Israel that would lead to a return of the Golan Heights and the acceptance of self-determination for the Palestinians, combined with well-defined security guarantees for Israel. Assad is in the best position because, as Margaret Hermann points out in this volume, he is a very effective leader, he has strong control over Syria

and he can play the "spoiler" role in relation to possible agreements by Hussein and Arafat with Israel that omit his interests.

6. *The Wall Street Journal*, June 19, 1986, p. 39.

7. Since the United States is more influential in the Middle East than the Soviet Union, such an initiative is more apt to get underway if it originates with the United States, but its success would require the endorsement and active participation of both superpowers. Secretary of State George Schultz, with the guidance of Henry Kissinger, might have been able to get such an initiative underway if he had been a more assertive foreign policy leader.

8. See Saunders, *The Other Walls*, and N. Kaplowitz, "Psychopolitical Dimensions of the Middle East Conflict," *Journal of Conflict Resolution* 20 (1976): 279–318.

9. See J. W. Burton, *Conflict and Communication* (New York: Macmillan, 1969), and H. C. Kelman and S. P. Cohen, "The Problem-Solving Workshop: A Social-Psychological Contribution to the Resolution of International Conflicts," *Journal of Peace Research* 13 (1976): 79–90.

13

CONCLUSION

Jeffrey Z. Rubin

This book was an intellectual (*Gedanken*) experiment designed to evaluate the critical role of leadership in international conflict management. We invited contributions from outstanding authorities on leadership; you have read their essays and can judge for yourself the high quality of their scholarship and insight. Based on these leadership profiles, two authorities on conflict and negotiation—one a political scientist, the other a social psychologist—were asked to evaluate the hypothesis that leadership information and analysis increase the opportunities for conflict management through negotiation.

Ultimately, of course, you the reader will have to decide whether our hypothesis has been supported by the available data. Are we better able to devise creative solutions to bring about joint problem solving based on leadership analysis? In the following pages, I will indicate why I have concluded that the answer is a qualified *yes*.

By the way of leading to my conclusion, I propose to do the following: first, place myself in the role of conflict analyst, adding my own commentary on the nine leadership profiles to those already provided by Saadia Touval and Morton Deutsch; second, as is only fitting for the author with the last word, to comment briefly on the two commentaries on negotiation; and finally, to return to the set of assumptions that gave rise to this enterprise in the first place, thereby responding to my coeditor's introductory chapter and commenting on the future role of leadership studies in international politics.

A PROVISIONAL INDEX FOR EVALUATING LEADERSHIP

To be considered a prime suspect for having committed a crime, two elements are required: motivation and opportunity. It must be ascertainable that one wished to commit the crime in question; second, it must be clear that one was in a position to do so. Both elements are necessary. I believe this is also the case in leadership. A leader may have ability, determination, and unbridled energy at his or her command, but unless this "motivation" is coupled with the opportunity conferred by what I will loosely refer to as a state of "situational ripeness," leadership will probably prove ineffective. The famous finger of that proverbial Dutch boy was able to save Holland from a terrible flood only because there happened to be a dike whose opening could be sealed with his finger. Had the entire dam wall collapsed, there is not much that that Dutch finger or determination could have done to save the day; and had the dam not sprung a leak, no finger at all would have been required.

Readers familiar with the writings of Thomas Carlyle and Sidney Hook[1] will recognize in the above story the "eventful hero": the individual who exercises leadership or heroism because he or she happens to be around when there is an available part requiring such a person. The eventful hero is distinguished from the "event-making" one: the individual who strides over the great wash of history, creating (rather than responding to) history through dramatic, transcendent acts. Most of us would like to believe in the possible emergence of such event-making heroes; how much simpler and more appealing to hold out hope for the few good men and women who will lead us from darkness into light than to rely on turgid explanations of "situational ripeness" or favorable circumstance.

I am inclined to believe, however, that despite the appeal of the legendary event-making hero—the leader with transcendent authority and charisma—such individuals rarely appear. Even President Anwar Sadat, cited by several of this book's authors as such an individual, was only able to stride into the Israeli parliament because of his strong, ongoing relationship with the United States and the previous contacts established between Egyptians and Israelis. His was a heroic act, to be sure, but one that was probably made possible by the larger context of political relationships in which it occurred.

Given these remarks, it will come as no surprise that, in reading through the leadership profiles, I have found it useful to pay attention both to the characterization of individual leaders (their style, personality, and so forth) and the context in which such leadership was exercised. I have also found it useful, as a way of attempting to move through some of the complexity and rich detail of the profiles, to summarize my observations in a crude index (see Table 13.1). Thus I have coded each of the nine chapters in terms of situational ripeness (Opportunity) and leadership strength, will, or potential (Motivation). Leadership "effectiveness" might then be thought of as the product of Opportunity $\times$ Motivation: what it is that the leader is actually able to do, given both talent and opportunity. In this crude index of leadership effectiveness, I have further found it useful to apply a modest three-point scale; scores can thus range from 1 (Low Motivation $\times$ Low Opportunity) to 9 (High Motivation $\times$ High Opportunity).

I do not advance this scheme as anything profound, only a convenient way

Table 13.1

A Subjective Index of Leadership Effectiveness in the 1982 Lebanese Crisis

	STATE	SITUATIONAL RIPENESS (Opportunity)	LEADERSHIP STRENGTH (Motivation)	PRODUCT
**	Lebanon (Sarkis/Gemayal)	Low (1)	Low (1)	1
	Israel (Begin)	Low (1)	High (3)--early Low (1)--late	3 1
	P.L.O. (Arafat)	Low (1)	High (3)	3
	Syria (Assad)	High (3)	High (3)	9
	Egypt (Mubarak)	Low (1)	Moderate (2)	2
	Jordan (Hussein)	Moderate (2)	High (3)	6
**	Saudi Arabia (Khaled/Fahd)	High (3)	Low (1)	3
	Soviet Union (Brezhnev)	Moderate (2)	Moderate (2)	4
	United States (Reagan)	High (3)	Low (1)	3

** Sarkis = Low Leadership Strength (1); B. Gemayal = Moderate (2); A. Gemayal = Low (1).

Khaled = Moderate (2); Fahd = Low (1).

of tracking the role of these two critical components.[2] Perhaps the relationship between Motivation and Opportunity is not multiplicative but additive, perhaps more than two elements are required, or perhaps they are related in a more complex way. The index is merely a heuristic that I have found helpful; I encourage you to devise one that makes sense for you.

Following is a brief chapter-by-chapter account of how these table entries were derived. I have tried to honor the leadership profiles, taking as truth the author's characterization of the situation and the leader.

Lebanon's Elias Sarkis and Bashir and Amin Gemayal

The overriding theme of David Rosen's chapter is that Lebanese society is structured in such a way that virtually no individual could have emerged as an effective leader. The Rosen chapter is, in fact, an excellent illustration of how, lacking opportunity (in this case, a society that makes possible the emergence of strong leadership), leadership ability does not count for very much.

Rosen says of Lebanese society:

> To be . . . successful . . . an individual must be a leader within both the national leadership system and the ethnic-communal leadership system. However, the conflicting demands and value orientations of these different systems continually undermine the legitimacy of presidential power and make it impossible to fill both roles properly. (p. 15)

The unwritten agreement known as the National Pact, including its amended form of 1976, simply does not allow reformist presidents to make changes or to exercise effective leadership. As a result, writes Rosen, "the Lebanese presidency has been an extraordinarily weak institution—so weak, in fact, that it has a long history of appealing to outside sources of power" (p. 20).

So much for situational ripeness. As far as the three Lebanese leaders are concerned, Elias Sarkis is characterized as weak, as having come into power because Syria backed him, and as unable to exercise much by way of leadership talent. "Recruited as a compromise candidate," writes Rosen, "he lacked legitimacy at the ethnic-communal level" (p. 25). More impressive as a leader is Bashir Gemayal, who was assassinated on September 14, 1982, shortly before he was to be inaugurated as president. Bashir Gemayal was able to convert the Christian militia into a trained and disciplined fighting force, and in this sense he demonstrated leadership ability. His death cut short any opportunity he might have had to grow as a leader. Finally, Amin Gemayal, who assumed the presidency after the assassination of his brother, enters the Lebanese story near the end of the four-month period under study, and hence does not play a major role. (Events subsequent to 1982, however, would appear to do nothing to indicate signs of strong leadership ability.)

To summarize what I read as Rosen's analysis, then, Lebanese leadership ability appears to have been generally moderate to low, while the situation made it all but impossible for leadership—no matter how motivated or talented—to prove effective.

Israel's Menachem Begin

Ofira Seliktar presents Menachem Begin as a remarkably effective leader, a cunning politician, someone able to maneuver skillfully amid the Scylla and Charybdis of Israeli domestic politics, and a man able to grasp "the historical forking" (p. 42) of Anwar Sadat's Egyptian overture.[3]

Nonetheless, it is this same Begin who is characterized by Seliktar as increasingly incompetent during the months of the Lebanese crisis. Both the decision to invade Lebanon and the events that followed managed to get away from Begin's control as his leadership deficiencies began to show. "Begin's faltering," writes Seliktar, "became even more evident during the decision-making process that culminated in the Sabra and Shatila massacre'' (p. 46). The same dogmatic worldview that made it possible for Begin to follow a straight and narrow pathway as a capable negotiator at some points also seems to have contributed to his growing rigidity (and therefore incompetence) during the months of the 1982 Lebanese crisis.

As far as "situational ripeness" is concerned, one need not look very deeply into the Israeli political system to understand that leadership emerges only through the labyrinthine workings of an elaborate coalition system. The several religious parties, for example, although they hold only a minority of seats in the Israeli parliament, are often able to bring the larger, ostensibly more powerful parties to their knees by forming winning coalitions with one side or another. Hardly any Israeli leader, no matter how talented or skillful, can elude the drag of domestic politics. As a maneuverer, Begin was about as skillful as they come, yet even he was pulled down by the system and the skillful maneuvering of Ariel Sharon.

Seliktar's "take" on the mix of what I have dubbed Opportunity and Motivation is perhaps best captured in her characterization of Begin at Camp David in 1978: "As Prime Minister, Begin was able to negotiate the historical treaty with Egypt through a rare combination of political opportunities and psychological compatabilities with Sadat and Carter. . . . Neither of these conditions was present in the Lebanon case" (p. 46). Clearly, talent and ability as a leader are not enough.

The PLO's Yasser Arafat

In this interesting portrait of a man about whom remarkably little seems to be known in Western circles, Rashid Khalidi depicts Yasser Arafat as a skillful and powerful leader who, through the strength of his personality, style, and craft, brought the PLO into existence, and then gave it shape. Khalidi portrays Arafat as a "master of survival" (p. 67), a complex, interesting and driven man who maintained his primacy in the Palestinian movement partly because "he works far harder than anyone else in the leadership, or indeed at any level of the movement" (p. 56).

It was under Arafat's leadership, Khalidi tells us, that Fateh grew into an important underground Palestinian nationalist movement. Indeed, although Khalidi stops short of saying so, one has the impression that the Palestinian movement would have taken a very different shape had it not been for the leadership of Arafat during its formative period.[4]

Despite Khalidi's often glowing portrait of Arafat, the author is careful to also point out the degree to which Arafat's leadership has been limited by a variety of situational circumstances. The fortunes of the PLO have been largely shaped by forces outside the control of a leader, even one as forceful as Arafat. The leadership succession in Saudi Arabia, Leonid Brezhnev's decline and death, the shifting fortunes of Egypt, changes in Israeli leadership, elections in the

United States, the Iran-Iraq conflict—each has been an important source of variation in PLO fortunes.

In sum, Arafat emerges as the determined and resourceful captain of a small ship that is bobbing about on turbulent seas. His leadership ability is high, we are told, even as situational ripeness and opportunity are perennially low.

Syria's Hafez al-Assad

In Margaret Hermann's careful analysis of Syria's Hafez al-Assad there emerges at last a strong leader who also appears to be in a situation that enables leadership to make a difference. One has the impression of a man swiveling in his chair and looking around constantly—not only to stave off threats but also to seize the latest opportunity to advance his interests and those of Syria. Assad is presented as a master maneuverer, akin to Arafat, but unlike the PLO leader, Assad is able to be not only reactive but also proactive in the leadership he provides. Based on this chapter, the conventional wisdom is confirmed: namely, that Syria must be included in any proposal for peaceful relations in the Middle East; Assad's leadership combines with relations between Syria and several key players to place Syria in a position of pivotal importance.

Assad's leadership style, Hermann tells us, is characterized by "behind-the-scenes maneuvering, broad consultation, control of information and attention to detail, use of incentives, pragmatism, and patience" (p. 74). He is a leader with a fine sense of political timing, a "workaholic" nature, a capacity for flexible decision making, and great skill in the strategy of creating interchangeable alliances: "he takes care to hit the adversary without knocking him out and help the friend without really bailing him out, for the roles could be reversed one day."[5] Like Arafat and Jordan's King Hussein, Assad seems to be very good at playing what Hermann refers to as "the traditional Middle Eastern game of opposing and cooperating at the same time."[6]

In Syria one can also see the immense complexity of the Middle East political situation. Thus, Hermann tells us that Syria and Iran are allies, partly because they share enmity with Iraq. However, Syria is also allied with Saudi Arabia, a source of its financial support, even though Saudi Arabia has been an opponent (now outspokenly so) of the Khomeini regime in Iran. Similarly, Syria has long wanted control over Lebanon and its politics—both back in 1982 and in the present day—but has also wished to avoid destabilizing the country, which would thereby justify Israeli military involvement.

In summary, we have in Assad a powerful and capable leader in a situation that (through relations with Saudi Arabia, Iran, Lebanon, and—perhaps most importantly—the Soviet Union) makes Syria a pivotal player in Middle East politics. At the very least, Assad's Syria has positioned itself in such a way that it can effectively play the role of "spoiler." Kissinger's observation, cited by Hermann, seems to the point: "no war is possible without Egypt, and no peace is possible without Syria."[7]

Egypt's Hosni Mubarak

Kenneth Dana Greenwald's essay on Hosni Mubarak makes clear that the Egyptian president's ability to lead effectively during the 1982 Lebanese crisis was seriously constrained by two situational factors: the long shadow cast by his illustrious predecessor, Anwar Sadat, and of even greater importance, the 1978 Camp David accords.

Mubarak emerges as a more capable and resourceful leader than might appear likely at first glance. Sadat handpicked Mubarak to be his successor, and this legacy helped to put Mubarak in a most difficult situation after Sadat's assassination: "it was soon evident that Mubarak would try to strike a balance: he would largely continue Sadat's policies but at the same time set himself apart from his predecessor" (p. 100). Where Sadat had been hard on his domestic opposition, Mubarak would be much softer; where Sadat had chosen a high-profile leadership style, Mubarak would choose to avoid the public eye; if Sadat referred to the Egyptian people as "my sons and daughters," Mubarak would address them as "my brothers and sisters." However, even as Mubarak was distinguishing himself from his predecessor in these ways, he nevertheless chose to adhere to the Camp David accords. As Greenwald points out, it was in Egypt's self-interest to do so for several reasons: "Egyptian soldiers were spared casualties; revenues flowed both from Sinai oil and the Egyptian-operated canal; and Egypt gained a magnanimous benefactor—the United States" (p. 103–4). In addition, Egypt no longer had to fear war with Israel.

Greenwald's portrait thus depicts a leader on a tight-rope—a fate that seems preordained for many Middle East leaders. Still, Mubarak emerges as a moderately capable leader, able to make necessary political adjustments, coping with domestic pressures and foreign policy constraints with skill, and ultimately able to move Egypt back a bit closer to the Arab fold.

The Egyptian story would not be complete without pondering what might have happened had Anwar Sadat lived to see the 1982 crisis in Lebanon. Surely he would not have kept his silence, as Mubarak did for at least part of the four-month period. He would have threatened, cajoled, and probably made one or more high-profile media appearances. Still, given the constraints imposed by Camp David, I believe that Sadat would have been no better able to change the course of events in 1982 than his successor, Mubarak. Situational constraints would probably have ruled the day.

Jordan's King Hussein

Aaron Klieman describes Jordan's King Hussein as a capable leader who has deliberately chosen to adopt a cautious leadership style. Another skillful manipulator and maneuverer in the rocky political terrain of the Middle East, Hussein managed to do virtually nothing during the 1982 crisis, yet still succeeded in strengthening his political hand; the Syrians and Israelis were bloodied and weakened, the PLO was temporarily driven out of the region, and the Soviet presence was (again temporarily) diminished as well. As Klieman puts it: Jordan "actually managed to convert a potentially threatening situation into political gain . . . without any major commitment, concession, or fundamental change in Jordanian bedrock policies" (p. 119).

While the above outcomes might appear to depict Hussein more as the beneficiary of good fortune than as a skillful statesman, Klieman makes clear that he regards the Jordanian king as a strong leader, with a clear sense of direction, sound instincts, and excellent timing: "He has known when to alternate coercion with persuasion; when to advance, to retreat tactically or, even better, to move sideways . . . in order to avoid confrontation or hard choices" (p. 121).

Hussein is a survivor (and a cautious ruler for more than three decades), someone skillful at straddling the middle, and an important player in the Middle East. He is also likely to be exceedingly careful about sticking his neck out too far, unless other necks are extended as well. Thus, when President Reagan proposed his initiative on September 1, 1982—a proposal to generate momentum toward peace in the Middle East that would have cast Jordan as a central player—Hussein refused to become entangled. The time was not yet right, and Hussein was not about to make a commitment that could expose and isolate him.

Klieman has portrayed in Hussein a strong and capable leader, with demonstrated ability to survive, maneuver, and adjust. The opportunities afforded by Jordan's situation in the Middle East appear to be neither outstanding nor dismal, but somewhere in between. Thus, as the neighbour of Israel, Syria, and Saudi Arabia, Jordan occupies a key geopolitical position in the region. Moreover, there are many Palestinians living in Jordan; I was surprised to discover that the figure is now up to 60 percent of the total population—a demographic consideration that may motivate Hussein to explore arrangements for Palestinian autonomy. It is therefore clear that Jordan will have to be included in any agreement that bears on a Palestinian state and, more generally, any agreement that encompasses Israeli-Palestinian relations. This very centrality in the future of Middle East politics affords Hussein special opportunities; his moves can make a difference. Offsetting this is Jordan's small size, landlocked position, and, therefore, its ultimate dependence on the goodwill and support of its Arab neighbors. Hussein can make moves that will matter, but he also has to be careful about exposing his flanks.

Saudi Arabia's King Khaled and King Fahd

If the story of leadership in the Middle East is starting to sound a bit repetitious—as concerns a moderately or highly capable leader trying to maneuver amid often difficult political circumstances—David Pollock's account of the Saudi leadership is quite different. Here is a nation with abundant situational ripeness and opportunity; the Saudis have managed to sustain reasonable relations with some of the most important players in the Middle East drama: the PLO,

Jordan, Syria, and the United States. Saudi Arabia is one of the few nations (perhaps the only one) to have such extensive crosscutting ties with nations who are adversaries of one another: for example, the PLO versus Syria, Syria versus the United States, and the PLO versus the United States. Saudi Arabia is clearly positioned, by virtue of these relationships as well as by its financial wealth, to make a difference.

However, what also emerges from Pollock's analysis of the two Saudi kings, Khaled and Fahd, is a portrait of weak leadership. As the author puts it:

a large part of the blame for the country's straitened circumstances and reduced leadership role lately must be laid at the door of a decline in the quality, and therefore also the unity, of Saudi leadership since the death of King Feisal. . . . Neither of his two successors to the throne exhibited the same imposing personal presence (p. 144).

Khaled, who assumed the throne after the assassination of Feisal in 1975, seems to have been a more capable leader than expected; his successor, Fahd, who came to power shortly after the Lebanese crisis began (in June of 1982) seems to have disappointed the high expectations that greeted his accession to the throne. Pollock gives us an interesting glimpse of the possible role of situation in the emergence of leadership when he describes the rather different support given to the two kings by the Saudi royal family: Khaled was given room to maneuver by the royal family because he was thought to be passive—while Fahd, who was expected to be more politically energetic, was constrained by ''countervailing royal family pressures'' (p. 152). This observation is reminiscent of Edwin Hollander's point that leadership cannot exist in a vacuum; it requires membership willingness, support, and acquiescence.[8]

In summary, Saudi Arabia emerges as a Switzerland of the Middle East: wealthy, concerned about protecting its wealth, and determined to prevent Arab instability in the region. Petrodollars seem to drive much of its foreign policy conservatism, which is characterized by a tendency to straddle the middle and to avoid taking sides if at all possible. The Saudi leadership, as represented by Khaled and Fahd, has been disappointing, especially so in light of the opportunities for making a difference that Saudi Arabia appears to have had by virtue of its relations with a set of odd political bedfellows.

The Soviet Union's Leonid Brezhnev

Under the leadership of Leonid Brezhnev, the Soviet Union was more effective than is commonly assumed during the 1982 Lebanon crisis. Dina Rome Spechler points out that Moscow was extremely active during the invasion, both diplomatically and militarily. ''Indeed,'' writes the author, ''the USSR succeeded either in inducing all the important parties in the conflict to heed its wishes or, when they refused to do so, in undermining their actions and plans'' (p. 167).

Largely responsible for these apparent successes was Brezhnev himself. While we are not given information about Brezhnev's personality, leadership style, history, and so on—information must surely be difficult or impossible to come by—the case history nevertheless presents Brezhnev as a capable leader, someone able to manage successfully a series of internal conflicts within the Soviet decision-making apparatus. While Brezhnev's views had been discounted or dismissed in the past, things went differently in the period leading up to and during the 1982 crisis in Lebanon. Brezhnev apparently had come increasingly to see the United States as a potential collaborator in the preservation of global peace, and this point of view—thanks to his skillful maneuvering—was accepted.

Perhaps driven by an interest in avoiding an open confrontation with the United States and its hawkish President Reagan, the Soviet Union seemed more to react rather than to take the initiative in the Middle East. As Spechler points out, it was the Camp David accords that created a crisis in Soviet circles and led Moscow to react by establishing increasingly strong political and military ties with Syria (its principal client state in the Middle East) and also the PLO. The Soviets were again placed in the position of the reactor in June of 1982; their response to the Israeli invasion was to call for a UN cease-fire resolution (vetoed by the United States), and to send warning signals to Israel, the United States and other countries. This is not to say that the Soviet moves were ineffective; Spechler is quick to point out that Brezhnev succeeded in getting exactly what he wanted during the crisis, virtually every time. Nevertheless, it is noteworthy that the Soviet Union always seemed to be in the position of making the second move. This was true after Israeli air strikes succeeded in destroying 20 percent of the Syrian air force, it was true after the United States announced that it intended to send in a multilateral peace-keeping force that would exclude the Soviet Union, and it was true when the Reagan Plan of September 1, 1982 was followed shortly thereafter by the so-called Brezhnev Plan of September 15.

In Brezhnev then, we have a leader who was at least moderately capable, and perhaps more so. The Soviet Union, by virtue of its global superpower status, its strong military and economic ties with two of the most central Middle East actors—Syria and the PLO—and its interest in becoming a possible broker of any peace in the region, also had ample opportunity to make a difference. Brezhnev thus had both "motivation" and "opportunity," not in the extreme, perhaps, but certainly in sufficient quantity to alter the course of events.

That was true back in 1982, and remains true to this day. As Spechler observes, the Soviet Union had—and probably still has—an interest in helping to resolve the conflict in the Middle East, provided that three conditions are met: "The USSR must play a major role in the negotiations, the agreement arrived at must meet the fundamental interests of the Arabs, and the Soviet Union must be accorded a major role in guaranteeing it" (pp. 168–69). This is important to keep in mind, particularly in conjunction with Morton Deutsch's appraisal of alternatives for future movement in the Middle East.

The United States's Ronald Reagan

The previous commentary on Brezhnev and the Soviet Union might appear to suggest that if it was the Soviet Union who was continually placed in the position of reacting during 1982, then surely the United States must have been the country taking the lead. This is not so, suggests Betty Glad. While the United States could have done a number of things to prevent the Lebanese crisis from ever taking place (for example, being clearer and firmer from the outset with Israel's Begin), and also could have helped bring the crisis to a close sooner, the United States was instead a surprisingly passive player. Why was this so? Glad offers two major reasons: First, the actions of the Israeli military were consistent with the U.S. foreign policy objectives of keeping the Soviet Union out of the Middle East, strengthening Israel's hand, and weakening the Syrians and the PLO. Second, Reagan was a fairly weak leader who didn't like to say no and didn't have the patience to pay attention to necessary detail. So while the situation—because of U.S. ties with Israel (the prime mover in this drama), as well as with many of the other actors (Egypt, Jordan, and Saudi Arabia, in particular)—conferred opportunities, Reagan failed to capitalize on them. Like his Soviet counterpart, he was more a reactor than an initiator. Thanks to his ineffectual leadership, the Israeli tail succeeded in wagging the U.S. dog for month after month of 1982.

As I understand Glad's profile of Reagan, at the heart of that leader's ineffectiveness was an ideology—like Begin's—that closed his mind to alternatives. Glad writes: "A feeling of anti-Communism that saw the USSR as the source of most of the conflict in the world would blind the administration to indigenous political conflicts and to the sensibilities of moderate Arab leaders in the area" (p. 200). Compounding this difficulty was his decision-making style. As Glad writes:

His apparent dislike of hard work and detail meant that he did not try to be his own secretary of state . . . but neither did he delegate major responsibility or foreign policy to one strong and experienced individual. . . . Instead, he loosely delegated power to several like-minded actors—a situation conducive to political and turf battles (p. 219).

In addition, Glad indicates that Reagan disliked controversy, and therefore tended to let conflicts simmer. This interfered with his ability to fire Alexander Haig at the appropriate time, and it led Reagan to avoid open confrontation with Israel's Begin.

The Perspectives of Touval and Deutsch

Before turning to my interpretation of the above "data," a brief comment or two is in order regarding the conflict analyses of Saadia Touval and Morton Deutsch. Touval has essentially responded to the book's major query by suggesting that the availability of better information about the leaders in the Middle East only enhances marginally the opportunities for conflict management. His thesis seems to be that while all kinds of elegantly rational solutions to conflict can be devised in the analyst's armchair, things look very different when one is down in the snake pit of international politics. Political leaders of necessity pursue self-interest; they care about winning, not about settling conflict.

I quite agree with this approach to the problem. Where I find Touval's argument unpersuasive, however, is when it comes to the possible uses of the leadership information that a book of this sort makes available. If, as Touval has suggested, the leaders in the Middle East do not care about conflict management but about ''winning'' (that is, about advancing their own interests), then why not use this sourcebook of leadership information for exactly that purpose: namely, appealing to the interests of the respective leaders? Analysis of leaders and situations may open up possibilities for more creative problem solving. This, I believe, is the challenge and the opportunity conferred by this book.

In fairness to Touval, he does make some use of the book's leadership information in his post hoc appraisal of the Lebanese crisis. He points out—I believe wisely—that had Begin and Arafat (and perhaps also Assad) had information about how extensive the costs of their conflict escalation would be, these leaders might have thought twice about continuing to up the ante in Lebanon. However, as he also points out, each of these leaders (particularly Begin) was constrained by a personality and a worldview that would have made it difficult to do other than he did.

It is not as if Touval dismisses the role of leadership in international politics. Rather, he seems to believe that differences of belief and value among these leaders are so profound that little can be done to move the Middle East conflict toward settlement. If this seems a rather gloomy portrait of the Middle East, then Morton Deutsch's view seems far more upbeat. Deutsch points out that in order to move parties out of what appears to be a non-negotiable conflict, it takes two things: disputant willingness to change their relations with one another (in my terms, motivation) and propitious circumstances (opportunity).

The way to create motivation among the parties to the Middle East conflict, Deutsch says in effect, is by getting them to recognize that their situation is not a viable one; they are in a stalemate in which none can any longer hope to dominate the others, and the parties must therefore accept the necessity of working with one another to reach settlement. The way to create a ripe situation, he argues, is to get U.S. and Soviet leaders to help create a venue in which comprehensive Middle East peace talks can take place. Such a joint U.S.–Soviet initiative, Deutsch indicates, could help successfully address the ''basic anxieties of the Israelis and Arabs,'' especially if the joint initiative is followed by informal meetings among the parties to keep the prenegotiation process moving along.

My primary quarrel with Deutsch's analysis is that he has largely ignored the role of leadership. His is a situational analysis with regard to the two concepts that I have dubbed ''motivation'' and ''opportunity.'' In creating both motivation and opportunity, Deutsch has largely sidestepped the possible role of working with particular regional leaders who have a demonstrated ability to be key players in the drama (Deutsch's mention of Assad's possible role is a notable exception). The key role he envisages for the United States and the Soviet Union appears primarily to be a function of their superpower clout, and the fact that they can apply pressure to their client states either as facilitators or spoilers, and therefore make a difference. Omitted from this analysis, unfortunately, is the important role of the leaders themselves. Surely a Mikhail Gorbachev is likely to make a different set of moves than his predecessor did; surely Reagan has shown a different leadership style and willingness to embark on Middle East initiatives than his predecessor, Jimmy Carter.

Implications and Conclusions

You, the reader, will have to judge for yourself whether I have done a reasonable job of summarizing the key arguments of the nine leadership analysts and the two negotiation commentators. All of this, however, leads to several key questions that I am now prepared to answer, at least provisionally.

Did the identity of the leaders during the 1982 Lebanese crisis make a difference? The answer, I believe, is clearly *yes*. Had there been a Peres at the Israeli helm rather than a Begin, I believe the Israelis would have been far less likely to invade Lebanon in June of 1982. Had George Habash been the acknowledged leader of the Palestinians rather than Arafat, a conflagration would probably have arisen sooner. Had there been stronger leadership in Saudi Arabia or in the United States, the invasion might not have occurred at all, and a ceasefire probably would have been arranged earlier. Thus, I believe that had there been different leaders at the helm, the situation might well have taken a different course in the four months of 1982.

Does this mean that there were missed opportunities back then, occasions where a particular intervention might have turned events around? Here I believe the answer is a resounding no. It follows from my analysis of motivation and opportunity that, while leaders can make a difference, their ability to do so is very much affected by the situational constraints in which they operate. Leadership talent and ability are forced through the tight mesh of situational opportunity. Based on the book's leadership profiles, I have characterized Begin (at least early in his career), Arafat, Assad, Hussein, and, to a lesser extent Mubarak and Brezhnev, as moderately or highly capable leaders. In principle, each of these people could have made a difference—and in the case of incumbents Arafat, Assad, Hussein, and Mubarak, still could make a difference. However, Begin was heavily constrained by the exigencies of Israeli domestic politics; Arafat and Hussein were "swiveling in their chairs" at all times, trying to figure out the right way of avoiding unnecessary, possibly dangerous exposure; and Brezhnev was constrained by internal decision-making conflict and a policy of caution in superpower confrontation. Only Assad seems to have had room to maneuver, as I see it—and Touval has even questioned that.

What about those leaders whose geopolitical situation or political relations placed them in a potentially influential position? Apart from Assad of Syria, it is the Saudi Kings Khaled and Fahd, and U.S. President Reagan who I would identify as having had the most important opportunities. As I have tried to indicate, the Saudi and U.S. leaders were decidedly incapable of exercising creative leadership.

Consequently, my response to the question of missed opportunities for dispute settlement in the Lebanon of 1982 is that a critical mass of talented players and opportune situations did not coexist. Only Syria's Assad and, to a lesser extent, Jordan's Hussein appear to have had a sufficient combination of leadership ability and situational ripeness to make a difference (see the "product" column in Table 13.1); and two players were probably not enough. My coeditor Barbara Kellerman believes that, to a considerable extent, Middle East politics consists of key men responding to what other key men do. I agree, but have tried to indicate why I believe that it will require a sufficient number of key men (and women) in ripe situations to create the basis for peace in the Middle East.

What, then, are the prospects for the future in this troubled corner of the world? Here I find the leadership profiles very helpful. As I indicated in my critique of Touval's analysis, I believe it should be possible to use leadership profiles to better understand the interests of nations and their leaders, and on that basis to try forging a pathway to possible agreement. The Middle East is a frustratingly complex puzzle, whose pieces—represented by the nations involved—must all be fitted together if a negotiated settlement is to be devised. Moreover, while it may be that these puzzle pieces can be assembled in different arrangements, some sequences may be better than others—making it easier to move to a solution. What I have derived from the leadership profiles is some sense of what one such sequence might look like, if we are able to take advantage of what these leaders are inclined to avoid or to do.

Syria's Assad appears to be a key player. The strategy thus far seems to have called for pressuring him to get involved only later in the process, after Israel, Jordan, Egypt, and the PLO. I read it differently, based on the materials in this book. I would include Syria as early in the peace process as possible.

How can we do this? It can be done in two ways: first, by taking advantage of the current era of *glasnost* in U.S.–Soviet relations (in keeping with Deutsch's analysis) and having the nations agree to approach Syria in two different ways. The Soviet Union would approach their client state, Syria, directly, and invite them to join what would eventually become a comprehensive Geneva-type negotiation. The United States would work to reach the Syrians through the Saudis (with whom the United States continues to have good relations—now even stronger because of the vagaries of the Iran-Iraq conflict in the Persian Gulf).

Once Assad is persuaded to become a key player (rather than continuing in his traditional role as spoiler), the next leader to include would be Jordan's

Hussein. Hussein seems willing to join in the negotiations, but only if it does not seem dangerous to do so—and especially if he can see opportunities for advancing his own national self-interest. Given the demographics of Jordan, where 60 percent of the population is now Palestinian (a situation that could destabilize the Hashemite kingdom), Hussein is likely to join the movement—assuming Assad joins first.

Once Jordan is included along with Syria, Egypt's Mubarak and the PLO's Arafat will probably find it safe to accept an invitation. Mubarak needs to keep trying to find ways back into the Arab community, which means that he cannot risk being an early player in the Middle East discussions—but he would clearly benefit from joining once others are already committed. Finally, Arafat, having to constantly watch on all sides for both external and internal threats, can only come to the negotiating party if others have already accepted their invitations.

What of the Israelis? Rather than begin with them, I would propose that their invitation be extended only later on—this invitation to be extended (with some pressure, as needed) by the United States, and sweetened by the promise of continued improvement of relations between Israel and the Soviet Union. Timing is important here, and it is my guess that the best time to push the Israelis to the negotiating table will be during the first two years of the next U.S. president's term of office. As William Quandt has wisely observed, the constraints of the four-year U.S. electoral cycle make it impossible for much innovative decision making to take place in the last two years of a president's term; hence it will have to be fairly early on, probably in Year Two of the next president's term—after he has acquired the necessary expertise to make policy moves—that the United States should invite the Israelis to the comprehensive negotiations party.

As concern the Soviets, as long as Mikhail Gorbachev is in office, there will probably continue to be openings for Soviet involvement in the Middle East process. The United States would be well advised to take advantage of *glasnost* by putting aside dreams of a Soviet-free Middle East and including their super-power counterparts as active players.

Finally, we must consider the Lebanese. Sad to say, their small devastated country has very little role to play in the future of the Middle East. They are victims and spectators, unable—no matter how strong the leadership that may someday emerge—to make much of a difference.

In summary, I have advanced the scenario above as one possible sequence of puzzle moves, based on a selective and interpretive reading of the book's profiles of leadership. There may well be other sequences that make sense, and I en-courage you to devise these as you see fit. One thing is certain: the puzzle of the Middle East will not be settled any time soon. Things are constantly changing as new actors enter the scene while others depart. Begin is in seclusion, Brezhnev is dead, and Reagan is on the way out—even though many of the other principals in the 1982 drama remain at their respective helms. On the other hand, the participants in the Lebanon drama have changed, and perhaps the most important addition has resulted from the Iranian revolution. The forces of Moslem fundamentalism are on the move, and Arab states throughout the Middle East have been driven to respond to this powerful movement originating in the Ayatollah's Iran. In addition, Libya, although clearly of secondary importance in the drama, has carved out its own place under the leadership of Colonel Khaddafi.

What all this means is simply that the frozen section of Middle East history that we chose to study in this book is only that: a slice of events, suspended in time. History is being made in the Middle East every day, and the challenge remains to use whatever information may be available in the service of increasing opportunities for negotiated settlement in that war-torn part of the world.

Finally, where does all this leave the study of leadership in international politics? What of our guiding thesis that opportunities for negotiated settlement of conflict can be enhanced through analysis of leaders and leadership? My own conclusion is that such analysis can help, although perhaps less than my coeditor believes possible. Required is the fortuitous mix of leadership motivation and talent with situational opportunity.

Still, I believe it remains very important to reach for whatever conceptual or practical handles may be available. In the Middle East, as elsewhere, analysts need all the help they can get. If leadership analysis changes the odds in favor of negotiated settlement, then no matter how slight this increment may be, we should take advantage of this opportunity. Perhaps profiles of leaders can help point the way to soft spots in the hard shell of international politics, and suggest a few unexpected opportunities. My reading of the Middle East leadership profiles has led me to the view that the order with which invitations are extended to a round of comprehensive negotiations may well be affected by who the leaders are, and what it takes to obtain their participation.

In her introductory chapter, my coeditor developed five propositions regarding the conditions under which the leader's role in international relations might be expected to be pivotal. Let us return to these propositions in light of the data that have been developed in this book.

What seems clear is that the propositions' predictive power is greatest if they are considered as a whole, rather than as five discrete and independent parts. Thus, while it is perfectly true that a leader's impact will vary in relation to the formal authority he has within his own national state—to wit, Assad—it is also true that great authority does not in and of itself ensure a powerful effect on international relations; as the Saudi regime attests, the will to play a strong participatory role must be there as well. Similarly, while foreign politics is important to the domestic politics of every nation in the Middle East, only some of the region's major players proved to have an impact on this particular regional crisis; others, for a variety of reasons, both personal and political, kept their distance. Only when all of Kellerman's five propositions are taken into account simultaneously do they provide good indicators of when individual leaders are likely to make an impression on world politics.

Moreover, I would reiterate the importance of opportunity. As I have tried to indicate at every turn, impact is a function not only of what the leader can and would do, but the extent to which the situation admits of restructuring. In short, I would argue that what I referred to earlier as "situational ripeness" is a sine qua non of leadership.

My coeditor asserted in the book's introduction that "we are convinced of the intellectual and perhaps also the ultimately practical value of deliberately focusing on those who are empowered to make the critical decisions" (p. 15). What I can say at journey's end is that our confidence was well founded, at least in part. Of the intellectual value of a briefing book of this kind, there can be little doubt. Under certain circumstances leaders do make a difference. Whether knowing this will create new opportunities for negotiation must remain an open question.

NOTES

1. See Thomas Carlyle, *On Heros, Hero-Worship, and the Heroic in History* (Boston: Houghton Mifflin, 1907); also Sidney Hook, *The Hero in History* (Atlantic Highlands, NJ: Humanities Press, 1943). The relevant excerpts from both Carlyle and Hook can be found in Barbara Kellerman (ed.), *Political Leadership: A Source Book* (Pittsburgh: Pittsburgh University Press, 1986).

2. After all, social scientists have been analyzing the role of the individual and the situation for years, and many have focused specifically on the issue of leadership, e.g., Fred E. Fiedler, *Leadership* (Morristown, NJ: General Learning Press, 1971) and Edwin P. Hollander ("Conformity, status, and idiosyncrasy credit," *Psychological Review*, 1958, *65*, 117–127).

3. See, in particular, William Quandt's insightful book, *Camp David* (Washington, DC: The Brookings Institution, 1986).

4. Khalidi's description of Arafat's influential role is reminiscent of Mao in China, Lenin in the Soviet Union, and the so-called "Founding Fathers" in the early history of the United States.

5. Karim Pakradouni, "Hafez al-Assad: The Arabs' Bismarck," *Manchester Guardian Weekly* 129 (December 11, 1985): 19, cited by Hermann, p. 74.

6. Robert G. Newmann, "Assad and the Future of the Middle East," *Foreign Affairs* 62 (Winter, 1983/1984): 253, cited by Hermann, p. 78.

7. James Kelly, "Bidding for a Bigger Role," *Time* 122 (December 19, 1985): 34, cited by Hermann, p. 90.

8. See the article, "Leadership," by Edwin P. Hollander and James W. Julian (in E. F. Borgatta and W. F. Lambert, eds., *Handbook of personality theory and research*, Chicago: Rand McNally, 1975).

SELECTED BIBLIOGRAPHY

Avineri, Shlomo. *Essays on Zionism and Politics*. Tel-Aviv: Sifrei Mabat, 1977.

Barly, Dan, and Salpeter, Eliahu. *Fire in Beirut*. Briarcliff Manor, N.Y.: Stein & Day, 1984.

Barrett, Laurence, I. *Gambling with History*. Garden City, N.Y.: Doubleday, 1983.

Carter, Jimmy. *The Blood of Abraham*. Boston: Houghton Mifflin, 1985.

Cobban, Helena. *The Palestinian Liberation Organization: People, Power and Politics*. Cambridge: Cambridge University Press, 1984.

Dallek, Robert. *Ronald Reagan: The Politics of Symbolism*. Cambridge, Mass.: Harvard University Press, 1984.

Dawisha, Adeed I. *Syria and the Lebanese Crisis*. London: Macmillan Press, 1980.

Eshel, David. *The Lebanon War, 1982*. Hod Hasharon, Israel: Eshel Dramit, Ltd., 1983.

Fisher, Roger, and Ury, William. *Getting to YES: Negotiating Agreement without Giving In*. Boston: Houghton-Mifflin, 1981.

Freedman, Robert O., ed. *The Middle East since Camp David*. Boulder, Colo.: Westview Press, 1984.

Gabriel, Richard A. *Operation Peace for Gallilee: The Israel-PLO War in Lebanon*. New York: Hill & Wang, 1984.

Galon, Galia. *The Soviet Union and the Palestinian Liberation Organization*. New York: Praeger, 1980.

George, Alexander, ed. *Managing U.S.-Soviet Rivalry*. Boulder, Colo.: Westview Press, 1983.

Gilmour, David. *Lebanon: The Fractured Country*. New York: St. Martin's Press, 1984.

Greenstein, Fred I., ed. *The Reagan Presidency: An Early Assessment*. Baltimore: Johns Hopkins University Press, 1983.

Gresh, Alain. *The PLO: The Struggle Within*. London: Zed Books, 1985.

Gubser, Peter. *Jordan: Crossroads of Middle Eastern Events*. London: Croom Helm, 1983.

Haig, Alexander. *Caveats: Realism, Reagan and Foreign Policy*. New York: Macmillan, 1984.

Haley, P. Edward, and Snider, Lewis W., eds. *Lebanon in Crisis: Participants and Issues*. Syracuse: Syracuse University Press, 1979.

Hart, Alan. *Arafat, Terrorist or Statesman?* London: Sidgwick and Jackson, 1984.

Herzog, Chaim. *The Arab-Israeli Wars.* Rev. ed. New York: Vintage, 1984.

Hussein, King. *Uneasy Lies the Head: The Autobiography of King Hussein I.* New York: Random House, 1962.

Katz, Mark. *The Third World in Soviet Military Thought.* Baltimore: Johns Hopkins, 1982.

Kellerman, Barbara, ed. *Leadership: Multidisciplinary Perspectives.* Englewood Cliffs, N.J.: Prentice-Hall, 1984.

Khalidi, Rashid. *Under Siege: P.L.O. Decision Making During the 1982 War.* New York: Columbia University Press, 1986.

Khalidi, Walid. *Conflict and Violence in Lebanon: Confrontation in the Middle East.* Cambridge, Mass.: Harvard Center for International Affairs, 1979.

Khuri, Fuad, ed. *Leadership and Development in Arab Society.* Beirut: American University of Beirut, 1981.

Klieman, Aharon. *Israel-Jordan-Palestine: The Search for a Durable Peace.* Berkeley: Sage Publications, and the Georgetown University Center for Strategic and International Studies, 1981.

Korany, Bahgat, and Dessouki, Ali E. Hillal, eds. *The Foreign Policies of Arab States.* Boulder, Colo.: Westview Press, 1984.

Lacey, Robert. *The Kingdom.* New York: Harcourt Brace Jovanovich, 1981.

Leitenberg, Milton, and Sheffer, Gabriel, eds. *Great Power Intervention in the Middle East.* New York: Pergamon, 1979.

Marantz, Paul, and Steinberg, Blema, eds. *Superpower Involvement in the Middle East.* Boulder, Colo.: Westview, 1985.

McLaurin, Rod, Peretz, Don, and Snider, Lewis W. *Middle East Foreign Policy: Issues and Processes.* New York: Praeger, 1982.

McLaurin, Rod, and Snider, Lewis W., eds. *Middle East Foreign Policies: Issues and Processes.* New York: Praeger, 1983.

Miller, Aaron David. *The P.L.O. and the Politics of Survival.* New York: Praeger, 1983.

Quandt, William. *Saudi Arabia in the 1980s: Foreign Policy, Security, and Oil.* Washington, D.C.: The Brookings Institute, 1981.

Rabinovich, Itamar. *The War for Lebanon.* Ithaca: Cornell University Press, 1984.

Rubinstein, Alvin Z. *Red Star on the Nile.* Princeton: Princeton University Press, 1977.

Safran, Nadav. *Saudi Arabia: The Ceaseless Quest for Security.* Cambridge, Mass.: Harvard University Press, 1985.

Saunders, Harold. *The Other Walls: The Politics of the Arab–Israeli Peace Process.* Washington, D.C.: American Enterprise Institute for Public Policy Research, 1985.

Schiff, Ze'ev, and Ya'ari, Ehud. *Israel's Lebanon War.* New York: Simon & Schuster, 1984.

Shevchenko, Arkady. *Breaking with Moscow.* New York: Alfred A. Knopf, 1985.

Silver, Eric. *Begin: The Haunted Prophet.* New York: Random House, 1984.

Sinai, Anne, and Pollack, Allen, eds. *The Syrian Arab Republic: A Handbook.* New York: American Academic Association for Peace in the Middle East, 1976.

Spechler, Dina Rome. *Domestic Influences on Soviet Foreign Policy.* Washington, D.C.: University Press of America, 1978.

Steele, Jonathan. *Soviet Power: The Kremlin's Foreign Policy—Brezhnev to Andropov*. New York: Simon & Schuster, 1983.

Wise, George S., and Issawi, Charles, eds. *Middle East Perspectives: The Next Twenty Years*. Princeton: Darwin Press, 1981.

INDEX

ABOUT THE EDITORS AND CONTRIBUTORS

MORTON DEUTSCH is Edward Lee Thorndike Professor of Psychology and Education at Teachers College, Columbia University. He has done considerable research and theoretical work on cooperation-competition, conflict, and justice; he is also a practicing psychoanalytic psychotherapist. Among his relevant publications are *Conflict Resolution: Constructive and Destructive Processes; Distributive Justice: A Social-Psychological Perspective;* and *The Prevention of World War III: Some Proposals.*

BETTY GLAD is Professor of Government and International Relations at the University of South Crolina at Columbia. She has long been interested in the impact of personality and ideology on foreign policy making—using in-depth biographies to develop theory. Her works include *Key Pittman: The Tragedy of a Senate Insider; Jimmy Carter: In Search of the Great White House; Charles Evans Hughes and the Illusions of Innocence: A Study in American Diplomacy.* She has served as Vice President of the International Society for Political Psychology.

KENNETH DANA GREENWALD received his B.A. from Haverford College and his M.A. in Middle Eastern Studies from Harvard University in 1986. After studying at the American University in Cairo as a Foreign Language and Area Studies fellow, he enrolled at the Georgetown University Law Center. Currently he is in his third year at the Law Center and is a staff member of the *Georgetown Law Journal.*

MARGARET G. HERMANN is a research scientist at the Mershon Center, Ohio State University. She received her Ph.D. from Northwestern University and held an NIMH Postdoctoral Fellowship at the Educational Testing Service in Princeton, New Jersey as well as taught at Princeton University before coming to Ohio

State. Her research has focused on how leaders shape foreign policy. Among her publications are *A Psychological Examination of Political Leaders* and *Political Psychology*. She was president of the International Society of Political Psychology in 1987–88.

BARBARA KELLERMAN is Dean of Graduate Studies and Research, and Professor of Political Science at Fairleigh Dickinson University. She has written widely on the American presidency and on political leadership in general. She is the author of *All the President's Kin* and *The Political Presidency: Practice of Leadership* and the editor of *Leadership: Multidisciplinary Perspectives; Political Leadership: A Source Book*; and *Women Leaders in American Politics* (with James David Barber). She is currently writing a book titled *The President as World Leader*.

RASHID KHALIDI recently joined the University of Chicago as Associate Professor of Modern Middle Eastern History after teaching at Columbia, Georgetown, and the American University of Beirut. He is author of *Under Seige: P.L.O. Decisionmaking during the 1982 War*, and author or editor of numerous articles and books on Palestinian politics, Lebanon, Arab nationalism, Soviet Middle East policy, and other related topics.

AARON S. KLIEMAN is Professor of International Relations, and former Chairman, Department of Political Science, Tel Aviv University. In 1979 he was first occupant of the chair for a visiting Israeli professor at Georgetown University, returning again in 1984–85. His recent publications include: *Israel's Global Reach: Arms Sales as Diplomacy*; and, in Hebrew, *Coexistence But Not Peace*, a study of Israeli-Jordanian tacit relations. In process is a book surveying forty years of Israeli foreign policy.

DAVID POLLOCK is the Near East Analyst, Office of Research, USIA. He has taught Mideast politics at Harvard, Cornell, and George Washington universities, and is the author of *The Politics of Pressure: American Arms and Israeli Politics Since the Six Day War*.

DAVID M. ROSEN is Associate Professor of Anthropology at Fairleigh Dickinson University. He has a Ph.D. in Anthropology and a J.D. degree, and his areas of specialization are political leadership and comparative law in Africa and the Middle East. Among his recent publications are "Third World Nations and Nuclear War: Not So Innocent Abroad," "Leadership in World Cultures," and "The Peasant Context of Feminist Revolt in West Africa." He is currently at work on a book on judicial ideology and the law on slavery in the antebellum south.

JEFFREY Z. RUBIN is Professor of Psychology at Tufts University and Executive Director, Program on Negotiation at Harvard Law School. He has written extensively on the topics of conflict and negotiation in interpersonal and international relations. Among his books are *Dynamics of Third Party Intervention: Kissinger in the Middle East; Social Conflict: Escalation, Stalemate, and Settlement* (with Dean G. Pruitt); and *Entrapment in Escalating Conflict* (with Joel Brockner).

OFIRA SELIKTAR is Visiting Professor of Political Science at Drexel University after several years of affiliation with the Middle East Research Institute at the University of Pennsylvania. She is author of *New Zionism and the Foreign Policy System of Israel*, co-editor of *The Emergence of Binational Israel: The Second Republic in the Making*, and has written other articles and chapters on Middle East politics.

DINA ROME SPECHLER is Associate Professor of Political Science at Indiana University. Her recent publications include "Soviet Policy Toward Third World Conflicts: Domestic Debate and Intervention in the Middle East," and "The Cost of Empire: Estimates and Re-estimates" (with Martin C. Spechler) in Daniel Nelson and Rajan Menon, *The Limits to Soviet Power*. Professor Spechler's current research focuses on superpower intervention in Third World conflicts, and economic constraints on Soviet foreign policy.

SAADIA TOUVAL is Professor of Political Science at Tel Aviv University. During the 1987–88 academic year, he was Visiting Professor of Political Science at the Graduate Center of the City University of New York, and Visiting Professor of Social Studies at Harvard University. He is also an Associate of Harvard's Center for International Affairs and of its Center for Middle Eastern Studies. Touval is the author of *The Peace Brokers: Mediation in the Arab-Israeli Conflict, 1948–1979* and co-author and co-editor (with I. William Zartman) of *International Mediation in Theory and Practice*.